virgin film

SCORSESE

Jim Sangster

First published in Great Britain in 2002
by Virgin Books Ltd
Thames Wharf Studios
Rainville Road
London
W6 9HA

A catalogue record for this book is available from the British Library.

ISBN 0 7535 0642 4

Typeset by TW Typesetting, Plymouth, Devon
Printed and bound in Great Britain by Mackays of Chatham PLC

Contents

Acknowledgements

Technically, this is my first book flying solo. But no book is truly written alone and the following people offered me inspiration, support, advice, friendship and strength when it was needed most. Thank you one and all.

David Bailey, John Brand, Joanne Brooks, Russell Coburn, Paul Condon, Peter Cooke, Paul Cornell, Neil Corry, Michael Cregan, Paul Evans, Bryon Fear, Gary Gillatt, Rebecca Levene, Louis Niebur, Rachel Phillips, Rakesh Rakhra, Paul Rhodes, Stuart Robb, Andy Roberts, Gareth Roberts, Eddie Robson, Michael Robson, Gary Russell, Jim Smith, Keith Topping, Kaff Trainer, John Trainer, Rob Tribe, Chris Vanderpijpen, Gary Wah, John Wilson, Mark Wright.

Thanks also to: Mrs Jones and Miss Riley for encouraging an early love for writing; Mr Cullen, who taught me the importance of the word 'unique'; Trevor Stent, who put me on the right path; and Dr Jackie Miller, who, despite opening my mind to the wonders of cinema, still didn't manage to change my mind about John Wayne – for which I can only apologise.

Massive gratitude to my editor, Kirstie Addis, for making this much less painful than it might have been.

This book is dedicated to Richy Moosbally, who first introduced me to a film called *Taxi Driver*. 'I think you'll like it,' he said, with usual understatement . . . and to my parents, whose complete lack of interest in Scorsese's work hasn't got in the way of their endless love and support.

Introduction

Ever since I can remember I've always wanted to be in the movies. Wet Saturday afternoons would be spent watching old MGM musicals, Warner Bros gangster flicks, even the odd black-and-white British film in anticipation of the appearance of Sam Kydd (he was in them all, y'know). We watched practically every major movie ever made . . . except Westerns – my mother hated them. (I can recall her praising only three Westerns: *The Searchers*, *The Man Who Shot Liberty Valance* and *The Magnificent Seven*.) When I went to uni, I made sure I was on all the film courses, and while everyone else trudged to the library or scrambled to borrow the department's sole copy of *Rear Window*, I went home, dived into my own Hitchcock collection with a copy of *Empire* or *Premiere* on my lap; and by the time I was earning a living, most of my wages went on trips to the cinema, eight, nine, ten times a week. I became a film junkie.

When Paul Condon and I kicked off the Virgin Film series with *The Complete Hitchcock*, it was as two film students eager to open discussion on The Master of Suspense rather than catalogue every frame of his hefty career. The 'Complete' banner in that instance was something of a millstone, as although there were many books already on his films, production histories and intense psychoanalysis of the man himself, there weren't any books around to tell us if the films are any *good*, and to be honest, that was what we were interested in writing about. *The Complete Hitchcock* therefore was written as a primer for any eager cineasts intending to dip their toes into Hitchcock's legacy. The following books in the series continued the trend, setting an incredibly high target for future authors. I should note that this is written from a British perspective by someone 25 years younger than Scorsese; someone whose primary experience of cinema was via a 29-inch Rediffusion colour TV set instead of a black and white 16-inch RCA Victor TV set. Perhaps I should have asked for it to be called 'A Personal Journey Through Scorsese's Movies' instead.

As with all the books in this series, *Scorsese* can be read in any order. Dip in and out as much as you like; you'll hear no complaints from me. In the format established in *The Complete Hitchcock* (which in turn was a variation on the one Cornell, Topping and Day set up with their TV guides – always steal from the best), each film entry is segmented into a number of subcategories:

1

SOUNDTRACK: Most Scorsese pictures have a soundtrack that would shame MTV. Songs marked with a * appeared on the soundtrack album.

TITLES: The opening sequence to a Scorsese picture is often a film in itself. Here you'll find information on music, editing and observations.

SUMMARY: Enough plot detail to give you an idea of what happens.

WHO'S WHO?: You recognise the face and feel you should know where you know them from. This section's here to give you a few pointers or to provide a little background.

THE USUAL SUSPECTS: Everyone knows De Niro is a regular participant in Scorsese projects, but he's by no means the most prolific. Regular cast members and principal production crew are recognised here.

SOURCE: The direct inspiration for the film, whether that be novel, biography or even, in one instance, the previous film version.

PRODUCTION: How the raw ideas reached the screen, the victories and defeats. Also incorporating subcategories such as **EDITING** and **MUSIC**.

ROOTS: Scorsese is possibly the most cinema-literate person on Earth. Though I have no hope of competing with that, this section goes some way to helping us all catch up a little, noting clear references to and inspiration from other works.

QUOTE/UNQUOTE: 'You talkin' to me?', 'Funny how?', 'Hello, Lazarus'. . . lines that add insight into characters, stand out as examples of exceptional dialogue or are simply destined to annoy the crap out of you every time you see them misquoted in a magazine article about De Niro.

THEMES AND MOTIFS: Those trick shots, recurring images and threads that make the pictures so recognisably Scorsese.

CONTROVERSY: Well, Scorsese's career hasn't been short of a bit of scandal and outrage. Here, you can keep up with the tabloids, the fundamental right, the moral majority and the politically correct.

THERE HE IS!: Like Hitchcock, Martin Scorsese often finds a small role for himself, even if it's just to make up the numbers.

KEEP IT IN THE FAMILY: Almost from the beginning, Scorsese liked to involve his parents in his work. Here's where I keep track of Catherine and Charles Scorsese's many appearances, plus other familial connections.

LEGACY: Some of Scorsese's films have left an indelible mark on our culture, *Taxi Driver*'s 'You talkin' to me?' being a prime example. Here are just some of the many examples of these films' influence on others.

SELLING THE FILM: Posters, taglines and other paraphernalia. There's also a separate entry for **TRAILERS**.

AWARDS: Scorsese has never won an Academy Award. There, I've tempted fate by saying that – let's hope that's the first part of this book to become out of date, eh?

AVAILABILITY: Many of Marty's pictures are now available on 'God's Own Format' (or DVD as some people call it), but some can only be found on VHS and a few have yet to see the light of day outside of the BFI and AFI vaults.

WHAT THE CRITICS SAID: Quotes from reviews at the time of the picture's release either at the cinema or on home video. Sometimes this shows how well the film was received, other times it shows how little critics actually know.

TRIVIA: Any spare bits of information that I can't shoehorn into a category of their own go here.

EXPERT WITNESS: Insights from the people who were there at the time and have the scars to prove it.

FINAL ANALYSIS: A few observations from myself.

SCORSESE ON . . .: As is fitting, the last word goes to Marty, always his harshest critic. These are from interviews held at the time or from more recent comments where hindsight has offered him a fresh perspective. A full list of references to the quotations in this book can be found on pages 283–7.

Vesuvius VI (1959)

(8 mm)

An 8 mm short film Scorsese made as a child, which the director describes as being a Roman epic inspired by the TV series *77 Sunset Strip*. Featuring the song 'Does Your Chewing Gum Lose Its Flavour on the Bedpost Overnight?' it was produced under the 'MarSco' banner, with the end credits featuring the caption 'Directed by Martin Scorsese' going up in flames.

What's a Nice Girl Like You Doing in a Place Like This? (1963)

(16 mm short – 9 min – B & W)

Produced by the New York University Department of Television, Motion Picture and Radio Presentations, Summer Motion Picture Workshop
Faculty Advisers: Haig P Manoogian, John Mahon
Written by Martin Scorsese
Cinematography: James Newman
Film Editor: Robert Hunsicker
Sound Editor: Mara Stoller
Sound: Sandor Reich
Still Photography: Frank Truglio
Unit Manager: Richard Klein
Assistant Director: Louise Stefanie
Music: Richard H Coll

CAST: Zeph Michaelis (*Harry*), Mimi Stark (*Wife*), Sarah Braveman (*Analyst*), Fred Sica (*Friend*), Robert Uricola (*Singer*), Lew Delgato, Ronnie Apres, Manny Stormiolo, Robert Gil, Peter Anson, Peter Osis, Mark Trail (*Performers*).

SOUNDTRACK: 'Swivel-hips Sal' (music by Richard H Coll, lyrics by Sandor Reich).

TITLES: With a fanfare, the title appears in a font near identical to the one Fellini used for *8 ½*.

SUMMARY: Writer Algernon – known to his friends as Harry – finds himself distracted by a photograph in his apartment of a man in a boat. It's not much to look at – even his friends say so – but it begins to affect him to the point where he begins to suffer from a bout of writer's block. He can't eat, can't sleep, and can't work, which Harry attributes to his sensitivity and vivid imagination. He decides to throw a party, where he meets a woman who's such a 'good catch' that it distracts him from the picture. He marries the girl and they live a normal life. But after a conversation with his analyst, Harry becomes fixated with another picture – this time, one depicting the ocean – to the extent that he eventually finds himself trapped inside the photograph.

THE USUAL SUSPECTS: Robert Uricola (*Who's That Knocking At My Door?*, *Raging Bull*) was a friend of Scorsese's from NYU, while Haig Manoogian (credited as Faculty Adviser for NYU) would also work with Scorsese on *It's Not Just You, Murray!* and *Who's That Knocking At My Door?*

PRODUCTION: Scorsese's first film at New York University, *What's a Nice Girl Like You Doing in a Place Like This?* was part-funded by the Edward L Kingsley Foundation, the Screen Producers' Guild and Brown University Film Festival, and produced by Scorsese's NYU professor, Haig P Manoogian. Scorsese had enrolled at NYU specifically because they had film classes, and it was Manoogian's class called 'The History of Motion Pictures, Television and Radio' which gave Scorsese his first true experience of film-making. In the second year of the course, students were exposed to practical lessons in film production, learning about lighting, camera speeds and other film-making techniques. Though their resources were limited (with student numbers exceeding thirty, the department had a budget for just six films a year), by the third year students were able to produce their own short films on the proviso that they had a script – and that Professor Manoogian liked them. It was Manoogian who encouraged Scorsese to write his own script instead of waiting round for someone else to write one. The result was *What's a Nice Girl Like You . . .*, completed in 1963.

QUOTE/UNQUOTE
The Analyst/The Friend: 'Harry, if you really want help, you must help yourself. You gotta fight it. You gotta hit it hard in the guts. Blood and thunder and all like. It's all in the mind, boy. The only way to do it is to stare it down, straight, cold. Stare it down, boy. Stare it down.'

What is strange about this particular line is how odd it sounds coming from the analyst, yet how right it sounds when repeated by Harry's mobsterlike friend.

Harry: 'I even found it hard to eat, but I figured that all this was because of my intense sensitivity, and because I have a vivid imagination. Even my friends say it.'

Harry's friend: 'Y'know Harry, you have a vivid imagination.'

Harry: 'Life is fraught with peril . . .'

ROOTS: Made just two weeks after Scorsese saw Fellini's *8½*, this short also reflects Scorsese's interest in the French New Wave led by Godard and Truffaut. The juxtaposition of the narrator and the photograph recalls Godard's placement of a Renoir painting alongside Jean Seberg in *À Bout De Souffle* (1960). The biggest influence on this project, however, was undoubtedly Ernest Pintoff's animated short *The Critic*, which has a frantic voice over from Mel Brooks.

THEMES AND MOTIFS: Scorsese describes *What's a Nice Girl . . .* as being a tale of 'pure paranoia', and in that at least it has links with most of Scorsese's work. That Algernon changes his name to the more commonplace Harry shows us an early example of a Scorsese character in search of identity. Look out for the extreme close-up on Harry's eyes, a shot we'll see again in the opening sequences of *Taxi Driver* and *Cape Fear*. Also, the idea of a show-within-a-show, seen here in the *Late, Late Show No. 3* sequence, which we see repeated in *Taxi Driver*, *New York, New York*, *The King of Comedy* and others. Catholic guilt is represented by Harry referring to his writing as his 'confessions'. Scorsese revisits the concept of a man trapped inside art years later. In Akira Kurosawa's *Yume* (AKA *Akira Kurosawa's Dreams*, 1990), Scorsese plays Vincent Van Gogh who steps into his own painting, 'Crows Over The Wheat Field'.

LEGACY: Although it's possible David Fincher has never even seen this picture, compare the way we see Harry's apartment filling with furniture with a similar shot in Fincher's *Fight Club* (2000).

AVAILABILITY: Released on VHS in the UK by Connoisseur Video in 1992 on the *Scorsese ×4* compilation (ASIN: B00004CMQW), which is still, at the time of writing, available from the British Film Institute.

FINAL ANALYSIS: Though early works can never be held as representative of what will follow, there's still a few elements of *What's a Nice Girl . . .* that are recognisably Scorsese. For the most part, however, it's very much a student's work, with literal humour (the narrator says he just hangs around his apartment – cut to a shot of him suspended by his arms) and obvious fan-boy enthusiasm for the New Wave film-makers of Europe.

It's Not Just You, Murray! (1964)

(16 mm short – 15 mins – B & W)

A New York University Department of Television, Motion
Picture and Radio Presentation
Faculty Advisers: John Mahon, Haig P Manoogian
Written by Martin Scorsese, Mardik Martin
Cinematography: Richard H Coll
Editor: Eli F Bleich
Music: Richard H Coll, performed by John W Dodd Junior
High School, Freeport, Long Island
Musical Director: Leo Ursini
Assistant Director: Mardik Martin
Costumes: Victor Magnotta
Costumes courtesy of Lancelot Braithwaite
Still Photography: Edwin Grant
Graphics: Marjorie Rosen
Production Associates: Edwin Grant, Larraine Brennan
Make-up: Teresa Brun
Sets: Lancelot Braithwaite

SOUNDTRACK: Elgar's 'Pomp and Circumstance, March No. 1' (best known in Britain as 'Land of Hope and Glory' and in America as 'The Graduation March').

CAST: Ira Rubin (*Murray*), Sam De Fazio (*Joe*), Andrea Martin (*Wife*), Catherine Scorsese (*Mother*), Robert Uricola (*Singer*), Bernard Weisberger, Victor Magnotta, Richard Sweeton, John Bivona.

'LOVE IS A GAZELLE' CAST: Robert Uricola, Susan Miller, Sydney Ann Seide, Vivian Thompson, Cynthia Koenig, Larraine Brennan.

UNCREDITED CAST: Mardik Martin.

TITLES: After a card informing us that the film won The Edward L Kingsley Award for 1964, the title is shown white on a black background while a fanfare plays.

SUMMARY: Businessman Murray introduces this film of his life, charting the highs and lows, crediting his success to one man – his best friend, Joe. But as Murray tells us about his bootlegging days, his links with organised crime and his relationship with his wife, he is slowly awakened to the fact that Joe has not been quite the perfect friend he's always seemed. However, the ever-persuasive Joe manages to bring his friend round with the offer of a new car, and Murray celebrates with his friends and business associates.

WHO'S WHO?: Mardik Martin was born in Iran and raised in Iraq. He fled his homeland to avoid the draft and eventually enrolled himself into NYU, where he met Scorsese in 1961. Martin would become one of Scorsese's principal collaborators. His sister, Andrea Martin (appearing here as 'the wife') was a regular in the sitcom *Kate and Ally*, and received ten Emmy nominations for her writing and performing in the long-running US series *Second City*. More recently, she's made a career for herself as a voice artist, playing Mad Harriet in the Warner Bros animated series *Superman* (first shown in 1996) and the lunch lady in Disney's *Recess* (1997–present).

THE USUAL SUSPECTS: Victor Magnotta (*What's a Nice Girl Like You Doing in a Place Like This?*, *Taxi Driver*, *Raging Bull*, *After Hours*); Mardik Martin (*What's a Nice Girl Like You Doing in a Place Like This?*, *New York, New York*, *American Boy*, *Raging Bull*, *The King of Comedy*, plus writing credits for *Mean Streets*, *Italianamerican*, *New York, New York*, *Raging Bull*); Robert Uricola (*What's a Nice Girl Like You Doing in a Place Like This?*, *Who's That Knocking At My Door?*, *Raging Bull*); producer Haig P Manoogian (*What's a Nice Girl Like You Doing in a Place Like This?*, *Who's That Knocking At My Door?*).

PRODUCTION: In his final year at NYU, and with the continued encouragement of Haig Manoogian, Scorsese made this satire of gangsters in Little Italy. Working with Mardik Martin, Scorsese set about writing a film that worked almost as a documentary of his neighbourhood, admittedly in ironic form, yet once again shot in the

style of his newly discovered obsession, the New Wave films from
Europe. With budget again almost non-existent, the picture was shot on
location in the Lower East Side of New York in the apartments and
cellars of family members. The cast comprised fellow NYU students,
many of whom also doubled or tripled up behind the camera. The
finished short premiered at the 4th New York Film Festival on 13
September 1966, two years after its completion.

QUOTE/UNQUOTE

Murray's mother: 'Murray, eat first!'

Joe: 'Remember that one day, Murray, one day you're gonna see
  somebody, some guy who's all those guys rolled into one, and then
  you can give him all he deserves.'

Murray: 'I was going places – really going places! . . . Jersey, Brooklyn,
  Staten Island . . .'

Murray: 'I refuse to answer on the grounds it may incriminal me . . . on
  the grounds I may discriminate myself.'

KEEP IT IN THE FAMILY: Marty's mother, Catherine Scorsese, makes
her first appearance here as Murray's mother, continually force-feeding
him with spaghetti.

ROOTS: As much a record of the street stories of Scorsese's youth, *It's
Not Just You, Murray!* is also a tribute to the many cinematic influences
he'd been exposed to by this time. Though the tone of the film, with its
stark black and white photography, can be seen as an ironic take on
Warner gangster flicks, such as *The Public Enemy* (William A Wellman,
1931) and the cheesy 'Love Is a Gazelle' musical number in the middle
seems to be mocking overambitious attempts at Busby Berkeley musicals,
Scorsese's passion for European directors is clear. The ending is a
deliberate reworking of Fellini's *8 ½*, which had been released the
previous year. Scorsese's use of the freeze-frame, lifted from the ending
of Truffaut's *The 400 Blows* (1959), makes its first appearance here,
while the look of Murray's wife is surely an intentional nod to
Antonioni's star, Monica Vitti.

THEMES AND MOTIFS: Murray's relationship with Joe seems to
foreshadow the destructive buddy relationships in *Who's That Knocking
At My Door?*, *Mean Streets*, *Raging Bull*, *GoodFellas* and *Casino*.
Another link to *Mean Streets* comes in the raid on the gin distillery,

which can be compared to the scene with the raid on the pool-room. Like Henry Hill in *GoodFellas*, Murray is defined not by who he is, but by what he owns and who he is associated with. As the saying goes, Murray knows the price of everything and the value of nothing, shown by his introduction, where he points to his tie, his shoes, his suit and his car before he even tells us his name. Though he tells us he's 'very rich . . . very influential . . . very well liked', he still attributes all of this to his friend Joe, a displacement of credit that contrasts with Joe's adept displacement of blame. The idea of a car being a status symbol is a recurring image, with most of Scorsese's films featuring an automobile of some kind to a significant degree, and here it acts as a signifier of Murray's foolish pride. Compare also Murray's boast, 'I always wanted to live good, ever since I was a kid' with Henry Hill's similar opening line in *GoodFellas*.

A common thread through Scorsese's work is the family structure and the Italian way of life, unsurprising considering Scorsese's own mother features in many of his pictures. Here, Catherine Scorsese embodies the overprotective mother whose words of wisdom can be boiled down to 'eat first'. The ritual of the meal is something that will come to figure highly in subsequent pictures.

ALTERNATIVE VERSIONS: The 16 mm print was blown up to 35 mm for its commercial theatrical run.

AWARDS: The picture was presented as The Edward L Kingsley Award Film for 1964, and later that year it won the Jesse L Lasky Intercollegiate Award. In the same year, Scorsese finally got his B.Sc. in Film Communications.

AVAILABILITY: Released on VHS in the UK by Connoisseur Video in 1992 on the *Scorsese × 4* compilation (ASIN: B00004CMQW), which is still available from the British Film Institute.

FINAL ANALYSIS: Technically Scorsese's first look into the world of the gangster, *It's Not Just You, Murray!* has much of the manic enthusiasm of his first picture, with less of the pretension. Heavy on the irony, with the narration rarely capturing the truth of the visuals, it's largely played for laughs: the big Dick Tracy-esque 'GIN' labels on the bottles in the bootlegging distillery and the slapstick routine that follows; the euphemistic reference to visiting 'Ossining, New York', the location of the famous Sing Sing prison; Murray's malapropisms during his trial;

and his suggestive and heavily loaded description of his part in 'one of the greatest financial syndicates in America' and its involvement in motel chains, politics, undertaking services, television, sports, private grants in foreign aids – all shown to be activities of the Mafia.

For all the comedy, it's hard to feel sorry for Murray, even though he's been cuckolded and betrayed by his supposed best friend, who's so low he even bums cigarettes off him while visiting Murray in prison. Murray's obsession with material wealth, which surely includes his trophy wife and handsome best friend, make him an unsympathetic foil, not helped by the climax to the picture, with Murray on the verge of realising the truth about Joe only for Joe to turn things round with the promise of a new car for just $10,000.

SCORSESE ON *IT'S NOT JUST YOU, MURRAY!*: 'Of all my films, Murray is the one that shows the old neighbourhood, the way it looked in the 60s, right before it began to die out.'

The Big Shave (1967)
(Working Title: *Viet '67*)

(16 mm – 6 mins – colour)

Film (producer, writer, editor): Martin Scorsese
Camera (Cinematography): Ares Demertzis
Blood (special effects): Eli Bleich
Bathroom (sets): Ken Gaulin
Whiteness: Herman Melville
Music: Bunny Derigan

SOUNDTRACK: 'I Can't Get Started with You', written by George and Ira Gershwin, performed by Bunny Berigan.

CAST: Peter Bernuth (*Young Man*).

TITLES: The title is shown in blocky black lettering on an off-white background.

SUMMARY: As 'I Can't Get Started with You' plays over the soundtrack, a young man shaves continually, drawing blood which splashes down into the brilliant white sink.

PRODUCTION: *The Big Shave* was shot on ten rolls of Agfa film, a grant from the Palais des Beaux Arts in Brussels, courtesy of Jacques Ledoux, curator of the Cinémathèque Royale de Belgique.

Originally intended to be screened as part of 'The Angry Arts Against The War', a week-long demonstration against the Vietnam conflict, Scorsese planned to end the picture with footage of the war. However, when it was finally shown on 28 September 1968 at the 4th New York Film Festival (along with Milos Forman's *The Fireman's Ball*), it was without the war footage, but with its cryptic end credits, including references to Herman Melville and 'Viet '67'.

THEMES AND MOTIFS: It's fitting that, as such a huge fan of Emmerich Pressburger and Michael Powell, Scorsese should load his first colour production with the colour red. The almost fetishistic joy with which the horrific shave is filmed is in some ways a clear early warning of a career that would be littered with accusations of unnecessarily graphic violence. But, even taking into account some of the images to follow, I'd argue this is the sole example of gratuitous body horror in Scorsese's entire filmography, being bloody simply for the sake of shock value.

AWARDS: Winner of Le Prix de L'Age d'Or at the 1968 Experimental Film Competition in Belgium, organised by Scorsese's patron, Ledoux.

AVAILABILITY: Released on VHS in the UK by Connoisseur Video in 1992 on the *Scorsese* × 4 compilation (ASIN: B00004CMQW), which is still available from the British Film Institute.

FINAL ANALYSIS: Most of the irony of *The Big Shave* would possibly be lost on a modern audience more accustomed to such bloodshed in movies. Both the use of Berigan's version of the Gershwin song 'I Can't Get Started with You' (with its opening lyric 'I've flown around the world in a plane/I've settled revolutions in Spain . . . Still I can't get started with you') and the credit to Herman Melville, an allusion to the determination and ultimately futile hunt of Captain Ahab from Melville's *Moby Dick*, should draw us to reading the picture as part of the anti-war feeling at the time. But for most of us it's just a very unpleasant viewing experience. Sickening and very effective, even if the message behind it is lost.

SCORSESE ON *THE BIG SHAVE*: 'Consciously it was an angry outcry against the war. But in reality, something else was going on inside of me, I think, which really had nothing to do with the war. It was just a very bad period.'

Who's That Knocking At My Door? (1969)

(35 mm – 90 min – B & W)

MPAA Rating: R

A Tri-Mod film
Producers: Joseph Weill, Betzi Manoogian, Haig Manoogian
Screenplay: Martin Scorsese
Cinematographers: Michael Wadleigh, Richard H Coll
Editor: Thelma Schoonmaker
Sound: John Binder, Jim Datri
Additional Dialogue: Betzi Manoogian
Directorial Assistant: Mardik Martin
Assistant Cameramen: Ron Clabeau, Ed Grant
Still Photographers: Neal Walder, Chuck Shipley
Club Designer: Victor Magnotta
Production Manager: Barbara Battle

SOUNDTRACK: 'Jenny Take a Ride' by Mitch Ryder and the Detroit Wheels; 'The Closer You Are' by the Channels; 'I've Had It' by the Bellnotes; 'El Watusi' by Ray Baretto; 'Don't Ask Me to Be Lonely' by the Dubs; 'Shotgun' by Jr Walker and All Stars; 'The End' by the Doors; 'Ain't That Just Like Me' by the Searchers; 'Who's That Knocking at My Door' by the Genies; 'The Plea' by the Chantells.

CAST: Harvey Keitel (*JR*), Zina Bethune (*Girl*), Lennard Kuras (*Joey*), Michael Scala (*Sally GaGa*), Anne Collette (*Young Girl in Dream*), Harry Northup (*Harry, the Rapist*), Robert Uricola (*Young Man at Party with Gun*), Bill Minkin (*Iggy/Radio Announcer*), Wendy Russell (*GaGa's Girlfriend*), Phil Carlson (*Guide on the Mountain*), Susan Wood (*Susan*), Marissa Joffrey (*Rosie*), Catherine Scorsese (*JR's mother*), Tsuai Yu-Lan, Saskia Holleman, Anne Marieka (*Dream Girls*), Victor Magnotta, Paul de Bionde (*Boys in Fight*), Martin Scorsese (*Gangster*).

TITLES: The opening scene cuts from shots of JR's mother preparing a meal for her family to religious iconography, miniature statues of the Virgin Mary. Though we don't return to this domestic scene for the rest of the picture, it sets the scene perfectly for it hints at a possible source for JR's repression, surrounded from an early age by images of Virgins and their association with the perfect woman – one's mother. From this, we cut to a street gang fighting. The credits consist of white lettering on black, intercut between scenes from the fight.

SUMMARY: JR is a young man leading a double life. Though, like his friends, he drinks hard and plays hard, sleeping with women and thinking nothing of it, he is also a man troubled by his faith. When he meets a young woman and falls in love with her, he tells her he will not sleep with her as he respects her too much. But when the girl confesses to him that she was once raped by an ex-boyfriend, he rejects her, believing her to be tainted and in some way guilty of betraying him by allowing herself to be violated.

JR looks for distraction in the crazy antics of his friends, but feels compelled to return to his girlfriend. She seems relieved that he hasn't abandoned her until he reveals that he 'forgives' her and wants to marry her anyway. In disgust, she tells him to leave. JR seeks solace in the church before arranging to meet with a friend the next day and walking off into the night alone.

WHO'S WHO?: Harvey Keitel makes his film debut here. Keitel's erratic career encompasses some astounding work in over a hundred pictures, including Ridley Scott's debut *The Duelists* (1977), Brian De Palma's *Wise Guys* (1986), and Quentin Tarantino's *Reservoir Dogs* (1992). He would later work for Scorsese on *Mean Streets*, *Alice Doesn't Live Here Anymore*, *Taxi Driver* and *The Last Temptation of Christ*.

Oscar-winning film editor Thelma Schoonmaker is the widow of British film-maker Michael Powell. Having worked with Scorsese on *Who's That Knocking At My Door?* and *Woodstock*, she would become the single most significant of Scorsese's collaborators, working almost exclusively for him on all of his directorial projects and many of his producer-only films from *Raging Bull* onwards.

THE USUAL SUSPECTS: Harvey Keitel (*Mean Streets*, *Street Scenes*, *Alice Doesn't Live Here Anymore*, *Taxi Driver*, *The Last Temptation of Christ*); Robert Uricola (*What's a Nice Girl Like You Doing in a Place Like This?*, *It's Not Just You, Murray!*, *Raging Bull*); Harry Northup (*Boxcar Bertha*, *Mean Streets*, *Alice Doesn't Live Here Anymore*, *Taxi Driver*, *New York, New York*, *Amazing Stories*: 'Mirror Mirror'); Bill Minkin (*Taxi Driver*, *The King of Comedy*); editor Thelma Schoonmaker (*Street Scenes*, *Taxi Driver*, *Raging Bull*, *The King of*

Comedy, *After Hours*, *The Color of Money*, *Bad*, *The Last Temptation of Christ*, *New York Stories*, *GoodFellas*, *Cape Fear*, *Age of Innocence*, *Casino*, *A Personal Journey with Martin Scorsese Through American Movies*, *Kundun*, *Bringing Out the Dead*, *My Voyage to Italy*, *Gangs of New York*); producer Haig Manoogian (*What's a Nice Girl Like You Doing in a Place Like This?*, *It's Not Just You, Murray!*); cinematographer Michael Wadleigh (director, *Woodstock*).

PRODUCTION: *Who's That Knocking At My Door?* was originally planned as the second part of a trilogy. Scorsese had written a forty-page script called 'Jerusalem, Jerusalem' about a group of eighteen-year-old boys on retreat at a Jesuit house, and had a vague idea for a third instalment, called 'Season of the Witch' (see **Mean Streets**). The central character, JR would become the focal point for *Who's That Knocking . . .*, and was a clearly autobiographical representation of Scorsese himself, dealing with his own religious doubt and sexual confusion.

In 1965 Scorsese put an advertisement in one of the trade papers recruiting for actors. One of the young hopefuls to reply was a 26-year-old man who had only recently begun acting after spending four years in the Marines, and then working as a court stenographer at Manhattan Criminal Court. His name was Harvey Keitel. Scorsese asked Keitel to read for him on three occasions before casting him as JR. In the role of The Girl, Scorsese cast nineteen-year-old Zina Bethune, who had been a child actress, and who shared an agent with Scorsese.

Scorsese's old film tutor, Haig Manoogian, took on the producer's role. Production began in 1965 when Scorsese tried to get it made as his graduate film. Scorsese's father raised $6000 from a student loan, but Scorsese Jr was unable to complete it. When the film was finally viewable in some kind of completed form, at just 65 minutes and entitled *Bring on the Dancing Girls*, it was poorly received and, in the words of Scorsese himself, 'a disaster'.

A year later, Scorsese went about trying to raise funds to complete the picture, at a time that coincided with the break-up of his first marriage. Manoogian and a theatrical agent and NYU film student called Joe Weill managed to pull together $37,000 to finish the picture (the final cost of production would be something in the region of $75,000), even shooting scenes at Manoogian's house. Scorsese, Manoogian, Weill and Thelma Schoonmaker cut the picture over four months. These sequences were filmed in 16 mm and then cut into the 35 mm scenes already shot. This second version was shown at the Chicago Film Festival in September 1969, billed as *I Call First*.

While Scorsese was in Europe making commercials, he met up with a distributor called Joseph Brenner, a soft-core pornographic film distributor and old army buddy of Manoogian's. Manoogian persuaded Brenner to distribute the film in Europe on the condition that a nude scene was added to the picture. The additional scene, which involved Keitel also performing nude, was shot in Amsterdam doubling for New York. Worried by the thought of getting the segment through customs, Scorsese smuggled it through in his pocket, and then shaved on the plane to look more respectable. The final picture, with its name changed again to *Who's That Knocking At My Door?*, was shown at New York's Carnegie Hall Cinema.

Brenner booked the Carnegie Cinema to run the picture, but the opening was delayed by an extended run of *The Crazy World of Laurel and Hardy*, one of a series of documentary compilations which had been released the previous year. When their film finally opened, Keitel, Scorsese and Brenner's son Steve stood outside distributing promotional flyers. But with little or no money to promote the picture, it soon died a death.

EDITING: A first credit for Thelma Schoonmaker. As JR and the girl talk on the ferry, the shots dissolve into each other, showing the dreamlike state of JR, as well as hinting at a passage of time. Generally, dissolves are not a common Scorsese–Schoonmaker technique – they prefer the fast, clean edits that become almost jump-cuts. There are plenty of those too: the insertion into the scene where the mother prepares dinner to shots of the Virgin Mary provides a fairly heavy-handed comparison that underlines JR's view of women. Later, as the boys fight in the street, we see a butcher cutting ribs as if in time to the music. When JR tells his girlfriend that he loves her, and that if she loves him she'd understand what he means by 'just not now' he's reflected in a mirror, but there are two reflections of her – mirrors are a common metaphor, particularly in literature, for views of the soul. In this shot, the girl is clearly 'divided' by her feelings for JR and her guilt over her past.

MUSIC: The use of the Doors' 'The End' isn't perhaps the most subtle use of music in Scorsese's work, with its Oedipal subtext ('Father, yes son, I want to kill you, mother I want to . . .') but it gets across a level of smutty innuendo that works effectively. Likewise, the use of the Dubs' 'Don't Ask Me to Be Lonely' in the scene where the girl describes her rape cannot be seen as anything other than deliberately ironic.

QUOTE/UNQUOTE

JR: 'Everybody should like Westerns.'

JR: 'There are girls and there are broads . . . a broad isn't exactly a virgin, you play around with them, you don't marry a broad, y'know what I mean?'

ROOTS: The characters Joey and Sally GaGa are named after real friends of Scorsese and, like *It's Not Just You, Murray!* and *Mean Streets, Who's That Knocking* . . . takes its inspiration from many of the events of Little Italy that Scorsese witnessed or heard about when he was younger. The title comes from a song by the Genies (featured on the soundtrack). Scorsese's use of contemporary music comes via *Scorpio Rising* (Kenneth Anger, 1964) which he saw in 1969 while tutoring at NYU. French actress Anne Collette was almost certainly cast after Scorsese saw her in a couple of films by Jean-Luc Godard. JR shares a passion for Westerns with Scorsese, specifically *The Searchers* (John Ford, 1956, see also **Mean Streets** and the structure of **Taxi Driver**), *The Man Who Shot Liberty Valance* (John Ford, 1962), which JR discusses with his girlfriend, *Rio Bravo* (Howard Hawks, 1959, which also features in the montage sequence at the centre of the picture) and *Scaramouche* (George Sidney, 1952), which JR takes his girlfriend to see at the cinema. *The Searchers* in particular has significant parallels with *Who's That Knocking* . . . John Wayne's character, Ethan Edwards, is looking for his niece, who has been captured by Indians. But his obsession in finding her is second to his obsession in finding her unviolated by the Indain chief, Scar. Like JR, Ethan's view of women is that they should be virgins or mothers; any sexual contact, even rape, makes them whores and beneath his concern. When the girl ultimately realises that JR considers her a whore that needs saving, she tells him to 'Go home', echoing the words of Natalie Wood's character in *The Searchers*. Mention of Jeffrey Hunter's role in *The Searchers* reminds JR that Hunter played Christ – in *King of Kings* (Nicholas Ray, 1961) – prompting the girl to ask 'Was he Swedish?' confusing him with Max Von Sydow in *The Greatest Story Ever Told* (George Stevens, 1965).

THEMES AND MOTIFS: As JR's gang fool around, we see one of the gang showing off his gun as the others fire their fingers (thumb as trigger) in the kitchen; we'll see variations on this action in *Mean Streets*, *Alice Doesn't Live Here Anymore*, *Taxi Driver* and *The Color of Money* to name but a few.

BIBLE CLASS: When the girl treats JR to dinner, he tells her off (lightly) for lighting a Holy Candle at the dinner table. In the final sequence, JR's guilt and confusion rage as he prays in church, and we see shots of him mixed with shots of The Sacred Heart (a statue of Christ bearing his heart), and, as with the opening sequence, the Virgin Mary. As JR kisses the feet of Christ on the crucifix, his lips begin to bleed, hinting at his own perception of his martyrdom in not sleeping with the girl. Note also the ever-present crucifix on JR's wall, which actually belonged to Scorsese's mother.

CONTROVERSY: The idea of women being either mother/the Madonna or whore/Mary Magdalene is one that we see again in *Taxi Driver*, but it's the element of the rape, played out again and again in JR's mind, that is the most disturbing, both in his obsession with it and his misappropriation of the blame. 'Who d'ya think you are, the Virgin Mary or something?' he asks her, and then goading her 'who else is gonna marry ya while you're at it? Tell me that while ya at it, you whore!' Throughout the picture, women are seen as an easy commodity, which makes JR's stance on not sleeping with his girlfriend such an odd one. But then, in her first scene, we do see the girl sitting next to a sign that reads, 'For Trash Only'.

Though *Who's That Knocking . . .*'s nude was by no means the first in cinema history (nudity's celluloid debut took place not long after trains and guns had their first nights), male nudity was still very much a taboo, and Keitel's scenes come very close to full frontal (evidently something Keitel has blocked out, if his claim that he's 'never done a nude scene' to unofficial biographer Marshall Fine is to be taken at face value).

THERE HE IS!: Scorsese plays a guest at the party, laughing along with JR and his friends.

KEEP IT IN THE FAMILY: Catherine Scorsese appears as the mother in the opening sequence.

LEGACY: Arguably the greatest legacy of *Who's That Knocking . . .* is everything that Scorsese revisits in *Mean Streets*. Characters discussing a film within a film is a trait that would be picked up by Quentin Tarantino, whose debut feature, *Reservoir Dogs*, would star one Harvey Keitel.

ALTERNATIVE VERSIONS: In addition to all its different incarnations prior to its completion, it was renamed JR for a limited reissue in 1970.

AWARDS: Won the Golden Siren at the 1970 Sorrento Festival.

AVAILABLITY: *Who's That Knocking At My Door?* was released by Warner Home Video on NTSC VHS only in 1991. It is not currently available in the UK, though it does pop up on cable and satellite movie channels occasionally.

EXPERT WITNESS: 'That whole first scene, with the discussion of the magazine and John Wayne, was totally improvised. There was no script. Martin created an environment and a scenario and wanted it to evolve. Harvey seemed to go with that mode and never questioned it. After a while, I started understanding how they devised the scenes and let the art happen. It was exciting but unnerving.' Actress Zina Bethune (*The Girl*).

FINAL ANALYSIS: Even putting aside its troubled production history, *Who's That Knocking . . .* fails to impress due to two main factors. Firstly, as Scorsese himself acknowledges, in an era of sexual liberation, few can begin to empathise with a young man unwilling to sleep with his girlfriend (even if a similar theme was explored by the Boulting brothers in the British production *The Family Way* at the same time), especially when he proves himself to be unworthy of her affection in the way he rejects her on learning that she has been raped. But the bigger problem is simply the knowledge that this is Scorsese's first attempt at a full-length feature, tackling subjects and characters we know he'll return to. Knowing that *Mean Streets* and *GoodFellas* are ahead of him, it's hard to warm to what amounts to a dress rehearsal for the big production.

SCORSESE ON *WHO'S THAT KNOCKING AT MY DOOR?*: 'I dislike it. Only because it took me three years to make. And, y'know, we'd make the film and we'd work on a weekend and then for three weeks we wouldn't shoot and then we'd work another weekend. So it wasn't really a professional film to make. . . . We were having a problem getting a distributor and my agents at William Morris said to me "Marty, what do you expect? You have a film here in which the guy loves a young woman so much that he respects her and he won't make love to her. Here we are in the age of the sexual revolution, and you're making a movie about repression! Total sexual repression. Who's gonna see it? Nobody!"'

Street Scenes (1970)

(16 mm – 75 mins – B & W/colour)

A Project of the New York Cinetracts Collective
Production Supervisor and Post Production Director: Martin Scorsese
Post Production Management: Raini Kaplan
Post Production Consultants: Diana Krumins, Maggie Koven, Peter Real
Post Production Co-ordinator: Nick Tanis
Editors: Peter Rea, Maggie Koven, Angela Kirby, Gerry Pallor, Larry Tisdall, Thelma Schoonmaker
Director/Cameramen 1: Don Lenzer, Harry Bolles, Danny Schneider, Peter Rea, The Big B (Bob Pitts), Bill Etra, Tiger Graham, Fred Hadley, Ed Summer, Nat Tripp
Director/Cameramen 2: Nancy Bennett, John Butman, Dick Catron, Frederick Elmes, Tom Famighetti, Peter Flynn, Robert Foresta, David Freeberg, Tony Janetti, Arnold Klein, Ron Levitas, Didier Loiseau, David Ludwig, Laura Primakoff, Gordon Stein, Oliver Stone, Bruce Tabor, Stan Weiser, Bob Zahn
Recordist/Interviewers 1: Jay Freund, Josh Stein, Michael Eppy, Harry Bolles, Danny Schneider, Marty Andrews, Bruce Tabor, David Ludwig

CAST: (all as themselves) William Kunstler, Dave Dellinger, Alan W Carter, David Z Robinson, Harvey Keitel, Verna Bloom, Jay Cocks, Martin Scorsese.

SUMMARY: The film documents public reaction to the American invasion of Cambodia. Protestors walk down a New York street and hand out leaflets, a heavy police presence visible on all sides. People for and against the fighting air their views to camera at a Wall Street rally. As speakers address the gathering, a group of construction workers bearing an American flag march through the crowd, and a vicious fight ensues. In a room some time afterwards, the film-makers discuss how they were attacked during the shoot. A later attempt to record a confrontation between a student and a network TV representative results in the crew's cameras being banned from the network's studio.

Another demonstration in Washington leads to the film-makers being granted access to the White House press room. Outside, we see the crowd tear-gassed into submission. Another discussion among film-makers erupts into a row over the best way to make political statements, finishing with Jay Cocks advocating 'reason' rather than 'force'.

WHO'S WHO?: Oliver Stone, who directed some of the footage used for the short, was later famous as a screenwriter and director responsible for a critically acclaimed trilogy of films about Vietnam consisting of *Platoon* (1986), *Born on the Fourth of July* (1989) and *Heaven and Earth* (1993). Jay Cocks first met Scorsese in 1968 when he was researching an article for *Time* magazine on student film-makers and would become one of Scorsese's closest friends and long-time collaborators.

THE USUAL SUSPECTS: Harvey Keitel (*Who's That Knocking At My Door?, Mean Streets, Alice Doesn't Live Here Anymore, Taxi Driver, The Last Temptation of Christ*); Jay Cocks (writer, *Made in Milan, The Age of Innocence, Gangs of New York*); editor Thelma Schoonmaker *Who's That Knocking At My Door?, Taxi Driver, Raging Bull, The King of Comedy, After Hours, The Color of Money, Bad, The Last Temptation of Christ, New York Stories, GoodFellas, Cape Fear, Age of Innocence, Casino, A Personal Journey with Martin Scorsese Through American Movies, Kundun, Bringing Out the Dead, My Voyage to Italy, Gangs of New York*).

PRODUCTION: This documentary project was inspired by the killing, in May 1970, of four students by heavy-handed state troopers who fired on a crowd of anti-war demonstrators at Kent State University. Scorsese and a group of his friends and some of his NYU students documented the groundswell of opinion. Harvey Keitel had been incensed by the slaughter and when he phoned Scorsese and learned about the project, he agreed to join them.

Scorsese directed only the last segment, dealing with a rap session among himself and some friends. The remaining parts were shot by student members of the NY Cinetract Collective during anti-war demonstrations on Wall Street and in Washington DC. As post-production supervisor, however, Scorsese had final cut, and in this sense, the picture can be said to represent his own feelings towards the public response to the US invasion of Cambodia, 'that no one political position, or any single individual holds the solution to such a complex issue'. *Street Scenes* premiered on 14 September 1970.

Neither the right nor the left agreed with the film's conclusion; individuals were beaten up during filming; Scorsese suffered massive asthma attacks; film stock came from donations. Indeed, all this added to the frustration of working with amateurs, students and makeshift equipment, coupled with an inconclusive subject matter that divided all who saw it, and led Scorsese to all but disown the film, rarely including it in his official filmography.

KEEP IT IN THE FAMILY: Actress Verna Bloom, who appears here in one of the discussion scenes, is the wife of Scorsese's friend Jay Cocks.

EXPERT WITNESS: 'I see the movie we did as more than entertainment. I resolved then to try to choose roles that have social meaning.' Participant Harvey Keitel.

SCORSESE ON *STREET SCENES*: 'I used footage that showed nobody knew what to do, neither radicals nor conservatives. Everybody was yelling at everybody and the picture ends in the middle of an argument because that was when the film literally ran out! I just left it that way. I thought "Perfect", it was godsent.'

Boxcar Bertha (1972)
(aka *Bloody Song of Freedom* German Title: *Die Faust der Rebellen*

(35 mm – 88 mins – colour)

MPAA Rating: R

Produced by American International Pictures
Written by: Joyce Hooper Corrington (as Joyce H
Corrington) & John William Corrington, based on the book
***Sister of the Road* by Bertha Thompson as told to Ben L**
Reitman
Producer: Roger Corman
Associate Producer: Julie Corman
Executive Producers: Samuel Z Arkoff, James H Nicholson
(not credited)
Executive in Charge of Production: Paul Rapp

Music: Gib Guilbeau & Thad Maxwell
Music Producer: Herb Cohen
Director of Photography: John M Stephens (credited as John Stephens)
Film Editor: Buzz Feitshans
Titles: The Golds West, Inc.
Script Supervisor: Bobbie Sierks
Costume Supervisor: Bob Modes

UNCREDITED CREW: Sound Editors: Fred J Brown, Roger Sword and Ross Taylor.

CAST: Barbara Hershey (*'Boxcar' Bertha*), David Carradine (*'Big' Bill Shelly*), Barry Primus (*Rake Brown*), Bernie Casey (*Von Morton*), John Carradine (*H Buckram Sartoris*), Victor Argo (*McIver 1*), David R Osterhout (*McIver 2*), Grahame Pratt (*Emeric Pressburger*), 'Chicken' Holleman (*M Powell*), Harry Northup (*Harvey Hall*), Ann Morell (*Tillie Parr*), Marianne Dole (*Mrs Mailler*), Joe Reynolds (*Joe Cox*).

UNCREDITED CAST: Gayne Rescher and Martin Scorsese (*Brothel Clients*).

TITLES: A title card announces: 'The following events are adapted from the experiences of "Box Car" Bertha Thompson as related in the book *Sister of the Road*'. We open on a shot of the young Bertha, who watches a plane fly by as men work on the railroad. The pilot is her father, a dust-cropper. He can't afford to repair his plane, but his employer forces him to continue flying. When the plane crashes, killing her father, Bertha attacks her father's boss and the workmen begin to beat him up. The titles begin with the credits daubed in thick paintbrush strokes, with the title in red and the rest in black. Then the mists come in and we see Bertha chase the morning train and jump up into a boxcar. Across sepia images of the railroad, a newspaper with the headline DEPRESSION CRIPPLES US and a montage of burnt out images, a circular inset appears and shows the main cast. As the final credit, Scorsese's name appears in white, then turns red before fading out.

SUMMARY: Arkansas, during the Great Depression. Drifter Bertha Thompson strikes up a relationship with 'Big' Bill Shelly, a union activist on the run from the railroad company's hired thugs (the McIvers). When Bill moves on, Bertha makes friends with a businessman from the North called Rake Brown. Sitting in on a card game between Rake and some business contacts, Bertha overhears the men speak of a plan to ensure Bill Shelly is punished for agitating the workers. But when one of the men accuses Rake of cheating and pulls a gun on him, Bertha shoots the man with Rake's gun. In a panic, Rake and Bertha go on the run.

Bertha drags Rake to where she knows the Unionists will be camped out, but before she can find Bill the camp is raided by company men led by the McIvers. Worried by the fact that the company men are carrying guns, Rake manages to persuade Bertha to escape with him in a train wagon which, coincidentally, is where they find Bill and his comrades hiding. Further down the line, the train is stopped by cops who begin to search the carriages, and Bill sends Bertha running for cover just before he, Rake and the others are arrested.

In jail, Bill is reunited with Von Morton, an old friend. When the sheriff sees Bill being so friendly with a 'nigger' he orders that Bill should be beaten until he too is black. The other cellmates start a riot until the McIvers arrive and begin to fire indiscriminately into the cage, killing a number of the prisoners and quickly putting an end to the riot. The surviving men are put to work on a chain gang. Bertha, dressed as a young missionary, pretends her car has broken down and distracts the guard while Bill hits him with a shovel and knocks him out. Bertha, Bill, Von Morton and Rake escape in Bertha's car, but after a close chase by a police car, the car breaks down. Ever resourceful, they use the car as a blockade to stop a train, which they then loot and hijack, leaving the bewildered train drivers behind.

The jailbreak makes the newspapers, but the escapees are far from happy when they see that the press have branded Rake a coward and Bertha a common prostitute and murderer. Learning about the shooting of the businessman for the first time, Bill panics and decides he wants to make off on his own with his share of the money. But after he is turned away from the union for being a trouble-causer, Bill returns to the fold to take part in the gang's crime spree, robbing a payroll office and a train full of passengers.

The actions of the gang begin to worry wealthy businessman Sartoris, who tells the McIvers that he and his associates are losing money every day because of Bill Shelly and his mob. As Sartoris plans his revenge, Rake and Morton prepare an attack on Sartoris's home and persuade Bill and Bertha to join them. Posing as guests, Rake and Bertha manage to gain access to the house and they proceed to rob Sartoris and his guests of their money and valuables. But, recognising Bill as one of the robbers, Sartoris mocks the ex-union man, saying that he'd assumed Shelly was a Bolshevik, but realises now that he's just a common crook.

Continuing their attacks on Sartoris, the gang sneaks aboard Sartoris's private train and attempts to kidnap him at gunpoint. But, when Sartoris reveals he has a small army of henchmen also aboard the train, Rake panics and is shot at point-blank range by the men. Bill manages to shout a warning to Bertha, who evades capture by jumping on to a passing train. Bill and Von Morton, however, are once again arrested and put back on to the chain gang.

Some time later, having spent time working as a prostitute in a brothel, Bertha goes to a bar where she is overjoyed to find Von Morton playing his harmonica. He tells her that Bill broke out of jail about a month ago and is on the run. He takes her to Bill's hide-out for an emotional reunion, unaware that the McIvers have also tracked down Bill's whereabouts. Bertha is knocked to the floor and Bill is easily overcome by the company men. As Bertha lies dazed on the ground, she can only watch as Bill is held against the side of a rail-wagon and crucified. Von Morton manages to gun down the company men and rescue Bertha, but the train pulls off with Bill's dying body still nailed to its side.

WHO'S WHO?: Eccentric actress Barbara Hershey's most famous role is probably that of the terminally ill Hilary in *Beaches* (Garry Marshall, 1988) opposite Bette Midler, though she did receive an Academy Award nomination for her portrayal of Madame Serena Merle in *Portrait of a Lady* (Jane Campion, 1996). She had a relationship with her *Boxcar Bertha* co-star David Carradine, the father of her child 'Free' (he later changed his name to 'Tom'). Hershey briefly changed her name to 'Barbara Seagull', allegedly to atone for accidentally killing a seagull while driving. Having played a number of minuscule roles in a number of early Universal horror movies back in the 30s, including James Whale's *The Invisible Man* (1933) and *Bride of Frankenstein* (1935), John Carradine was a major player in Universal's revival of the genre a decade later, playing Count Dracula in Erle C Kenton's *House of Frankenstein* (1944) and *House of Dracula* (1945), a role, or variants of which he'd play many more times. By the end of his career, he was working almost exclusively in cheap horror movies designed for the video market, the best of these being *The Monster Club* (Roy Ward Baker, 1980) opposite Vincent Price. One of these roles, that of the ghost of Dr Frankenstein in *Frankenstein Island* (Jerry Warren, 1981), at least allowed him to lay claim to the boast that he'd played both Frankenstein and Dracula. David Carradine is the eldest son of John Carradine and half-brother of actors Keith and Robert. A familiar face from over 150

TV and cinema projects, he'll forever be remembered for his leading role in the long-running TV series *Kung Fu*. Like his father, he holds that rare distinction of having played a character called Frankenstein – in the Carmageddon action thriller *Deathrace* 2000 (Paul Bartel, 1975) – and the infamous Count Dracula – in *Sundown* (Anthony Hickox, 1989).

After *Boxcar Bertha*, ex-NFL American football star Bernie Casey found a number of roles in the Blaxploitation genre, in pictures such as *Cleopatra Jones* (Jack Starrett, 1973) and *Dr. Black, Mr. Hyde* (William Crain, 1976). Later he found himself moving into comedy with parts like Jefferson in *Revenge of the Nerds* (Jeff Kanew, 1984) and its sequels, and Mr Ryan the History Teacher who was partly responsible for kick-starting *Bill & Ted's Excellent Adventure* (Steven Herek, 1989). Producers Roger Corman and Samuel Z Arkoff have between them been responsible for some of the most varied, exciting and, above all, cheaply made films ever, riding every genre trend from sci-fi and horror right through to such transient cinematic obsessions as gangsters, bikers, blaxploitation, women in prison and teen slashers. The Corman 'school' of film-making counts among its graduates Francis Ford Coppola, Jonathan Demme, Peter Bogdanovich and Joe Dante. Musician Gib (real name Floyd August) Guilbeau has been a member of numerous bands, including Nashville West, Swampwater (who toured with Linda Ronstadt) and the Flying Burrito Brothers (who later shortened their name to simply the Burrito Brothers). Guilbeau's songs have been recorded by, among others, the Byrds, Rick Nelson and Rod Stewart.

THE USUAL SUSPECTS: Barbara Hershey (*The Last Temptation of Christ*); David Carradine (*Mean Streets*); Barry Primus (*New York, New York*); Victor Argo (*Mean Streets, Taxi Driver, After Hours, The Last Temptation of Christ*); Harry Northup (*Who's That Knocking At My Door?, Mean Streets, Alice Doesn't Live Here Anymore, Taxi Driver, New York, New York, Amazing Stories*: 'Mirror Mirror').

SOURCE: As the opening titles inform us, the script, by Joyce Hooper Corrington and John William Corrington, was loosely based on *Sister of the Road*, the autobiography of Bertha Thompson 'as told to' Ben L Reitman (reprinted in May 2002 with an introduction by Kathy Acker), first published in 1937. As might be expected with an exploitation picture, certain liberties were taken with the truth. The two months Bertha spent working at the Globe brothel are boiled down to just two scenes – her arrival at the house and an evening where one of her clients turns out to be an anthropologist studying prostitutes. The anthropologist is based on Dr Harry Fredericks, who Bertha met on a train journey (not, as claimed in the film, as one of her clients at the brothel). Bertha's mother is completely excised from the script, as is Bertha's pregnancy, and although Bertha acknowledges that her time as a prostitute left her with over fifteen hundred possible fathers for her child, she generally attributed paternity to her long-time companion Big Otto (who in the film becomes 'Big Bill'). Unlike the sensationalist lynch-mob execution of Bill in the picture, Otto was executed by the State, hanged for murder after he killed a cashier in a bungled robbery.

PRODUCTION: In the early 70s, the gangster genre was enjoying a brief revival thanks to the unexpected success of *Bonnie and Clyde* (Arthur Penn, 1967). Ever quick off the mark, Roger Corman, the notorious producer of low-budget exploitation movies, had already cashed in on the trend with the hastily prepared *Bloody Mama* (1970), starring Shelley Winters as the infamous gangster Ma Barker and a young Robert De Niro as her bewildered son. Keen to capitalise on *Bloody Mama*'s success, Corman began preparing an unofficial sequel and, at the recommendation of his bride-to-be Julie, began preparing a production based on the life of activist and ex-criminal Bertha Thompson. Taking Thompson's ghost-written autobiography as his source, Corman hired Joyce and John William Corrington (who had scripted *The Red Baron* for Corman the previous year) to adapt the book for the screen, but with the strict edict to keep the sex and the violence – highly exploitable commodities – to the fore.

Introduced to Corman by his agents at William Morris, Scorsese was invited to direct. Scorsese later claimed that he'd been initially tempted because the film promised 'costumes and guns'. Corman told Scorsese that the script would be called 'Boxcar Bertha' and would be ready for filming in six months. With that, Corman went off to get married. As Scorsese waited for Corman to get back to him, he managed to get work as a sound editor for his friend and mentor John Cassavetes on his latest film *Minnie and Moskowitz* (1971), which effectively secured Scorsese $500 a week just to hang around the set.

Having almost given up hope of hearing from Corman again, Scorsese was relieved when the producer finally called to confirm him as director on *Boxcar Bertha*. Corman provided a budget of $600,000 and instructed Scorsese to produce a picture that incorporated some form of nudity or titillation every fifteen minutes, even if that meant merely a flash of leg. The sound mixing for the picture would have to be completed within just three days, at a rate of three reels a day, an incredibly tight schedule. Corman also advised Scorsese to ensure the first and last reels received the most attention, apparently telling Scorsese without a hint of sarcasm that 'the first reel has to be good because people coming to the drive-in have to hear what's going on. Forget the rest of the film until you get to the last reel, because they just want to know how it turned out.'

Having been fired from *The Honeymoon Killers* for attempting to film the entire picture in master shots (see **Unseen Scorsese**), Scorsese was determined not to make the same mistake again. He decided to plan ahead and storyboard the entire picture. When Corman asked to see the initial preparation for the project, Scorsese began showing him individual sketches for every single shot – some five hundred in total. This surprised Corman, but it at least showed that his young director appeared to know what he was doing and convinced him to leave Scorsese to it.

The shoot was scheduled to take place on location, in Reader, Arkansas, over 24 continuous days with little in the way of incident. By chance, while on a location scout, Scorsese found a church with a large mural of Mary Magdalene on one wall and incorporated it into the picture. During production, Corman visited the set and Scorsese took the opportunity to negotiate for an extra day to film a car chase that had not appeared in the original script but was to be inserted at Corman's instruction. Corman refused more time, asserting that Scorsese would simply have to work it into his current schedule. Undeterred, Scorsese managed to wrap the shoot within its scheduled time. The picture opened as part of a double bill with Ray Austin's *1000 Convicts and a Woman*.

EDITING: Though Buzz Feitshans is credited as editor, Scorsese insists that he himself cut the picture, simply because he didn't feel he could trust anyone else with it. However, this really doesn't feel like a Scorsese picture, with many scenes dissolving into the next instead of the usual jump-cuts we'd expect. The sound, though, owes much to *Bonnie and Clyde* and the Westerns of John Ford, with gunshots echoing across invisible canyons and exploding out of the screen with an unnatural exuberance.

MUSIC: Singer-songwriter Gib Guilbeau, working with old friend Thad Maxwell, contributed three songs to the picture: 'Bertha's Theme', 'Boxcar Bertha Blues' and 'Boxcar Bertha Cues'. Gib's frenzied fiddle-and-harmonica tunes really give a sense of the Deep South during the Depression from the very first scene. Sadly, the soundtrack was never released commercially, though Guilbeau has recorded many albums both as a solo artist and as a member of many different American folk bands. A brief comical moment occurs just before the jail riot as an irritable guard shouts at the harmonica-playing Von Morton: 'If you're gonna play, you play Dixie – or shut up!'

QUOTE/UNQUOTE

Shelly: 'I'm not a criminal; I'm a Union man.'

Rake: 'I had a dog in New York once.'
Bill: 'What'd ya do – lose him in a craps game?'
Rake: 'No, as a matter of fact I didn't lose him in a craps game – he started a union!'

ROOTS: Bertha's hair in the first scene is a nod to Judy Garland's Dorothy in *The Wizard of Oz* (Victor Fleming, 1939). We get another reference to Oz later on, with Bertha telling one of her guests at the brothel to 'pay no attention to that man behind the curtain'. As already noted, the sound recordings of the gunshots really try to outmatch the sheer volume of those in Bonnie and Clyde. The two McIvers (who are led a merry dance for most of the movie) bear an uncanny resemblance to slapstick comedians Laurel and Hardy, a possible dig at the compilation of their work that delayed the release of *Who's That Knocking At My Door?* back in 1969.

Two characters are named after Michael Powell and Emmerich Pressburger, whose film-making partnership was responsible for some of the greatest British films of the post-war period, including *The Thief of Bagdad* (1940), *A Matter of Life and Death* (1946), *Black Narcissus* (1947) and *The Red Shoes* (1948). Michael Powell would eventually become a close friend of Scorsese and went on to marry Scorsese's long-time collaborator Thelma Schoonmaker.

THEMES AND MOTIFS: As in *Who's That Knocking At My Door?*, *Taxi Driver* and others, the central issue with Bertha here is the dichotomy between whore and virgin. The mural of Mary Magdalene on the back wall of the church reminds us that in the eyes of many men, women polarise into saints/mothers or whores. Indeed, the anthropologist–punter at the brothel asks her lots of questions, including 'Was your mother a whore?' Significantly, both Bertha's mother and her own experience of motherhood are missing from the finished picture. A mirror again plays an important part, reflecting Bertha and her client on the bed in the brothel, yet tilted at an angle, as if to show us 'God's view' of the proceedings.

BIBLE CLASS: The bloody climax to the picture, depicting a crucifixion, was already a part of the script before Scorsese's involvement, something he took as a sign: 'I liked the way we shot it, the angles we used, and in particular the way you saw the nails coming through the wood, though they were never seen piercing flesh.' As Bill hangs from the side of a rail-wagon, the McIvers nail a playing card above his head, a visual reference to the sign INRI nailed at the head of Christ's cross.

CONTROVERSY: Ah, the exploitation genre. Structured to give maximum titillation at the beginning, at regular intervals throughout, and then a big climax. Almost the first shot has a quick flash of Barbara Hershey's thigh, which, considering she's supposed to be a young girl no more than about fifteen is a little worrying. In the build-up to the first sex scene there's some playful innuendo, where Bertha calls Bill a 'real straight shooter', he assures her he's 'the best straight shooter', noting that she's never seen him shoot. The first flash of nudity is bang on the ten-minute mark, halfway through the first reel as Bill and Bertha make love (both David Carradine and Barbara Hershey have claimed that their sex scenes were not faked). Though Bill is one of the few who seems to have any respect for Bertha, after they make love he leaves her some money. Whether this is to tide her over or to be considered payment for services rendered is unclear.

A film set in America's Deep South would be somewhat less than believable if the issue of racism wasn't tackled in some way. A guard complains about the jail being 'full of communists and coons' shortly before he's instructed by the sheriff to 'go make a nigger' out of Bill by beating him until he too is black. And Bill's return to the union office is met with concern by his old colleague Joe who exclaims: 'Whores and niggers, my God, ain't that a nice image for unionism?!'

THERE HE IS!: Is that really Scorsese as the painter at the brothel about 1 hour 14 minutes in? It certainly looks like him, but whose is that voice?

LEGACY: During the filming of *Boxcar Bertha*, Barbara Hershey showed Scorsese a novel by Nikos Kazantzakis called *The Last Temptation of Christ*. The book became a personal obsession for the director, who eventually filmed it fourteen years later, casting Hershey in a pivotal role and structuring significant shots of crucifixion almost identically to the final scenes of *Boxcar*.

Incidentally, an episode of the British comedy series *The Goodies* entitled 'Kung Fu Capers' featured a song about the Queen of Northern Soul, 'Black Pudding Bertha'.

TRIVIA: Watch the spare tyre that seems to appear and disappear from the back of the car in scenes set after Bertha frees Bill Shelly from the prison gang. President Franklin D Roosevelt makes an appearance in the film thanks to the archive film footage used in the opening montage.

SELLING THE FILM: With a strange attempt at impersonating the speech patterns of the American South, the tagline for the lobby posters boasted: 'America in the 30's was a Free Country. Bertha was jes' a little bit free'er than most.' The poster art depicted Bertha in sultry pose, Bill grimacing as he's nailed to the train-carriage (rather spoiling the film's climax) and a montage of Von Morton's face, a train racing across an exploding track and a small image of Bertha and Bill embracing.

AWARDS: Regardless of what John Cassavetes thought (see **WHAT THE CRITICS SAID** below), *Boxcar Bertha* was considered good enough to get Scorsese into the American Director's Guild.

AVAILABILITY: *Boxcar Bertha* was released on full-screen VHS in the UK by Virgin Video in 1989 as part of their Gangster collection alongside *Bloody Mama*, *Dillinger* (John Milius, 1973) and *A Bullet for Pretty Boy* (Larry Buchanan, Maury Dexter, 1970). In the USA, Vestron video relcased both the VHS and laserdisc versions, long since deleted.

WHAT THE CRITICS SAID: John Cassavetes, veteran actor and director, told Scorsese, 'You just spent a year of your life making a piece of shit.' (Subsequently, Cassavetes has modified this view, saying it was a good picture, but unworthy of Scorsese's talent.)

In a retrospective on Scorsese's work for *Empire*, Andy Gill wrote: '*Boxcar Bertha* eschews overt action and gunplay in favour of a more realistic, if not fully realised, portrayal of life in the Depression,' awarding the picture just two stars.

FINAL ANALYSIS: Though it's more a Roger Corman production than a Scorsese one, Cassavetes's dismissal of *Boxcar Bertha* as 'a piece of shit' is still unfair. The narrative is tightly plotted, with a fine balance between provocative sexuality, comedy and raw action even if much of it is played out in a series of set pieces rather than a clear, developing story. The performances are all fine, too, with Barry Primus (Rake), stealing the film with a number of humorous segments (trying to divide their loot into even piles of $1s, $20s, $50s and $100s, bitching about being dressed in a tux instead of tails as they prepare to rob Sartoris's guests. The only real problem is the love affair between Bertha and Bill which isn't really convincing, perhaps because, with Hershey's little-girl-lost act and Carradine's lack of real screen charisma, there really isn't much of a spark between them.

SCORSESE ON *BOXCAR BERTHA*: 'Mostly I attempted to show the characters as people acting like children, playing with violence until they start getting killed – then they're stuck in a real game, a life and death game. I used the element of surprise violence to emphasise that when you least expect it, things are destroyed, people are killed – that's very important to the picture.'

Mean Streets (1973)

(35 mm – 110 min – colour)

MPAA Rating: R

A Taplin–Perry–Scorsese Production for Warner Bros.
Producer: Jonathan T Taplin
Executive Producer: E Lee Perry
Cinematographer: Kent Wakeford
Film Editor: Sid Levin
Production Manager: Paul Rapp
Second Assistant Director: Ron Satlof
First Assistant Director: Russell Vreeland
Property Master: Bill Bates
Sound: Glen Glenn
Sound Re-recording Mixers: Walter Goss, Charles Grenzbach, John Wilkinson
Sound Mixer: Don Johnson
Boom Operator: Kenneth Schwarz
Special Effects: Bill Bales
Visual Consultant: David Nichols
Assistant Visual Consultant: Doyle Hall

Director of Photography, New York: Norman Gerard
Director of Photography, Second Unit: Alec Hirschfeld
Wardrobe: Norman Salling
Animal Trainer: George Toth

SOUNDTRACK: 'Jumping Jack Flash', 'Tell Me' by The Rolling Stones; 'I Love So' by the Chantells; 'Addio Sogni di Gloria', 'Canta Per' Me', 'Munasterio Di Santa Chiara' by Giuseppe De Stefano; 'Marruzella', 'Scapricciatiello' by Renato Carosone; 'Please Mr Postman' by the Marvelettes; 'Hideaway', 'I Looked Away' by Eric Clapton; 'Desiree' by the Charts; 'Rubber Biscuit' by the Chips; 'Pledging My Love' by Johnny Ace; 'Ritmo Sabroso' by Ray Baretto; 'You' by the Aquatones; 'Ship of Love' by the Nutmegs; 'Florence' by the Paragons; 'Malafemmina' by Jimmy Roselli; 'Those Oldies But Goodies' by Little Caesar and the Romans; 'I Met Him on a Sunday' by the Shirelles; 'Be My Baby' by the Ronettes, 'Mickey's Monkey' by the Miracles.

CAST: Robert De Niro (*Johnny Boy*), Harvey Keitel (*Charlie*), David Proval (*Tony*), Amy Robinson (*Teresa*), Richard Romanus (*Michael*), Cesare Danova (*Giovanni*), George Memmoli (*Joey Catucci*), Victor Argo (*Mario*), Lenny Scaletta (*Jimmy*), Murray Moston (*Oscar*), David Carradine (*Drunk*), Robert Carradine (*Assassin*), Jeannie Bell (*Diane*), Lois Walden (*Girl at Bar*), D'Mitch Davis (*Black Cop*), Dino Seragusa (*Old Man*), Julie Andelman (*Girl at Party*), Peter Fain (*George*), Harry Northup (*Soldier*), Robert Wilder (*Benton*), Jaime Alba (*First Young Boy*), Ken Konstantin (*Second Young Boy*), Nicki 'Ack' Aquilino (*Man on Docks*), Ken Sinclair (*Sammy*), B Mitchell Reed (*Disc Jockey*).

UNCREDITED CAST: Catherine Scorsese (*Woman on Landing*), Martin Scorsese (*Jimmy Shorty, Michael's hired killer*), Ron Satloff (*Carl*), Anna Uricola (*Neighbour at Window*), Barbara Weintraub, Heather Weintraub (*Girls with Johnny Boy*).

TITLES: In blackness, we hear Michael assert that you make up for your sins on the streets (see **QUOTE/UNQUOTE** below). Michael wakes up in bed with a start. He goes over to his mirror, checks his reflection and then, exhausted, goes back to bed. As he tries to get back to sleep, a series of jump-cuts bring us close in on Michael's face and the opening music begins: 'Be My Baby' by the Ronettes. Next, courtesy of an ancient projector, we're treated to some home movie footage of Charlie greeting people in the streets, attending a christening and generally showing us the nice guy that he is. The image is projected centre screen with the title MEAN STREETS spanning the screen in red and the credits either above or below image in a white typewriter font.

SUMMARY: We are introduced to Charlie's friends: Tony owns the bar where they all spend their time; Michael, a would-be Don, supervises a haul; 'Johnny Boy' Cervello, meanwhile, blows up a mailbox for kicks. Michael is annoyed that Johnny Boy has once again defaulted on the repayments on a loan Michael gave him. Michael goes to see Charlie, who has the respect of the guys thanks in no small part to the influence of his uncle, Giovanni. Michael hopes Charlie will talk some common sense into his friend, especially as it was Charlie who vouched for Johnny in the first place. Johnny doesn't help matters by turning up at Tony's bar later that evening with a couple of girls. When Charlie confronts him about the repayments, Johnny initially claims that he paid Michael his money before eventually confessing that actually he didn't. Charlie shakes Johnny Boy down, cleaning out his wallet and leaving him just a little money to entertain his girlfriends for the evening. When they bump into Michael later, Johnny promises he'll make his payment the next week without fail.

Charlie goes to see his Uncle Giovanni and tells him that he thinks that Oscar, a man who owes them money, is faking poverty to avoid making payments. Giovanni tells Charlie not to worry, to let things take their course.

After another late night at Tony's bar, a skinny young guy tells Tony he's waiting for a friend, and indicates a drunk staggering to the bathroom, knocking chairs over and generally making a nuisance of himself. The skinny guy follows the drunk into the bathroom, pulls out a gun and shoots him, to everyone's shock. The drunk goes to attack the gunman, but collapses in the street outside the bar. Hearing the police sirens, Charlie and Johnny leave the bar and accept a lift from Michael part of the way home.

Charlie has secretly been dating Johnny's cousin Teresa, who is epileptic. Charlie tells her about the shooting, and explains that it all happened because the drunk insulted Mario, a rival wiseguy, and that the kid shot the drunk to climb the ranks of the mob. Teresa tells Charlie she's going to move to an apartment away from her parents, but she's waiting for him, despite him telling her he cannot leave the neighbourhood because of his responsibilities. Knowing how Charlie looks after Johnny, she warns him that her cousin is insane. Later, at Giovanni's restaurant, Charlie hears his uncle discussing the shooting.

Mario claims there was no insult in the first place and that he never asked anyone to shoot the guy for him. The father of the assassin tells Giovanni that his son is in hiding and begs for protection, but Giovanni refuses, suggesting the father should send his son away for a year until things have been forgotten. Charlie dines with Giovanni and Mario at Oscar's. Giovanni tells Charlie to inspect the restaurant, intending to hand control of the place over to his nephew soon, but Giovanni also warns him to stay away from Johnny and Teresa as he feels they are both likely to cause trouble.

Michael comes to see Charlie and tells him he can't give Johnny Boy any more chances. Charlie promises he'll talk to Johnny that night at the welcome home party they are throwing for their friend Jerry, back from Vietnam. Predictably, Johnny doesn't show up at the party and Michael tells Charlie that Johnny now owes him $3,000. Charlie now understands why Johnny couldn't make the payments, and is appalled that Michael would charge someone from his own neighbourhood so much in interest. Out of respect for Charlie, Michael agrees to lower the debt to $2,000, but threatens to break Johnny's legs if he has to go looking for him again. Teresa comes to the bar to find Charlie. She tells him Johnny Boy is up on a roof with a loaded gun. With some difficulty, Charlie manages to talk the distressed Johnny Boy down. Johnny asks him to speak to his uncle about a loan, but Charlie refuses.

Johnny spends the evening hiding out from Michael. He goes to Charlie's apartment via the fire escape and sees Charlie and Teresa together. Making his way into the apartment, Johnny Boy teases Charlie and Teresa before losing his temper and threatening to tell Charlie's uncle about them. The men fight, but then Teresa begins to fit. Eventually they all calm down and Charlie gives Johnny some more money for Michael. But when Michael finally catches up with them at Tony's bar, Johnny offers him just $10. Michael tells him it's an insult. Johnny replies that nobody in the neighbourhood is stupid enough to lend him money – except Michael. Enraged, Michael lunges at Johnny, who in turn pulls a gun on him. Michael leaves and Charlie goes berserk at Johnny. Tony lends them his car so they can get away. After a brief stop-off at a cinema, they decide to drive off to Greenwood Lake. Teresa insists on coming with them. As they drive towards Brooklyn, Michael drives up next to their car and one of his crew starts shooting at them and their car skids off the road and crashes. Teresa and Charlie are taken away by paramedics as Johnny Boy limps off into the night clutching his neck where he has been shot.

WHO'S WHO?: Robert De Niro is the actor most regularly associated with Martin Scorsese. Their almost instinctive understanding of each other's methods has led to them collaborating on some of the most important films in the last 30 years. De Niro has acted in almost 80 feature films, including Brian De Palma's *Greetings* (1968), *Hi Mom* (1970) and (as Al Capone) *The Untouchables* (1987), *The Godfather Part II* (Francis Ford Coppola, 1974) (as the young Vito Corleone, for which he won a Best Supporting Actor Oscar), *The Deer Hunter* (Michael Cimino, 1978), *Once upon a Time In America* (Sergio Leone, 1984) and *Meet the Parents* (Jay Roach, 2000). In 1993, he finally stepped behind the camera to direct an adaptation of Chazz Palminteri's play *A Bronx Tale*. Despite being one of cinema's most famous Italian–American actors, he is not actually an Italian–American, coming from French–Irish stock. Robert and David Carradine, along with their brother Keith, followed their father, legendary actor John Carradine, into show business. David previously appeared in Scorsese's *Boxcar Bertha*. More than twenty-five years after *Mean Streets*, David Proval would also play Richie Aprile in the gangster drama TV series *The Sopranos*, which, in its third season also featured an appearance by Richard Romanus.

THE USUAL SUSPECTS: Robert De Niro (*Taxi Driver, New York, New York, Raging Bull, The King of Comedy, GoodFellas, Cape Fear, Casino*); Harvey Keitel (*Street Scenes, Who's That Knocking At My Door?; Alice Doesn't Live Here Anymore, Taxi Driver, The Last Temptation of Christ*); Victor Argo (*Boxcar Bertha, Taxi Driver, After Hours, The Last Temptation of Christ*); Harry Northup (*Who's That Knocking At My Door?, Boxcar Bertha, Alice Doesn't Live Here Anymore, Taxi Driver, New York, New York, Amazing Stories*: 'Mirror Mirror'); Murray Moston (*Alice Doesn't Live Here Anymore, Taxi Driver, New York, New York, After Hours*); George Memmoli (*New York, New York, American Boy*); Peter Fain (*New York, New York, Raging Bull, The King of Comedy, GoodFellas*); Amy Robinson (producer, *After Hours*).

PRODUCTION: *Mean Streets* started life as 'Season of the Witch', the third part of a planned trilogy, following on from *Who's That Knocking At My Door?* and the abandoned *Jerusalem, Jerusalem*. Having seen *Who's That Knocking At My Door?*, Scorsese's mentor, Haig Manoogian, read 'Season of the Witch' and begged him not to make 'more pictures about Italians'. However, Scorsese's friend Jay Cocks showed *Who's That Knocking* . . . to John Cassavetes, who suggested to Scorsese he should make films more like that and less like *Boxcar Bertha*. The script of 'Season of the Witch', following on from *Who's That Knocking* . . . was still very much concerned with the religion of the characters. Scorsese's partner at the time, Sandra Weintraub, felt that the script needed lightening up and suggested he make more of the comedy, drawing from the kind of anecdotes Scorsese would tell Sandra about his own upbringing in Little Italy. Out came much of the religion, and in came scenes such as the one set in the pool-hall.

During one of its many subsequent rewrites, Scorsese's friend Jay Cocks suggested the title 'Mean Streets', inspired by a phrase from Raymond Chandler. Scorsese's producer on *Boxcar Bertha*, Roger Corman, was interested in producing the script, and offered him $150,000 towards production costs – but only if he'd rewrite it more in line with the latest trend – blaxploitation. Mindful of Cassavetes's words on *Boxcar Bertha*, and aware that rewriting the script for a black cast would take him too far away from the personal film he wanted to make, Scorsese declined Corman's offer.

While Scorsese was working as an editor on *Elvis on Tour* (Robert Abel, Pierre Adidge, 1972), Jay Cocks's wife, actress Verna Bloom, introduced him to Jonathan Taplin, ex-road manager for the Band (see **The Last Waltz**) who was keen to move into film production. Taplin read Scorsese's script and viewed both *Who's That Knocking* . . . and *Boxcar Bertha* before he agreed to produce *Mean Streets*. With a budget of about $600,000, and with Scorsese still considered an untested director, Taplin insisted the bulk of the picture was made in LA where they could keep an eye on him. As a compromise, Scorsese managed to persuade Taplin to let him have eight days of filming in New York.

Verna Bloom was also instrumental in setting Scorsese up with one of the most important working relationships of his career. Then a virtually unknown actor, Robert De Niro had worked on three low-budget pictures for Brian De Palma as well as a few other pictures in supporting roles. Though Scorsese and De Niro had been brought up mere streets away from each other and, it turned out, knew a lot of the same people, they hadn't met previously. Scorsese asked De Niro to read his script with the role of Johnny in mind, but De Niro turned it down, eager to play the more central character of Charlie. Scorsese had really wanted Keitel for Charlie, but had been persuaded by the backers to cast Jon Voight, thinking that his clout from the Oscar-nominated performance in *Midnight Cowboy* (John Schlesinger, 1969) might help the picture. But just before they went into production, Voight changed his mind, leaving Scorsese free to cast his first choice, and within days he was filming Keitel walking through the streets during the San Gennaro Festival. It was Keitel who eventually persuaded De Niro to take the lesser part of Johnny Boy. As he would often do, Scorsese taped the actors improvising in rehearsals and incorporated any interesting developments into the script. Some scenes, such as the one where Keitel and De Niro fight with trash cans, were improvised on location.

For the New York footage, Scorsese set to work with a largely inexperienced crew of students from NYU (even though Scorsese had been fired from NYU for missing classes, he managed to acquire most of what he needed just by pretending he was shooting a student film). The first night of shooting was the scene with Charlie and the black girl, shot on 8th Street and 6th Avenue. Improvising, Scorsese just hired a cab, paid the driver $25 for the night and shot the footage he needed. Other locations included the hallways and the cemetery of St Patrick's Cathedral, and some shots of Chinatown. For the scenes with Keitel strolling through the San Gennaro festival, Scorsese neglected to obtain permission to film. When the festival organisers sent him the bill for $5,000, Scorsese borrowed the money from Francis Coppola. Scorsese paid back the loan when Warner Bros picked up the picture.

An invaluable person on the shoot was the production manager Paul Rapp who had worked with the director on *Boxcar Bertha* and who advised him to get all the shots to be lit in one direction to be done first. This resulted in most of the scenes being shot backwards so they could get the close-ups and medium shots first to reduce the number of set-ups they needed, then pick up the master shot last. This technique saw them through the remaining 21 days of shooting in LA. Even taking into consideration the savings Scorsese had made throughout the production, it was slightly over budget, largely thanks to the cost of obtaining usage rights for the twenty or so songs used on the soundtrack.

After assembling a rough cut, De Niro and Scorsese discussed intently how the final cut should look. Taking advice from old friend, Brian De Palma, Scorsese considered removing the celebrated improvised segment where Keitel harangues De Niro about his loan. Thankfully, Jay Cocks persuaded him to leave it in.

Scorsese and Taplin began looking for a distributor for the picture and though Universal dismissed it out of hand, both Paramount and Warner Bros seemed keen. With Paramount riding high after Coppola's box-office smash adaptation of *The Godfather*, Scorsese was convinced that he would close a deal there and suggested to Taplin that maybe they wouldn't need Warners after all. But after a disastrous screening where the Paramount representative left after just ten minutes, Scorsese and Taplin were relieved they still had Warners. John Calley, head of production at the studio, and Leo Greenfield, head of distribution, were both New Yorkers and quickly identified with the setting and the characters. The deal was set.

While hawking the picture round the Cannes Film Festival in the May of 1973, Scorsese and Taplin were introduced to legendary New Wave auteur and Scorsese's idol, Federico Fellini. As the men talked, Fellini was interrupted by his distributor. In an act of generosity, Fellini persuaded his distributor to pick up Scorsese's film despite not having watched it himself. That autumn, *Mean Streets* was premiered at the New York Film Festival. The audience loved it, giving the director a standing ovation, and the reviews in the *New York Times*, notably from Pauline Kael, were glowing. However, though box-office takings were healthy, they were seriously dwarfed by another film, coincidentally also produced by Warner Bros – William Friedkin's *The Exorcist*.

EDITING: Taking his inspiration from a sequence in Alfred Hitchcock's *The Birds* (1963), Scorsese begins the picture with three quick cuts that zoom in on Charlie's face. Johnny Boy's entrance – to the sounds of the Rolling Stones – was filmed slightly faster so it could be slowed down to show Charlie's mounting frustration with his friend. An unusual technique was used to convey the sensation of the drunken Charlie. Harvey Keitel was fitted with an Arriflex body harness that was covered by his jacket. A camera was attached to this, locked on to his movements and giving the impression that it's the room that's moving. Other shots in the sequence were achieved by having Keitel stand on the dolly to make him look as though he's floating.

MUSIC: Though Scorsese had eschewed the traditional specially composed score in preference for existing music for *Who's That Knocking . . .*, it is in *Mean Streets* that he first gets to grips with how this can be an effective – if cost-consuming – way of conveying a specific era. Scorsese deliberately chose songs not just from the current charts but from the previous two or three decades. 'A lot of places you had jukeboxes,' he told Gavin Smith of *Film Comment* in 1990, 'and when The Beatles came in, you [still] had Benny Goodman, some old Italian stuff, Jerry Vale, Tony Bennett, doo-wop, early rock'n'roll, black and Italian.' From the opening drumbeats of 'Be My Baby', *Mean Streets* is Scorsese's first – but by no means last – attempt at the feature-length rock promo.

QUOTE/UNQUOTE

Charlie: 'You don't make up for your sins in church. You do it on the streets. You do it at home. The rest is bullshit and you know it.'

Charlie: 'It's all bullshit except the pain, right? The pain of Hell. The burn from a lighted match increased a million times. Infinite . . . well ya don't fuck around with the infinite. There's no way you do that.'

Everyone: 'What's a "mook"?'

Charlie: 'You know what the Queen said? "I had balls, I'd be a King." '

Johnny Boy: 'Y'know what we can do, she [Teresa] can have a seizure and we can watch.'

Johnny Boy: 'I fuck you right where you breathe.'

End credits: 'Good night, good luck and God bless you.'

ROOTS: The film showing as Johnny and Charlie hide at the cinema is Roger Corman's *Tomb of Ligeia* (1965), which Scorsese inserted as a tribute to the man who got him started. As Tony shows off his pet lion cub, and tells him he really wanted a tiger, he mentions William Blake, in reference to Blake's poem 'Tyger, Tyger'. Johnny Boy quotes the John Wayne war film *Back To Bataan* (Edward Dmytryk, 1945). There's also a clip from Fritz Lang's *The Big Heat* (1953) to underline the inspiration Scorsese drew from the old Warner Bros gangster pictures, such as William A Wellman's *The Public Enemy* (1931). Charlie's apartment contains posters for *X: The Man with the X-Ray Eyes* (Roger Corman, 1963), *Husbands* (John Cassavetes, 1970) and *Point Blank* (John Boorman, 1967). Look out for the dolly shot in which Harvey Keitel enters the bar and appears to be floating – there's a similar shot in *The Railway Children* (Lionel Jeffreys, 1970), where Jenny Agutter glides into her birthday party.

The ending is partly inspired by an event in Scorsese's own life. In the autumn of 1963 he and his friend Joey accepted a lift from a local man. A few minutes after he dropped Scorsese and Joey off, the man got into an argument with another driver and was shot dead. The name for the picture was inspired by the Raymond Chandler essay, 'The Simple Art of Murder', in which Chandler wrote: 'Down these mean streets a man must go who is not himself mean, who is neither tarnished nor afraid.' Much of the interplay between Johnny Boy and Charlie is inspired by the interaction of comedy legends Abbott and Costello.

THEMES AND MOTIFS: Charlie holds his hand above the candle, testing his will against the flame. We later see both Travis Bickle and Max Cady do the same. This is Scorsese's first full-length colour picture and we already get a sense that the colour red is significant. Tony's bar – which looks startlingly like the one we see in *GoodFellas* where Henry introduces his crew – with its permanently fiery hue, looks like the entrance to Hell.

Charlie's routine for getting ready matches that of JR from *Who's That Knocking . . .*, including the pan down the length of his tie. See also **GoodFellas,** in which we see young Henry's new gangster suit eyed from foot to head in disgust by his mother, and Tommy De Vito admiring his tie on the day he expects to be Made. A variation on the fingers-as-gun motif comes where, after we've seen Charlie pretend to fire his finger, we hear the real gunshot. Later, as Giovanni tells Charlie that Groppi committed suicide, this time we see a real gun, overdubbed by Giovanni's click of his fingers. Charlie, like JR (and Scorsese) is a fan of John Wayne.

After they've made love, Teresa asks Charlie not to look as she gets dressed. He covers his eyes but then peeks and we see a close shot of his eyes peering through his fingers. Scorsese's cinema is all about the gaze; his camera often takes the place of a person, giving us their point of view, or at least making us empathise with the character – Charlie is drunk, so the camera falls about, or he's confident, so it glides with him. We see here a familiar shot of an extreme close-up on a pair of eyes (*Taxi Driver*, *Cape Fear*). It makes the audience the character's accomplice, or at least entreats us into being complicit with whatever they do.

The Italian–American gangster tradition of the Made Man is introduced here. The kid assassin thinks that by avenging the honour of his boss he can rise through the ranks. In *GoodFellas* we see Tommy DeVito, who expects to be Made because he believes he has it coming to him. But as he is suspected of being the killer of a Made man, he is instead whacked. It's a strict code of honour. *GoodFellas* also explains to us the reason why Charlie would be taking over a restaurant: as a Long Firm, a front for a silent partner to run up bills through the front door and sell off stock at discounted profit. Had Charlie taken over the business, he would no doubt have been forced to torch the restaurant for insurance within a year.

CONTROVERSY: Though Charlie is attracted to a dancer, he is at pains to explain in his narration that there'd be no point in doing anything about it as the girl is black. Although he invites her out to dinner, ostensibly to discuss her being the hostess of the restaurant he hopes to open, at the last minute he changes his mind as he doesn't want to be seen taking out a black girl. We also have Tony telling Michael that he saw Michael's girlfriend 'kissing a nigger under the bridge in Jersey', news that Michael takes badly, and it's not certain which Michael finds more upsetting – his girlfriend's unfaithfulness or the race of the man she cheats on him with. The gay couple whom Michael gives a lift to after the shooting do appear distressingly stereotypical, ogling passers-by and being insensitively over-the-top, so even considering accusations of homophobia on the part of the characters, it's not surprising Michael kicks them out of his car (they do provide one unintentional moment of humour as one of them says the word 'suck' but it is beeped out by a well-timed blast of car horns).

BIBLE CLASS: Charlie, like JR, is a man trying to reconcile his life with his faith. In church, he prays 'Lord I'm not worthy to eat your flesh, I'm not worthy to drink your blood', full of humility, but then tells God that he doesn't believe in the penance the priest gives him week after week: 'They're just words.' He wants to do the penance his way, to pay for his own sins but remain proud. His friends certainly don't understand Charlie's apparent devout Catholicism. Tony recounts the story that a priest told Charlie when he went on retreat (a reference to the 'Jerusalem, Jerusalem' script – see **Unseen Scorsese**). The priest claimed he once lent his car to an unmarried couple and they decided to make out in it when – boom! – a truck crashed into the car. Tony says that two years earlier a different priest told him the same story, which he says just goes to show you shouldn't believe what priests tell you.

THERE HE IS!: Scorsese plays Shorty, who Charlie mocks for being so short and who later pulls the trigger that leads to the bloody finale. For the ultimate in back-seat cameos though, see **Taxi Driver**.

KEEP IT IN THE FAMILY: The neighbour who looks after Teresa when she fits is played by Catherine Scorsese. Anna Uricola, mother of Scorsese's old friend Robert from NYU, plays a neighbour. Barbara and Heather Weintraub (the girls with Johnny) are the daughters of Fred Weintraub (vice-president of creative services at Warners). His third daughter, Sandra, became Scorsese's girlfriend during production of the picture.

LEGACY: Remade as *Wong Gok Ka Moon* (Kar-wai Wong, 1988). As a result of seeing *Mean Streets*, Bernardo Bertolucci cast De Niro in his epic *1900*, and Coppola, who had screen-tested the unknown De Niro for *The Godfather*, cast him as the young Vito Corleone in *The Godfather Part II*.

DELETED SCENES: Scorsese speaks of one scene lost due to the carelessness of a crew member which featured an extension of the scene with the two gay guys in Michael's car. The original script also contained a line from Bob Dylan's 'Subterranean Homesick Blues': 'Twenty years of schooling and they put you on the day shift'.

TRIVIA: At one point, Johnny suggests that he and Charlie can pass the time watching Teresa have a seizure – De Niro has trouble with an epileptic girl again in Bernardo Bertolucci's sprawling historical epic *1900* (1976).

TAGLINE: A line from Charlie's opening monologue: 'You don't make up for your sins in church. You do it on the streets . . .'

POSTERS: There's a nice variety of posters available for *Mean Streets*. The 25th Anniversary release in the USA was accompanied by a stunning art deco one-sheet depicting a smoking gun against a stylised cityscape (this image later appeared on the American DVD release). The British quad poster for the rerelease featured a black and white photo of Harvey Keitel's face obscured by his hands, as if in confession or wracked with either guilt or shame. Various campaigns across the world used one of two images: either De Niro cockily waving a gun about, or a more sombre photo of Keitel and De Niro in conversation (the latter appearing on the cover of the UK DVD and 4Front VHS releases).

TRAILER: Over a series of clips from the film, we are told that '*Mean Streets* is about Tony . . . Michael . . . Giovanni . . . Johnny . . . and about Charlie. About Charlie who played . . . and he laughed and prayed . . . and fought . . . but most of all he cared . . . he cared for his friends in these mean streets. Charlie cared for them all.' The trailer concludes with quotes from reviews by *The New York Times*, Pauline Kael, *Newsday* and *Newsweek*.

AWARDS: Robert De Niro won the 1974 National Society of Film Critics Awards for Best Supporting Actor, while Mardik Martin and Martin Scorsese were nominated by the Writers Guild of America for

Best Drama Written Directly for the Screen. In 1997, *Mean Streets* was entered in the American National Film Preservation Registry.

AVAILABILITY: Released in the USA on laserdisc in 1991 by Warner Home Video in both pan-and-scan and original aspect ratios, it was later reissued by Encore along with a trailer (and a selection of trailers for other Encore releases). The picture was released on DVD by Warner Bros in Region 1 (USA) in 1998, with both pan-and-scan and original ratio versions of the film as well as a trailer and brief production notes. Universal Pictures' Region (UK) release in January 2001 contained just the full-screen version, but with an additional photo gallery. The film has also been released on VHS in both pan-and-scan and widescreen versions

WHAT THE CRITICS SAID: 'A true original, and a triumph of personal filmmaking. This picture about the experience of growing up in New York's Little Italy has an unsettling, episodic rhythm and it's dizzyingly sensual. The director, Martin Scorsese, shows us a thicker-textured rot than we have ever had in an American movie, and a riper sense of evil.' Pauline Kael, *New York Times*.

EXPERT WITNESSES: 'Perhaps I got the part of Charlie because Marty sensed that I came from a similar background . . . I was new, I was raw, I hadn't had much experience. I don't think it was my experience at acting that landed me that work, but the experience Marty saw in me. Our neighbourhoods said to a young man, "You have a place and you will not go beyond that place because you do not belong anywhere beyond this place." Marty and I rebelled against it.' Harvey Keitel (Charlie)

'Sometimes as an actor you get this thing: I don't know if I can take that part because I've taken stronger supporting roles and now I'm taking a lesser part and blah blah; and I was saying that to myself. It's like takin' a position, you know, careerwise. But I wanted to work with Marty.' Robert De Niro (Johnny Boy)

FINAL ANALYSIS: A real turning point for the director, this is the film that made people start to notice him. In many ways a rehash of some of the ideas in *Who's That Knocking . . .*, and a precursor to the greater depth of *GoodFellas*, yet still with an identity very much of its own. The introductions tell us as much as we need to know about the characters. Charlie troubled by sleeplessness; he, Tony and Michael all feel they're surrounded by idiots who always let them down. In contrast, Johnny

Boy seems carefree, yet reckless, casually blowing up a mailbox and running away. As ever, he makes a mess and leaves others to tidy up after him.

Of course, *Mean Streets* is significant in one other way as it marks the transition between Keitel being replaced by De Niro as Scorsese's on-screen alter-ego. For although Keitel receives top billing, his calm, easygoing performance is overshadowed by De Niro's electric turn as the whirlwind Johnny Boy. He's dangerous, unrestrained and wild, bumming off everyone he can and then turning on them for being stupid enough to let him get away with it. But behind the bravado, De Niro also manages to create a character that up to the end provokes our interests and keeps us rooting for him, making the violent ending all the more unsettling.

SCORSESE ON *MEAN STREETS*: '*Mean Streets* is always a favourite of mine because of the music and because it was the story of myself and my friends. It was the movie that I made that people originally took notice of. But I certainly couldn't watch it. I've watched scenes of it. I could never watch the whole thing. It's too personal.'

Alice Doesn't Live Here Anymore (1974)

(35 mm – 112 min – colour)

MPAA Rating: PG

Produced by Warner Bros
Producers: David Susskind, Audrey Maas
Associate Producer: Sandra Weintraub
Production Executive: Larry Cohen
Screenplay: Robert Getchell
Director of Photography: Kent Wakeford
Editor: Marcia Lucas
Original Additional Music: Richard La Salle
Production Designer: Toby Rafelson
Unit Production Manager: John G Wilson
Second Assistant Director: Michael Kusley
Assistant Director: Mike Moder
Hair Stylist: Lola 'Skip' McNalley
Make-up Artist: Bob Westmoreland

Property Master: Edward Aiona
Sound Mixer: Don Parker
Key Grip: Tom Conley
Gaffer: Bill Curtis
Men's Wardrobe: Lambert Marks
Women's Wardrobe: Lucia De Martino
Title Designer: Wayne Fitzgerald
Camera Operator: Owen Marsh
Assistant Editor: C Timothy O'Meara
Script Supervisor: Julie Pitkanen
First Camera Assistant: Reynaldo Villalobos

SONGS: 'All the Way from Memphis' by Mott the Hoople; 'Roll Away the Stone' by Leon Russell; 'Daniel' by Elton John; 'Jeepster' by T-Rex; 'Cuddle up a Little Closer, Lovey Mine' by Betty Grable (from the film *Coney Island*); 'You'll Never Know' by Alice Faye (from the film *Hello Frisco, Hello*); 'Where or When' (written by Rodgers & Hart), 'When Your Lover Has Gone' (written by EA Swan), 'Gone with the Wind' (written by by Allie Wrubel and Herb Magidson), 'I've Got a Crush on You' (written by George and Ira Gershwin), all sung by Ellen Burstyn; 'I'm So Lonesome I Could Cry' (written by Hank Williams), sung by Kris Kristofferson; 'I Will Always Love You' by Dolly Parton.

CAST: Ellen Burstyn (*Alice Hyatt*), Kris Kristofferson (*David*), Alfred Lutter (*Tommy*), Diane Ladd (*Flo*), Billy Green Bush (*Donald*), Vic Tayback (*Mel*), Jodie Foster (*Audrey*), Harvey Keitel (*Ben*), Lelia Goldoni (*Bea*), Lane Bradbury (*Rita*), Valerie Curtin (*Vera*), Harry Northup (*Joe & Jim's bartender*), Murray Moston (*Jacobs*), Mia Bendixsen (*Alice Graham – Alice, Aged Eight*), Ola Moore (*Old Woman*), Dean Casper (*Chicken*), Martin Brinton (*Lenny*).

UNCREDITED CAST: Henry M Kendrick (*Shop Assistant*), Mardik Martin (*Customer in Club*), Martin Scorsese, Larry Cohen (*Patrons at the Diner*), Laura Dern (*Girl Eating Ice-cream Cone*).

TITLES: The picture begins with the Warner Bros logo in a cropped, almost square frame, which remains throughout the opening credits and prologue. 'You'll Never Know' plays over the credits themselves, which are presented as scrolling red letters over a blue silk backdrop. The end credits consist of a split screen, with pink-lettered credits on the right, and on the left side of the screen a top-down view of Alice's hands playing us out on a piano.

SUMMARY: Socorro, New Mexico. Alice is now married with one precocious son, Tommy. Her husband, Donald, spends his days working as a truck driver and his evenings snarling at Alice and Tommy. Tommy doesn't help by being cheeky and wilful. Alice is clearly unhappy and confides in a friend that she could easily live without a man (though she'd probably make an exception for Robert Redford). But at that moment, fate deals her an unexpected card – Donald has been killed in an accident on the freeway. His funeral leaves Alice penniless. Alice hasn't worked in some time, certainly since Tommy was born. The only job she ever had was as a singer, so she decides she and Tommy are going to Monterey, where she grew up, so she can earn some money singing.

After a long and trying journey, Alice stops off at Phoenix to look for work. She buys a new dress and gets a new hairstyle in the hope she can make herself look under thirty, and heads out to look for work. Sadly, none of the clubs is hiring. After a long and fruitless day, she eventually comes to the bar of a Mr Jacobs and manages to convince him to give her a job. But when she discovers that a man she's been dating is actually violent and married, Alice and Tommy pack their belongings and hit the road again.

They reach Tucson with just $90 and in desperation Alice takes a job waitressing at Ruby's Café, a local diner, where she meets the dizzy Vera and the coarse, brash Flo, who, after a shaky start, becomes Alice's best friend. Alice also attracts the attention of a regular customer, David, a divorcee, who invites Alice and Tommy out to his ranch, showing Tommy how to milk a cow. He also plays guitar and plays along with Tommy. Alice and David begin spending more and more time together until Tommy's birthday comes along and David throws a small party for him. As David tries to teach Tommy a chord, Tommy moans that he can't do it and becomes more and more insistent until David loses his temper and smacks the boy. Alice and David row: he accuses her of not being able to make up her mind between him or Monterey; she says he's just helped her make up her mind and walks out. As she drives home, Tommy reproaches her for not keeping her promise to get them to Monterey by his birthday. In frustration, Alice pulls over, bundles him out of the car and drives off. She reaches home and regrets what happened, frantically searching the town until she gets a phone call. Tommy has been arrested for shoplifting. He went to stay with a friend called Audrey, a streetwise tomboy, and ended up getting drunk.

At work the next morning Alice confesses to Flo that she spent all the money she'd saved up on the cowboy outfit she bought Tommy for his birthday. She tells Flo how scared she was of her late husband, Donald, but how she'd always known he'd look after her, and that she doesn't feel she can live without a man. Flo cheers Alice up, reminding her that she needs to figure out what it is that she wants and then 'jump right in'.

David comes to the diner and tells Alice he'd like her and Tommy to come out to his place, that he knows things have got to be different and that he wants to understand her, or at least try to. Remembering what Flo said, she tells him she still intends to go to Monterey and this time she's not going to let anyone stop her. He asks her who's stopping her and that, if she wants, he'll take her. To the cheers of the diner patrons Alice and David kiss.

WHO'S WHO?: Coming to prominence in *The Last Picture Show* (Peter Bogdanovich, 1971), Ellen Burstyn will be forever remembered as the mother of possessed Regan MacNeil in *The Exorcist* (William Friedkin, 1973). Known more for his country-and-western music than his acting, Kris Kristofferson can be seen at his best as Billy the Kid in *Pat Garrett and Billy the Kid* (Sam Peckinpah, 1973), opposite Barbra Streisand in the second remake of *A Star is Born* (Frank Pierson, 1976) and in Michael Cimino's notoriously slated Western, *Heaven's Gate* (1980).

Having cornered the market in feisty tomboy juvenile roles in films such as *Freaky Friday* (Gary Nelson, 1977), Jodie Foster has emerged as one of Hollywood's leading players. Winning Best Actress Oscars for both *The Accused* (Jonathan Kaplan, 1988) and *The Silence of the Lambs* (Jonathan Demme, 1991), she made her directorial debut with *Little Man Tate* (also 1991) (see also **Taxi Driver**).

Diane Ladd received her second Oscar nomination when she starred alongside her real-life daughter, Laura Dern, in David Lynch's mad road movie *Wild at Heart* (1990), and her third nomination, also alongside Laura, for *Rambling Rose* (Martha Coolidge, 1992). She also appeared in the TV version of *Alice Doesn't Live Here Anymore*, although as a different character, alongside Vic Tayback, who recreated his role of Mel from the movie. Valerie Curtin played Judy in the TV version of *9 to 5*.

THE USUAL SUSPECTS: Harvey Keitel (*Street Scenes, Who's That Knocking At My Door?, Mean Streets, Taxi Driver, The Last Temptation of Christ*); Harry Northup (*Who's That Knocking At My Door?, Boxcar Bertha, Mean Streets, Taxi Driver, New York, New York, Amazing Stories:* 'Mirror Mirror'); Murray Moston (*Mean Streets, Taxi Driver, New York, New York, After Hours*); Dean Casper (*Casino*); editor Marcia Lucas (*Taxi Driver, New York, New York*).

PRODUCTION: After her Oscar nominations for *The Last Picture Show* and *The Exorcist*, Ellen Burstyn was in a powerful position to choose her next project. Invited by Jonathan Calley, head of production at Warners, to make another picture with the studio, Burstyn was disappointed with the scripts she saw, which mainly cast her as either a victim or a prostitute. Finally, a script caught her eye – called 'Alice Doesn't Live Here Anymore' and written by Robert Getchell. It had already been read by, among others, Diana Ross, and had been through a number of rewrites to accommodate different leading actresses. She approached Calley with the script and asked if he might be able to find someone young and exciting to direct it. Calley and Burstyn initially contacted Francis Ford Coppola, who suggested they consider Scorsese. After viewing *Mean Streets*, Burstyn was convinced – which is more than Scorsese was. The prospect of directing his first studio picture was both exciting and terrifying, and he confessed to his girlfriend Sandra Weintraub that he felt he knew nothing about directing women. But Scorsese also knew that if he didn't accept the project he might face being cornered solely as a gangster director.

When it came to casting, Ellen Burstyn had considerable influence. She had been impressed by Harvey Keitel in *Mean Streets* and wanted him for the part of her suitor, Ben, but Warner Bros were not keen, ironically because they believed the Polish–Jewish actor, raised in Brooklyn, to be too East-Side Italian for the role of a smooth Westerner. Scorsese managed to persuade Keitel to accept just $3,000 for the small part instead of the expected $10,000. Despite this pay-drop, Keitel's performance was as dedicated as ever. Indeed it was way more intense than the part probably called for, and certainly more intense than he'd been in rehearsals. In the first take for the scene where he forces his way into Alice's motel room, he broke the glass in the door and cut his hand. For the part of Alice's friend Bea, Burstyn suggested her real-life friend, Lelia Goldoni. Scorsese had seen Goldoni in John Cassavetes's *Shadows* (1959) and was pleased to get her, even for such a small part. Diane Ladd was suggested for Flo by Burstyn and separately by Scorsese's friends Jay Cocks and Verna Bloom and was, Scorsese admitted at the time, his favourite bit of casting. Scorsese managed to persuade singer-songwriter Kris Kristofferson to take the role of David. With Kristofferson about to embark on a tour, his schedule allowed him just two weeks to complete his sequences.

Around 300 children were auditioned for the role of Alice's son. Sandra Weintraub found Alfred Lutter and Scorsese put him into the read-through with Burstyn. She improvised to see how each child responded. Most children in this situation either faltered and stared at the floor or jumped straight back to the script unable to improvise around it, but Alfred impressed them by being flexible with the text and, if anything, Scorsese had trouble keeping the enthusiastic boy quiet.

With studio backing came Scorsese's first major budget – $1.6 million – and the luxury of several weeks of rehearsal time prior to the beginning of principal photography. Scorsese began rehearsals with just Burstyn and Lutter to allow them time to get to know each other, then brought other actors in for a couple of days at a time. One of the main sequences to come out of improvisation with mother and son was the water fight, and Tommy's joke was one that Lutter himself had told Scorsese. Encouraging the cast to improvise around the script, Scorsese had Robert Getchell on hand to take notes and incorporate any interesting elements into the script.

The set for the opening sequence, the last to be built on the old Gower Street Columbia lot, took a hefty $85,000-sized chunk out of the budget (which was more than twice the entire production cost for *Who's That Knocking At My Door?*). It was the first set Scorsese had ever commissioned, comprising a huge 180-degree diorama. The budget also allowed for a seven-week shoot, mainly on location in Tucson, Arizona and the film was shot almost completely in continuity apart from some scenes near the end involving Kris Kristofferson. The crew had to find locations in Tucson to double up for Phoenix because, with the fuel crisis sending transportation costs soaring at the time, they couldn't afford to get to Phoenix. On location in Tucson, they stumbled across a sign saying MONTEREY in big neon, which Scorsese felt was perfect serendipity and incorporated the sign into the final shot of the movie. The shoot wrapped one week over schedule.

The ending to the picture had proven troublesome. Calley and Burstyn had argued at length about the final outcome. While the actress was excited by the very un-Hollywood idea of ending the picture with Alice taking a job as a singer and leaving her boyfriend (Kristofferson) behind, Calley was insistent that the character should end up with a man. Scorsese was aware that the old guard at Warners eyed these new directors with suspicion, and despaired with their demands that all 'artistic statements' should have downbeat endings. Eventually, Scorsese managed to find a compromise, allowing for a theatrical ending (with the patrons at the café applauding as Alice agrees to head off to her new job with her boyfriend in tow) that happily matched the staged look of the picture's opening.

EDITING: As a (relatively new) member of the Director's Guild of America Scorsese was not allowed to take credit for editing the picture himself, and he was afraid the studio would appoint someone as their spy from within, so he hired his friend Marcia Lucas. At least with Marcia there he could exercise some control over the way the picture would be edited. But Lucas had her own agenda. Worried that people believed she only worked on films made by her husband (George Lucas), she was eager to prove she was a strong editor in her own right, and ultimately she gained Scorsese's confidence enough for him to let her cut the picture largely unsupervised.

MUSIC: With musicals growing slowly out of vogue, they have evolved into what can generally be divided into two sorts of picture: the two-hour music promo or the kind where the music comes from the narrative. Scorsese is well known for making the former, but here we get his first stab at a modern musical, casting Burstyn as a bar singer. Aside from the songs of her act, Scorsese applies some inventive techniques in shoehorning some more samples from his extensive music library. As the prologue stutters into the present (with young Alice's voice echoing 'You'll never know if you don't know now-now-now-now-now . . .'), we cut to the intro to Mott the Hoople's 'All The Way from Memphis'. After a series of establishing shots leading to the Hyatt household, we discover that the music is coming from Tommy's speakers. Later, we realise that Elton John's 'Daniel' is playing on the car radio (note how the music drops out when the shot moves to outside of the car again).

QUOTE/UNQUOTE
Tommy: (as they drive past the border of New Mexico) 'Booo! Booo!'
Alice: 'Don't turn back, you'll turn into a pillar of shit.'
Tommy: 'The whole state is shit.'
Alice: 'Don't talk dirty, Tommy, how many more times do I have to tell ya?'

Tommy: 'Mom, are we in Arizona yet?'
Alice: (driving) 'If you ask me that one more time I'm gonna beat you to death. Just sit back there and relax and enjoy life, huh?'
Tommy: 'Life is short.'
Alice: (dismissive) 'So are you.'
Tommy: 'Mom, I'm *bored*!'
Alice: 'Well so am I! Whadda you want from me, card tricks?'

Tommy: 'What?'
Alice: 'Whadda you mean "What"? What are you, Helen Keller?'

Alice: (after a prospective employer asks her to turn around so he can look at her): 'Look at my face, I don't sing with my ass!'

Flo: 'Mel, what you doin' back there, pullin' on you' puddin'? Or are ya givin' it a whack with a hammer? I heard the only way you can get it up is to slam it in a door [laughs].'
Mel: 'Don't wanna get too close to you, honey. I'll get you all bothered up early in the morning.'
Flo: 'Sure. Man, I could lie under you, eat fried chicken and do a crossword puzzle at the same time – that's how much you'd bother me.'

Flo: 'My old man? Honey, he ain't talked to me since the day Kennedy got shot.'
Alice: Why, does he think you had something to do with it?'

ROOTS: The cropped frame of the prologue is a reminder of a bygone age, before Cinemascope and Panavision, when the cinema image would be almost square (in a ratio of 1.33:1). Of course, this reminder of early cinema would be completely lost on modern audiences used to the similar '4:3' ratio of TV screens. This feeling continues with the farmstead, deliberately made to look like a set. The fiery red-orange lighting might well remind one of *Gone with the Wind* (Victor Fleming, 1939), *Invaders from Mars* (William Cameron Menzies, 1953) or *Duel in the Sun* (King Vidor, 1946), while the look of young Alice comes via Dorothy Gale, Judy Garland's character in *The Wizard of Oz* (Victor Fleming, 1939). The establishing shots in Socorro are reminiscent of Hitchcock's *Psycho* (1960), which opens with shots of Phoenix, finishing with a slow tracking shot leading up to and through a window.

Other references include mentions of screen idol Robert Redford; *The Postman Always Rings Twice* (Tay Garnett, 1946); the long-running soap opera *All My Children*; and Dale Evans, star of many musical Westerns in the 40s and 50s, and partner of Roy Rogers, both on- and off-screen. One of the nightclubs Alice goes to in Phoenix is called 'Quo Vadis', after the sword-and-sandal epic directed by Mervyn LeRoy (1951). Tommy watches the Betty Grable film, *Coney Island* (Walter Lang, 1943) and an edition of *The Tonight Show*, with king of the chat-shows Johnny Carson (see **The King of Comedy**). The recording of

Alice Faye singing 'You'll Never Know' is taken from the film *Hello Frisco, Hello* (Bruce Humberstone, 1943).

THEMES AND MOTIFS: Typical of a road movie, it's the signs the characters *don't* see that are the important ones. As Alice begins to look for work in Phoenix, there's a sign pointing ONE WAY in the opposite direction to the one she walks in. At the end of the picture, we see Alice and Tommy walking down a Tucson street towards a neon sign that just happens to read MONTEREY, which, as they are walking away from their motel must have been looming down on them the whole time they were there. The colour red features heavily here: the vivid sunset at the beginning; the carpet of their first motel room; and the red of Alice's dress that she wears when she sings in the bar, which, like all Scorsese bars, is lit red. Harvey Keitel, as Ben, continues to be Scorsese's John Wayne signifier, dressed like a cowboy and making bullets for a living. As Ben sees Alice home for the first time, he turns and fires his finger at her like a gun.

BIBLE CLASS: As they drive out of New Mexico, Alice quips 'don't look back, you'll turn into a pillar of shit,' a reference to Lot's wife, who, according to the book of Genesis (19:17), looked back as she and her husband rushed away from Sodom and was promptly turned into a pillar of salt. There's an almost biblical element to the death of her husband too: she learns of it mere seconds after telling her friend that she could live without a man. Though the accident must have happened some time earlier, the way she learns of the news, with a cut-away to the truck itself, does seem closer to an act of God than mere coincidence.

CONTROVERSY: For the prologue, the production team had trouble with the welfare officer on set to look after Mia Bendixsen (playing the young Alice). After they got one take of Mia delivering the lines, 'blow it out your ass' and 'Jesus Christ', the welfare officer complained, forbidding them from forcing the girl to speak such profane language. Fortunately, they already had that one take of her saying the line and were able to overdub a later take with the original dialogue.

KEEP IT IN THE FAMILY: Associate producer, Sandra Weintraub, daughter of Fred Weintraub (vice-president of creative services at Warners), was Scorsese's girlfriend at the time of production. Diane Ladd's daughter Laura Dern (*Jurassic Park*, *Wild at Heart*) plays a girl eating ice cream.

LEGACY: Inspired the sitcom *Alice* (1976), which starred Linda Lavin and briefly co-starred Diane Ladd, who replaced Polly Holliday, the actress who'd been cast in the role Ladd had played in the original picture. A fairly faithful recreation of the diner can be found at Universal Studios, Florida.

POSTER: The US one-sheet designs tended to focus on a rather touching monochrome shot of Burstyn and Kristofferson arm in arm, with the tagline announcing the film as: 'A picture for anyone who has ever dreamed of a second chance!'

TRAILER: 'Alice has a 12-year-old kid,' a lugubriously throaty voice tells us over a montage of clips. 'She hasn't got a job . . . and she's on her own . . . How come she has such a good time?' The trailer manages to include a clip of David and Alice making up in the diner, spoiling any kind of surprise.

AWARDS: Ellen Burstyn picked up the American Academy Award for Best Actress in a Leading Role (which Scorsese collected on her behalf), while Diane Ladd and Robert Getchell received nominations for Best Actress in a Supporting Role and Best Writing (Original Screenplay) respectively. Ellen Burstyn couldn't make the Academy awards as she was rehearsing for a play in New York. The statuette was given to her two nights later by Walter Matthau and Jack Lemmon. At the British Academy Awards, the picture won BAFTAs for Best Film, Best Actress (Burstyn), Screenplay and Supporting Actress (Ladd), and nominations for Best Direction, Best Newcomer (Alfred Lutter III) and Supporting Actress (Lelia Goldoni). Burstyn and Ladd also received nominations at the Golden Globes, and Getchell was nominated for a Writer's Guild Award. Finally, Scorsese himself chalked up a nomination for the Palme d'Or at the 1975 Cannes Film Festival.

AVAILABILITY: The US laserdisc was released by Warner Home Video in a two-sided widescreen format. The UK release from Tartan was a basic pan-and-scan presentation. In the UK, Warner Home Video released both pan-and-scan and widescreen VHS versions.

WHAT THE CRITICS SAID: 'Full of funny malice and breakneck vitality, it's absorbing and intelligent even when the issues it raises get all fouled up.' Pauline Kael, *The New York Times*.

FINAL ANALYSIS: Thankfully proving himself wrong, Scorsese shows here that he can not only direct women but also children, bringing out a superb performance from Alfred Lutter, who sadly would appear to have given up acting just three years later. Completely unlike almost every other picture in Scorsese's filmography, *Alice . . .* succeeds in being both dramatic and surprisingly funny, with some genuine laugh-out-loud moments (although Tommy's laborious joke about a gorilla falling out of a tree isn't one of them).

SCORSESE ON *ALICE DOESN'T LIVE HERE ANYMORE*: 'We never intended it to be a feminist tract. It was a film about self-responsibility and also about how people make the same mistakes again and again. There was even thought of her getting divorced and running away from her husband at the beginning, but we decided to make it very different, that he died and she was left with no choice.'

Italianamerican (1974)

(16 mm – 45 mins – colour)

Produced by the National Communications Foundation
Producers: Elaine Attias & Saul Rubin
Associate Producer/Editor: Bert Lovitt
Treatment: Mardik Martin & Lawrence D Cohen (credited as Larry Cohen)
Production Manager: Dale Bell
Assistant to Producers: Susan Rubin
Production Assistant: Constantine Makris
Sound Man: Lee Osborne
Electrician/Still Photographer: Martin Andrews
Cameraman: Alec Hirschfeld (credited as Alec Hirshfeld)
Assistant Camera: Marc Hirschfeld (credited as Marc Hirshfeld)
Associate Editor: Tom Walls
Assistant Editor: Randy Jon Morgan
Still Photos courtesy of the Scorsese Family

CAST: (as themselves) Charles Scorsese, Catherine Scorsese

UNCREDITED CAST: Martin Scorsese, Mardik Martin

TITLES: Traditional Italian music plays over the title card, which reads: ITALIANAMERICAN in plain white lettering on a blue background.

SUMMARY: Catherine and Charlie Scorsese talk about growing up in Little Italy, coming from a large Italian family and about their honeymoon, which they finally took after 39 years of marriage. Catherine also talks her son through her recipe for pasta sauce.

THE USUAL SUSPECTS: Charles Scorsese (*Raging Bull, The King of Comedy, After Hours, The Color of Money, Cape Fear, The Age of Innocence*); Catherine Scorsese (*It's Not Just You, Murray!, Who's That Knocking At My Door?, Mean Streets, The King of Comedy, GoodFellas, Cape Fear, Casino*); Mardik Martin (*What's a Nice Girl Like You Doing in a Place Like This?, It's Not Just You, Murray!, Mean Streets, New York, New York, American Boy, Raging Bull, King of Comedy*).

PRODUCTION: Scorsese was approached by the National Endowment for the Humanities to make a programme for *Storm of Strangers*, a television programme made for the 1976 American Bicentennial. The show would take a fresh look at ethnic diversity in contemporary America, and Scorsese was asked to film a thirty-minute documentary on the Italian American experience of coming to America as immigrants. Initially, he declined, worried that it would conflict with the completion of *Alice Doesn't Live Here Anymore*, but then he remembered the stories he'd heard all his life about members of the family coming over from Italy and approached the producers of the programme with the idea of interviewing his own parents for the show. Mardik Martin, who knew Scorsese's parents, worked on some questions and the entire production was shot over six hours in the Scorsese's Elizabeth Street apartment. The finished film came in at 45 minutes, so was cut down for the TV version, but was shown in full at the 1974 NY Film Festival. Catherine Scorsese attended the screening, enjoying the star treatment for a night, and was overjoyed when the credits rolled and her recipe for spaghetti sauce (which was printed in full) received a standing ovation.

QUOTE/UNQUOTE
Charlie: 'There wasn't anything to do anyway; you had no radio; you had no television, and every now and then you used to get a paper. A guy would come on out, "extra, extra!" You'd buy the paper – there was nothing in the paper.'

Charlie: 'We used to be like one family. It was different.'

Catherine: (pointing at the cameraman) 'Is he still taking this? I'll murder you – you won't get outta this house alive.'

THEMES AND MOTIFS: It's no small wonder that the nature of identity is so regularly questioned in Scorsese's work when we learn that his mother, Catherine, is a twin, whose brother was christened Salvatore but also known as Charlie. Her father's name was Martin, but he was called Filipo by many people, and that Charles Scorsese's real first name is Luciano.

BIBLE CLASS: Charlie used to make a little money on Saturdays lighting the stoves for Jewish families on Delancey Street – Jews are forbidden from doing anything classed as work on their Sabbath day.

CONTROVERSY: Charlie tells of the development of the immigrant ghettos in New York: that the Irish were there first; then the Italians arrived, setting up Little Italy, and that bred resentment; then the Chinese began to arrive, with their Chinatown confined to the other side of Canal Street. Catherine tells a story about her father, who never learned to speak English. When he applied for American citizenship, the woman accepting his application said she was disgusted he couldn't speak English after thirty years, so he told her in English to go f*** herself.

THERE HE IS!: Scorsese interviews his parents and is visible in some scenes, notably the beginning, where they set up, and the end.

ALTERNATIVE VERSION: As part of the *Storm of Strangers* series, the thirty-minute edit of *Italianamerican* sits alongside the two other films: *Jung Sai: Chinese-American*, directed by Frieda Lee Mock & Terry Sanders, and *The Irish*, directed by Chris Jenkyns and narrated by Edmond O'Brien.

AWARDS: Exhibited theatrically in its full length, *Italianamerican* won First Prize & the Red Ribbon at the American Film and Video Festival and has also been awarded a CINE Golden Eagle and Association of Visual Communicators Cindy Award.

AVAILABILITY: Released in the USA by Home Vision Cinema alongside *The Big Shave* (ASIN: 6302969719), and in the UK by

Connoisseur Video in 1992 as part of the *Scorsese* ×4 compilation (ASIN: B00004CMQW).

SCORSESE ON *ITALIANAMERICAN***:** [His father didn't attend the premiere at the Lincoln Center during the New York Film Festival] 'He felt he'd come off terrible so he saw it privately. That was OK. My mother went instead. I couldn't be there, my mother took over anyway. She threw kisses to everybody, signed autographs.'

Taxi Driver (1975)

(35 mm – 113 mins – colour)

Produced by Columbia Pictures
Associate Producer: Phillip M Goldfarb
Producers: Julia Phillips and Michael Phillips
Screenplay: Paul Schrader
Music: Bernard Herrmann
Cinematography: Michael Chapman
Supervising Film Editor: Marcia Lucas
Editors: Tom Rolf, Melvin Shapiro
Art Direction: Charles Rosen
Set Decoration: Herbert F Mulligan
Costume Design by Ruth Morley
Title Designer: Dan Perri

CAST: Robert De Niro (*Travis Bickle*), Jodie Foster (*Iris*), Cybill Shepherd (*Betsy*), Harvey Keitel (*Sport/Matthew*), Steven Prince (*Andy, the Gun Salesman*), Albert Brooks (*Tom Harvey*) Peter Boyle (*Wizard*), Leonard Harris (*Charles Palantine*), Diahnne Abbott (*Concession Girl*), Frank Adu (*Angry Black Man*), Richard Higgs (*Secret Service Agent*), Gino Ardito (*Policeman at Rally*), Garth Avery (*Iris's Companion*), Copper Cunningham (*Hooker in Cab*), Harry Fischler (*Cab Dispatcher*), Harry Cohn (*Cabbie in Cafeteria*), Brenda Dickson (*Soap Opera Woman*), Beau Kayser (*Soap Opera Man*), Nat Grant (*Stick-up Man*), Robert Maroff (*Mafioso*), Victor Magnotta (*Secret Service Photographer*), Norman Matlock (*Charlie T*), Murray Moston (*Caretaker at Iris's Apartment*), Harry Northup (*Doughboy*), Bill Minkin (*Tom's Assistant*), Gene Palma (*Street Drummer*), Peter Savage (*The John*), Robert Shields (*Palantine Aide*), Robin Utt (*Campaign Worker*), Joe Spinell (*Personnel Officer*), Maria Turner (*Angry

Prostitute on Street), Carey Poe (*Campaign Worker*), Ralph Singleton (*TV Interviewer*), Martin Scorsese (*Passenger Watching Silhouette*), Victor Argo (*Melio, the Deli Owner*).

UNCREDITED CAST: Jean Elliott (*Clerk at Sam Goody Store Selling Record*), Debbi Morgan (*Girl at Columbus Circle*), Billie Perkins (*Friend of Iris*), Connie Foster (*Jodie Foster's stand-in*).

TITLES: On a black background, the first title cards appear in vivid red: COLUMBIA PICTURES PRESENTS . . . ROBERT DE NIRO IN . . ., Then, through a cloud of steam from a manhole cover, a yellow cab slowly emerges, like a predatory animal. The title appears in its wake in glowing yellow letters. Then we see the eyes of the driver in close-up as he scans the sidewalks for his next fare, and a shot through the cab's rain-soaked windscreen of the blurry neon city around him.

SUMMARY: Having been granted an honourable discharge from the marines, Travis Bickle takes a job as a taxi driver in New York. Travis suffers from insomnia and finds himself working long shifts, unable to rest. As he drives through the City That Never Sleeps, he is witness to the underbelly of society: drunks, thugs, gangs, junkies, and prostitutes. Though he is able to converse on some superficial level with his fellow drivers, Travis remains a loner and seeks solace in regular visits to a downtown porn cinema.

Maybe as a result of his experiences in Vietnam, maybe something already in his psyche, Travis develops an obsession about cleaning up the streets, like a biblical purging of all that is bad and rotten in the city. His obsession, combined with his loneliness and hypochondria, convinces Travis that he must prepare himself for a tour of duty as 'God's Lonely Man'.

From the safety of his cab, Travis spies a beautiful young woman, a campaign worker for Senator Palantine's election bid. Plucking up the courage to approach her, he at first pretends that he wishes to volunteer for the campaign before finally asking her out for a date. The girl, Betsy, is at first reluctant, but then gives in. They meet for coffee later that day, and although Travis fails to notice how awkward and stilted their conversation is, the date goes without incident. Through persistence, and perhaps because Betsy finds him genuinely intriguing, Travis manages to convince her to go on another date, offering to take her to the movies. But he makes a serious misjudgement when he takes her to a 'dirty movie'. Disgusted, Betsy storms out of the theatre.

Despite Travis calling her and sending her flowers, Betsy refuses to have any more to do with him. He returns to her office to talk to her and is escorted off the premises. This rejection is the inspiration for Travis to 'get in shape'. Through a contact at the cab company, Travis meets Andy, a travelling salesman, and purchases an arsenal of guns. He begins a regime of vigorous exercising and practises his shooting at a target range.

When a young and visibly distressed prostitute is pulled from his cab by her pimp, Travis seeks her out and befriends her. The girl, Iris, appears to be little more than twelve years of age and her situation troubles Travis greatly. He begs her to give up prostitution and let him 'save' her, but she refuses.

The pressures of Travis's loneliness and insomnia finally take their toll on him. He shaves his head and prepares himself for a mission – he aims to assassinate Senator Palantine. When this attempt fails, Travis turns his attentions to the pimps that hold Iris in their grasp. He storms the brothel, gunning down everyone in his way. As the last man falls, and as Iris cowers, terrified in the corner of her room, Travis puts his gun to his head and pulls the trigger . . . but the chamber is empty.

The press hails Travis a hero and soon he returns to his old job as if nothing has happened. Iris's parents write to thank him for rescuing their daughter, and even Betsy appears impressed by his short-lived celebrity status. But inside the mind of Travis, his loneliness continues.

WHO'S WHO?: Actor/writer/director and *Saturday Night Live* alumnus Albert Brooks starred in *Broadcast News* (James L Brooks, 1987), and the critically acclaimed *Out of Sight* (Steven Soderbergh, 1998) as well as directing, writing and starring in *Defending Your Life* (1991) and *The Muse* (1999). Brooks also guest-starred in Eddie Murphy's reworking of *Dr. Dolittle* (Betty Thomas, 1998) alongside Peter Boyle (Wizard), who can also be seen as Sandra Bullock's confidant in *While You Were Sleeping* (1995) and as the hilarious monster in *Young Frankenstein* (Mel Brooks, 1974). Despite producing a self-titled sitcom in the 1990s, Cybill Shepherd will forever be identified with her long run as Maddie Hayes in the cult series *Moonlighting*. Norman Matlock can be spotted as a police commissioner in both *The Blues Brothers* (John Landis, 1980) and *Ghostbusters* (Harold Ramis, 1984). Robert Shields was, at the time of *Taxi Driver*'s release, a regular performer on *The Sonny and Cher Show*.

Bernard Herrmann had worked on a number of Orson Welles's radio shows, including the notorious *War of the Worlds* broadcast, before making the move west for *Citizen Kane* (1941). Almost immediately he become a highly sought after composer of film scores. He became the 'sound' of Alfred Hitchcock for nearly a decade, composing the haunting suites for *Vertigo* (1958) and the much-imitated shrieking strings for *Psycho* (1960).

Oscar-winning make-up artist Dick Smith worked on *The Godfather* and *The Godfather Part II*, among many others. His most famous creation is the possessed make-up for Linda Blair/Eileen Dietz for *The Exorcist* and *The Exorcist II: The Heretic*. Michael and Julia Phillips also produced Best Picture Oscar-Winner *The Sting* (George Roy Hill) and Steven Spielberg's science fiction blockbuster *Close Encounters of the Third Kind*. Julia Phillips was also the author of the controversial exposé of Hollywood, *You'll Never Eat Lunch In This Town Again*.

THE USUAL SUSPECTS: Robert De Niro (*Mean Streets, New York, New York, Raging Bull, The King of Comedy, GoodFellas, Cape Fear, Casino*); Harvey Keitel (*Who's That Knocking At My Door?, Mean Streets, Street Scenes, The Last Temptation of Christ*); Jodie Foster (*Alice Doesn't Live Here Anymore*); Diahnne Abbott (*New York, New York, The King of Comedy*); Harry Northup (*Who's That Knocking At My Door?, Boxcar Bertha, Mean Streets, Alice Doesn't Live Here Anymore, New York, New York, Amazing Stories*: 'Mirror Mirror'); Victor Magnotta (*It's Not Just You, Murray!, Raging Bull, After Hours*); Bill Minkin (*Who's That Knocking At My Door?, The King of Comedy*); Murray Moston (*Mean Streets, Alice Doesn't Live Here Anymore, New York, New York, After Hours*); Steven Prince (*New York, New York, American Boy*, associate producer, *The Last Waltz*); Peter Savage (*New York, New York, Raging Bull*); writer Paul Schrader (*Raging Bull, The Last Temptation of Christ, Bringing Out the Dead*); cinematographer Michael Chapman (*The Last Waltz, American Boy, Raging Bull, Bad*); Thelma Schoonmaker (editor, *Who's That Knocking At My Door?, Street Scenes, Raging Bull, The King of Comedy, After Hours, The Color of Money, Bad, The Last Temptation of Christ, New York Stories, GoodFellas, Cape Fear, Age of Innocence, Casino, A Personal Journey with Martin Scorsese Through American Movies, Kundun, Bringing Out the Dead, My Voyage to Italy, Gangs of New York*); Marcia Lucas (editor, *Alice Doesn't Live Here Anymore*); title designer Dan Perri (*New York, New York, The Last Waltz, Raging Bull, The King of Comedy, The Color of Money*).

PRODUCTION: After the break-up of his marriage and his forced departure from the American Film Institute (following a public disagreement over the way it was being run), Paul Schrader was at his lowest ebb. Out of this black period in the summer of 1972 came a script about isolation and depression the likes of which had never been seen before. Schrader wrote the script in ten days, presenting it in chapter form, with headings such as 'Travis gets a job' and 'Travis gets organised'. Once it was finished, he handed the manuscript to his agent and then went travelling.

Some time later, Paul Schrader met director Brian De Palma and, having struck up a friendship, he decided to tell him about his script, which he'd called 'Taxi Driver'. De Palma was immediately impressed by it but couldn't imagine who might direct such material. He passed it on to producers Michael and Julia Phillips. They too were enthusiastic and optioned the screenplay for $1,000. At this time, Scorsese was already interested in directing the project, but with just *Boxcar Bertha* under his belt, Schrader and the Phillipses were dismissive of him. The Phillipses instead tried to court interest from Robert Mulligan to direct, with Jeff Bridges as Travis, but neither party could be persuaded to commit to the project. Also considered at some point were Robert Blake and (strangely) Neil Diamond. Then the Phillipses saw *Mean Streets*. By the time *Alice Doesn't Live Here Anymore* was released, they were convinced Scorsese was the right man for the picture.

Since the Phillipses had first persuaded Columbia Pictures to make *Taxi Driver*, their main players had grown in status. Their own previous production, *The Sting* (George Roy Hill, 1973) had won them an Academy Award for Best Picture; De Niro had just won his first Oscar for *The Godfather Part II*; Scorsese was getting rave reviews for *Alice Doesn't Live Here Anymore*; Paul Schrader's script 'The Yakuza' (1975) had been picked up by Sydney Pollack, and another, the Hitchcock tribute *Obsession* for Brian De Palma, was already in production. What really impressed Julia Phillips was that despite De Niro's new-found success, and his invitation to work with Bernardo Bertolucci on the ambitious *1900*, the actor didn't try to increase the fee they'd already agreed with him. He was paid $35,000, Schrader $30,000 and Scorsese $65,000 with an arranged budget of $1.5 million (although the project would eventually cost $1.9 million).

With De Niro already attached, Scorsese set about finding the two pivotal female roles: Betsy and Iris. Late one night, Schrader sent Scorsese a note, telling him he had found their 'Iris'. He'd met a girl the previous night and invited her back to his hotel room at which point he'd discovered she was a prostitute, under age and a drug addict. Schrader introduced Scorsese to the girl and they both decided to base the details of Iris's character on her. She had a very short attention span; she poured sugar on to her bread; she wore sunglasses indoors. Later on, they introduced her to Jodie Foster and she can be seen in a number of scenes as Iris's companion.

Having worked with Foster for just two days on *Alice Doesn't Live Here Anymore*, Scorsese suspected the young actress would be capable of much more than they'd given her, and approached her for the part of Iris. Foster's mother was understandably unhappy with the idea of her daughter playing an under-age prostitute, and brought her to the audition dressed in her school uniform. But Foster's ability to perform way beyond her years convinced Scorsese that she'd be more than able to find the range needed for such a difficult part. Concerned by the idea of a juvenile playing such a sexually provocative role, the Board of Education insisted that Jodie Foster visit a psychiatrist to ensure her morals were not likely to be damaged by the picture. The production team agreed not to allow Foster to film any excessively sexual scenes, so for those, Foster's elder sister Connie – eight years her senior, but of about the same colouring and build – stood in for her. A naturally conservative child, Jodie Foster later said that the clothes she was given for Iris embarrassed her – she was mortified by the heels, hotpants and make-up, and confesses that when they first went shopping for her character's look she began to cry.

Throughout pre-production Scorsese and Schrader would refer to Betsy as a 'Cybill Shepherd type'. Shepherd had been a top model at one time, but since then her relationship with director Peter Bogdanovich had led to her being a high-profile actress. At this time though, her reputation had been soured somewhat by a number of flops. Shepherd's agent, Sue Mengers, approached Scorsese, saying she'd heard rumours he was looking for a 'Cybill Shepherd type' and that he should consider casting the real thing. Despite reservations that they couldn't afford her (Mengers got her to take $35,000 for the role) and that maybe she didn't have the required range for the part they cast her. After all, as Schrader noted, how much worse could she be than a Cybill Shepherd type? Cybill Shepherd and De Niro improvised around Schrader's script, with Scorsese recording their improvisations on black and white videotape so he could come back to their work and write it into the script. Shepherd also did her own make-up and kept checking it in the mirror, something she came to realise irritated Albert Brooks. Brooks was doing a lot of stand-up comedy at the time on TV, which caught Scorsese's eye. Brooks's role wasn't fully written and Brooks believes he was cast partly so he could write his own dialogue.

In Schrader's original script, all of Travis's victims were black, including the character of the pimp, Sport. Concerned by the possibility of accusations of racism, Scorsese decided to cast a white actor as Sport. According to Keitel, Scorsese originally approached him to play the campaign worker (the part which eventually went to Albert Brooks), but after reading the script, he asked to play the pimp. In the script, the character was sketched out in barely a few lines, but Keitel worked with Scorsese to flesh out the role, coming up with the idea for the scene where he comforts Iris and begins his strange Barry White monologue. Keitel did, however, experience resistance from the producers to some of his ideas for his character, notably the wig, which they told him would be too expensive to get for him. Scorsese fought Keitel's corner, however, and also encouraged other touches, such as the single long nail on the small finger, a detail Keitel had heard about, as some pimps grew a pinky nail to scoop cocaine up with.

Another role was cast thanks to Scorsese's girlfriend Sandra Weintraub, who introduced him to Steve Prince, who she knew through her father. Steve was known as someone who could not only handle a gun but could bring his own. Prince and Scorsese connected immediately and became friends.

De Niro finished making *1900* with Bertolucci, and returned to the USA with two weeks to go before starting on *Taxi Driver*. He acquired a hack licence from the Motor Vehicle Department and began to practise being a cabby. For his costume, De Niro borrowed some clothes from Paul Schrader – his boots, jacket, shirt and jeans. He also lost thirty pounds to give himself the gaunt, underfed look he felt would suit the character (see **Raging Bull**).

Victor Magnotta, who appears as the Secret Service photographer, was a friend of Scorsese's from NYU and had been in Vietnam. He told Scorsese and De Niro about how certain soldiers on special missions would cut their hair into a Mohawk, a sign that they were psychologically preparing to kill, and that others should give them a wide berth. Both Scorsese and De Niro have laid claim to the idea of putting it in the movie. Surprisingly, given De Niro's reputation for method acting, the shaven head is in fact a bald-cap provided by make-up effects genius Dick Smith. As the latex cap was very thin, a fresh cap would be used every day, with Dick Smith painting on the stubble and then attaching the centrepiece. Smith later commented that De Niro, ever the perfectionist, would inspect the cap thoroughly. When it came to the final shoot-out, Smith was given the task of designing the hand that would be shot by Travis. In normal circumstances, he'd have used mono-filaments to pull the false hand at the required time, but because of the restrictions of the corridor the scene would be shot in, Smith was forced to use explosive squibs. He crafted a fake hand from wax, with the fingers and upper palm made of wax. The fake hand slipped over the real hand of Murray Moston, and contained the squibs and some pockets of fake blood, so that when the gunshot went off, the wall behind would be sprayed with blood.

For the scene where Keitel shoots De Niro in the neck, Smith developed a new effect. A thin tube filled with fake blood was placed on De Niro's neck. The tube had a small cut where the bullet was supposed to slice past. A small filament was then attached to the area, and plastered over, so that when Keitel shot, the filament could be ripped out, revealing the cut and then the blood would flow as if De Niro had been shot. All this was achieved via a fishing rod to enable Smith to gain access to the tight corridor. A similar technique was used to create the shot where Travis shoots one of the pimps in the face.

The tracking shot through the brothel after the bloodbath was one of the last sequences to be shot. As he had done on *Boxcar Bertha*, Scorsese storyboarded the sequence so he and Michael Chapman had a clear idea what they'd need to do. Schrader's script was very clear as to how the scene would be shot, with the camera up above looking down, panning across the set in slow motion, carefully making its way outside, and taking in the devastation, the police crew tentatively entering the building and the crowds of people outside. As the crew had taken over an entire disused brownstone, they were able to rip open the ceiling and shoot from up there, and spent three weeks preparing the set (the shoot was delayed slightly because of the discovery that the removal of vital struts had weakened the structure of the already derelict building, forcing the crew to install props around the set to hold up the ceiling). On the night, with Jodie Foster required for the scene, and with child labour laws clear about how late she could work, the scene was eventually shot in just twenty minutes.

Scorsese had decided not to edit the picture as he went along, but to save all the editing until shooting had wrapped. Unfortunately, this left him with very little time to cut the picture, as Columbia's contract stipulated that a finished cut had to be supplied by the middle of February. Marcia Lucas began cutting the picture, and Scorsese also brought in Tom Rolf, and later, Melvin Shapiro and an uncredited Thelma Schoonmaker. At one point, Steven Spielberg visited Scorsese and chipped in with some contributions towards the final edit. Despite the tight deadline, the picture was delivered on time to Columbia.

During production, a political journalist called Julia Cameron came to do an interview with Schrader for *Oui* magazine. She decided to hang around the set for a while and eventually met with Scorsese. Cameron has claimed that she rewrote the political speeches, the campaign office dialogue and the scene with the cab drivers at the cafeteria. It has been said that Scorsese was advised not to give Cameron a writing credit to avoid getting a bad review from celebrated New York critic Pauline Kael, who it was believed gave women in the industry a hard time (see **WHAT THE CRITICS SAID**). Within a few weeks of meeting, she and Scorsese were dating (despite Scorsese officially still being with Sandra Weintraub). By the end of the year they were married.

When the final cut was submitted to the Motion Picture Association of America, the board threatened to slap an X certificate on the picture, a surefire kiss of death. Worse, Stanley Jaffe, vice president of production at Columbia, wasn't at all supportive, saying that if the picture wasn't cut back to earn a more acceptable 'R' rating, the studio would reclaim the film and cut it themselves. In a panic, Scorsese got his friends, including Brian De Palma and Steven Spielberg to rally around. Producer Julia Phillips even went to the extent of taking the film to New York to screen for Pauline Kael and selected other critics. Kael offered to write an open letter in her column in support of the picture should they need it. As Scorsese and the Phillipses tried to find a solution to the problem, they met with Eric Pleskow from MGM/UA, who had no problems in taking *Taxi Driver* as an X-certificate picture. Though they were unable to take him up on the offer at the time, United Artists would end up being Scorsese's home for his next picture.

As a concession, Scorsese trimmed some of the more violent excesses of the final climactic bloodbath, and desaturated the film to make the blood look less real, which appeased the MPAA who granted the picture the required 'R'. Ironically, the director felt the desaturated scenes made the picture even more shocking (see **ROOTS**). When supervising the original transfer of the picture to laserdisc, Michael Chapman tried to find the original negatives of the shoot-out before the colour was desaturated. Sadly, the film had deteriorated to the extent that the colour had faded almost completely.

The picture was finally released on 8 February 1976 to massive public acclaim, raking in $58,000 in its first weekend in New York alone.

EDITING: Director of Photography, Michael Chapman, notes how the crew felt uneasy with Scorsese's direction, specifically with the scene in the cab office where Travis walks to the right but the camera pans away from him, turns left and completes a circle before rejoining Travis where we left him, showing us Travis's world instead of following Travis as normal. 'They'd made hundreds of shots following somebody, but the idea of letting him go that way, and the camera go *that* way, almost offended their sensibilities. After a while they got used to that, because they realised it was Marty, and none of them had worked with Marty before.'

Editor Tom Rolf has said that Scorsese insisted on certain shots being longer than instinct would usually allow, to build tension and force the audience to re-examine what they were looking at (such as the Alka-Seltzer shot). For the 'You talkin' to me' scene, De Niro is almost out of shot and remains at the extreme right of the frame for most of the scene, leaving a great, blurry void almost consuming the screen. In the speech that follows the mirror scene, we hear the voice-over begin, and then halt and start over again, and this restart also happens in the shot where De Niro begins slowly to rotate towards the camera, then a jump-cut returns him to his original position as the narration begins again. Throughout the picture, Scorsese uses a familiar technique: by filming all of De Niro's non-dialogue scenes at 48 frames a second, he is able to slow him down to make him appear more monstrous.

MUSIC: While in preparation for *Taxi Driver*, Scorsese was introduced to Bernard Herrmann by Pim de la Parra and Wim Verstappen, who he'd worked with on a Dutch film called *Obsessions* (1969). Scorsese had a tough time convincing the veteran composer to consider scoring what Herrmann dismissively referred to as 'a film about a cab driver'. Eventually he sent Herrmann the script, and then met him in his adopted home, London, and persuaded him that the film would be a worthwhile project. This would be Scorsese's first time working directly with a composer, especially one so well regarded.

Herrmann struggled to find a suitable tone for the running theme for the picture. His long-time associate Christopher Palmer remembered a piece Herrmann had written some time ago and suggested he could rework it. That became the basis for the haunting saxophone music that flows through the picture. Unbeknown to Scorsese, Herrmann was seriously ill and was in no fit state to fly over the Atlantic. The score was recorded over two days, with Herrmann conducting the first day and Jack Hayes, who'd unofficially collaborated with him on the score, conducting the second. That night, Herrmann died.

As we enter the cab office at the start of the film, there's a lift from Charlie Chaplin's *City Lights* (1931). Also, it's Herrmann's music that's the biggest clue that, at the film's climax, Travis is still a deeply disturbed man; listen out for the sound of a cymbal played in reverse just as Travis's eyes dart up to his rear-view mirror.

In among all this, we find Gene Palma, a real-life street drummer spotted by Peter Boyle. Palma used to stand on street corners with shoe polish in his hair and drum away, an element Scorsese liked and wanted to include in the picture for some street-life colour.

The soundtrack also includes 'Late for the Sky' (Jackson Browne) and 'Hold Me Close', performed by George 'Obie' McKern (lyrics by Keith Addis, music by Bernard Herrmann), plus Betsy misquotes 'The Pilgrim' by Kris Kristofferson.

QUOTE/UNQUOTE

Travis: 'All the animals come out at night; whores, skunk-pussies, buggers, queens, fairies, dopers, junkies . . . Sick! Venal! Some day a real rain'll come and wash all the scum off the streets.'

Travis: 'Loneliness has followed me my whole life, everywhere, in bars, in cars, sidewalks, doors, everywhere. There's no escape, I'm God's lonely man.'

Travis: [to his reflection in a mirror] 'You talkin' to me? . . . You talkin' to me? . . . Well who the hell else are you talking to, you talkin' to me? Well I'm the only one here . . . Who the fuck do you think you're talking to? . . . oh yeah? [then in voice-over] Listen you fuckers, you screwheads, here is a man who would not take it any more, a man who stood up to the scum, the cunts, the dogs, the filth, the shit. Here is someone who stood up!'

ROOTS: The plot bears some similarities to *Shane* (George Stevens, 1953), and to *The Searchers* (John Ford, 1956), while Scorsese claims a point-of-view shot from Hitchcock's *The Wrong Man* (1957) influenced the similar technique on display throughout. The lines Scorsese himself speaks regarding what different calibre bullets can do to a person is inspired by *Murder by Contract* (Irving Lerner, 1958). The vivid blood in the final shoot-out, while desaturated to make it look less real, is reminiscent of the similarly vibrant blood effects in the British Hammer Horror pictures of 1958–1974; it was a technique Scorsese had wanted to try ever since seeing John Huston's *Moby Dick* (1956). And while the political campaign was a part of Schrader's original script, it may also have been influenced by Scorsese's own work, filming Hubert Humphrey's unsuccessful presidential election campaign in 1968. As

we'd expect, there's also a strong New Wave influence here. The scene
with the Alka-Seltzer fizzing away in the glass is a lift from Godard's *2
Ou 3 Choses Que Je Sais D'elle* (1967), while Scorsese has compared
Travis to the character of the priest in Robert Bresson's *Journal d'un
Curé de Campagne* (1950). The documentary approach comes via
Scorsese's mentor John Cassavetes. And it could be argued that the scene
where Travis is on the phone to Betsy and the camera slowly pulls away,
owes more than a little to the scene in Hitchcock's *Frenzy* (1972) where
the camera pulls away from the apartment of the killer, to spare us the
pain of watching.

The scene where Travis buys the gun from Salesman Andy and follows
pedestrians with his sights is partly inspired by a story film-maker John
Millius told Scorsese about Paul Schrader buying a gun for himself. After
writing the script, Schrader read the autobiography of Arthur Bremer,
the man who tried to assassinate governor of Alabama and presidential
candidate George Wallace. Though tempted to use sections of it in his
rewrites, he resisted, fearing legal ramifications. Schrader does, however,
cite *The Stranger*, *Pickpocket* and Dostoevsky's *Notes From
Undergound* as influences. Also, Travis's description of himself as 'God's
lonely man' comes from the Thomas Wolfe essay of the same name
(which, incidentally, Schrader quoted in his introduction to the script).
The narration technique, via Travis's diary, is a method of storytelling
that can be traced back to the dawn of literature from Samuel
Richardson's *Clarissa* right through to Mary Shelley's *Frankenstein* and
beyond.

On Travis's TV, we see a clip of Brenda Dickson-Weinberg and Beau
Kayser from the daytime soap *The Young and The Restless*. Through the
rain-soaked windscreen of Travis's cab we can just make out the words
'Texas Chainsaw Massacre'. And the speech from Sport as he seduces
Iris is surely inspired by 'The Walrus of Lurve', Barry White.

THEMES AND MOTIFS: Compare Travis's narration with that of
Charlie in *Mean Streets*, full of guilt, uncertainty and self-examination.
The importance of identity, or more specifically the loss of identity, runs
through *Taxi Driver*. In the 'You talkin' to me?' monologue, Travis goes
on to ask: 'Well who the hell do you think you're talkin' to?' As he
provokes his imaginary aggressor, Travis unconsciously questions
himself, asserting and reasserting that he is 'a man who would not take it
any more . . . someone who stood up'. Throughout, Travis questions his
own identity, and is left with an increasing sense of alienation. The
people around him similarly fail to identify who he is. The manager of

the cab company suspects he's a joker and reacts badly to his claim that his driving licence is 'clean . . . like my conscience'; his fellow cabbies think he's a ladies' man; Matthew the pimp, whether serious or joking, identifies him as a police officer; to Iris's parents and to the newspapers, he's a local hero. Only Betsy comes close, in her comparison of Travis to a song by Kris Kirstofferson: 'He's a prophet and a pusher/Partly truth, partly fiction/A walking contradiction.' Typically, Travis takes offence at the word 'pusher'.

In constructing such a fractured identity, screenwriter Paul Schrader consciously gave Travis a name that works against itself – a heroic name like 'Travis' that is somehow undermined by the name 'Bickle', to rhyme perhaps with 'fickle'. When Travis adopts a pseudonym to avoid detection from the Secret Service agent, he chooses 'Henry Krinkle', a name with similar cadences to his own, both in syllables and in the contrast between the respectable and the comic. Note how Travis is concerned that he twice forgets to ask Betsy her surname (does she consciously withhold this information, like Travis does with the agent, only with subtler elements of subterfuge?) We can link this with both the Black power preaching of Elijah Muhammad, head of the nation of Islam, and with the feminist movement, both of which have identified surnames as labels of ownership, either patriarchal or as a reminder of slave ownership. That Betsy never reveals her family name to Travis is surely an indication that he will never 'own' her. Like many of Scorsese's characters, Travis reveals a heavy glut of misogyny in his private conversations with his diary, admitting: 'I realise now [Betsy] is just like all the rest – cold, distant – many people like that; women for sure. They're like a union.'

CONTROVERSY: As with any story that depicts violence, *Taxi Driver* has been cited as the cause of, or at least the catalyst for, a number of real-life incidents. It was blamed for inspiring John Hinckley's attempted assassination of Ronald Reagan in March 1981. Hinckley had become obsessed with Jodie Foster after another of his heroes, John Lennon, was killed in 1980. He claimed to have watched *Taxi Driver* fifteen times, and that he wanted to kill Reagan to get her attention. The irony of being inspired by a psychopath like Travis Bickle somehow eluded Hinckley, however. Prior to the 1976 Oscar ceremony, at which *Taxi Driver* was up for Best Picture, Scorsese received a letter threatening his life for what he did to 'little Jodie'. The FBI were contacted.

Paul Schrader also claimed that, for a time, he endured his fair share of obsessives, and on one occasion found himself face to face with a man who was certain Schrader had somehow uncovered his 'plan' to assassinate a senator. It would seem that one of the unfortunate side effects of being involved in such a commanding picture is its influence on an ever-expanding number of wackos. Schrader points to the scene where Travis takes Betsy to see a 'dirty movie': 'There's something inside him that wants to sully her, and there's something inside of him that says "I'm worthless and I should be alone".'

KEEP IT IN THE FAMILY: The picture of Iris's parents that accompanies a newspaper clipping on Travis's wall is actually a picture of Scorsese's parents. Diahnne Abbott, (the concessions attendant) would later become De Niro's wife (see also **New York, New York** and **King of Comedy**).

THERE HE IS!: Scorsese appears twice. His planned cameo is as Betsy makes her first appearance – he's sitting on a wall just behind her. Then later he plays the cuckolded husband who hires Travis to take him to his soon-to-be-ex-wife's apartment. This second cameo came about because George Memmoli, the actor scheduled to play the role of the passenger, had an accident on another movie.

LEGACY: In *You Talkin' to Me?* (Charles Winkler, 1987) told the story of a would-be actor and De Niro fan who finds his life taking parallel lines to the events in *Taxi Driver*. The infamous mirror scene has been spoofed by everyone, from the agoraphobic Matthew in the BBC sitcom *Game On* to the Genie of the Lamp in Disney's *Aladdin* (Ron Clements & John Musker, 1992). And of course De Niro himself parodied the scene in *The Adventures of Rocky and Bullwinkle* (Des McAnuff, 2000) (most of his fans wished he hadn't). In what must be an ironic bit of casting, Leonard Martin also appears in the family film *Hero at Large* (Martin Davidson, 1980) as the Mayor of a town protected by unwilling superhero, John Ritter.

POSTER: The theatrical poster's now iconic image of De Niro ambling along the street is accompanied by some powerful, insightful copy: 'On every street in every city in this country there's a nobody who dreams of being a somebody. He's a lonely forgotten man desperate to prove that he's alive.'

TRAILER: The trailer trades on De Niro as the hot rising actor, with the introductory narration focusing on De Niro's recent successes in *Bang* *the Drum Slowly*, *Mean Streets* and *The Godfather Part II* and praising his 'terrifying portrait of life on the edge of madness'. 'People do anything in front of a taxi driver,' explains De Niro's voice-over, 'I mean anything. People too cheap to rent a hotel room, people wanna embarrass ya, it's like you're not even there. It's like, y'know, a taxi driver doesn't even exist.' The grave narrator then warns us that 'The taxi driver is looking for a target, getting ready, getting organised, preparing himself for the only moment in his life that will ever mean anything.'

WHAT THE CRITICS SAID: Pauline Kael, in her column in the *New Yorker*, praised Scorsese's nightmare: 'Part of the horror implicit in this movie is how easily [Travis] passes. The anonymity of the city soaks up one more invisible man; he could be legion.'

Jack Kroll in *Newsweek* raved: 'First and last, Taxi Driver belongs to Robert De Niro, the most remarkable young actor of the American Screen. What the film comes down to is a grotesque pas de deux between Travis and the City, and De Niro has the dance quality that most great film actors have had, whether it's allegro like Cagney, or largo like Brando. De Niro controls his body like a moving sculpture. Once, seething with frustration, he takes a swig from a beer can and his head snaps into a quick, complex spasm of thwarted rage. Trying to ingratiate himself with a Secret Service man, his entire conversation comes out of a tilted-up, twisty-smiling face that's a diagram of social unease.'

On the film's release in the UK, David Castell of *Films Illustrated* made *Taxi Driver* a cover story in his retraction of an earlier, less favourable review after seeing the film at Cannes in what he felt were less than ideal circumstances. 'It is a measure of Robert De Niro's brilliant performance (he is barely off the screen for the whole running time) that the film binds together as well as it does. After the gentleness of *Alice Doesn't Live Here Anymore*, Martin Scorsese proves not only his skill and his vision, but his range. If 1976 produces another film as good, it will indeed have been a vintage year.'

TRIVIA: Assistant director Ralph Singleton can be seen briefly playing a TV interviewer. In the cab stand, there's a sign that reads: 'Be alert – the SANE driver is ALWAYS READY for the UNEXPECTED', a hint of what is to come.

AWARDS: The 1976 Cannes Film Festival awarded Scorsese the Palme d'Or for *Taxi Driver*, despite jury chief Tennessee Williams's outburst against violence in movies. It was also nominated in the 1977 American Academy Awards (Oscars) for Best Actor, Best Music, Original Score (Herrmann), Best Picture, Best Supporting Actress (Jodie Foster). At the British Academy Awards (BAFTAs) it was nominated for Best Actor, Best Direction, Best Film, Best Film Editing, and won the Anthony Asquith Award for Film Music, with Best Newcomer and Best Supporting Actress again going to Foster. At the Golden Globe Awards, there were nominations for Best Motion Picture Actor – Drama (De Niro) and Best Screenplay – Motion Picture (Schrader). Finally, the Los Angeles Film Critics Association Awards, the National Society of Film Critics and the New York Film Critics Circle all awarded De Niro a Best Actor, with additional awards for Herrmann (LA Critics) and Foster (New York Critics). In 1994, *Taxi Driver* was registered with the National Film Preservation Board, USA, and in 1999 it was named the American Film Institute's number 47 in 100 best films of the Century.

AVAILABILITY: *Taxi Driver* is regularly rereleased on VHS, most recently by Columbia TriStar Home Video in commemoration of the film's 25th anniversary. Originally released by RCA/Columbia in a two-sided pan-and-scan laserdisc presentation, it was later released in a four-sided widescreen presentation by Criterion, who added a commentary by Scorsese and Paul Schrader, plus an examination of Bernard Herrmann's score by Herrmann's biographer, Steven C Smith.

Columbia TriStar Home Video released a basic widescreen DVD back in 1997, but their collectors' edition re-release (released in 2000 in both the USA and Europe) is vastly superior. Boasting an anamorphic transfer, its extras comprise a thorough 'making of' documentary, branched storyboard and screenplay that allows access to and from the relevant sections in the movie, advertising materials and a photo gallery with commentary by the DVD's producer, Laurent Bouzereau.

EXPERT WITNESS: 'You can work to cure cancer for 40 years and never be acknowledged. But take a shot at the president and you can be a hero, because in a world of media and fame and celebrity there are no values.' Writer Paul Schrader.

'Paul Schrader, Marty and myself, we all felt that we could relate to the character, the loneliness and so on. I was raised in New York City – I'm in the middle of New York City, but I'm still alone in it. There have been many times in my life I've been very alone and felt isolated and we could identify with that . . . the talking in the mirror scene is something that a lot of people I'm sure do in one form or another and they can relate to that.' Robert De Niro (*Travis Bickle*), interviewed by James Lipton.

'I remember [De Niro] being kind of directive . . . he would run the lines ad nauseam with me. It was so boring, it was just like, "Oh God. Do we have to?" And he wouldn't talk to me. In his Method-y way, he'd just kind of sit there and go, "Yeah". By the time I got to the actual shooting of the scene, I knew the dialogue so well that when he went off into a surprise area, it never threw me because I could always go back to the text. But I would see the text in a new way.' Jodie Foster (*Iris*), interviewed by Rachel Abramowitz.

FINAL ANALYSIS: Like *Jaws* for Steven Spielberg, or *The Godfather* for Francis Ford Coppola, *Taxi Driver* really is the film that typifies Scorsese's film-making, with its disinterested documentary style, a script that was given greater depth by lengthy improvisation sessions prior to filming and a staggering performance by De Niro.

Such is the ferocity of the portrayal of New York here, and coming so soon after *Mean Streets*, some might think that Scorsese had a downer on his native city. With the grimy streets, seedy nightlife and the menagerie of different characters, some beautiful, some hideous and some just plain weird, it's almost no surprise at all that Travis finds it hard to cope. From the start, a sense of menace pervades every shot. In the opening sequence, the dark, steam-filled street is suddenly divided by the relentless cheery yellow of a taxi-cab. With an entrance like this, the cab takes on the form of a predator – a huge, squat tiger with one chequer-coloured stripe running along its flank, unblinking and deadly. Ex-marine Travis Bickle trades the jungles of South East Asia for a human jungle, to which he is equally unable to adapt. Yet in this grim tale there can be found many lighter moments; the mad street drummer with the boot-polish hair; the way Travis completely fails to pick up on Betsy's incredulity at his clumsy seduction technique (most probably lifted from a porno film he's seen). Yet the level of cynicism and repulsion in *Taxi Driver* is relentless, unflinching and unrepentant; the inherent racism and 'morbid self attention' of its central character is at odds with Cinema's usual factory-produced pretty boys in romantic comedies or the solemn-faced loners played by John Wayne in numerous Westerns. In fact, the subject of the effects of the Vietnam War were rarely touched, the war still being too recent for many to allow any sense of decency.

Since its birth at the end of the nineteenth century, the cinema has been the scapegoat for any number of organisations and movements. *Taxi Driver*, in its bold depiction of racism and sexual deviance, is very much an easy target. For instance, few film-makers would risk the career of an encouraging newcomer like Jodie Foster by casting her as a child prostitute. That Foster's portrayal has a self-assurance, a confidence that belies her age is almost as frightening and unsettling as the reality of the situation, that for some people this is merely an everyday facet of their lives. Fortunately, few of us are able to identify with it.

That is the true power behind *Taxi Driver*; though most of us have played no part in a war like the Vietnam conflict, have never seriously considered becoming a vigilante, or even a cab driver, the essence of Travis' plight – his alienation from all around him, his loneliness, his paranoia – is as honest a discussion into the human condition as we're likely to see.

SCORSESE ON *TAXI DRIVER*: 'I felt all those feelings in the story at that time. I was 32 years old. I really felt that way at times and so really felt it was special to express. De Niro felt very strongly about it too. I thought at the time we were making sort of a labour of love; a picture that wouldn't necessarily speak to many people – maybe to a darker side of some people – and was surprised when it had such an acceptance of an audience.'

New York, New York (1977)

(33 mm – 153 mins – colour)

MPAA rating: PG

Produced by United Artists
Producers: Irwin Winkler, Robert Chartoff
Executive in Charge of Production: Hal W Polaire
Screenplay: Earl Mac Rauch, Mardik Martin
Associate Producer: Gene Kirkwood
Original Songs by Fred Ebb & John Kander
Cinematography by László Kovács
Supervising Editor: Marcia Lucas, Irving Lerner
Film Editors: Bert Lovitt, David Ramirez, Tom Rolf
Technical Consultant: Georgie Auld
Casting: Lynn Stalmaster

Production Design: Boris Leven
Art Direction: Harry Kemm
Set Decoration: Robert De Vestel, Ruby R Levitt
Costume Design: Theadora Van Runkle
Title Designer: Dan Perri

MUSIC AND SONGS: 'Theme from New York, New York', 'There Goes the Ball Game', 'But the World Goes Round', 'Happy Endings', 'You Brought a New Kind of Love to Me', 'Once in a While', 'You Are My Lucky Star', 'The Man I Love', 'Taking a Chance on Love' all sung by Liza Minnelli; 'Blue Moon' by Mary Kay Place; 'Honeysuckle Rose' sung by Diahnne Abbott; 'Opus One', 'Song of India', 'I'm Getting' Sentimental over You', 'Don't Blame Me', 'It's a Wonderful World', 'For All We Know', 'South America Take It Away', 'Just You, Just Me', 'Do Nothing Till You Hear from Me', 'Don't Get Around Much Anymore', 'Hold Me Tight', 'Bugle Call Rag', 'Avalon', 'Night in Tunisia', 'Wonderful Girl', 'Billets Doux' performed by the Hot Club of France Quintet.

CAST: Liza Minnelli (*Francine Evans*), Robert De Niro (*Jimmy Doyle*), Lionel Stander (*Tony Harwell*), Barry Primus (*Paul Wilson*), Mary Kay Place (*Bernice*), Georgie Auld (*Frankie Harte*), George Memmoli (*Nicky*), Dick Miller (*Palm Club Owner*), Murray Moston (*Horace Morris*), Lenny Gaines (*Artie Kirks*), Clarence Clemons (*Cecil Powell*), Kathi McGinnis (*Ellen Flannery*), Norman Palmer (*Desk Clerk*), Adam David Winkler (*Jimmy Doyle Jr*), Dimitri Logothetis (*Desk Clerk*), Frank Sivera (*Eddie Di Muzio*), Diahnne Abbott (*Harlem Club Singer*), Margo Winkler (*Argumentative Woman*), Steven Prince (*Record Producer*), Don Calfa (*Gilbert*), Bernie Kuby (*Justice of the Peace*), Selma Archerd (*Wife of Justice of the Peace*), Bill Baldwin Sr (*Announcer in Moonlit Terrace*), Mary Lindsay (*Hat Check Girl in Meadows*), Jon Cutler (*Musician in Frankie Harte Band*), Nicky Blair (*Cab Driver*), Casey Kasem (*DJ*), Jay Salerno (*Bus Driver*), William Tole (*Tommy Dorsey*), Sydney Guilaroff (*Hairdresser*), Peter Savage (*Horris Morris's Assistant*), Gene Castle (*Dancing Sailor*), Louie Guss (*Fowler*), Shera Danese (*Doyle's Girl in Major Chord*), Bill McMillan (*DJ*), David Nichols (*Arnold Trench*), Harry Northup (*Alabama*), Marty Zagon (*Manager of South Bend Ballroom*), Timothy Blake (*Nurse*), Betty Cole (*Charwoman*), DeForest Covan (*Porter*), Phil Gray (*Trombone Player in Jimmy Doyle's Band*), Roosevelt Smith (*Bouncer in Major Chord*), Bruce L Lucoff (*Cab Driver*), Bill Phillips Murry (*Waiter in Harlem Club*),

Clint Arnold (*Trombone Player in Palm Club*), Richard A Berk (*Drummer in Palm Club*), Jack R Clinton (*Bartender in Palm Club*), Wilfred R Middlebrooks (*Bass Player in Palm Club*), Jake Vernon Porter (*Trumpet Player in Palm Club*), Nat Pierce (*Piano Player in Palm Club*), Manuel Escobosa (*Fighter in Moonlit Terrace*), Susan Kay Hunt, Teryn Jenkins (*Moonlit Terrace Girls*), Mardik Martin (*Well Wisher in Moonlit Terrace*), Leslie Summers (*Woman in Black in Moonlit Terrace*), Brock Michaels (*Man at Table in Moonlit Terrace*), Washington Rucker (*Musician at Hiring Hall*), Booty Reed (*Musician at Hiring Hall*), David Armstrong, Robert Buckingham, Eddie Garrett, Nico Stevens (*Reporters*), Peter Fain (*Greeter in Up Club*), Angelo Lamonea (*Waiter in Up Club*), Charles A Tamburro, Wally McCleskey – credited as Wallace McCleskey – (*Bouncers in Up Club*), Ronald Prince (*Dancer in Up Club*), Robert Petersen (*Photographer*), Ottaviano Dell'Acqua – credited as Richard Raymond – (*Railroad Conductor*), Hank Robinson (*Francine's Bodyguard*), Harold Ross (*Cab Driver*), Eddie Smith (*Man in Bathroom in Harlem Club*).

UNCREDITED CAST: Allison Caine (*Additional Voice*), Joey Forman (*Argumentative Man*), Larry Kert.

TITLES: A MARTIN SCORSESE FILM appears in red on a black background, then it fades out to make way for a graphic of the Manhattan skyline at night while the overture (a compilation of the songs from the movie, in the style of the big musicals of the 1940s) plays on. (On the video release, this sequence is preceded by a card informing us that the film is in its full version, and includes the 'Happy Endings' sequence that marked the film debut of Larry Kert.)

SUMMARY: VJ Day, 1945. As the whole of New York celebrates the end of the war, Jimmy Doyle tries to get himself a girl for the night. He tries his luck with a number of women with no success, and then approaches a girl from the Women's Army Corp sitting on her own. He's persistent but she tells him she's waiting for her friends and is not interested in talking with him. Her friend shouts over to her, and Jimmy learns her name: Francine Evans. Jimmy gives up on her and goes to speak to one of his friends who has just found himself a girl; she happens to have a friend he'd like to introduce to Jimmy. Unfortunately, it is the one Jimmy has just struck out with. Jimmy lends his hotel-room key to his friend, who runs off with his girl leaving Jimmy and Francine together. Francine is not impressed with his persistence and walks out on him.

The next day, Francine goes to Jimmy's hotel to find her friend and bumps into Jimmy who, it appears, is trying to scam the hotel and avoid paying his bill. Suddenly going up to Jimmy's hotel room, Francine finds Jimmy's luggage and smuggles it out of the hotel just as Jimmy is escorted off the premises. They get a cab together and Francine accompanies Jimmy to an audition. Jimmy is a saxophonist and likes to play free-form jazz. Unfortunately, the man holding the auditions is not a fan and Jimmy almost blows his chance, until Francine steps in, placates Jimmy and begins to sing along and dance. The man is impressed and books Jimmy and Francine as a double act. Surprised by this turn of events, the pair spend the night celebrating and it's only after Jimmy sees her to her hotel and leaves that Francine learns that her agent has got her an audition of her own.

Jimmy is disappointed when Francine doesn't show up for their rehearsal, and when she sends him a note via her agent telling him that she's been booked on to a tour, Jimmy rushes to follow her. He hitch-hikes up to Ashford and finds her in the middle of her act. His presence there alarms Francine, especially when he drags her outside in the middle of her set. He tells her that he loves her – and then quickly downplays this, saying that he 'digs' her. Francine manages to get Jimmy into the band she's singing with, but Jimmy's brash manner and insistence on hogging the limelight and showing off begins to wear on the other band members. One night, Jimmy reads some poetry that Francine has written and when she tells him it's about him he seems to be furious. He grabs her by the arm and bundles her into a cab, driving out to a small town to see the Justice of the Peace in the middle of the night to ask him to marry them. The suddenness of all this, coupled with the complete lack of a proposal throws Francine, and it's only when Jimmy threatens to throw himself under a cab that she realises he's serious. He kneels at her feet and urgently tells her he loves her and asks her to marry him. She agrees.

As the tour progresses, the band-leader, Frankie, confides in Francine that he's considering cancelling the rest of the tour due to the low turn-out of the audiences. Francine convinces him that Jimmy could take over the band, and though Frankie considers her husband to be a 'top pain in the ass', he consents. The tour continues, despite some of the booking agents' dismay at Frankie's departure. The reviews come in, and Francine gets singled out for praise. Rehearsals are strained with Jimmy's brusque methods and his constant bickering with Francine beginning to spread tension through the band. Then, during a performance, Francine falls ill. Much to Jimmy's annoyance, Francine tells him that she's pregnant and wants to return to New York. Back home, Francine continues to work thanks to bookings from her agent. Her ability to mimic popular stars like Jo Stafford and Peggy Lee gains her a good reputation. Meanwhile, Jimmy has hired a replacement singer for the tour. She's not a patch on Francine and bookings begin to cancel. As key members of the band begin to quit, Jimmy is forced to cancel the tour and return home.

Jimmy and Francine are invited to the opening night of The Paul Wilson orchestra to meet a representative from Decca, Mr Kirks. Jimmy holds a grudge against Paul Wilson since he left Jimmy's band, and when he reaches the club he sulks for most of the night, refusing to sit with Francine and her friends and in the end he picks a fight with Paul and is thrown out. The next morning, Francine goes for tests and finds Jimmy waiting for her, his Buick filled with flowers. He apologises for his behaviour and begs for her forgiveness. A second meeting with Mr Kirks is arranged. Kirks eulogises about Francine's talent, and offers to provide a nurse, day care for the baby when it arrives and a car. Kirks goes out of his way to reassure Jimmy and make sure he's happy. Later in the evening, Jimmy is playing with the band, and Francine walks towards the stage as if to join him to sing, so he quickly changes the tempo to something faster, a clear signal that she is not welcome on his stage. She slowly returns to her seat, grabs her coat and leaves. Jimmy runs after her and jumps in his car to chase after a cab he's just seen drive off, but is startled to find Francine in the back of his car. He roars at her for being drunk and for getting pregnant. They break into a fight until she suddenly goes into labour. Jimmy immediately drops the argument and rushes her to hospital. After their son is born, Jimmy is angry that Francine names the baby after him without consulting him. Though he's apologetic and tells her he loves her, they both know they have no future together. Jimmy leaves without seeing his new-born son.

Some years later, Jimmy has his own club and the song he wrote for Francine, 'New York, New York' looks set to be a hit. Francine meanwhile has become a big star, and her face is on the cover of every magazine. After the release of her latest movie, 'Happy Endings,' and the opening of her own show on Broadway, Jimmy goes to visit her. He tells Francine how proud of her he is, but their conversation is awkward, both regretting the distance between them. He leaves, and meets his son for the first time. On his way out, he passes a phone booth and calls Francine to arrange to meet her after the show the next night. But when the next evening comes, Jimmy waits outside the stage door and Francine waits inside. Both are disappointed that the other doesn't show, but both seem resigned to the fact. Jimmy walks off alone into the night.

WHO'S WHO?: Daughter of Judy Garland and director Vincente Minnelli, Liza Minnelli made her film debut at just fourteen months old. She won an Oscar for her performance in the film version of the show *Cabaret* (Bob Fosse, 1972) and developed a breathless stage repertoire which earned her three Tony Awards and an Emmy for her TV special *Liza with a Z* (1972). In the 1980s, her collaboration with pop band the Pet Shop Boys led to the hits 'Losing My Mind' and 'Don't Drop Bombs' as well as the hit album 'Results'.

Lionel Stander's massive filmography is completely overshadowed by his supporting role of Max in *Hart to Hart*, for which Stander provided the opening voice-over. Mary Kay Place played Camille Cherski in the teen drama *My So-Called Life*. Dick Miller began his career as a jobbing actor for Roger Corman in such B-movie hits as *A Bucket of Blood* (1959) and the original *Little Shop of Horrors* (1960). Having worked with director Joe Dante during the production of *Fly Me* (Cirio H Santiago, 1972) (which Dante worked on as dialogue coach), Miller would later make appearances in most of Dante's films, most notably as paranoid ex-airpilot Murray Futterman in *Gremlins* (1984) and *Gremlins II: The New Batch* (1990). Clarence Clemons is the saxophonist from Bruce Springsteen's backing group, The E-Street Band. DJ Casey Kasem is famous for playing the voice of Shaggy in the many series of Scooby Doo cartoons.

Producer Irwin Winkler first met Scorsese at the New York Film Festival screening of *Mean Streets*. After *New York, New York*, Winkler produced *Raging Bull* and *GoodFellas*, while Scorsese appeared in Winkler's *Round Midnight* (Bertrand Tavernier, 1986) and Winkler's directorial debut, *Guilty by Suspicion*, which also starred De Niro. Husband to actress Margo Winkler and father of Charles Winkler, who was also the production assistant on both *New York, New York* and *Raging Bull*.

THE USUAL SUSPECTS: Robert De Niro (*Mean Streets, Taxi Driver, Raging Bull, The King of Comedy, GoodFellas, Cape Fear, Casino*); Diahnne Abbott (*Taxi Driver, The King of Comedy*); Harry Northup (*Who's That Knocking At My Door?, Boxcar Bertha, Mean Streets, American Boy, Alice Doesn't Live Here Anymore, Taxi Driver, Amazing Stories*: 'Mirror Mirror'); Steven Prince (*Taxi Driver, American Boy, The*

Last Waltz); Barry Primus (*Boxcar Bertha*); George Memmoli (*Mean Streets, American Boy*); Peter Savage (*Taxi Driver, Raging Bull*); Mardik Martin (*It's Not Just You, Murray!, American Boy, Raging Bull, The King of Comedy*, plus writing credits for *Mean Streets, Italianamerican*); Peter Fain (*Mean Streets, Raging Bull, The King of Comedy, GoodFellas*); Producer Irwin Winkler (*Raging Bull, GoodFellas*); Margo Winkler (*The King of Comedy, After Hours, GoodFellas*); production assistant Charles Winkler (*Raging Bull*); title designer Dan Perri (*Taxi Driver, The Last Waltz, Raging Bull, The King of Comedy, The Color of Money*); Marcia Lucas (*Alice Doesn't Live Here Anymore, Taxi Driver*).

PRODUCTION: It was during the making of *Alice Doesn't Live Here Anymore* that Martin Scorsese first read about *New York, New York*. An article in The Hollywood Reporter announced that producer Irwin Winkler had bought a script from Earl Mac Rauch and had yet to decide on a director. Scorsese immediately put himself forward. Scorsese envisaged the film as a tribute to the Hollywood of old, with big musical numbers and the gloss and glamour of the musicals of the 1940s and 50s, yet also combining modern film-making techniques to merge the old and the new together. Having worked extensively with Robert De Niro on both *Mean Streets* and *Taxi Driver* (which had still to receive the green light), Scorsese knew he wanted him on board. He also managed to gain the interest of Liza Minnelli to play Francine. With Minnelli's versatility as a singer, dancer and actress and – significantly – her background, being the daughter of Judy Garland and director Vincente Minnelli, she would bring much to the production. Scorsese began pre-production on the picture just as confirmation came through that *Taxi Driver* would be going ahead after all. *New York, New York* would have to be put aside until *Taxi Driver* was completed. Scorsese flew out to Parma, Italy, where De Niro was completing *1900* to confirm that the actor would be willing to commence filming of *New York, New York* straight after *Taxi Driver*. De Niro was happy.

Taxi Driver brought massive critical acclaim to both Scorsese and his leading man. When the pair returned to start on their big musical it was, by Scorsese's own admission, with vastly inflated egos. Suddenly, the small picture as outlined in Earl Mac Rauch's script wasn't big enough. Scorsese requested a number of rewrites from the writer but, being more familiar with the techniques of prose, the scripts came back bigger and bigger each time. Scorsese's wife, Julia Cameron, was despatched to work with Earl, but eventually, after nearly two years working on the same script he announced that he had no more to contribute and left the production. Mardik Martin stepped in to help provide some kind of structure to the spiralling script but by that time the window in which they could make the picture was coming to an end due to Minnelli's existing commitments. Despite having such a long lead-time on the picture, Scorsese was forced to begin production without a final shooting script.

The technique of improvisation had worked for him in the past, but here he was preparing to pin the entire picture on that method. Now he, De Niro and Minnelli were all contributing ideas to the picture and rehearsing on the set itself instead of some time before. While this had worked when he was working with three actors in a basement in New York, it was a different matter when there were hundreds of extras standing round waiting for the scene to be written and rehearsed. The proposal scene, which had been scripted almost as a farce, took longer than expected to film simply because of concerns over the window that De Niro was supposed to punch. Worried that his leading man could injure himself, Scorsese spent much of the first day arranging for replacement windows to be constructed and ensuring De Niro would be as safe as possible. Waiting around for the issue with the window to be resolved, De Niro came up with the idea that he should threaten to put his head under the cab wheels.

Just like the old musicals, *New York, New York* would be filmed on soundstages in LA, and the job of recreating the New York of old fell to set designer Boris Leven, who'd worked on musicals such as *West Side Story* (Jerome Robbins & Robert Wise, 1961). Leven's brief was to make everything on the soundstages, from New York streets and music halls to an open-air winter forest and a small mid-west town just after a heavy snowfall. Songwriters Fred Ebb and John Kander, whose music for *Cabaret* had helped Minnelli win an Oscar, were commissioned by United Artists to write original songs, including the title track.

Neither Scorsese nor Winkler had made an all-out musical before, and they together worked out that they would need $7 million and fourteen weeks to complete the picture, with the first ten days of the schedule dedicated to the big production number, dubbed 'Happy Endings'. As it turned out, 'Happy Endings' was the only part of production that managed to stay on schedule. Part of the problem was the issue of synchronised sound. Keeping the action on-screen in synch with the music over every shot was a constant drain of energy, with De Niro's sax teacher Georgie Auld (who also appears as bandleader Frankie Harte) acting as technical adviser to ensure that De Niro's fingering matched the soundtrack Auld had recorded. The fight inside the car that leads to Francine going into labour was shot over two days, one for the master shots, one for everything else. Working in the confined space of the car prop proved difficult and Minnelli hurt her arm as she hit De Niro, and De Niro bruised his knuckles, necessitating a trip to the hospital for x-rays.

Publicity for the picture was huge, with celebrity visits to the set including Minnelli's father, Vincente, directors Milos Forman and Bernardo Bertolucci, and actors Sylvester Stallone (who was working with Winkler on his rags-to-riches boxing movie, *Rocky*), Jeanne Moreau and Jack Nicholson. All of these visits, however, provided the team with more distractions that slowed them down.

The production eventually wrapped twenty-two weeks later. With his private life falling apart and his recreational drug-use escalating, Scorsese was reaching burn-out. Given three weeks to rest before commencing the editing process, Scorsese accepted an invitation to film a documentary about the final performance of rock group The Band, working behind Winkler's back to get both productions completed.

Frantically trying to cut *New York, New York* by day and *The Last Waltz* (as the documentary would be called) by night, Scorsese was showing no signs of completing either project and so eventually he begged Marcia Lucas to help him out. Lucas was editing a picture by her husband George, a science fiction B-movie that no one, let alone Marcia, had any faith in, so she dropped everything to work with Scorsese again. Concerned by the buzz surrounding Scorsese's picture and his own, George Lucas came to visit Scorsese and, puzzled by the bleak tone to what was supposed to be a musical, suggested that he'd probably add $10 million to his box office if he just made the film with a happy ending. It was advice that Scorsese ignored. The film stood at four hours, twenty-nine minutes and while Scorsese was personally happy with the cut, he knew that commercially, it had to be much shorter. Setting up a few re-shoots to blend the massive cuts needed, Scorsese managed to assemble an edit closer to an acceptable length (although still more than an hour longer than most commercial movies).

New York, New York finally opened on 21 June 1977. It was a darker movie than United Artists had wanted. The critics hated it (even Pauline Kael, one of Scorsese's champions, dismissed it as a pastiche) and the box-office receipts were not good. Scorsese had his first flop on his hands. George Lucas's picture – *Star Wars* – was a massive commercial success, the biggest hit anyone had seen in years, while Scorsese's 'grown-up' picture, $2 million over budget, sank, leaving Marty on the brink of a period of depression.

EDITING: Taking inspiration from the likes of Vincente Minnelli, Scorsese shaped the musical sequences around the structure of the music, panning across the band for a few bars with no master shot, then panning across the other way, almost like the camera is conducting the orchestra. It's a technique Scorsese would use again in *Raging Bull* and *The Color of Money*, choreographing the fight/pool sequences to a regular structure. We also get the first use of a flashbulb to mask the cut to the next scene when Francine takes a picture (which Scorsese would use again in *Raging Bull* and *GoodFellas*). The most significant nod to the past comes in the 'Happy Endings' sequence, which merges the classic Busby Berkeley production numbers of the 1930s, with their spinning kaleidoscopic choreography, with the later story-within-a-story segments of Stanley Donen.

Towards the end, as Francine looks into her mirror and sees Jimmy arrive to see her, Scorsese cheats a deep focus shot by using a split screen, with Jimmy in the background and Francine in extreme close-up in the foreground.

MUSIC: *New York, New York* relies upon existing tunes to create a sense of the era, including 'You Are My Lucky Star', sung by Debbie Reynolds/Jean Hagen in *Singin' in the Rain*, Glenn Miller's 'Pennsylvania 6-5000', and 'Taking a Chance on Love, made famous by the Benny Goodman Orchestra. In among these are Ebb and Kander's new tunes which, to modern audiences will now be as familiar as the standards (see **LEGACY**).

In among the improvisation-gone-mad, De Niro was still sticking to his regime of dedicated research for the part. He'd begun hanging out in jazz clubs, soaking up the atmosphere, and taking lessons on how to play the saxophone from musician Georgie Auld. When, as Frankie Harte, Auld tells Francine that Jimmy is a 'top pain in the ass' he could just as easily be referring to De Niro himself, who, he later claimed, dogged him with question after question about the life of a saxophonist.

QUOTE/UNQUOTE
Jimmy: 'I guess a little small talk's in order.'
Francine: 'Could it get any smaller?!'

Jimmy: 'That's a major chord'.

Francine: 'What's a major chord?'

Jimmy: 'A major chord is when everything in your life works out perfectly. When you have everything you could ever possibly want – everything. You have the woman you want, and you have the music you want and you have enough money to live comfortably. And that's a major chord.'

ROOTS: De Niro here could pass for a young Gene Kelly, and with Barry Primus bearing a striking similarity to Dan Dailey this could almost be a remake of *It's Always Fair Weather* (Stanley Donen, Gene Kelly, 1955). Francine's costume for the 'Happy Endings' sequence was inspired by a painting by Edward Hopper of an usherette, while the colouring of the clothes worn by Jimmy (burgundy) and Francine (green) when she tells him she's pregnant paint an image of Vivien Leigh and Clark Gable in *Gone with the Wind* (Victor Fleming, 1939).

Jimmy Doyle signs himself into the hotel as Mr Powell, another tribute to Scorsese's friend and idol, British film-maker Michael Powell.

THEMES AND MOTIFS: Again, use of colour is important, particularly red and green. Francine's clothes are often a vivid red, which makes her stand out on stage, including the woollen top she wears during the rehearsals where Jimmy tells her off for counting in the band; in the 'Happy Endings' sequence she has the usherette uniform (white and red), then the piano singer in black and white with a red scarf (in a red room), then a red sequinned dress; and then for her performance of the title song it's another red top with black pants. And when Jimmy begins having an affair with the replacement singer, we see him in a loose red shirt in a dark green room. There's also deliberate use of red or green lighting with Jimmy captured in a red halo for his audition for the Frankie Harte band, or Paul West's club flooded with red – except the side bar, which is green. Throughout the picture, this harmony continues with red and green balancing each other out until – significantly – the end, where Jimmy waits outside of the theatre, bathed in red light, while Francine waits against a cornflower-yellow wall.

KEEP IT IN THE FAMILY: Diahnne Abbott was, by this time, Robert De Niro's wife.

LEGACY: *Gremlins II: The New Batch* features a stunning musical number where the gremlins (including a glamorous lady gremlin) stage a production of the song 'New York, New York' (including a gremlin chorus doing all the 'Dah dah dahdedah' bits). Frank Sinatra did, of course, steal the song and make it his own, which in turn led to the song making an obligatory appearance on every karaoke song-list across the globe. 'Just You, Just Me' features prominently throughout Woody Allen's *Everybody Says I Love You* (1996).

ALTERNATIVE VERSIONS: Initially standing at a whopping 4-hour, 29-minute edit, Scorsese and Lucas managed to snip it down to 153 minutes for its release, removing the bulk of the 'Happy Endings' section and adding a few reshoots to soften the cut. The European release was cut down further to just 136 minutes, but in preparing the TV version in 1981, Scorsese was persuaded to restore a number of edited scenes, including the show-stopping 'Happy Endings', bringing the 'full' and final version up to a 164-minute special edition.

TRIVIA: Sydney Guilaroff, who appears as a hairdresser, was a legendary Hollywood hairstylist, the first to receive an on-screen credit and responsible for the styles of thousands of actresses, including Lucille Ball. The blonde woman dancing with the sailor who Jimmy watches from the fire escape is actually Liza Minnelli in a wig.

POSTERS: The tagline read: 'The war was over and the world was falling in love again.' 'A love story is like a song. It's beautiful while it lasts.' 'The magic that is MINNELLI. The power that is DE NIRO. The force, the life, the music, the explosion that is NEW YORK, NEW YORK.'

TRAILER: 'Robert De Niro is a fast-talking saxophonist who's trying to make it in the Big Apple,' announces the excited voice-over. 'Liza Minnelli's a singer who's on her way to the top. When two of today's hottest stars team up, a stormy relationship makes for beautiful music in Martin Scorsese's brilliant feature film'.

AWARDS: At the Golden Globes, USA Year Result Award Category/Recipient(s) *New York, New York* was nominated for Best Motion Picture – Musical/Comedy, De Niro and Minnelli were nominated for Best Motion Picture (Musical/Comedy) Actor and Actress respectively and 'The Theme from *New York, New York*' received a nod for best original song. At the British Film and Television Awards later that year, Michael Colgan, James Fritch, Larry Jost, Richard Portman and Kay Rose were nominated for Best Soundtrack and Theadora Van Runkle was nominated for Best Costume Design.

AVAILABILITY: *New York, New York* has enjoyed a number of releases and re-releases. It received a full unedited VHS release in 1992. MGM home video released a widescreen laserdisc edition in 1989, across three sides and complete with the restored 'Happy Endings' segments.

WHAT THE CRITICS SAID: '*New York, New York* has superb performances from its two principles, De Niro's contribution perhaps being the greater in that he makes sympathetic a character of considerable unattractiveness. Minnelli's vocabulary of nervous giggles and swallowed sobs hasn't been better used since *Cabaret* and her singing style has the fullness and soul-felt ache of the mature Judy Garland.' David Castell, *Film Illustrated*, October 1977.

EXPERT WITNESS: 'In all those other forties movies, you never really knew about the woman, what she felt or said after going home. Women get angry and swear and in this movie I get angry and swear. It's a story I can relate to. When a man leaves, it's not her undoing, she has fulfilment in her work . . . for the first time in my life I didn't play a kook. I'm just an intelligent girl-woman in the movie. Robert De Niro has the wacky role for a change. And he's incredible. I think he's probably the greatest actor around today.' Liza Minnelli (*Francine Evans*).

FINAL ANALYSIS: *New York, New York* received a critical mauling on its release and it's not hard to see why: Hollywood, and specifically the movie critics, hate to see self-indulgence on such a grand scale. It's what crippled Francis Ford Coppola with his similarly overambitious and downbeat musical *One from the Heart* (1982) and it very nearly crippled Scorsese. Over-long and pulling in too many directions at the same time, it's unclear whether it really is trying to be an old-style musical or merely trying to ape their style to re-invent the genre. On that level at least, *New York, New York* is a failure.

However, what we are left with is yet another superb performance from De Niro as the self-obsessed musician, managing to gain our admiration for his bloody-mindedness and refusal to quit (at one point, seeing his train pull away, he runs after it and tries to push it back in the opposite direction), while at the same time provoking revulsion at his abject selfishness and his abominable treatment of a woman he loves yet is envious of. Only when he has finally managed to make it on his own terms, with a small club and a band consisting largely of black musicians (who are generally regarded to be the best) can he return to Francine, flush with her own, greater level of stardom. Even then though, he cannot resist a dig at her latest feature, which he dubs 'Sappy Endings'.

New York, New York is, more than anything, Minnelli's picture, showcasing her as an all-round entertainer with a staggering vocal range – fragile, barely audible one minute, belting it out with all the power her lungs can stand the next. Though the picture could survive perfectly well without that big production number that seems to slow the film down completely, it's her performance of the title song that really brings the film to a climax, making the (very long) wait all the more worthwhile.

SCORSESE ON *NEW YORK, NEW YORK*: 'I was extremely disappointed when the movie was finished because I had had a really bad experience making it. But over the years I've been able to see that it has a truth to it. I still don't really like it, yet in a way I love it.'

The Last Waltz (1978)

(35 mm – 117 mins – colour)

MPAA rating: PG

Produced by FM Productions/Last Waltz Inc. for United Artists
Producers: Robbie Robertson, Joel Chernoff (not credited)
Line Producer: LA Johnson
Line Producer, Studio & Documentary: Frank Marshall
Associate Producer: Steven Prince
Executive Producer: Jonathan T Taplin
Cinematography by Michael Chapman, Michael W Watkins, Vilmos Zsigmond
Additional Cinematographers: Bobby Byrne, László Kovács, David Myers, Hiro Narita
Production Designer: Boris Leven
Set Decoration: Anthony Mondell
Title Designer: Dan Perri

SOUNDTRACK: 'Don't Do It', 'Theme From *The Last Waltz*', 'Up on Cripple Creek', 'Shape I'm In', 'It Makes No Difference', 'Stagefright',

'The Night They Drove Old Dixie Down', 'Chest Fever', 'Ophelia', 'Old Time Religion', 'Genethic Method', 'Sip the Wine' by The Band; 'The Weight' by the Staples; 'Evangeline' by Emmylou Harris; 'Who Do You Love' by Ronnie Hawkins; 'Such a Night' by Dr John; 'Helpless' by Neil Young; 'Dry Your Eyes' by Neil Diamond; 'Mystery Train' by Paul Butterfield; 'Coyote' by Joni Mitchell; 'Mannish Boy' by Muddy Waters; 'Further on up the Road' by Eric Clapton; 'Caravan' by Van Morrison; 'Forever Young', 'Baby Let Me Follow You Down' by Bob Dylan; 'I Shall Be Released' by Bob Dylan, Ringo Starr, Ron Wood et al.

CAST: (all as themselves) Dr John, Robbie Robertson, Ringo Starr, Muddy Waters, Ron Wood, Neil Young, Paul Butterfield, Eric Clapton, Rick Danko, Neil Diamond, Bob Dylan, Emmylou Harris, Ronnie Hawkins, Levon Helm, Garth Hudson, Howard Johnson, Richard Manuel, Joni Mitchell, Van Morrison, Martin Scorsese, Roebuck 'Pops' Staples.

TITLES: A MARTIN SCORSESE FILM appears in red letters on a black background. Then 'THE BAND' appears in yellow lettering, followed by the distinctive logo of *The Last Waltz*. The remaining credits appear in yellow or red over footage of couples waltzing.

SUMMARY: After sixteen years of touring, rock group The Band decide to go out in style, throwing a massive concert, featuring special guests and personal friends from the world of rock, at the Winterland, the first venue they ever played together as The Band. The movie features footage from that night as well as interviews with the band-members telling their story.

THE USUAL SUSPECTS: Steven Prince (*Taxi Driver*, *New York, New York*, *American Boy*); Robbie Robertson (*Raging Bull*, promo video 'Somewhere Down That Crazy River'); cinematographer Michael Chapman (*Taxi Driver*, *Raging Bull*); title designer Dan Perri (*Taxi Driver*, *New York, New York*, *Raging Bull*, *The King of Comedy*, *The Color of Money*).

PRODUCTION: In September 1976, during the final week of filming of *New York, New York*, producer Jonathan Taplin (Scorsese's producer on *Mean Streets*) approached Scorsese with a proposition. The Band was about to break up and he invited Scorsese to shoot a documentary of their final concert on Thanksgiving Day 1976. A big fan of Robbie Robertson and The Band, Scorsese accepted instantly, planning on editing the concert footage at night while he was cutting *New York, New York* during the day. The only snag was he had to film the concert and edit it without the knowledge of Irwin Winkler, his producer on *New York, New York*. While Winkler believed Scorsese was in New York editing that picture, he was in fact on the opposite coast, in San Francisco.

Scorsese chose to film the concert on 35 mm stock in full synch sound and with seven cameras. As Bob Dylan was worried the picture might be in competition with his own movie *Renaldo and Clara* (eventually released in 1978), he insisted that Scorsese would only be allowed to shoot two of his numbers, 'Baby, Let Me Follow You Down' and 'Forever Young'.

As the editing of *New York, New York* dragged on, Scorsese was forced to put *The Last Waltz* to one side. In the meantime, Robbie Robertson and Scorsese became good friends; Robertson actually moved into Scorsese's LA home in early 1977 soon after Scorsese's wife left him. As some of the concert footage was incomplete, Robertson suggested doing a montage sequence of some of the numbers, including 'Evangeline,' 'The Last Waltz' and 'The Weight'. Scorsese and Robertson also persuaded United Artists to give them more money to re-record some songs on a sound stage, with Emmylou Harris, Ray Charles and the Staple Sisters, and later, to add some interviews, with Scorsese as the interviewer. In the spring of 1978, Scorsese and Robertson took *The Last Waltz* to Cannes.

EDITING: Just as he'd done on *New York, New York*, Scorsese chose to cut the concert footage every few bars, giving the editing a rhythm in time with the music.

MUSIC: The sound recording from the concert was released in 1978 as a triple vinyl LP and later re-released as a double CD. In 1995 the entire undubbed concert was released on a 4-disc bootleg CD.

QUOTE/UNQUOTE
Robbie Robertson: (quoting Ronnie Hawkins) 'He said, "Well, son, you won't make a lot of money, but you'll get more pussy than Frank Sinatra".'

CONTROVERSY: It will come as no surprise to anyone that many of the interviewees were stoned or drunk or both during the production (and see also **EXPERT WITNESS** below).

THERE HE IS!: Scorsese interviews the band members and, it has to be said, can barely contain his excitement.

LEGACY: Spoofed by Rob Reiner (who appears in the picture as director and interviewer Marty DiBergi) in *This Is Spinal Tap* (1984). Despite this, *The Last Waltz* is still seen as a textbook example of how rockumentaries should be made.

AVAILABILITY: Warner Home Video have been kind to fans of The Band, releasing *The Last Waltz* on both laserdisc (now deleted) and on VHS (re-released in 2001).

EXPERT WITNESS: Producer Jonathan Taplin recalls the first time they projected *Waltz* and the face of Neil Young, looking wasted and very big, appeared on the screen: 'There was a rock of cocaine falling out of his nostril. His manager was freaking out – "I'm refusing to let you put this song in the movie!" I went to an effects house run by these older guys who didn't know cocaine from . . . a booger in his nose. I told them, "This guy has got a booger in his nose. Can you fix it?" They called back in a couple of days and said, "We've invented a travelling booger matte".'

SCORSESE ON *THE LAST WALTZ*: 'I had the feeling that the movie audience could become more involved with the concert if we concentrated on the stage. Besides, after *Woodstock*, who *wants* to see the audience any more?'

American Boy: A Profile of Steven Prince (1978)

Working Title: *All-American Boy*

(16 mm – 55 mins – colour)

A New Empire Films/Scorsese Film
Produced by Bert Lovitt
Executive Producers: Jim Wheat, Ken Wheat
Treatment: Mardik Martin, Julia Cameron
Cinematographer: Michael Chapman

Film Editing: Amy Holden Jones, Bert Lovitt
Production Manager: Tikki Goldberg

SOUNDTRACK: 'Time Fades Away' by Neil Young.

CAST: (all as themselves) Steven Prince, Martin Scorsese, George Memmoli, Mardik Martin, Julia Cameron, Kathy McGinnis.

SUMMARY: Steven Prince tells Scorsese and a group of friends about his experiences of growing up in an army barracks and the life that followed.

THE USUAL SUSPECTS: Steven Prince (*Taxi Driver, New York, New York, The Last Waltz*). George Memmoli (*New York, New York*). Mardik Martin (*Mean Streets, Italianamerican, New York, New York, Raging Bull, The King of Comedy*).

PRODUCTION: After the completion of *Taxi Driver, New York, New York* and *The Last Waltz*, Scorsese was finally able to edit the footage of an interview he'd done with his friend Steven Prince at the home of actor George Memmoli. As Prince delivered what were effectively monologues, Scorsese edited in home movie footage of Prince as a boy. Prince's stories centred around his sense of survival, the army, drugs and his time as manager of a rock group. Prince managed to keep the mood light, even when discussing how, in self defence, he killed a man who tried to rob him while he was working at a petrol station. Prince concluded the interview with the revelation that he'd learned that his father was dying. The film eventually premiered at the 16th NY Film Festival, on 6 October 1978.

AVAILABILITY: Though at one time, *American Boy* was available on the 'Three By Scorsese' Voyager laserdisc alongside *Italianamerican* and *The Big Shave*, it is currently not available in any format.

LEGACY: Steve's description of how to revive someone from a drug overdose made its way into a scene in *Pulp Fiction* (Quentin Tarantino, 1994).

Raging Bull (1980)

(35 mm – 129 mins – B & W/colour)

A Chartoff-Winkler Production for United Artists
Producers: Robert Chartoff & Irwin Winkler
Associate Producers: Hal W Polaire and Peter Savage
Screenplay: Paul Schrader, Mardik Martin, from the book
Raging Bull by Jake LaMotta with Joseph Carter and Peter
Savage
Cinematographer: Michael Chapman
Film Editor: Thelma Schoonmaker
Casting: Cis Corman
Production Designer: Gene Rudolf
Art Direction: Sheldon Haber (New York)
Set Decoration: Phil Abramson, Frederic C Weiler (credited
as Fred Weiler)
Costume Design: John Boxer, Richard Bruno
Consultant: Jake LaMotta
Title Designer: Dan Perri

SOUNDTRACK: 'Intermezzo from Cavalleria Rusticana' by Mascagni;
'Stornelli Fiorentini' by Carlo Buti; 'Scapricciatiello' by Renato
Carosone; 'Turi Giuliano' by Orazio Strano; 'Cow Cow Boogie' by Ella
Fitzgerald & the Ink Spots; 'Whispering Grass', 'Do & Worry' by the
Ink Spots; 'Stone Cold Dead in the Market' by Ella Fitzgerald & Louis
Jordan; 'Till Then' by The Mills Brothers; 'Big Noise from Winnetka' by
Bob Crosby & The Bobcats; 'Heartaches' by Ted Weems; 'Blue Velvet'
by Tony Bennett; 'Flash', 'Two O'Clock Jump', 'All or Nothing at All'
by Harry James; 'Drum Boogie' by Gene Krupa; 'Jersey Bounce' by
Benny Goodman; 'Come Fly With Me', 'Mona Lisa' by Nat King Cole; 'I
Ain't Got Nobody' by Louis Prima & Keely Smith; 'Nao Tenho
Lagrimas' by Patricio Teixerra; 'Prisoner of Love' by Perry Como;
'Prisoner of Love' by Russ Colombo; 'Just One More Chance', 'That's
My Desire' by Frankie Laine; 'Bye Bye Baby' by Marilyn Monroe;
'Lonely Nights' by The Hearts; 'Tell the Truth' by Ray Charles.

CAST: Robert De Niro (*Jake LaMotta*), Cathy Moriarty (*Vickie
LaMotta*), Joe Pesci (*Joey LaMotta*), Frank Vincent (*Salvy*), Nicholas
Colasanto (*Tommy Como*), Theresa Saldana (*Lenore LaMotta, Joey's
Wife*), Mario Gallo (*Mario*), Frank Adonis (*Patsy*), Joseph Bono

(*Guido*), Frank Topham (*Toppy*), Lori Anne Flax (*Irma*), Charles Scorsese (*Charlie – Man with Como*), Don Dunphy (*Himself/Radio Announcer*), Bill Hanrahan (*Eddie Eagan*), Rita Bennett (*Emma – Miss 48's*), James V Christy (*Dr Pinto*), Bernie Allen (*Comedian*), Floyd Anderson (*Jimmy Reeves*), Harold Valan (*Referee, Reeves Fight*), Victor Magnotta (*Fighting Soldier*), Johnny Barnes (*Sugar Ray Robinson*), John Thomas (*Sugar Ray's Trainer*), Kenny Davis (*Referee, 1st Robinson Fight*), Paul Carmello (*Ring Announcer, 1st Robinson Fight*), Jimmy Lennon Sr (*Ring Announcer, 2nd Robinson Fight/Dauthuille Fight*), Bobby Rings (*Referee, 2nd Robinson Fight*), Kevin Mahon (*Tony Janiro*), Marty Denkin (*Referee, Janiro Fight*), Shay Duffin (*Ring Announcer, Janiro Fight*), Eddie Mustafa Muhammad (*Billy Fox*), 'Sweet' Dick Whittington (*Ring Announcer, Fox Fight*), Jack Lotz (*Referee, Fox Fight*), Kevin Breslin (*Heckler*), Louis Raftis (*Marcel Cerdan*), Frank Shain (*Ring Announcer, Cerdan Fight*), Coley Wallace (*Joe Louis*), Fritzie Higgins (*Woman with Vickie*), George Latka (*Referee, Cerdan Fight*), Fred Dennis (*Cornerman 1*), Robert B Loring (*Cornerman 2*), Johnny Turner (*Laurent Dauthuille*), Vern De Paul (*Dauthuille's Trainer*), Chuck Hassett (*Referee, Dauthuille Fight*), Ken Richards (*Reporter at Phone Booth*), Peter Fain (*Dauthuille Corner Man*), Count Billy Varga (*Ring Announcer, 3rd Robinson Fight*), Harvey Parry (*Referee, 3rd Robinson Fight*), Ted Husing (*Himself*), Michael Badalucco (*Soda Fountain Clerk 1*), Thomas Beansy Lobasso (*Beansy*), Paul Forrest (*Monsignor*), Peter Petrella (*Johnny*), Serafino Tomasetti (*Webster Hall Bouncer*), Geraldine Smith (*Janet, Joey's Date at Copa*), Mardik Martin (*Copa Waiter*), Maryjane Lauria (*Girl 1*), Linda Artuso (*Girl 2*), Peter Savage (*Jackie Curtie*), Daniel P Conte (*Detroit Promoter*), Joe Malanga (*Bodyguard*), Sabine Turco Jr, Steve Orlando, Silvio Garcia Jr (*Bouncers at Copa*), John Arceri (*Maitre D'*), Joseph A Morale, James Dimodica, (*Men at Table 1*), Robert Uricola (*Man outside Cab*), Andrea Orlando (*Woman in Cab*), Allan Malamud (*Reporter at Jake's House*), DJ Blair (*State Attorney Bronson*), Laura James (*Mrs Bronson*), Richard McMurray (*JR*), Mary Albee (*Underage ID Girl*), Lisa Katz (*Woman with ID Girl*), Candy Moore (*Linda*), Richard A Berk (*Musician 1*), Theodore Saunders (*Musician 2*), Noah Young (*Musician 3*), Nick Trisko (*Bartender Carlo*), Lou Tiano (*Ricky*), Rob Evan Collins (*Arresting Deputy 1*), Wally K Berns (*Arresting Deputy 2*), Allen Joseph (*Jeweller*), Bob Aaron (*Prison Guard 1*), Glenn Leigh Marshall (*Prison Guard 2*), Martin Scorsese (*Barbizon Stagehand*).

UNCREDITED CAST: Bruno DiGiorgi (*Soda Fountain Clerk 2*), Bill Mazer (*Reporter*), John Turturro (*Man at Table, Webster Hall*), McKenzie Westmore (*Jake's Daughter*).

TITLES: As the Intermezzo from Cavalleria Rusticana plays in, LaMotta shadow-boxes in the ring. The credits appear in white, while the title is written in red.

SUMMARY: New York, 1964. In the dressing room of a nightclub, ex-boxing champion Jake LaMotta rehearses his lines for a one-man show. He is overweight, his speech slurred through years of boxing.

Cleveland Arena, 1941. A young LaMotta at the peak of fitness loses against Jimmy Reeves on points. A riot breaks out, the crowd furious that LaMotta has been denied a victory. After the fight, Jake's brother Joey speaks with Salvy, a local mobster who wants Jake to work with them – with Jake in their pocket, they could make a lot of money from him. Joey goes to see his brother right in the middle of another domestic situation as Jake and his wife fight. Jake moans to his brother that he'll never be given the chance to fight Joe Louis because he's a middleweight and Louis is a heavyweight. Then he goads Joey into hitting him in the face. Joey asks him in despair what he's trying to prove.

Jake talks Joey into introducing him to Vickie, a young, beautiful blonde girl from the neighbourhood who happens to be friends with certain local mobsters. Jake invites her to go for a ride with him, teaches her to play putting golf and then takes her home and seduces her. At around this time, Jake and 'Sugar' Ray Robinson begin a friendly rivalry. The first time they meet, LaMotta becomes the first boxer to defeat Robinson. Later that year, they meet again, largely because no one else will face them so they can only fight each other. Despite LaMotta knocking him down, Robinson is declared the winner, to the audible disgust of the crowd. Back in the dressing room, Joey smashes the place up, saying Robinson only got the win because he was about to go into the army. Jake is stoical, saying that he's done a lot of bad things and maybe this is just a sign of things coming back to him. He can't face seeing anyone and asks Joey to take Vickie home.

1947. Jake and Vickie are married, and Jake has had an impressive run of victories, yet has still not been able to get a title shot. Jake berates Joey for putting him down for a fight against well-known 'pretty-boy' Janiro. Joey has registered Jake at 155 pounds, which is way below his current weight, and if he doesn't make the fight he'll be fined $15,000. Joey reminds him that all he's ever wanted is a title shot. If he loses the fight because of his weight, then all the guys who are too afraid to fight him will then be willing to face him and he should get a title shot. If he wins, he still has to have a shot at the title because there's no one else to fight. While their wives are out of the room, Jake asks Joey if he thinks Vickie is cheating on him. Joey reassures him, but Jake asks him to watch her for him while he spends time at a health spa to lose some weight. On Joey's advice, Jake takes Vickie out for the night, though he's none too happy that his wife is still very familiar with members of the mob.

While Jake is away at the training camp, Joey sees Vickie out with her old male friends. She tells him she's tired of being a prisoner at twenty years old, even though she loves Jake. Joey tells her she's making an ass out of his brother and even the reassurances of Salvy aren't enough to placate him. Joey flips and attacks Salvy. News of the fight reaches mob boss Tommy Como, who orders Joey and Salvy to shake hands and hold no grudges. Tommy then tells Joey that Jake is causing them an embarrassment, making things hard on himself and making it look like Tommy can't even deliver a kid from his own neighbourhood. He says he has no respect and that they will never give Jake a title shot unless he begins to work with them. By the time Jake takes on Billy Fox at Madison Square Garden, rumours are already flying that he intends to throw the fight. Fox is not a strong enough contender and the crowd turn ugly when it becomes obvious that Jake isn't even trying to fight him. Fox is declared the winner by a technical knockout. Back in his dressing room, Jake sobs.

1949. After serving his suspension from boxing for the fixed fight, Jake prepares for his title shot against middleweight champion Marcel Cerdan. He receives a hero's welcome from the crowd and as thanks he gives Cerdan a punishing ten rounds and is declared the world middleweight champion. Jake has finally got what he wanted all this time and openly sobs with joy. Becoming the World Champion isn't enough to change Jake's domestic life however. His jealousy continues to grow and after Joey nags at him once again for piling on weight, Jake asks Joey how the fight with Salvy came about. Joey tells him it had nothing to do with him, but Jake tells him it's not what he heard and accuses Joey of fucking Vickie. Joey storms out, disgusted, but Jake follows him, beats him viciously and punches Vickie, knocking her out cold. Though Jake and Vickie are eventually reconciled, he and Joey part ways.

1951. LaMotta takes on Robinson again, but by the 13th round he finds himself struggling. Believing he deserves to be punished for his actions, he stands back and goads Robinson into giving him everything he's got. Jake takes a savage beating, spraying the horrified crowd with his blood. Though Robinson is crowned the victor and Jake's face beaten to a pulp, Jake still taunts his opponent that even after such a savage defeat, Robinson never managed to knock him down.

1956. Jake has retired from boxing and opened a club named (imaginatively) Jake LaMotta's in Miami with himself as compere. One morning he's roused from bed by an officer from the DA's office telling him a complaint has been made that he has served a 14-year-old girl and introduced her to men. The insinuations cripple him. He's thrown into prison. At his lowest ebb, Jake begins to beat the wall of his cells until his fists are bloody pulps. His reputation in tatters, Jake is unable to fight again. Even his own brother refuses to speak to him.

By the time Jake has entered the cabaret circuit in the 1960s, he is doing recitals of the famous speech from *On the Waterfront* by Brando. 'I coulda been a contender' he tells himself in the mirror. 'I coulda been somebody.'

WHO'S WHO?: Joe Pesci's earlier career as a guitarist and singer has been eclipsed by his acting career, especially since the triple-whammy of foul-mouthed psycho Tommy De Vito in *GoodFellas*, Harry, one of the 'Wet Bandits' in *Home Alone* and *Home Alone 2* (Chris Columbus, 1990, 1992) and motormouth moaner Leo Getz in *Lethal Weapon 2–4* (Richard Donner, 1989, 1992, 1998). Despite the initial fame brought by *Raging Bull*, Cathy Moriarty's career sadly never lived up to initial expectations. Her most high-profile roles post-*Raging Bull* include the female lead in Joe Dante's B-Movie comedy *Matinee* (1993) and a villainous turn in the live action version of the cartoon *Casper* (Brad Silberling, 1995). Nicholas Colasanto was at one time a TV director on shows such as *Columbo, Starsky & Hutch* and *CHiPs*, though he's most famous for playing barman Ernie 'Coach' Pantusso in the long-running sitcom *Cheers*. Soda Fountain Clerk Michael Badalucco might be familiar from his dark, disturbing portrayal of serial killer David Berkowitz in Spike Lee's *Summer of Sam* (1999) and as the brash, self-obsessed bank-robber George 'Babyface' Nelson in the Coen Brothers' *Oh Brother, Where Art Thou?* (2000) (which also starred John Turturro, who makes an uncredited appearance in a scene at Webster Hall in *Raging Bull*). McKenzie Westmore grew up to play Sheridan Crane in the US daytime soap *Passions*, and made an appearance as herself in an episode of *Friends*.

THE USUAL SUSPECTS: Robert De Niro (*Mean Streets, Taxi Driver, New York, New York, The King of Comedy, GoodFellas, Cape Fear,*

Casino); Joe Pesci (*GoodFellas, Casino*); Frank Vincent (*GoodFellas, Casino*); Peter Savage (*Taxi Driver, New York, New York*); Victor Magnotta (*It's Not Just You, Murray!, Taxi Driver, After Hours*); Robert Uricola (*It's Not Just You, Murray!, What's a Nice Girl Like You Doing in a Place Like This?, Who's That Knocking At My Door?*); Peter Fain (*Mean Streets, New York, New York, The King of Comedy, GoodFellas*); Frank Adonis, Joseph Bono, Daniel P Conte (*GoodFellas, Casino*); cinematographer Michael Chapman (*Taxi Driver, The Last Waltz, American Boy, Bad*); writer Paul Schrader (*Taxi Driver, The Last Temptation of Christ, Bringing Out the Dead*); producer Irwin Winkler (*New York, New York, GoodFellas*); editor Thelma Schoonmaker (*Who's That Knocking At My Door?, Street Scenes, Taxi Driver, The King of Comedy, After Hours, The Color of Money, Bad, The Last Temptation of Christ, New York Stories, GoodFellas, Cape Fear, Age of Innocence, Casino, A Personal Journey with Martin Scorsese Through American Movies, Kundun, Bringing Out the Dead, My Voyage to Italy, Gangs of New York*); screenwriter Mardik Martin (*It's Not Just You, Murray!, Mean Streets, Italianamerican, New York, New York, American Boy, The King of Comedy*); title designer Dan Perri (*Taxi Driver, New York, New York, The Last Waltz, The King of Comedy, The Color of Money*).

SOURCE: *Raging Bull: My Story* was first published in hardback in 1970 (and later republished under the banner *Raging Bull: The Autobiography of Jake LaMotta*). It was co-written by Joseph Carter and Peter Savage – aka LaMotta's lifelong friend Peter Petrella. For the purpose of the film, much of Petrella's influence on LaMotta's life is transferred to his brother, Joey. Paul Schrader stripped the book in half, removing the story of LaMotta's early life (half of the book) completely, which is strange considering how easily identifiable that section is as (for want of a better phrase) a typical Scorsese project. It begins with LaMotta's assault and apparent murder of bookie Harry Gordon, the guilt stemming from which dogged LaMotta for most of his life until the night he learned that Gordon hadn't died and indeed had no idea that it had been LaMotta who had mugged him. We then follow LaMotta's life as a petty criminal, his eventual arrest and his experiences in prison where, after being beaten in a fight, he began to train hard as a boxer. Instead, as it turned out, wisely, Schrader concentrated solely on the period leading up to LaMotta's title shot and his later decline, topping and tailing the story with scenes of Jake as a stand-up comedian rehearsing his patter before leaping straight into the first fight with 'Sugar' Ray Robinson.

PRODUCTION: In the early 60s, while Scorsese was still a student at NYU, *Variety* announced that he was in pre-production on a student film starring an ex-world champion boxer turned actor, Jake LaMotta. Though the news report was an error, Scorsese later remembered this detail when, nearly twenty years later, he was speaking to journalists to promote his film *Raging Bull*. From the very beginning though, *Raging Bull* was De Niro's project. Having read Jake LaMotta's autobiography while on the set of *The Godfather, Part II*, De Niro identified something in the boxer's story that appealed to him as an actor. He first approached Scorsese with the book during the filming of *Alice Doesn't Live Here Anymore*. Scorsese was dismissive, largely because he couldn't find a way to make it interesting for himself. He had little faith in the (ghost-written) autobiography, and even less faith in the events depicted in it. As De Niro pestered him relentlessly over the next few years, Scorsese briefly entertained the notion of producing the book as a play, and filming the results. But really, he couldn't find the enthusiasm he felt he'd need. At one point, his friend Mardik Martin, who had been attempting to adapt the book to script form, provided the first breakthrough to convince Scorsese he might do the picture. He described one scene, where two boxers attack each other, like gladiators in Rome, surrounded by the wealthy crowd dressed in tuxedos and fur coats. Martin described how he imagined the scene, saying that as LaMotta gets punched in the face, his nose squirts blood in a spray over the rich onlookers.

Scorsese became slightly more interested in the project, but Martin noted how the director was steering the script to be closer to his own upbringing than that of the legendary boxer. When De Niro saw the script he was not happy. He could tell that Scorsese still wasn't that sold on the idea, and wasn't taking it seriously. The anecdotes from Scorsese's own life, his own family, were not true to the book. Exasperated, De Niro asked if Paul Schrader could be brought in to give the script a much-needed rewrite. But when Schrader read the script, he knew he had to go right back to the beginning. While he edited his own film, *Hardcore*, by day, he rewrote *Raging Bull* by night.

Although structurally the script was sound, its content proved too much for United Artists – both the repellent characters and the graphic descriptions of LaMotta attempting (and failing) to masturbate in his prison cell – and it looked like they might consider dropping the picture.

Producer Irwin Winkler, who'd been attached to the project largely on his success with *Rocky*, was forced to play dirty. *Rocky* had been so successful the studio wanted a sequel desperately. Still in possession of the rights to Rocky, Winkler offered them a deal – *Rocky II* in return for *Raging Bull 1*.

Schrader, De Niro and Scorsese battled out the script, with De Niro still having reservations about some of the stronger stuff. But, exhausted after editing *New York, New York*, *The Last Waltz* and *American Boy* back-to-back, and depressed after *New York, New York* received a critical roasting, Scorsese was heading for burn-out. On Labor Day 1978, he was rushed to hospital and told he could suffer a brain haemorrhage at any moment. His excessive partying, drug-taking and late nights had taken their toll. De Niro visited him in hospital and again asked him to commit to his pet project. It took such a near-death experience as this for Scorsese to finally understand why *Raging Bull* was something he needed to do – living like there was no tomorrow, with no respect for himself or anyone else, damaging his potential with stubbornness and overindulgence – he *was* Jake LaMotta. Once he was safe to be discharged from hospital, he and De Niro escaped to St Martin in the Caribbean to work on rewriting the script. By the time the pair returned, script in hand, the studio was too busy ramping up production on Michael Cimino's epic Western *Heaven's Gate* to trouble them and they left Scorsese and De Niro to continue with a picture they felt was probably doomed.

In preparation for the picture, Scorsese took some 8 mm footage of De Niro boxing and showed it to Michael Powell, who noted how the colour seemed too bright. Cinematographer Michael Chapman agreed, and noted how the colour distracted from the action. Remembering that he'd seen some of LaMotta's fights on newsreels at the time, Scorsese decided to make *Raging Bull* in black and white, both to add a sense of the documentary feel of it, and because it would help make it different to all the other boxing movies at the time. Additionally, as the colour film stock people were using then was at risk of fading, he thought the picture might survive longer on black and white film. This of course meant that the cameramen needed to light the sets differently to get a greater depth with the black and white film stock. Chapman had never shot in black and white, and found it difficult lighting the low-ceilinged apartments needed for the shoot. As so few film-makers used anything other than colour film, few of the photographic laboratories were able to process the film stock. Strangely, Technicolor was able to help. The only colour segments would be the opening title over the black and white image of the boxer in the ring, and the colour home movie footage, which were desaturated to make them look faded.

De Niro had been in training with the real Jake LaMotta for a year, both as a fighter and as a convincing native of the Bronx, and had, as was the custom, pestered him for intricate details of his life at the time. He also interviewed Jake's second wife, Vickie and their daughter Stephanie. But unlike any other role, this was one that De Niro would have to prepare for physically as well as mentally. Thanks to an intensive training programme, he built up his 145 pounds to a taut, muscular 160 pounds. To test his training, LaMotta entered De Niro into three professional fights, billed as 'The Young LaMotta' and he managed to win two of them. But there was also the matter of the older Jake, described in the script as being bloated and overweight. Both Scorsese and De Niro felt that padding the actor up in a fat suit would look fake. De Niro volunteered to put on the weight, necessitating a shut-down of production to allow him enough time to eat his way around some of the restaurants he'd found during the filming of *The Godfather Part II* and *1900*.

For the part of Jake's younger brother Joey, Scorsese and De Niro chose Joe Pesci, who they'd seen some years earlier in *The Death Collector* (Ralph De Vito, 1975). At the time, Pesci was a frustrated, struggling actor slugging it out as one half of a musical act alongside fellow actor Frank Vincent. Disillusioned with movie acting, however, Pesci had to be convinced to take the part. In turn, it was Pesci who found them their Vickie LaMotta. He first saw a photograph in a nightclub in Mount Vernon, New York of Cathy Moriarty, a local beauty contest winner and realised the girl bore an uncanny resemblance to LaMotta's wife. He told Scorsese about her and she was invited in to audition. Moriarty would be called back many times over the next three months, not even knowing if she had the part until the very end.

Raging Bull finally came before the cameras in April 1979. Though the scenes of LaMotta's life would be shot on location in Hell's Kitchen in New York, the complicated fight sequences were staged on soundstages in Los Angeles. Whenever possible, he wanted the camera to be inside the ring, putting the audience in the shoes of the boxers, instead of the safety of the audience. Indeed, with sequences that showed the blood of the fighters shower across the audience, the feeling was that even in the seats of the auditorium, the audience would not be safe. Scorsese, cinematographer Michael Chapman and production designer Gene Rudolf worked hard to make each fight look different. For instance, LaMotta's first, victorious fight with 'Sugar' Ray Robinson was brightly lit. But in a later fight, in which LaMotta lost to Robinson on a technicality, the ring is smaller, and flames were put in front of the camera to create a mirage-like haze effect on the image and fill the ring with smoke, giving the impression that LaMotta was beginning his descent into his own personal Hell. The fuzzy, badly framed sequences also represented LaMotta's state of mind. For the recreation of the fight between LaMotta and Laurent Dauthuille in Detroit, 1950, Scorsese was lucky enough to have some actual footage of the original fight, and strove to match it with a literal blow-by-blow re-enactment, even down to the wide punch that LaMotta threw to knock Dauthuille out, and the way Dauthuille's head bounced off every rope until he came to rest on the canvas.

While De Niro was off eating his way across Italy, Scorsese married actress Isabella Rossellini. He also began editing the picture together – minus the 'fat Jake' scenes – with Thelma Schoonmaker. After four months of binge-eating, De Niro had gained a staggering 60 pounds in weight. Scorsese was concerned by the actor's weight gain and noticed how his breathing had become like the director's own just before an asthma attack. Though worries about De Niro would prove unfounded, Scorsese was not so lucky, and when he fell ill again, his own father, Charles, stepped in to direct the home movie sequence of Joey LaMotta's wedding, basing the action on his own wedding to Catherine (including filming the reception on the rooftops because it was too hot inside).

The 'An Evening With Jake LaMotta' scene, filmed on the last day of the shoot just before Christmas 1979, took nineteen takes, with De Niro attempting different interpretations of the speeches each time. With filming completed, De Niro sank into a depression as he struggled to lose the weight and realised that LaMotta might have been a once in a lifetime experience. Meanwhile, Scorsese began post-production unaware that United Artists were struggling to find a distributor for the picture.

The sound effects for the picture were specially created from scratch by Frank Warner, who'd also worked on *Taxi Driver*. Warner became very defensive of his work, not even allowing Scorsese to know how he'd achieved all of the effects, and after the film's completion he burned the tapes to prevent anyone else using them. In addition to the sound effects, Warner also used absence of sound, such as at the beginning of the LaMotta v Robinson fight of 1951, in which a low, primal roar drops to silence until the first blow is thrown, at which point the cries of the crowd crash in. Additionally the fight sequences would be recorded in Dolby stereo to get the best of Warner's sound design, but the day-to-day life of LaMotta was recorded monoaurally, as with a TV documentary.

Finally, after nearly a year in post-production, the picture was ready to be previewed. When the lights went up, the audience didn't clap. But neither did they boo – or complain, They were literally stunned into silence. One woman, overwrought with emotion, simply burst into tears. That was when Scorsese and De Niro knew they'd made a picture that was unlikely to be a commercial success. With the eventual domestic box office stalling at around $10 million, *Raging Bull* was neither a success nor a failure. Critics too were divided, with many of the team's previous fans disgusted by the picture, but many more instantly recognising the effort that had gone into making Raging Bull something unique.

EDITING: Scorsese employs two distinct methods of editing throughout the film. Outside the ring, scenes are shot in a flat documentary style with little music and few visual tricks, apart from a brief use of slow motion, usually to represent Jake's own point of view of the world around him: his first wife, the gangsters, Vickie or his brother. A couple of other interesting point-of-view shots not to do with Jake occur during and after Joey's brawl with Salvy. During the fight itself we see the view from inside the cab where Joey repeatedly slams the door against Salvy's torso as the would-be passenger pushes herself into the corner of the cab and screams. In the next scene, we see the bruised Salvy and the apologetic Joey from over Tommy Como's shoulder, at once positioning Tommy as a powerful man.

In the ring, Scorsese can afford to be more experimental, as is shown by the cut from the overweight Jake of 1964 to the muscular Jake of 1941, a startling juxtaposition, especially considering how unrecognisable De Niro is as the bloated LaMotta. In the first fight, Jake is shot from below to enhance the sense of his power (although significantly, the overhead shot of the two fighters pushing their gloves together reveals that Jake has small hands, something that we learn has always worried him). By the time of the third fight, Scorsese wants to show us the beginning of LaMotta's descent into Hell. For this, he shot everything with long lenses, placing fire just below the lens to give the hazy rippled effect to the image and fill the screen with a gauze-like fog.

Taking his lead from Eisenstein, much of the fighting is textbook montage, with Scorsese and Schoonmaker following slowed-down shots of the fighters approaching each other with fast cuts of the fight itself, trimming certain shots back and back until they become almost subliminal images flashing before our eyes (seen at its best in the gruesome Janiro fight). After Jake's pummelling from Robinson, note the extreme close-up on the ring which waits for four drops of blood to drip from the rope, a shot that bears comparison with the crucifixion scenes in *The Last Temptation of Christ*.

After the judges rule against him in the third Robinson fight, we see Jake holding his hands in a bucket of ice. The shot lingers just like the one of the Alka-Seltzer in *Taxi Driver* until we almost will it away, the tension building way beyond comfortable levels. This then leads into the colour home movie footage, interspersed with stills of the fights that work almost like stop motion animation, showing whole fights in just four or five stills. Finally, we have one long continuous shot for the scene where Jake is dragged kicking and punching into his cell and then begins to rage his frustration on the wall. There is actually a cut here, just as Jake sits down on the bed, but it's a surreptitious one, suggesting the intention was there to 'fake' a continuous shot and maintain the documentary feel to the sequence.

MUSIC: Scorsese sculpted the soundtrack from music he had heard throughout his childhood, deliberately using contemporary sounds, but playing them in as live instead of dubbing them on as normal. A notable exception to this is his use of the Intermezzo from Pietro Mascagni's 'Cavalleria Rusticana' (a tragic Sicilian love story), which plays over the home movie and still photography montage at the centre of the film, and again during the wake of Joey's brawl with Salvy (although Joey was also a fighter, this is all we ever see of his own abilities – a vicious attack making use of anything he can lay his hands on to attack the man, including a car door). Never has opera been used with such irony in a movie, contrasting the grace and swelling emotion of the music with a different kind of artistry in the ring.

QUOTE/UNQUOTE
Jake LaMotta: (rehearsing his routine) 'I remember those cheers they still ring in my ears, and for years they'll remain in my thoughts. 'Cause one night I took off my robe and what'd I do – I forgot to wear shorts. I recall every fall, every hook, every jab, the worst way a guy could get rid of his flab. As you know, my life was a jab . . . Though I'd rather hear you cheer when I delve into Shakespeare. "A Horse, a Horse, my Kingdom for a Horse," I haven't had a winner in six months. I know I'm no Olivier, but if he fought Sugar Ray, he would say that the thing ain't the ring it's the play. So gimme a stage where this bull here can rage. And though I can fight I'd much rather recite – that's entertainment!'

Tommy Como: 'He's a nice kid. A pretty kid too. I mean I dunno, I got a problem if I should fuck 'im or fight 'im.'

Tommy Como: (watching LaMotta destroy Janiro) 'He ain't pretty no more . . .'

Jake LaMotta: (sobbing after being imprisoned for soliciting minors) 'They call me an animal . . . I'm not an animal! Why do they treat me like this? I'm not that bad. Not that bad! I'm not that guy!'

Jake LaMotta: (quoting Marlon Brando as Terry Malone in *On the Waterfront*) ' "I could have been a contender – I could have been somebody, instead of a bum, which is what I am. Let's face it." '

ROOTS: Scorsese screened *Body and Soul* (Robert Rossen, 1947) and *Force of Evil* (Abraham Polonsky, 1948) for De Niro during their preparations, with the brother relationship in *Force of Evil* influencing their depiction of the brothers LaMotta. The decision to use black and white film stock was partly motivated by the brash colour of *Rocky* (John G Avildsen, 1976). There's a scene set in LaMotta's apartment that is reminiscent of *Frenzy* (Alfred Hitchcock, 1972), where the camera tracks Vickie walking towards the stairs but doesn't follow her, then returns to the LaMotta brothers rowing, then after Joey leaves and Jake follows Vickie upstairs, the camera pauses in the living room, afraid or unwilling to follow him up there. Copying a technique used in Hitchcock's *Psycho* (1960), Scorsese used chocolate for the blood in certain sequences to give it a darker appearance in black and white. On the LaMottas' television we see a clip from *Of Mice and Men* (Lewis Milestone, 1939), which Scorsese chose partly because he knew the film was showing on television at that time and partly because of the similarities between the two films.

The billboard for 'An Evening With Jake LaMotta' says that it features the works of a number of different authors: Paddy Chayefsky was the writer of the play *Marty*, the film version of which starred Ernest Borgnine; Rod Serling was the creator of *The Twilight Zone*, though LaMotta was more likely to have been performing an extract from *Serling's Requiem for a Heavyweight*, which had been remade for television two years earlier; we hear LaMotta mock Shakespeare's *Richard III* in the opening sequence ('a horse, a horse, my kingdom for a horse . . .'); Budd Schulberg was the screenwriter of *On the Waterfront* (Elia Kazan, 1954); and Tennessee Williams, whose play *A Streetcar Named Desire* was almost certainly the text LaMotta would have performed from.

THEMES AND MOTIFS: Self destruction once more rears its head, with LaMotta joining De Niro's growing list of characters (Johnny Boy,

Travis Bickle, Jimmy Doyle) whose lives seem inextricably linked to violence or to a way of life that will ultimately leave them on their own by the end of the picture. LaMotta's enforced celibacy before a fight recalls Charlie from *Who's That Knocking At My Door?* and here we see LaMotta taking this test of will further as he brings Vickie to him only to push her away. 'You made me promise not to get you excited,' purrs Vickie. 'Can't do it,' he boasts, but as they get more and more intimate, he pushes her back. Significantly, where Charlie, Travis and, later, Max Cady test their will with fire, here Jake's is connected to ice, which he pours down his shorts to control his visible excitement. Ice is also used to suppress his bruising, his fists held in iced water between rounds, his face packed with ice after the fight. And of course, we have another scene where a character, LaMotta (De Niro again) speaks to himself in a mirror, as he rehearses his act.

BIBLE CLASS: Either side of the bathroom door in Jake's apartment are pictures of the Sacred Heart and the Virgin Mary. Scorsese's use of the biblical quote at the end ('Once I was blind and now I can see') might be seen to refer to Jake's repentance until we realise it's actually in the context of a dedication to his old professor from NYU, Haig Manoogian, who died just before the film's release. The quote then takes on the meaning that it was Manoogian who literally taught Scorsese to 'see' in a filmic sense.

CONTROVERSY: When De Niro, as Jake, had to ask Joe Pesci, as Joey, if he'd slept with Jake's wife, Scorsese wasn't happy with some of Pesci's reactions. De Niro garnered a specific response by asking Pesci, unrehearsed: 'Did you fuck your mother?' which resulted in a shocked Pesci asking him: 'What? How could you ask me that?' His reaction was then cut after De Niro asked the scripted question: 'Did you fuck my wife?' Pesci, not to be outdone, threw in the line where he calls De Niro a 'fucking whacko', foreshadowing the character he'd play in Scorsese's *GoodFellas* ten years later.

THERE HE IS!: Scorsese appears as a stage-hand at the Barbizon, asking Jake to go on stage.

KEEP IT IN THE FAMILY: Charles Scorsese plays Tommy Como's right-hand man, Charlie. Behind the scenes, Irwin Winkler's son Charles worked as a production assistant. McKenzie Westmore is the real-life daughter of make-up artist Michael Westmore.

LEGACY: In the 1990s, British comedy duo Hale & Pace performed a sketch, in black and white, that mocked the constant bickering between the two LaMotta brothers, focusing on the repetition of insults. Though, it has to be said, this was ten years too late. Better was *Harry Enfield's Television Programme*'s mockery of the redubbing of profanity for TV audiences, with Enfield asking Paul Whitehouse: 'Did you *fun* my wife?' 'No,' replies Whitehouse, 'she just sucked my *duck* and I ate her *puppy*'.

DELETED SCENES: Paul Schrader's original script included a scene of LaMotta trying to masturbate in his prison cell. Every time he imagines a woman and remembers how badly he treated her. He ends up taking it out on his hands, pummelling the walls. De Niro understandably raised questions about the scene and it was dropped. Schrader also included more of LaMotta's first wife, including a version of an anecdote LaMotta told in his book where he punched his wife at a party and knocked her out so cold he thought he'd killed her. Drunk and in a panic, he and his friend Pete argued over how to get rid of the body. This scene was cut by Scorsese who felt that it brought the ugliness of LaMotta's domestic violence in too soon. Originally, the last scene, depicting another rehearsal for 'An Evening With Jake LaMotta' would have had LaMotta performing a speech from *Richard III*, but on Michael Powell's suggestion it was replaced with a scene from *On the Waterfront*, which Scorsese felt was not only truer to LaMotta's state of mind, but also spoke of his own difficulties in making the film.

An extract of one scene that was cut from the final film made it into the trailer: LaMotta holds a press conference in the ring and tells the journalist that he wants a title shot because 'there's no one else around who wants to fight me, they're all afraid.'

TRIVIA: Scorsese used many of the original fight announcers and referees: Don Dunphy was a legend in boxing commentary, having presided over more than 2,000 fights, including the infamous 1974 'Rumble in the Jungle' with Muhammad Ali and George Foreman in Zaire. Others include Jimmy Lennon Sr and Count Billy Varga, and Ted Husing, one of radio's most familiar sports broadcasters. Allan Malamud was a sports journalist for the *Los Angeles Times* until his death in 1996. Incidentally, when the real LaMotta got married for the sixth and, to date, final time, his best man was his old nemesis, 'Sugar' Ray Robinson.

POSTERS: The US one-sheet for *Raging Bull* depicted a black and white portrait of De Niro, his brow low, his nose swollen, as in the mid-stages of the picture. International variants of the poster use the same image of De Niro but with images of Cathy Moriarty and De Niro (as the older and fatter LaMotta) superimposed.

TRAILER: To the strains of the title music, the voice-over tells us 'He was a fighter . . . a lover . . . a sinner . . . a winner . . . a loser . . . a man.'

AWARDS: At the Golden Globe Awards of 1981, *Raging Bull* featured in seven categories: Best Director (Scorsese), Best Motion Picture (Drama), Best Motion Picture Actor in a Supporting Role (Joe Pesci), Best Motion Picture Actor (Robert De Niro), Best Motion Picture Actress in a Supporting Role (Cathy Moriarty), Best Screenplay – Motion Picture (Mardik Martin, Paul Schrader) and New Star of the Year in a Motion Picture – Female (Cathy Moriarty). As the winners were announced, only De Niro came away with an award.

It was, perhaps, unlikely that a film as brutal as *Raging Bull* might actually clean up at the Oscars, but, despite the disappointment of the Golden Globes, and with eight nominations, expectations were still high: David J Kimball, Les Lazarowitz, Donald O Mitchell and Bill Nicholson were nominated for Best Sound; Joe Pesci and Cathy Moriarty were nominated in the suporting actor/actress categories; Michael Chapman was up for Best Cinematography; plus of course nominations for Best Picture and Director. In the Best Picture category, *Raging Bull* lost out to the favourite, *Ordinary People*, which marked the directorial debut of Hollywood sex symbol Robert Redford (See also **GoodFellas**). But it wasn't all bad news. Thelma Schoonmaker collected the award for Best Editing, while De Niro's mammoth physical effort in creating both versions of LaMotta was rewarded with the Oscar for Best Actor. In his acceptance speech, he thanked Joey LaMotta, despite (he revealed) the fact that Joey was at the time trying to sue them for defamation of character.

Thelma Schoonmaker picked up an 'Eddie' from the American Cinema Editors awards. At the Boston Society of Film Critics Awards, *Raging Bull* won Best Picture, Best Cinematography for Michael Chapman, and Best Actor for De Niro. The British Academy of Film and Television gave awards to Thelma Schoonmaker for editing and Joe Pesci for Most Outstanding Newcomer, for which Cathy Moriarty also received a nomination. Sadly, De Niro, up also against Bob Hoskins (for a superb performance in John Mackensie's *The Long Good Friday*) and Jeremy Irons (for *The French Lieutenant's Woman*) lost out to Burt Lancaster for his performance in Louis Malle's *Atlantic City*. The Los

Angeles Film Critics Association awarded De Niro, however, and named *Raging Bull* as their choice for Best Picture. The National Board of Review and the New York Film Critics Circle awarded De Niro and Pesci for best Actor and Supporting Actor respectively.

At the National Society of Film Critics Awards, Michael Chapman, Joe Pesci and Martin Scorsese all went home with awards. Finally, in 1990, *Raging Bull* entered the National Film Registry of the National Film Preservation Board, its place in history assured.

AVAILABILITY: VHS copies of *Raging Bull* are available from MGM Home Video in both full- and widescreen versions. Criterion released a fine laserdisc in 1991 containing an audio commentary by Martin Scorsese and Thelma Schoonmaker, interviews with Jake LaMotta and critics Siskel & Ebert and a selection of storyboards. Sadly the disc is long since deleted. MGM Home Video's 1997 US DVD release contained both pan-and-scan and widescreen versions of the picture (the European release offered just the widescreen version). For the 20th Anniversary, MGM re-released a European version of the disc in smart, white, cardboard packaging with a second bonus disc featuring the theatrical trailer, a specially commissioned 26-minute documentary 'The Bronx Bull', containing interviews with Jake LaMotta and editor Thelma Schoonmaker, footage of LaMotta doing his old stand-up routine to camera, three postcards, a 16-page booklet plus two hidden features: a photo gallery of stills taken during production of the documentary and rare footage of LaMotta from a title fight in his heyday. All in all, an impressive edition!

WHAT THE CRITICS SAID: For the first time in his career, De Niro received a negative review from his usual champion, Pauline Kael. Writing in *The New York Times*, she described his performance as LaMotta as 'a swollen puppet with only bits and pieces of a character inside, and some semi-religious, semi-abstract concepts of guilt'. Turning to the film itself, like many of the critics of the time Kael reserved no mercy for the director: 'By removing the specifics or blurring them, Scorsese doesn't produce universals – he produces banality. What we get is full of capitals: A Man Fights, A Man Loses Everything, A Man Bangs His Head Against The Wall. Scorsese is putting his unmediated obsessions on the screen, trying to turn raw, pulp power into art by removing it from the particulars of observation and narrative. He loses the lowlife entertainment values of prizefight films; he aestheticizes pulp and kills it.'

EXPERT WITNESS: 'I thought it would be interesting to see how somebody could fall apart graphically just by gaining this weight, just get totally out of shape.' Actor Robert De Niro.

'I've never seen anybody dedicate himself the way [De Niro] did. One time, he asked me what kind of cigars I smoke. I said, "What difference does it make? Smoke any kind you want," and he said, "Oh no, I gotta smoke the same brand." . . . He psychoanalysed me too. I found out more about myself than I ever did before while making the film.' Jake LaMotta.

FINAL ANALYSIS: Despised on its release, revered ten years later by critics hailing it the best movie of the decade, *Raging Bull* only really became a landmark film once its moment had already passed. Though the characters are unsympathetic and the violence both in and out of the ring unforgiving, there's still an amazing beauty in the way Scorsese captures the brutality and atavism of a sport that calls for two adult men to wound each other in the name of entertainment.

Much of the praise for the film is, rightly, placed on De Niro's shoulders. It was, after all, De Niro who hounded Scorsese for nearly six years before the director began to take the project seriously. It was De Niro who risked his reputation as an Oscar-winning actor to play a character even the most charitable people would call a monster. And, as if we could forget, it was he who built up twenty pounds of muscle to look the part of a world-class fighter, only to bulk up even further for the final scenes of an overweight Jake in decline. But arguably, De Niro could have done all of this only to appear in a rushed-out cash-in on *Rocky*. Once Scorsese finally accepted that he had to make the picture, his dedication and commitment were unquestionable. The single decision to film the picture in black and white placed *Raging Bull* so far removed from Stallone's working-class fantasy as to make it one of the most highly regarded sports movies – and one of the most intense dramas of any kind – you're ever likely to see.

SCORSESE ON *RAGING BULL*: 'Knowing Jake personally at that time, he was a very interesting man, he was very subdued. It's an odd thing. Sometimes I'll look at an animal and the animal is at peace. Sometimes fighters are like that, real fighters who get in the ring every day. Part of the brutality, part of being human, I don't know what it is, but Jake had gone through a terrible journey and come out the other side alive and reached some kind of understanding of himself. That's what I saw in him and that's what ultimately made me make this picture.'

The King of Comedy (1982)

(35 mm – 108 mins – colour)

MPAA Rating: PG

An Embassy International Pictures Production for 20th
Century Fox
Producer: Arnon Milchan
Associate Producer: Robert F Colesberry
Executive Producer: Robert Greenhut
Original Music: Robbie Robertson
Cinematographer: Fred Schuler
Film Editor: Thelma Schoonmaker
Casting: Cis Corman
Production Design: Boris Leven
Art Direction: Lawrence Miller, Edward Pisoni
Set Decoration: George DeTitta Sr, Daniel Robert
Costume Design: Richard Bruno
Title Designer: Dan Perri

SONGS: 'Jerry Langford Theme', 'Rupert's Theme' by Bob James;
'Come Rain or Come Shine'*, 'Sweet Sixteen Bars' by Ray Charles; 'The
Finer Things'* by David Sanborn; 'Back on the Chain Gang'* by The
Pretenders; 'Fly Me to the Moon' by Frank Sinatra; 'Swamp'* by
Talking Heads; 'Rainbow Sleeves'* by Ricki Lee Jones; 'Between
Trains'* by Robbie Robertson; 'T Ain't Nobody's Buziness If I Do'* by
BB King; 'Steal the Night'* by Ric Ocasek; 'The Best of Everything' by
Tom Petty; 'Wonderful Remark' by Van Morrison.

CAST: Robert De Niro (*Rupert Pupkin*), Jerry Lewis (*Jerry Langford*),
Diahnne Abbott (*Rita*), Sandra Bernhard (*Masha*), Ed Herlihy (*Himself*),
Lou Brown (*Band Leader*), Loretta Tupper, Peter Potulski, Vinnie
Gonzales (*Stage Door Fans*), Whitey Ryan (*Stage Door Guard*), Doc
Lawless (*Chauffeur*), Marta Heflin (*Young Girl*), Katherine Wallach
(*Autograph Seeker*), Charles Kaleina (*Autograph Seeker*), Richard Baratz
(*Cartoonist*), Catherine Scorsese (*Rupert's Mom*), Cathy Scorsese
(*Dolores*), Chuck Low (*Man in Chinese Restaurant*), Liza Minnelli
(*Herself*), Leslie Levinson (*Roberta Posner*), Alan Potashnick, Michael
Kolba, Ramón Rodríguez, Robert Colston, Chuck Coop, Sel Vitella
(*Men at Telephone*), Margo Winkler (*Receptionist*), Tony Boschetti (*Mr
Gangemi*), Shelley Hack (*Cathy Long*), Mick Jones, Joe Strummer, Paul

Simonon, Kosmo Vynil, Ellen Foley, Pearl Harbour, Gary Salter, Jerry Baxter-Worman, Don Letts (*Street Scum*), Matt Russo (*Cabbie*), Thelma Lee (*Woman in Telephone Booth*), Dr Joyce Brothers (*Herself*), George Kapp (*Mystery Guest*), Victor Borge (*Himself*), Ralph Monaco (*Raymond Wirtz*), Rob-Jamere Wess (*Security Guard*), Kim Chan (*Jonno*), Audrey Dummett (*Cook*), June Prud'Homme (*Audrey*), Frederick De Cordova (*Bert Thomas*), Edgar J Scherick (*Wilson Crockett*), Thomas M Tolan (*Gerrity*), Ray Dittrich (*Giardello*), Richard Dioguardi (*Captain Burke*), Jay Julien (*Langford's Lawyer*), Harry Ufland (*Langford's Agent*), Scotty Bloch (*Crockett's Secretary*), Jim Lyness (*Ticket Taker*), Bill Minkin (*McCabe*), Diane Rachell (*McCabe's Wife*), Dennis Mulligan, Tony Devon, Peter Fain, Michael F Stodden, Jerry Murphy (*Plainclothesmen*), Jimmy Raitt (*Stage Manager*), Martin Scorsese (*TV Director*), Tony Randall (*Himself*), Charles Scorsese (*First Man at Bar*), Mardik Martin (*Second Man at Bar*), William Jorgensen, Marvin Scott, Chuck Stevens, William Litauer (*Newsmen*), Jeff David (*Announcer*).

UNCREDITED CAST: Mary Elizabeth Mastrantonio (scenes deleted), Mike Tremont (*Talk Show Contestant*).

TITLES: White title cards on a black background announce ARNON MILCHAN PRESENTS . . . A MARTIN SCORSESE PICTURE . . . STARRING ROBERT DE NIRO. Cut to the opening sequence to another Jerry Langford show, where Jerry chats with his announcer and jokes with the band. Outside, Rupert Pupkin purposefully makes his way to the studios of the Jerry Langford Show and joins the crowd who jostle each other for prime position to see their idol as he leaves for the night. When Jerry finally appears, he pushes his way through the crowd desperate to get to the safety of his limousine, but is startled when he finds that Masha, a crazed obsessive fan, has somehow found her way into his car and begins to maul him. Jerry scrambles out of the vehicle and slams the door, trapping Masha inside. As Rupert Pupkin looks at Masha in revulsion, her outstretched hands span the window, obscuring Rupert's face. A camera flash, a freeze-frame and then the title logo slowly drops into place in between Masha's hands before the credits continue.

SUMMARY: Rupert jumps to Jerry's assistance, dragging Masha out of the way for Jerry to get into the car – with him by his side. As the car drives off, Rupert explains that he is a comedian and that he feels that he is now ready for his 'big break'. Jerry politely explains that he can't just expect to walk on to a networked show without experience, but at 34 years old, Rupert says he doesn't want to wait. Jerry brushes him off by telling him to call his secretary. Jerry reaches his destination and after a number of false starts he finally escapes from Rupert, leaving him out on the street.

Cut to some time later. Rupert has now made it in show business and Jerry is begging him to take over the Langford Show for six weeks just to give him some time off. Of course, this is merely a fantasy of Rupert's, shattered by his mother calling to him. Rupert goes to see Rita, an ex-cheerleader who he knew in high school and who now works as a bartender. He invites her to dinner and spends the evening boring her with stories of his show-business contacts and 'personal friends'. Rita is more than a little unsettled by his fantasies and asks to be taken home. The next morning, Rupert acts out his talk show in a set he's built in his mother's basement. His 'guests', Liza Minnelli and Jerry Langford, are merely life-sized black and white photographs. The show is interrupted by Rupert's mother telling him that his bus is due and he'll be late for work.

Having failed to arrange an appointment with Jerry through his secretary, Rupert goes to Jerry's office where he meets Cathy Long, the secretary to the Executive Producer, Bert Thomas. Cathy echoes Jerry's words when she tells him that if he manages to get a booking in a club they'll send someone down to see him. Rupert tells her he's working on new material just now, and Cathy asks him to send them a tape. As he leaves the office, he is accosted by Masha, the crazy fan, who wants to know if Jerry spoke about her. She begs him to give Jerry a message, claiming Rupert owes her a favour, which riles him. Rupert reminds her about all the things he's done for her, like letting her have his spot next to Jerry after he waited eight hours to see him, or the time he gave her his copy of 'The Best of Jerry' album. It's only after she throws a wad of cash into his hand that he resentfully agrees to pass on her letter.

The next morning, Rupert hand-delivers a tape of his 'act' to Cathy and asks when he can expect to hear back from Jerry about it. Cathy is clearly embarrassed by his pushiness and gives him a vague 'tomorrow or Monday'. Rupert tells her he'll wait, even when she stresses that it'll probably be Monday. He begins to daydream again – Jerry tells him how envious he is of Rupert's talent and invites him out to his house to thrash out some new ideas.

The next day, Jerry decides to walk to his offices. Wherever he goes, members of the public recognise him and call out to him. As he approaches his offices, he notices he is being followed by Masha.

Breaking into a sprint he dives through the doors of his building leaving Masha outside just as Rupert walks by and enters the building. Inside, Rupert waits for Cathy and fantasises about being a guest of the Jerry show. When Cathy finally comes to see him as she says Jerry's not in, she tactfully tells him they think he has a lot of potential but that they don't think he's ready yet. She again suggests he should test his material out in one of the comedy clubs in the city and that when he does, she'll send someone to check him out. Disappointed, Rupert tells her that he doesn't have faith in her judgement. Firmly, Cathy repeats that there's little they can do about that and walks back to her office. Rupert returns to sit in the reception until the head of security arrives to politely remove him from the premises. Outside, when Masha comes over to harangue him about giving the letter to Jerry, he says that Jerry wasn't in, but when Masha tells him that she saw him go in herself he marches back into the offices in a desperate search for Jerry. Instead he finds himself confronted by the head of security and a number of guards who forcibly eject him from the building, much to Masha's amusement.

Rupert takes Rita to Jerry's country estate as (he thinks) he arranged with Jerry. Rita's suspicions are aroused when she sees that the table is only set for one, but Rupert tells her that they're just the first guests to arrive. When Jerry returns home, Rupert tries to bluff his way by saying he's brought his material to work on with Jerry. Losing patience, Jerry threatens to have them arrested, and Rita quickly realises that Rupert has drawn her into one of his fantasies and begs Rupert to take her home. Trying to rescue what little dignity he might have left, Rupert accuses Langford of having a bad attitude now that he's famous, and thanks him for proving that he can't count on anyone but himself. He boasts that he's going to work fifty times harder and end up fifty times more famous than him, and Langford roars that when he does he'll end up being harassed by people like himself. Rupert leaves, slamming the door behind him.

Joining forces with Masha, Rupert stakes out Jerry's office and kidnaps the star at gunpoint, bundling him into the back of their car. They take him to Masha's home (revealing she comes from a very wealthy family) and tie Jerry to a chair. Rupert tells him to call his producer and warns him to do exactly what he tells him. Jerry phones his producer but the receptionist hangs up on him thinking it's a prank call. Calling back, Jerry finally gets through to his producer, Bert Thomas and is forced to answer a number of questions to prove his identity. Then Jerry reads from Rupert's cue-cards, telling Bert that a man will come to the studio, identify himself as 'The King' and that he must be allowed to be the first guest on that night's show or they'll never see Jerry alive again.

The kidnapping has sent the studio executives into a blind panic as they try to work out the best course of action. Should they give in to the ransom demands and broadcast the show or should they pull it in case the act contains a coded terrorist message. The senior executive, however, says that they should tape his routine and then show it, if that's what he wants, simply because all they're talking about is ten minutes of a talk show against a man's life. Rupert arrives at the studio and manages to find Cathy Long. Tired and worried by the prospect of the evening, she asks him what he's doing there and seems stunned when he tells her he's 'The King'. Once Bert Thomas assures Rupert that he can have anything he wants, Rupert admits to Inspector Gerrity that he kidnapped Langford and Gerrity is forced to read him his rights.

While Rupert is at the studio, Jerry has been subjected to the banal, obsessed ravings of Masha, who has arranged a candlelit dinner for them. She's clearly unstable, mentioning that her doctors won't allow her to have fun, and then, to Jerry's terror, she begins to strip for him. Convinced that Jerry will make love with her, she releases him. Free at last, he grabs her gun, but on discovering that it was just a toy all along, he slaps her and escapes. Masha tries to run after him in her underwear.

With Tony Randall standing in for Jerry, Rupert is introduced to the studio audience. With the performance taped, Rupert insists on seeing the show air at Rita's bar. He is taken there by the policemen who reassure Rita and allow him to watch his show in peace. Surprisingly, though the routine seems fairly tame; it gets a good response from the audience. He even tells them all how he only got on to the show by kidnapping Jerry Langford. With the broadcast finished, Rupert is finally arrested. The press and TV stations report the bizarre tale that Rupert's appearance on the Langford show was watched by a record 87 million households. Pupkin is sentenced to six years for the abduction, though in the event, he serves just two years, nine months. His memoirs, which are due to be made into a major motion picture, are reportedly picked up for $1 million. By the time of his first television appearance since he gate-crashed the Langford show, Rupert has got what he wanted – he is now a huge star.

WHO'S WHO?: Jerry Lewis was, with Dean Martin, one half of one of the world's all-time most popular screen duos, despite alleged friction between the pair off-screen. Away from Martin, Lewis was also the biggest box-office draw on and off from 1959 to 1964, during which time he starred in, directed and co-wrote the original screen version of *The Nutty Professor*. In recent years he's been the host of an annual telethon for the Muscular Dystrophy Association, a charity he supports passionately.

At one point, Sandra Bernhard ran the risk of being merely another member of Madonna's entourage. An aggressive comedian, actress and singer, her unconventional approach may have denied her leading roles, but have helped make her a genuinely unique supporting artist. She appeared in Michael Lehmann's hit-and-miss action comedy *Hudson Hawk* (1991) opposite Bruce Willis, and had a regular role in long-running sitcom Roseanne as Roseanne's bisexual best friend, Nancy. Her awesome cover version of 'You Make Me Feel Mighty Real' has to be heard to be believed.

Ed Herlihy provided voice-overs for numerous newsreels through the 1940s and was a familiar voice to American audiences thanks to stints on *The Perry Como Show* and *The Tonight Show with Johnny Carson*. In the 1960s, Lou Brown was the musical director for *The Jerry Lewis Show*. Shelley Hack was one of the lesser-known members of the glam crime-fighting organisation *Charlie's Angels*. Mick Jones, Joe Strummer and Paul Simonon (the street scum who cat-call after Masha) were members of the influential British rock band, The Clash. Dr Joyce Brothers is a well-known psychologist on American TV. Victor Borge, known as The Clown Prince of Denmark, was an all-round entertainer, musician and comedian. Kim Chan played the sinister Uncle Benny in *Lethal Weapon 4*. Frederick De Cordova was the producer of, among others, *The Tonight Show with Johnny Carson* for many years. Edgar J Scherick is a movie producer, responsible for *The Stepford Wifes* (Bryan Forbes, 1975) and its many TV-movie sequels. Tony Randall appeared in the Rock Hudson/Doris Day romantic comedy *Pillow Talk* (Michael Gordon, 1959) as Hudson's best friend, and played all seven faces of Lao in *The Seven Faces of Dr Lao* (George Pal, 1964). He's most famous for playing the fussy Felix in the TV version of *The Odd Couple* for which he won an Emmy.

THE USUAL SUSPECTS: Robert De Niro (*Mean Streets, Taxi Driver, New York, New York, Raging Bull, GoodFellas, Cape Fear, Casino*); Diahnne Abbott (*Taxi Driver, New York, New York*); Murray Moston (*Mean Streets, Alice Doesn't Live Here Anymore, Taxi Driver, New York, New York*); Mardik Martin (*Mean Streets, Italianamerican, New York, New York, American Boy, Raging Bull*); Peter Fain (*Mean Streets, New York, New York, Raging Bull, GoodFellas*); Margo Winkler (*New York, New York, After Hours, GoodFellas*); George Memmoli

(*American Boy*); Bill Minkin (*Who's That Knocking At My Door?*, *Taxi Driver*); Kim Chan (*Kundun*). Richard Dioguardi, Katherine Wallach, Chuck Low (*GoodFellas*); editor Thelma Schoonmaker (*Who's That Knocking At My Door?*, *Street Scenes*, *Raging Bull*, *After Hours*, *The Color of Money*, *Bad*, *The Last Temptation of Christ*, *New York Stories*, *GoodFellas*, *Cape Fear*, *Age of Innocence*, *Casino*, *A Personal Journey with Martin Scorsese Through American Movies*, *Kundun*, *Bringing Out the Dead*, *My Voyage to Italy*, *Gangs of New York*); title designer Dan Perri (*Taxi Driver*, *New York, New York*, *The Last Waltz*, *Raging Bull*, *The Color of Money*).

PRODUCTION: In the early 70s, *Newsweek* critic Paul Zimmerman had seen a TV talk show about autograph hunters which inspired him to write a screenplay about celebrity stalkers. The script came to Martin Scorsese but, perhaps mindful of such subject matter so soon after *Taxi Driver*, he passed, saying it would make for little more than a one-gag film. But, in the wake of the murder of John Lennon by Mark Chapman and the attempted assassination of Ronald Reagan (alleged to have been inspired by *Taxi Driver*), De Niro approached Scorsese with the idea of telling the story of an obsessive fan, which reminded the director of Zimmerman's script. Scorsese set about working Zimmerman's screenplay into something a little darker. With Scorsese combining De Niro's idea with the existing script he set about bringing the picture together. De Niro, meanwhile, began to research the part of a comedian, hanging out in comedy clubs, as well as speaking with autograph hunters about their obsessive collections.

Though the script was written with Dick Calvert in mind for the TV show host, Scorsese's first choice was Johnny Carson, the host of the popular *Tonight* talk show. Mindful of his own limited screen success (having appeared in *Looking for Love* in 1964) and the possibility of fact being inspired by fiction, Carson declined the offer. Trying to think his way around the issue of having a big, recognisable star, Scorsese next considered Orson Welles, then Frank Sinatra, which led him to think of Dean Martin, which led him to Martin's old on-screen partner, Jerry Lewis. For the part of loony fan Masha, Scorsese approached Meryl Streep, who had displayed real chemistry working with De Niro in *The Deer Hunter* (Michael Cimino) a couple of years earlier. Streep had other commitments so instead Scorsese hired Sandra Bernhard, who had arrived on the comedy scene in the last few years, but whose film experience extended to the part of a 'nut girl' in the slapstick farce *Cheech & Chong's Nice Dreams* (Tommy Chong, 1981).

With a director's strike looming, the team had to have four weeks of major scenes in the can or else the film would be stopped. Producer Arnon Milchan, heading his first film, insisted that the production must begin shooting on 1 June, some weeks earlier than Scorsese had been planning. This, coupled with Scorsese's growing apathy with the material, led to an unhappy shoot. Scorsese's temper began to fly in all directions as he grew more and more frustrated with the unhelpfulness of people around him. Diahnne Abbott agreed to appear as Rupert's friend Rita.

Surprisingly, Scorsese hadn't planned on using much improvisation, and stuck closely to the script. A couple of scenes were improvised, however: the scene where Jerry Lewis tells De Niro that he's 'just a human being', and the scene where Jerry suffers a horrific seduction from the voracious Sandra Bernhard. For the scene where Rupert and Rita arrive uninvited at Jerry's house, De Niro unleashed an unceasing barrage of anti-Semitic remarks to anger Jerry Lewis. Lewis, who had never worked with method actors, was shocked and appalled, but managed to channel his anger into an extremely credible performance – which of course had been De Niro's plan all along. Despite the tension on the set, Lewis threw his efforts into making his fellow performers laugh to keep the atmosphere as light as possible. His stream of anecdotes and personal experiences of fame helped Scorsese shape Langford's character, to the point where the story of a woman wishing cancer on Lewis for refusing to speak to her relative on the phone was incorporated into the script.

The picture was shot on location over twenty slow weeks, with the director realising late on that his lack of enthusiasm for the project had slowed him down. His marriage to Isabella Rossellini was on the rocks, and after the still-painful disappointment of *Raging Bull*'s failure, he was flat out. Faced with nearly a million feet of footage, Scorsese sat from December 1981 to March 1982 unable to motivate himself to begin to edit the picture. When the picture was finally released in February 1983, it would be one of his most lacklustre films so far, with flat direction and hollow characters that failed to excite critics or audiences. Having cost over $20 million to make, it recouped just $2.5 million in its initial domestic theatrical run. After just a month on release, the studio informed Scorsese that they were going to pull the plug on *The King of Comedy* and remove it from cinemas. Similarly, in Britain, it enjoyed the briefest of runs, and was broadcast on British television at the end of the same year, which perhaps in some way helped it gain five BAFTA nominations (see **AWARDS**) in 1984.

MUSIC: *The King of Comedy* begins with Ray Charles singing 'Come Rain or Come Shine', a song which receives a 'unique' interpretation from Masha later in the film as she tries to seduce Jerry Langford. Masha confides in Jerry that she wishes she was Tina Turner – it's worth noting here that Ms Turner had yet to effect her comeback with the Private Dancer album. At this time, she was famous more for the double act she had once had with her famously abusive husband.

Robbie Robertson, Scorsese's old friend from The Band, produced the soundtrack, taking samples from existing tracks, newly recorded versions of songs by Ray Charles, David Sanborn, Bob James, BB King and Van Morrison, whose 'Wonderful Remark' brings the picture to a close. Robertson dedicated one of his own songs, 'Between Trains', to 'Cowboy' Don Johnson, a member of Scorsese's staff, who had died suddenly of meningitis.

QUOTE/UNQUOTE

Rupert: 'My name is Rupert Pupkin, and I know the name doesn't mean a lot to you but it means an awful lot to me.'

Jerry: 'I know it's an old hackneyed expression but it happens to be the truth – you've got to start at the bottom.'
Rupert: 'I know. That's where I am. At the bottom.'
Jerry: 'That's the perfect place to start.'

Rupert: 'Just a couple of hours ago, guess who I was talking to.'
Rita: 'Your shrink?'

Construction Worker: 'Hey Jerry, ya lookin' good.'
Jerry: 'You should see me in my white taffeta.'

Rupert: 'My lawyer will be calling you.'
Raymond Wirtz (Head of Security): 'Yeah, well I hope he gets my name right.'

Rupert: 'Alright, so I made a mistake –'
Jerry: 'So did Hitler!'

Jay, Jerry's Lawyer: 'There is nothing polite about a kidnapping, let me tell ya something. It is one of the most stupid offences ever created. Where's the defence of kidnapping? How can you say "I was crazy"? How can you say "I didn't know what I was doing, I did it on the spur of the moment"? Only an idiot kidnaps.'

Rupert: 'Better to be king for a night than schmuck for a lifetime.'

ROOTS: The Jerry Langford Show is, of course, a blatant mirror of the real-life *Tonight Show* presented by Johnny Carson from 1962 to 1992. Having already told Rupert that she likes Marilyn Monroe, it's no surprise that the white dress Rita wears on her trip to Langford's house is modelled after the one Monroe wore in *The Seven Year Itch* (Billy Wilder, 1955) for the infamous scene where her skirt is lifted up by a gust of air from the subway. The wedding speech delivered by the Principal in Rupert's fantasy is a parody of Casablanca's immortal 'hill of beans' speech.

THEMES AND MOTIFS: Thematically similar to *Taxi Driver*, *The King of Comedy* presents assassins who have traded in their guns for pens. As Rupert makes his way through the crowd there's a dour-looking man at the back – a Paul Schrader lookalike, author of *Taxi Driver*. Rupert's often contradictory responses to people (when asked if Jerry knows him, Rupert answers 'Yes – I don't think he does') makes him even more the 'walking contradiction' that Betsy calls Travis. And Rupert's explanation of his need to be a comedian – 'I see the awful, terrible things in my life and turn it into something funny' – mimics Travis's diary entries.

The King of Comedy also addresses the nature of identity. Rupert's name, which might remind us of Travis's pseudonym 'Henry Krinkle', is a deliberate comic device which shows how Rupert's fight for recognition is more basic than his need for fame. He suffers the indignity of people calling him 'Crupkin', 'Pumpkin', 'Pimpkin', 'Parkin', even 'Mr Pumgi' to the extent where he replaces his own identity with that of the mastermind kidnapper, significantly Mr 'King'. But just as there are shades of celebrity, so we see here that while everyone knows the name of Jerry Langford, one of the guests scheduled to appear on his show to promote his book finds that he cannot get on to the set because his name is not on the security guard's list. When the writer is later questioned by the FBI, he reveals that he writes under a pseudonym, his real name protected by a fake.

Look out for the red tie which clashes with Rupert's pastel suit, and the bright red suit and tie he wears for his return after two years in prison.

THERE HE IS!: Scorsese plays the director of the edition of the 'Jerry Langford Show' that Rupert hijacks.

KEEP IT IN THE FAMILY: Catherine Scorsese plays Rupert's mother, Charles Scorsese plays a man at the bar where Rita works and Cathy

Scorsese, his daughter from his first marriage, plays Dolores, the autograph hunter. Diahnne Abbott, who had only recently split from De Niro (though they wouldn't divorce for another six years), plays Rupert's friend Rita.

ALTERNATIVE VERSION: The Warner Home Video release is slightly different from the one from RCA/Columbia. The moment in the network office where the secretary calls for security when Rupert refuses to leave is cut out in the Warner video; so it appears the security guard shows up for no reason.

TRIVIA: Jay, the litigious lawyer, is played by Scorsese's then-lawyer, Jay Julien.

POSTER: The US one-sheet depicted two playing cards with caricatures of a gagged and bound Lewis as the King and De Niro as the victorious joker.

AWARDS: At the British Film and Television Awards, the gong for best original screenplay went to Paul D Zimmerman. *The King of Comedy* also received nominations for Best Actor (De Niro), Best Director, Best Editing (Schoonmaker), and Best Supporting Actor (Jerry Lewis). The film was also nominated for a Palme d'Or at the 1983 Cannes Film festival, and Sandra Bernhard won Best Supporting Actress at the National Society of Film Critics Awards.

AVAILABILITY: RCA/Columbia released a basic 2-sided pan-and-scan laserdisc for the US market, now deleted. VHS versions are, however, still available (see **ALTERNATIVE VERSION** above).

WHAT THE CRITICS SAID: Pauline Kael again led a backlash against the picture in her *New York Times* column. 'Putting a grossly insensitive, coldhearted deadhead at the centre of a movie is a perverse thing to want to do, and Martin Scorsese's *The King of Comedy* isn't an ordinary kind of bad movie. It's so – deliberately – quiet and empty that it doesn't provide even the dumb, mind-rotting diversion that can half amuse audiences at ordinary bad movies.'

David Denby of New York wrote that it was 'a clever, sometimes brilliant movie, but ice-cold and not really likeable,' adding that 'it produces, at best, a nervous giggle – too bitter, too angry to make anyone laugh.' But just a decade later, the popular opinion had swung in

The King of Comedy's favour. In his appraisal of De Niro's work for his fiftieth birthday, Matt Snow declared that it was '. . . perhaps the funniest film ever about celebrity and the most serious about laughs.'

EXPERT WITNESS: 'Before we started the production, during those four months that we worked together, I talked to [De Niro] one night about dinner and he said "Listen Jerry, you better know that where I'm coming from, I'm going to want to kill you in this picture; I certainly don't want to have dinner with you." I looked at him as if I was finally seeing Stanislavsky come alive. It shook me, but I understood it.' Jerry Lewis (*Jerry Langford*).

FINAL ANALYSIS: Films about the business of comedy rarely show it as anything other than a miserable way to make a living. In this reworking of *Taxi Driver*, we see Rupert Pupkin wanting to remove everyone who stands in his way of making it as a comedian with the intention of slaying people with jokes instead of bullets.

Initially, Rupert's image acts as both a mirror to and a parody of Langford, with his hair parted the same, his coloured shirts (with white collars and cuffs), pale suits and carefully chosen ties. Nowhere does this become more apparent than in Rupert's increasingly ludicrous daydreams. At first we almost suspect that some time has passed and that Rupert truly is a big star. It's only when the voice of Rupert's mother interrupts and we return to Rupert's room that we realise we've been watching a fantasy. As the dream continues we see a marked contrast between the suave confidence of Rupert's imagined self and the harsh, manic over-egging of the reality. But as we begin to learn, it is not enough for Rupert to reach the same level of status as Jerry. For him to truly achieve his ambition, he must *become* him, usurp him as the rightful King of Comedy and rule in his place. We get our first whiff of suspicion when, in the dream, Rupert has Jerry beg him to take over his TV show for just six weeks. Later, as many of us have dreamed, Rupert imagines being greeted by his old high-school principal who apologises for telling him he'd never amount to anything in a sequence that, were it real, would be sickening and embarrassing. But then, as a person with little or no self-awareness, Rupert wouldn't recognise that.

What is most disturbing about *The King of Comedy* is not Rupert's eagerness for fame at any cost, or Masha's desperate need for validation from a man she only knows through the television (though this is very, very unpleasant) but that after everything, Rupert does indeed receive acceptance as a star. His book, 'King for a Day' becomes a best-seller

and on his return to television after his release from prison, the
announcer's overexcited cries for 'the wonderful Rupert Pupkin' seem
too much of a grotesque to be realistic. Though it's perhaps easy to want
this all to be another of Rupert's deluded fantasies (indeed many critics
have read the ending this way), it's more likely that Scorsese's
commentary on the essence of celebrity is much more cynical than that –
that it is a particular kind of borderline psychotic that craves that level of
attention so greatly, and a curious kind of disturbed person that wants to
be just like them.

SCORSESE ON *THE KING OF COMEDY*: 'I must say, that was
painful. Because the film came out and died in four weeks, and they were
right – the picture was a bomb. It's called *The King of Comedy*, it's Jerry
Lewis, and it's not a comedy. I mean, already it's a problem.'

After Hours (1985)

(35 mm – 97 mins – colour)

MPAA Rating: R

Produced by: Double Play/The Geffen Company
Producers: Robert F Colesberry, Griffin Dunne, Amy Robinson
Associate Producer: Deborah Schindler
Music: Howard Shore
Cinematographer: Michael Ballhaus
Film Editor: Thelma Schoonmaker
Casting: Mary Colquhoun
Production Design: Jeffrey Townsend
Art Direction: Stephen J Lineweaver
Set Decoration: Leslie A Pope
Costume Design: Rita Ryack
Title Designer: Dan Perri

SOUNDTRACK: Symphony in D Major K73N, 1st Movement,
composed by Wolfgang Amadeus Mozart; 'Air Ouverture' Nr 3 in D,
composed by Johann Sebastian Bach; 'En la Cueva' by Cuadro
Flamenco; 'Sevillanas' by Manitas de Plata; 'Night and Day' words and
music by Cole Porter; 'Body and Soul' lyrics by Edward Heyman, Robert
Sour & Frank Eyton, music by John Green; 'Someone to Watch over

Me', 'You're Mine', 'We Belong Together' by Robert and Johnnie; 'Angel Baby' by Rosie and the Originals; 'Last Train to Clarksville' by the Monkees; 'Chelsea Morning', 'I Don't Know Where I Stand' by Joni Mitchell; 'Over the Mountain and Across the Sea' by Johnnie and Joe; 'One Summer Night' by the Danleers; 'Pay to Cum' by the Bad Brains; 'Is That All There Is?' by Peggy Lee.

CAST: Griffin Dunne (*Paul Hackett*), Rosanna Arquette (*Marcy*), Verna Bloom (*June*), Thomas Chong (*Pepe*), Linda Fiorentino (*Kiki*), Teri Garr (*Julie*), John Heard (*Tom the Bartender*), Cheech Marin (*Neil*), Catherine O'Hara (*Gail*), Dick Miller (*Waiter*), Will Patton (*Horst*), Robert Plunket (*Street Pickup*), Bronson Pinchot (*Lloyd*), Rocco Sisto (*Coffee Shop Cashier*), Larry Block (*Taxi Driver*), Victor Argo (*Diner Cashier*), Murray Moston (*Subway Attendant*), John P Codiglia (*Transit Cop*), Clarke Evans (*Neighbour 1*), Victor Bumbalo (*Neighbour 2*), Bill Elverman (*Neighbour 3*), Joel Jason (*Biker 1*), Rand Carr (*Biker 2*), Clarence Felder (*Bouncer*), Henry Baker (*Jett*), Margo Winkler (*Woman with Gun*), Victor Magnotta (*Dead Man*), Robin Johnson (*Punk Girl*), Stephen J Lim (*Club Berlin Bartender*), Frank Aquilino (*Angry Mob Member*), Maree Catalano (*Angry Mob Member*), Paula Raflo (*Angry Mob Member*), Rockets Redglare (*Angry Mob Member*).

UNCREDITED CAST: Charles Scorsese, Martin Scorsese (*Club Berlin Searchlight Operator*).

TITLES: The logo appears with a swirling white font for the 'After', slim yellow letters for the 'Hours', and a blue pair of watch hands inside the 'O'.

The closing credits are displayed over a moving shot of Paul's office, during which more and more employees show up for work. When the camera passes Paul's desk again, he has disappeared.

SUMMARY: Office worker Paul Hackett finds himself unable to rest after a demoralising day at work. Heading out to a late-night café, he strikes up a conversation with an attractive young woman called Marcy. Marcy shares an apartment with a sculptress whose latest work is plaster of Paris cream-cheese bagel paperweights. Asking Paul if he'd like one of the paperweights, she gives him her phone number and then departs for a prior engagement with a friend.

Back at home, Paul calls Marcy's number and learns that Marcy is upset because she and her friend had a row. Paul politely suggests that perhaps she and her friend won't fall out for long and encouraged by his optimism she invites him over to her apartment in SoHo. Paul gets a cab to her address, but when his money, a $20 bill, is blown out of the window, he finds himself unable to pay the cab driver, who speeds off in a fury. Paul is let in by Marcy's room-mate Kiki, who tells him that Marcy had to pop out to an all-night pharmacist. Kiki is in the middle of adding papier maché to a sculpture and invites Paul to take over for her while she rests. As Paul begins nervously adding the plaster-soaked strips of paper to the sculpture, the phone rings. Kiki answers it and from what she says to the caller, Paul gets the impression it's Marcy telling her to get rid of him, but Kiki refuses to help and returns to her work. Paul manages to get a piece of paper stuck to his shirt so Kiki offers to clean it for him and lends him a replacement. She confesses that sculpting all day often leaves her shoulders sore, so Paul offers to give her a massage. He begins to tell her a story about his childhood, but notices that she has fallen asleep.

Paul decides that it's time to leave just as Marcy returns carrying something from the pharmacy. She invites him to wait in her room while she showers. There, Paul sneaks a look into the bag Marcy brought back from the pharmacist and is startled to find burn cream in there. Marcy enters the room and Paul moves in to kiss her, but she seems troubled and pushes him away. It's then that he looks at her thigh and thinks he sees three horrific scars running along her inside leg. She chooses that moment to tell him that she was once raped by her boyfriend in that very room. Though Paul is surprised, she seems unconcerned and suggests they go to an all-night café she knows. As they leave, Paul notices a $20 bill stuck to one of Kiki's statues.

At the café, Marcy tells Paul about her ex-husband. It is he who owns the loft apartment where she and Kiki are staying. They were married for only three days, mainly because of his obsession over *The Wizard of Oz*, though they still write to each other every day. Paul offers to get the bill but the café manager tells him it's on the house. They return to her apartment and Marcy gives Paul a joint, which has a peculiar effect on him, making him aggressive and rude. He orders her to go and fetch him one of the cream-cheese plaster bagels he came to see, but as soon as she leaves the room, he makes a bolt for the door and escapes.

Making his way to the subway, Paul learns that the toll-fares increased at midnight meaning he doesn't have enough change to catch his train. It begins to rain heavily so Paul rushes into a nearby bar to dry off.

The bar is almost empty apart from a dancing couple, a waitress and a barman. The waitress comes over to take his order. Paul asks if he can just sit and dry off. She scribbles a note on a tab-sheet and walks back to the bar. The note reads: 'Help! I hate this job!!' Paul sits at the bar and tells his story to the barman, saying that he just wants to get out of the rain or go home. The barman, Tom, generously offers to give him the money to get home but then discovers his till has suddenly and inconveniently jammed and the key is back at his apartment. As Tom can't leave the bar he asks if Paul would go and fetch it. Paul reassures the barman that he can be trusted and gives him his own house-keys as collateral.

Paul heads over to Tom's apartment straight away, picks up the key for the till and leaves. A gay couple who live in the same block accuse him of being responsible for a spate of burglaries in the area. He shows them the keys that Tom gave him and reassures them that he's innocent. On the way back to the bar, he passes by Marcy's apartment and sees two men apparently stealing one of Kiki's statues. He scares them off and takes the statue back to Kiki. He finds her gagged and bound and rushes over to ungag her. Telling her about the burglars, he's surprised to learn that they were in fact friends of hers and that she sold them her TV. Paul suddenly realises too late that he's actually interrupted an S&M sex romp between Kiki and a leather-man who calls himself 'Horst'. Horst and Kiki chastise Paul for walking out on Marcy and talk him into finishing off what he started. Paul goes to Marcy's room and finds her lying in bed. But it's only after he's finished a lengthy apology that he realises she's dead, having taken a bottle of pills. He shouts for help but Kiki and Horst have gone, leaving behind a note saying they've gone to the Club Berlin.

Paul phones 911 to tell them about the dead body. As he waits for the police, curiosity gets the better of him again and he lifts the covers off Marcy to check out what he thought he saw earlier. It wasn't scar tissue, it was a tattoo of a skull in a top hat. He looks her over and can't find any burns at all. The tattoo reminds him that Tom's keys had a keyring on them – a white metal skull in a top hat. Leaving notes around the apartment saying DEAD PERSON with arrows pointing to Marcy's corpse, Paul leaves the apartment to meet up with Tom.

On the way back to the bar, he meets the waitress who gleefully tells him she's just quit her job. He tells her all he wants is to go to the bar, get his keys and go home. But the bar is closed. The waitress tells him she only lives across the street and invites him back with her to wait for Tom to return to the bar. She tells him her name is Julie and asks if he's had a rough night. Paul breaks down crying. She tries to get him to talk while she sketches him. She tells him that she hates her other job, in the Xerox shop, but jokes that at least she can get free copies whenever she wants to, prompting Paul to exclaim 'Gee whizz'. Julie takes offence at his flippancy and begins to get hysterical. He quickly apologises for being rude. Just then he sees Tom returning and makes to leave just as Julie asks him to stay. Aware that if he rejects her now she might go nuts again, he promises her he'll go and get his keys and be straight back. Julie doesn't seem convinced. Back at the bar, Tom tells him he'd been worried when Paul didn't return so he had to lock up and check his apartment. Paul tells him about what just happened with Julie and Tom suggests he should just take off, saying, 'what's she gonna do, kill herself?' Just then the phone rings. Paul decides he'll take Tom's advice and just shoot off without returning to Julie, but then Tom puts the phone down and reveals that he's just learned his girlfriend has taken an overdose and killed herself. He blames himself as earlier that night they had a row and he told her to get out of the apartment. He cries out her name – 'Marcy! Marcy!'

Taking this to be a bad omen, Paul runs straight back to Julie. She's pleased that he kept his word and, as a reward, she presents him with a plaster bagel and cream-cheese paperweight she bought from a local artist. Seeing the night take a strange turn, he tells her that he came back as he said he would, but that now he really needs to go home and sleep. He promises to see her again and takes her phone number. Pausing outside her apartment, Paul is startled when Julie leaps out and says he forgot his plaster bagel. Paul snaps at her and leaves; a spurned Julie threatens that he'll be sorry.

Typically, when Paul returns to the bar it's closed. He heads back to Tom's apartment but he's not home, and as he goes to leave, the two gay men and another neighbour see him and chase after him, again believing him to be the burglar. Paul hides down a stairwell as the three men run off into the night. Paul decides to go to Club Berlin to find Kiki. Unfortunately, it's 'Mohican Night' and when a bouncer tries to shave Paul's head he is forced to flee before he can speak with Kiki. Next, Paul returns to Kiki's apartment and takes the $20 from the statue Kiki was making. Careful to avoid the growing mob of vigilantes patrolling the streets for the burglar, Paul spies a cab bringing home a blonde woman. He runs towards the cab and the woman manages to gash his arm on the door as she steps out. Ignoring this for a moment, Paul speaks to the driver. It's the same one who brought him downtown earlier in the evening and so Paul shows him his $20 bill to prove that he now has the fare he needed. The driver snatches the money from Paul's grasp and drives off without him.

The woman passenger, Gail, notices that his arm is bleeding and, feeling guilty, offers to take him back to her place to get patched up. Back at Gail's place, Paul uses her phone to get a number from directory enquiries, but as he tries to memorise it, the woman playfully begins to shout numbers into his ear and he forgets it. Losing patience, he explains that he just wants to sleep or go home, but she refuses to listen, insisting that as she hurt his arm with the cab door, she will fix it. She notices a sliver of papier maché still stuck to his arm and suggests maybe she could burn it off. Paul immediately bolts for the door and runs downstairs only to find Gail waiting for him – she took the lift. She tells him she is an ice-cream vendor and has a van that could get him home. Paul gratefully accepts her offer. As they walk towards her van, Gail stops to look at a sign. Paul asks her if there's something the matter and Gail pulls out a whistle and blows it to call the vigilantes. Once again, Paul is on the run – and soon he discovers why. Julie, the waitress/Xerox girl, has photocopied the sketch she drew of Paul and stuck it all around SoHo as a WANTED poster.

He finds his way back to Club Berlin, where an art exhibition is now being held. Unsurprisingly, the place is deserted apart from one barman and the artist, a sculptor called June. Realising that she looks depressed, Paul asks June to dance with him. Baring his soul, he tells her about the vigilante mob persecuting him. She invites him downstairs to her studio. Outside, the vigilantes force their way into the club in search of Paul. Paul panics and knocks a bucket of plaster over himself. June quickly gets an idea and begins covering Paul in plaster, turning him into a work of art. As she goes to distract the mob, the two thieves from Kiki's place break into the studio and 'steal' Paul, bundling him into the back of their van. As they drive through the city, dawn breaks. Turning a corner, their van doors fly open and Paul is catapulted out on to the road. The plaster shatters away from him and, stunned, he looks up to find himself back outside the gates to his office. Exhausted, but relieved, Paul heads back to his desk.

WHO'S WHO?: Actor and director/producer Griffin Dunne will forever be remembered for playing a rather unattractive, but talkative, corpse in *An American Werewolf in London* (John Landis, 1981). Rosanna Arquette is the sister of fellow actors Alexis, David and Patricia, and star of *Desperately Seeking Susan* (Susan Seidelman, 1985), for which she won a BAFTA. Verna Bloom might be familiar as the dean's wife from *National Lampoon's Animal House* (John Landis, 1978) (see also **THE USUAL SUSPECTS, KEEP IT IN THE FAMILY**). Cheech Marin and

Tommy Chong were one of the top counter-culture comedy acts of the late 70s/early 80s with films such as *Up in Smoke* (Lou Adler, 1978) and *Still Smokin'* (1983), which Chong also directed. Dissolving their partnership in 1985, Chong went on to play Leo in the sitcom *That '70s Show*, while Marin wrote and directed *Born in East LA* (1987) before allying himself with wunderkind director Robert Rodrigues for *Desperado* (1995), *From Dusk Till Dawn* (1996) and *Spy Kids* (2001).

Linda Fiorentino first came to prominence in *Visionquest* (Harold Becker, 1985), before playing the scheming Bridget in *The Last Seduction* (John Dahl, 1994) and the hapless Dr Laurel Weaver in *Men in Black* (Barry Sonnenfeld, 1997), a role she allegedly won in a poker game with the director. Teri Garr played Richard Dreyfuss's wife in *Close Encounters of the Third Kind* (Steven Spielberg, 1977) and Dustin Hoffman's on-off girlfrind in *Tootsie* (Sydney Pollack, 1982). In 1998, she took a guest role in the sitcom *Friends*, playing Phoebe's long-lost birth-mother. John Heard's filmography is extensive, but he'll still probably be most familiar as Macaulay Culkin's father in the first two *Home Alone* films (Chris Columbus, 1990/1992). He recently played Detective Vin Makazian in TV mafia drama *The Sopranos*. Coincidentally, Catherine O'Hara (Gail) also starred in the *Home Alone* films, as Culkin's mother.

Bronson Pinchot usually plays uptight assholes. He played The Prankster in episodes of the TV series *Lois & Clark: The New Adventures of Superman*, and ended up with a faceful of cocaine in *True Romance* (Tony Scott, 1995). Taking into account the special interests of Marcy's ex-husband, I should probably also mention that Pinchot organised the 1975 Wizard of Oz convention.

Rocco Sisto is another connection to mafia TV drama *The Sopranos*, having played Young Uncle Junior in the episode 'Fortunate Son'.

THE USUAL SUSPECTS: Rosanna Arquette (*New York Stories*); Verna Bloom (*The Last Temptation of Christ*); Victor Magnotta (*It's Not Just You, Murray!, Taxi Driver, Raging Bull*); Victor Argo (*Boxcar Bertha, Mean Streets, Taxi Driver, The Last Temptation of Christ*); Murray Moston (*Mean Streets, Alice Doesn't Live Here Anymore, Taxi Driver, New York, New York*); Margo Winkler (*New York, New York, The King of Comedy, GoodFellas*); producer Amy Robinson (*Mean Streets*); Dick Miller (*New York, New York*); Frank Aquilino (*GoodFellas*); editor Thelma Schoonmaker (*Who's That Knocking At My Door?, Street Scenes, Raging Bull, The King of Comedy, The Color of Money, Bad, The Last Temptation of Christ, New York Stories, GoodFellas, Cape*

Fear, Age of Innocence, Casino, A Personal Journey with Martin Scorsese Through American Movies, Kundun, Bringing Out the Dead, My Voyage to Italy, Gangs of New York); title designer Dan Perri (*Taxi Driver, New York, New York, The Last Waltz, Raging Bull, The King of Comedy, The Color of Money*).

PRODUCTION: After the crushing disappointment of the collapse at that time of *The Last Temptation of Christ* (see **THE BATTLE FOR THE LAST TEMPTATION**), Martin Scorsese became determined to prove he could make a commercial picture on a low budget, just as he'd done right at the start of his career. His lawyer, Jay Julien, had come into possession of a script, called 'Lies' (later retitled 'A Night in SoHo' before finally being called 'After Hours'), which he passed on to Scorsese. The script had been written by film student Joe Minion in his class at Columbia University (where it had been given an A by his tutor), and was currently owned by producer Amy Robinson, who'd worked with Scorsese as an actress on *Mean Streets*, and actor Griffin Dunne. They were joined by Robert Colesberry, who had been Scorsese's associate producer on *The King of Comedy*. The team had already secured the backing of Fox Classics, with a comparatively small budget of $3.5 million. Returning to his roots, Scorsese was back working with independents away from the Hollywood Studios, where, he felt, he really belonged.

The producers introduced Scorsese to cinematographer Michael Ballhaus, who from this picture would become Scorsese's regular director of photography. With a tight schedule and no money for over-runs, Ballhaus was a gift. Scorsese did his customary storyboards and worked out that the script required about sixteen set-ups a day, but they only had time for five. Nevertheless, Ballhaus felt confident he could do it. As Scorsese began to work, he realised he had no time to sit down or mope in his trailer as he had been doing regularly since part-way through the production of *New York, New York* some seven years earlier. Encouraged by working with a fresh, new team and a young, enthusiastic crew, Scorsese found his energy bolstered.

Originally, the ending to the picture would have had Paul simply leaving to buy June the sculptor an ice cream. This was replaced by a scene of Paul climbing into the womb of a gigantic June and being reborn naked on the streets of New York. But when head of the production company David Geffen read the ending he felt it was wrong, like they were trying to remake *2001: A Space Odyssey*; it was just too surreal. A new ending was written, which had Paul drive off with Cheech and Chong. But when he screened this version of the film at different times to Michael Powell, Terry Gilliam, Steven Spielberg, even his own father, Charlie, they all hated the ending and generally agreed that Paul should fall out of the truck. Scorsese recalled Griffin Dunne and shot a new ending, suggested by Michael Powell, that Paul should just return to work, bringing the film full circle. The film completed at a cost of just $4.5 million, slightly over-budget. Released in October 1985, it was fairly well received and went on to gross over $10.6m in the USA alone. Phase one of Scorsese's return to form was complete.

EDITING: Compare the lacklustre direction of *The King of Comedy* with the tight camerawork here. From the very beginning, the camera seems energised, zooming across Paul's office to see him train a dismissive new employee. When Paul gets to Kiki's apartment and she drops the keys down to him, they take on an air of menace plummeting down to the ground like a stone slab, forcing Paul to step back from them warily. The crash-zooms become a regular fixture of the film as they begin to feature every time a phone is seen or heard, until by the end the cutting between the sight of a phone and Paul rushing towards it to dial for help becomes almost too intense to watch. Thanks to the editing, telephones suddenly become objects of menace, which makes the unanswered ringing of the phone in Marcy's room all the more suspenseful.

Paul's frantic buzzer-pressing as he tries to get past the security door to escape the angry mob foreshadows Karen Hill in *GoodFellas* alerting the neighbours in her husband's mistress's block that she is 'a whore'.

QUOTE/UNQUOTE
Pepe: 'Art sure is ugly.'
Neil: 'Shows how much you know about art. The uglier the art, the more it's worth.'
Pepe: 'This must be worth a fortune, man.'

Paul: 'What do you want from me?! I'm just a word processor!'

Paul: (after witnessing a murder through a window) 'I'll probably get blamed for that.'

Street Pickup: 'Why don't you just go home?'
Paul: 'Pal, I've been asking myself that all night.'

ROOTS: Though it might not seem so at first, *After Hours* is Scorsese's tribute to Alfred Hitchcock. Why else would there be so many blonde women determined to complicate Paul's life? Why else would he be punished for the simple and understandable desire to have sex? And why would he find himself an innocent man on the run? The extreme close-up of Paul's finger phoning the police after the death of Marcy comes from Hitch's *Dial M For Murder* (1954) – another film where telephones are objects of peril – while Paul's return to the Club Berlin with his invitation is, according to the director, inspired by a shot in *Marnie* (Alfred Hitchcock, 1964) in which Tippi Hedren carries a gun to shoot her lame horse. And of course, the phone that continues to ring unanswered is a textbook Hitchcock trick, building suspense to near breaking point.

Marcy tells Paul her ex-husband was obsessed by *The Wizard of Oz* (Victor Fleming, 1939); he insisted on crowing 'SURRENDER DOROTHY!' at the moment of climax. A subtler reference to the film comes in Julie's kitchen – take a look at the rainbow on her cupboard. And of course, in both films, the lead character simply wants to get home. There's also an oblique reference to the John Wayne Western *Three Faces West* (Bernard Vorhaus, 1940) – the branding on Paul's clock at home reads 'FACES WEST', though this might also be a further Hitchcock reference, the ultimate innocent man-on-the-run film being *North by Northwest* (1959). Marcy reads Henry Miller's *Tropic of Cancer* [see **Cape Fear**] and Paul misremembers the title of Norwegian artist Edvard Munch's most famous work, *The Scream*.

Puzzled by Paul's bizarre behaviour, the subway cop surmises that there 'must be a full moon out there', a reference to Griffin Dunne's role as werewolf food in John Landis's superb *An American Werewolf in London* (1981), while Paul's mummification by June in the film's climax echoes views of the Egyptian killer in Hammer's *The Mummy's Shroud* (John Gilling, 1967).

THEMES AND MOTIFS: *After Hours* is one gigantic nightmare in which everyone would be much happier if they just learned to listen to each other. As Lloyd talks to Paul, his attention drifts; when he tells Kiki his (frankly disturbing) tale about his time in a burns ward as a child, she falls asleep before she (and therefore we) can hear the end of the tale, leaving us in suspense (another Hitchcock trick); Paul's unwillingness to listen to Julie moaning about her job leads to her freaking out on him; and, for some strange reason, Gail seems to mishear everything he says.

From a Freudian perspective, many of Paul's problems come from castration anxiety. His libido brings him to Marcy's apartment, but it is the sight (or perceived sight) of the deep scars on her leg and her violation at the hands of her ex-boyfriend that are the initial barriers (compare his reaction to her tale here with that of JR in *Who's That Knocking . . .*). There's also the graffiti in the restroom at the bar depicting a shark emasculating a crudely drawn man, and his blind panic as he is pinned down at the Club Berlin and faced with the threat of having his head shaved (which of course also harks back to *Taxi Driver*).

THERE HE IS!: Scorsese can be seen operating a searchlight at the Club Berlin.

KEEP IT IN THE FAMILY: Verna Bloom is the wife of Scorsese's old friend Jay Cocks.

POSTER: Griffin Dunne's head forms the wind mechanism on top of a pocket watch. The fingers of a woman, with red painted nails, grip his head and twist. The tagline reads: 'When it's after midnight in New York City, you don't have to look for love, laughter and trouble. They'll all find you!'

AWARDS: At the British Academy Awards, Rosanna Arquette was nominated for Best Actress in a Supporting Role. At the Cannes Film Festival Martin Scorsese won Best Director – and the film was nominated for the Palme d'Or. The Casting Society of America nominated Mary Colquhoun for an Artios award for Best Casting for a Feature Film (Comedy). Griffin Dunne received a nomination for a Golden Globe for Best Performance by an Actor in a Motion Picture (Comedy/Musical). Finally, the Independent Feature Project (an organisation set up to support the west-coast independent film community) presented 'Spirit Awards' for Best Feature to the producers, Robert F Colesberry, Griffin Dunne and Amy Robinson. Also nominated were Michael Ballhaus (Cinematography), Martin Scorsese, Rosanna Arquette and Joseph Minion (Screenplay).

AVAILABILITY: Warner Home Video have released the film on VHS. In 1991 they also released both widescreen and pan-and-scan NTSC laserdiscs.

WHAT THE CRITICS SAID: Roger Ebert: 'This is the work of a master filmmaker who controls his effects so skillfully that I was drained by this film – so emotionally depleted that there was a moment, two-thirds of the way through, when I wondered if maybe I should leave the theater

and gather my thoughts and come back later for the rest of the
"comedy".' He concluded by saying 'After Hours is a brilliant film, one
of the year's best.'

EXPERT WITNESS: 'The anxiety of the movie struck all of us as
hilariously funny. We always thought it was a nightmare, and it was so
scary that it was funny. The expression on Marty's face when we'd
watch Paul Hackett go through something was something like, "Oh no!
Oh, my God, oh!" I could hear him out of the corner of my ear during
takes, saying "Oh God, that's awful." He had to turn away to not look
at the take, because he was laughing.' Griffin Dunne (*Paul Hackett*).

FINAL ANALYSIS: *After Hours* has an almost perfect symmetry to it –
Scorsese's most tightly structured picture by far. The key to it all is
repetition. Note how Paul's obsessive-compulsion manifests itself in him
washing his (clean) hands five times in the picture. It begins and ends
with Paul seated at his desk in his office, and is topped and tailed by an
encounter with a sculptor, the first encouraging Paul to become a part of
the art process, the second turning him into a work of art. Both pieces of
art are removed by Cheech and Chong's inept burglars, who are the
legitimate owners of the first, but are mistaken for burglars by Paul, and
who are later revealed to *be* the burglars that the mob should be looking
for (instead of Paul) when they steal him from June's studio. The
elements that return to thwart Paul's attempts to return home, the
cream-cheese bagel paperweights, the array of paranoid women in SoHo,
the telephones, Tom's gay neighbours who twice accuse Paul of being a
thief, the ice-cream van . . . and the elements that remain permanently
just out of his grasp, like his house-keys and that $20 bill.

The elements of coincidence, frustration and plain bad luck mount
until there really is nowhere for Paul to go but right back to the start. By
the end, Paul seems to accept this, indeed his aside after witnessing the
point-blank murder of a man (see **QUOTE/UNQUOTE**) suggests as
much. *After Hours* knows it's a farce, and so does Paul which is all the
more frustrating for him.

SCORSESE ON *AFTER HOURS*: 'The final cost was $4.5 million,
including a quarter of my normal salary. When I subsequently went to
Hollywood to promote my next film I found, to my surprise, some
people resented that we had made it for so little.'

Amazing Stories: 'Mirror, Mirror' (1986)

(35 mm – 24 mins – colour)

MPAA Rating: PG

Produced by Amblin for Universal TV
Supervising Producers: Joshua Brand, John Falsey
Production Executives: Kathleen Kennedy, Frank Marshall
Producer: David E Vogel
Developed by Steven Spielberg, Joshua Brand, John Falsey
Associate Producers: Stephen Semel, Steve Starky, Skip Lusk
Teleplay: Joseph Minion, from a story by Steven Spielberg
Cinematography (colour): Robert Stevens
Editor: Joe Ann Fogle
Music: Michael Kamen
Production Designer: Rick Carter
Story Editor: Mick Garris
Theme: John Williams
Fireside Storyteller: Ray Walston

CAST: Sam Waterston (*Jordan*), Helen Shaver (*Karen*), Dick Cavett (*Himself*), Tim Robbins (*Jordan's Phantom*), Dana Gladstone (*Producer*), Valerie Grear (*Host*), Michael C Gwynne (*Jail Attendant*), Peter Lacangelo (*Limo Driver*), Jonathan Luria (*Cameraman*), Harry Northup (*Security Guard*), Glenn Scarpelli (*Jeffrey Gelb*), Jack Thibeau (*Tough Guy*).

TITLES: Each episode of *Amazing Stories* began with a montage of clips depicting storytelling, beginning with a shaman with his tribe huddled around a fire, then with books and knights in armour flying towards the camera until finally we return to the image of the shaman, this time transmitted via television.

SUMMARY: Returning home after a TV appearance publicising his latest film, horror writer Jordan Manmouth finds a young man sitting outside his front door. The man tells him he is Manmouth's number one fan and proceeds to struggle with a manuscript he has written. Manmouth tells him he is trespassing and orders him off his property.

Hoping for a relaxing night alone, Jordan finds himself terrorised by a phantom he can only see in mirrors. He phones the local police department but is kept on hold so long that he passes out with exhaustion only to wake up the next morning unharmed. Driving into a car park later that morning, however, he sees the phantom in the back seat of his car holding a garrotte. As he scrambles from his car he is stopped by a guard wearing sunglasses. Jordan sees the phantom reflected in the glasses too and jumps towards the guard to get away from the killer he is certain is behind him. As a consequence, he is locked up in a holding cell until his friend Karen can come and bail him out. She finds his story hard to believe and takes him back to his house to show him that it is safe. But, after she coaxes him to look in the mirror, he sees the phantom in there and breaks down sobbing. Karen decides to cover all the mirrors and remove everything reflective. Unfortunately, a TV crew arrive for a scheduled interview with Jordan and, despite insistences from Karen that he's sick, he is forced to conduct the interview. Before the first question is completed, however, he looks into the camera, sees the reflection of the phantom again and screams. Taking control, Karen bustles the crew out of the house and helps the distraught writer to bed. She kisses him and, in her eyes, he sees the phantom – all too late. As Karen watches in horror, he clutches his throat and then turns into the monster that has been stalking him. In horror he leaps through his bedroom window and falls to his death.

WHO'S WHO?: Sam Waterston starred in *The Great Gatsby* (Jack Clayton, 1974) and *The Killing Fields* (Roland Joffé, 1984), and played Kathleen Turner's husband in *Serial Mom* (John Waters, 1994). Comedian and TV personality Dick Cavett has been a popular face on American TV since the early 60s, fronting his own talk show on and off since 1969. Tim Robbins went from this small but pivotal role to become one of Hollywood's leading players as an actor, director and political activist alongside his partner, actress Susan Sarandon. His films include *Bull Durham* (Ron Shelton, 1988), *The Player* (Robert Altman, 1992), *The Shawshank Redemption* (Frank Darabond, 1994), and *Dead Man Walking* (1995), which he wrote, produced and directed. Glenn Scarpelli is the son of Archie comics artist Henry Scarpelli.

THE USUAL SUSPECTS: Harry Northup (*Who's That Knocking At My Door?*, *Boxcar Bertha*, *Mean Streets*, *American Boy*, *Alice Doesn't Live Here Anymore*, *Taxi Driver*, *New York, New York*). Helen Shaver (*The Color of Money*).

PRODUCTION: As arguably the most powerful film-maker in the Western world, and with hits like *Jaws*, *Close Encounters of the Third Kind*, *Raiders of the Lost Ark* and *ET The Extra-Terrestrial* under his belt, Steven Spielberg was in a unique position in 1985. Approaching Sid Sheinberg, then head of MCA, with the idea of doing an anthology series, Spielberg left with a two-year deal with NBC to produce over forty episodes regardless of ratings success or failure, a move unprecedented in television history. What is even more unusual is that anthology shows had all-but died off at the tail end of the 60s after *Alfred Hitchcock Presents*, *The Outer Limits* and, of course, *The Twilight Zone* had glutted the market with their one-off teleplays about the weird and not-so wonderful. In more recent times, HBO's *The Hitchhiker* had enjoyed limited success, due in no small part to its regular slice of nudity, while George Romero's *Tales from the Crypt* went down the horror route with similar results. Spielberg set about assembling the best directors and writers he could find to create his vision of self-contained stories from across all genres, from old hands like Joe Dante and Clint Eastwood (who had already had some success in moving from in front of the camera to the director's chair) to newcomers like Tim Burton. For Scorsese, it significantly represented his further move towards gaining acceptance of his work from Hollywood, as well as being the first official collaboration with Spielberg (though Spielberg had helped him unofficially with a few of his films over the years). Shot over six days, it was Scorsese's first foray into the horror genre, drawing on his love of old Hammer productions and hiring composer Michael Kamen for the music, as he'd liked his work on David Cronenberg's adaptation of Stephen King's *The Dead Zone* (1988).

Spielberg wasn't the only one trying to launch a new anthology show in 1985, however. A series of *Alfred Hitchcock Presents* episodes (complete with 'colourised' introductions from the Master of Suspense's original episodes) was also debuting on NBC, while on CBS, *The Twilight Zone* was also being revived, alongside *George Burns' Comedy Week*, co-produced by Steve Martin and Carl Gottlieb. And ABC were ramping up their revival of *The Outer Limits* as either a movie or a TV show.

Amazing Stories was scheduled for 8 p.m. on Sunday evenings, not a particularly strong slot. Coupled with this was the issue of publicity. To create a buzz for the series, Spielberg had requested that, to maintain an air of surprise, none of the storylines would be released to the press in advance, and no footage would be broadcast in trails for the programme ahead of its transmission. Instead of creating a buzz, however, it created a backlash, with the press lining up to knock Spielberg's latest project down. Still, it was ahead of the competition in the Nielson ratings at least. In their first month, *Amazing Stories* averaged 22nd, *Alfred Hitchcock Presents* 32nd, *The Twilight Zone* 39th and *George Burns' Comedy Week* 59th.

Scorsese's episode, 'Mirror, Mirror' was broadcast in September 1986 as episode 19 of the first season. It would not receive a terrestrial transmission in the UK, however, until the BBC began using *Amazing Stories* as a schedule-filler in the spring of 1992.

EDITING: Jordan runs through his apartment to escape the phantom and we see a montage of jump-cuts as he locks the windows and doors (see **CAPE FEAR**).

QUOTE/UNQUOTE
Jordan: (discussing monsters in movies) 'It's the live ones you gotta worry about, not the dead ones. Agents, ex-wives, journalists . . . those are the people that scare me.'

ROOTS: Spielberg's career began working on Rod Serling's other anthology show *Night Gallery*. *Amazing Stories* was named after a pulp magazine from the 1950s. The clip from *The Plague of the Zombies* (John Gilling, 1966) is Scorsese's tribute to the British Hammer horror pictures of the 50s, 60s and early 70s. One of the movie posters in Jordan's lounge features a reproduction of Edvard Munch's *The Scream* (see **AFTER HOURS**). The phantom itself is reminiscent of Lon Chaney's *The Phantom of the Opera* (especially the shot where Jordan realises he has turned into his tormentor), while the ending to the piece could be seen as an interpretation of the climax to *The Exorcist* (William Friedkin, 1974) where the priest, having become possessed by the demon, flings himself through a window to his death.

THEMES AND MOTIFS: It's no surprise that the most significant recurring motif here is the use of mirrors. Jordan's chauffeur is only really seen through the rear-view mirror, his eyes framed like Travis Bickle's in *Taxi Driver*. Jordan talks to himself in the mirror and, for a large proportion of the episode, it is his reflection and not him that we see. The sterile whiteness of Jordan's apartment recalls the bathroom from *The Big Shave* and makes the redness of the lamp in his room and the other sparse bits of décor seem all the more lurid and incongruent. Fan obsession is examined in greater detail in *The King of Comedy*.

LEGACY: The *Amazing Stories* series did spawn one spin-off, the animated series *Family Dog*, based on the characters created for his Amazing Story of the same name.

AVAILABILITY: 'Mirror, Mirror' was released on Laserdisc as part of the *Amazing Stories* collection (*Amazing Stories Book 4*) alongside two other episodes, 'Blue Man Down' and 'Mr. Magic'; and originally released on VHS in compilation form as *Amazing Stories: The Movie IV* alongside episodes 'Life on Death Row', 'The Amazing Falsworth' and 'Vanessa in the Garden'.

FINAL ANALYSIS: Where *Alfred Hitchcock Presents* and *The Twilight Zone* succeeded was the introductions (from Hitchcock and Rod Serling, respectively), bringing a sense of continuity between the many unconnected stories they churned out. Spielberg, however, turned down the chance to present his anthology (even the tag 'Steven Spielberg Presents . . .' was vetoed), preferring the device of the off-screen narrator. It's a decision many felt was a mistake. Spielberg's claim that he didn't want to step out from behind the camera and become a familiar face just doesn't hold water either (as anyone who's queued for the *ET* ride at Universal Studios, Florida can verify). Secondly, calling the show '*Amazing Stories*' was not only giving critics ammunition to shoot it down but assembling, loading and aiming the gun for them. Many of the stories just weren't that . . . well, amazing. Which all makes Scorsese's effort all the more surprising as it is genuinely scary at times, contains many visual references that are familiar to students of Scorsese's work and seems very unlike the kind of story one might expect to have come from the mind of Spielberg.

SCORSESE ON 'MIRROR, MIRROR': 'I just wanted to work fast again, to think fast on my feet again . . . My last feature, *After Hours*, was a fast shoot, too, so I was ready to do a six-day shoot . . . But, before that, I'd worked on movies that took a lot of time. Maybe too much time.'

The Color of Money (1986)

(35 mm – 119 mins – colour)

A Silver Screen Partners production for Touchstone
Pictures
Screenplay by Richard Price, based on the novel by Walter
Tevis
Producers: Irving Axelrod, Barbara De Fina
Associate Producer: Dodie Foster
Music: Robbie Robertson
Cinematographer: Michael Ballhaus
Film Editor: Thelma Schoonmaker
Casting: Gretchen Rennell
Production Design: Boris Leven
Set Decoration: Karen O'Hara
Costume Design: Richard Bruno
Title Designer: Dan Perri
Production Accountant: Elizabeth Yanoska
Acknowledgements: Marion Billings, James Hendricks,
Harold L Simonsen, Shari Simonsen, Christopher Tellefsen

SOUNDTRACK: 'Strangers in the Night', lyrics by Charles Singleton and Eddie Snyder, music by Bert Kaempfert; 'I'll Never Smile Again', written by Ruth Lowe; 'Anema E Core', Italian lyrics by Tito Manlio, English lyrics by Mann Curtis and Harry Akst, music by Salve D'Esposito; 'The Day the Rains Came', French lyrics by Pierre Delanoe, English lyrics by Carl Sigman, music by Gilbert Bécaud; 'The Girl from Ipanema', English lyrics by Norman Gimbel, Portuguese lyrics by Vinicius De Moraes, music by Antonio Carlos Jobim; 'I'll Remember April', written by Don Haye, Gene de Paul and Pat Johnston, performed by Charlie Parker; 'Feel Like Going Home' by The Del Lords; 'Va Pensiero' from *Nabucco* by Giuseppe Verdi; 'Walk on the Wild Side', lyrics by Mack David, music by Elmer Bernstein, performed by Jimmy Smith; 'Still a Fool' by Muddy Waters; 'My Baby's In Love with another Guy' by Robert Palmer; 'She's Fine – She's Mine' by Bo Diddley; 'It's My Life Baby', written by Don Robey and Ferdinand 'Fats' Washington, performed by Eric Clapton and The Big Town Playboys; 'Who Owns This Place?' by Don Henley; 'Let Yourself in for It' by Robert Palmer; 'It's in the Way You Use It' by Eric Clapton; 'Two Brothers and a Stranger' by Mark Knopfler; 'Don't Tell Me Nothin'' by Willie Dixon; 'Standing on the Edge' by BB King; 'One More Night' by Phil Collins;

'Still the Night' by Bodeans; 'Werewolves of London' by Warren Zevon; 'Out of Left Field' by Percy Sledge.

CAST: Paul Newman (*'Fast' Eddie Felson*), Tom Cruise (*Vincent*), Mary Elizabeth Mastrantonio (*Carmen*), Helen Shaver (*Janelle*), John Turturro (*Julian*), Bill Cobbs (*Orvis*), Robert Agins (*Earl at Chalkies*), Alvin Anastasia (*Kennedy*), Randall Arney (*Child World Customer 1*), Elizabeth Bracco (*Diane at Bar*), Vito D'Ambrosio (*Lou in Child World*), Ron Dean (*Guy in Crowd*), Lisa Dodson (*Child World Customer 2*), Donald A Feeney (*Referee 1*), Paul Geier (*'Two Brothers/Stranger' Player*), Carey Goldenberg, Lawrence Linn, Rick Mohr, Rodrick Selby (*Congratulating Spectators*), Joe Guastaferro (*Chuck the Bartender*), Paul Herman (*Player in Casino Bar*), Mark Jarvis (*Guy at Janelle's*), Keith McCready (*Grady Seasons*), Jimmy Mataya (*Julian's Friend in Green Room*), Grady Mathews (*Dud*), Carol Messing (*Casino Bar Band Singer/Julian's Flirt*), Peter Saxe, Brian Sunina, Jim Widlowski (*Casino Bar Band Members*), Steve Mizerak (*Dale, Eddie's First Opponent*), Lloyd Moss (*Narrator – Resorts International*), Michael Nash (*Moselle's Opponent*), Mario Nieves (*Third Latin Guy*), Miguel A Nino (*First Latin Guy*), Andy Nolfo (*Referee 2*), Ernest Perry Jr (*Eye Doctor*), Jerry Piller (*Tom*), Iggy Pop (*Skinny Player on the Road*), Richard Price (*Guy Who Calls Dud*), Juan Ramrez (*Second Latin Guy*), Alex Ross (*Bartender Who Bets*), Charles Scorsese (*High Roller 1*), Christina Sigel (*Waitress*), Harold L Simonsen (*Chief Justice Tournament*), Fred Squillo (*High Roller 2*), Wanda Christine (*Casino Clerk*), Forest Whitaker (*Amos*), Bruce A Young (*Moselle*).

UNCREDITED CAST: Martin Scorsese (*Opening Voice-over*).

TITLES: The pre-titles appear red on a black background in a chunky font that looks more akin to the credits from a Western (helped by the lone whistling of the intro music). TOUCHSTONE PICTURES PRESENTS ... IN ASSOCIATION WITH SILVER SCREEN PARTNERS II ... A MARTIN SCORSESE PICTURE ... PAUL NEWMAN ... TOM CRUISE. Then we hear Scorsese explain the concept of 9-Ball while smoke from a cigarette wafts across the screen. The remaining titles appear as a red haze around black text over images of a bar.

SUMMARY: Eddie Felson is a liquor salesman, but in his youth he'd been a hustling pool player until one of his hustles caught up with him. But he still finds the addiction for the game in his blood. So when he

meets Vincent, a brash new player at the local pool hall, Eddie knows the
kid has a talent. Unfortunately he also has an uncontrollable ego and an
ambitious girlfriend, Carmen. Working through Carmen, Eddie invites
Vincent to dinner to discuss his playing. He notes that Vincent may have
a gift, that he has an attitude that makes men want to kill each other to
take a shot at him but that he doesn't think the kid could convert that
into being a great player. Excellence in Pool, he asserts, is not about
excellent pool. To achieve excellence, he needs to become a 'student of
human moves'. That is Eddie's area of excellence. Vincent seems
unimpressed so Eddie bets him that a man standing by the bar, who he
has observed trying to chat up a woman, will give up on her and leave
within thirty seconds. Vincent gets his watch and counts him out, but the
man is still there. But just as Vincent declares Eddie the loser, the man
gets up and walks away. Eddie stoically suggests he was out by a couple
of seconds and that they raise the bet. For the price of the dinner they've
just enjoyed, he bets that he will leave with the woman himself in two
minutes. Vincent laps up the bet. Eddie walks over to the woman,
excuses himself and invites her, enigmatically, to take a look at his car.
The woman, intrigued, stands up and he escorts her to the door. As he
passes Vincent's table, he casually throws down a $10 bill and says
generously 'the cab's on me' and leaves with the woman. But as they
leave the restaurant it's clear that he and the woman are old friends and
he offers to drive her home.

Eddie visits Vincent and invites him to take part in a forthcoming
9-ball tournament in Atlantic City, all expenses paid for him and
Carmen by Eddie. The catch is that they would need to leave the very
next day so that they can get six weeks of practice before the
tournament. Vincent seems unsure, but Eddie sagely points out that
Carmen seems to be the kind of girl who bores easily and asks him if
she's as excited with him working in a shop as she would be if he were a
champion player. He leaves Vincent to think the proposition over. The
next day, Vincent comes by the bar with a few questions. Eddie shows
him his pool cue – a prized Balabushka – and offers it to Vincent. Eddie
sends him out into the pool hall to try it out. As he leaves, Vincent tells
Eddie he was wrong about Carmen, that she's happy to be with him.
Eddie tells him absently that he's glad to be wrong. As Vincent shows the
cue off to the guys in the pool hall, Eddie goes over to the bar where
Carmen is watching her boyfriend. He whispers something in her ear and
she leaves. Vincent goes looking for her and when she comes back she's
very frosty with him. Vincent begins to play a game, but he's distracted
and after his break he tells Eddie he's decided to go for the Atlantic City

tournament. Eddie lays out his terms to Vincent and Carmen. He'll cover all their expenses – room, travel, the lot. In return, he expects 60 per cent of all of Vincent's winnings, which he sees as fair considering he'll also be covering his losses. He also tells him that often the real money can be made in the practice room. A guy can wipe out in the first round of the tournament, hang around in the practice room and make more money than the winner.

They arrive at their first practice venue. Eddie tells Vincent to leave his new cue in the trunk of his car as it'll put people off – he will play with a house cue. But when they enter the hall it's full of junk – the pool hall has long closed down. Eddie is bitterly disappointed. At the next pool hall, Vincent plays an old man with a hole in his throat for a stake of just $60. Eddie tells him to get on with it, but it's clearly pricking Vincent's conscience so Eddie tells him to turn it around; if he's going to dump the game, he should dump like a professional, make it a real performance. As Vincent begins deliberately to throw the game, Eddie sends Carmen to bring the car round front and then slips up to the viewing gallery. When Vincent loses the game and can't find Eddie to pay the old man a fight breaks out – the old man's clearly not as infirm as he's pretended to be. Eddie lets Vincent get close to taking a beating and then jumps in, pretending to be his angry father. He drags Vincent outside and throws him into the waiting car and tells Carmen to drive. The lesson – nice guys finish last.

At the next hall, Eddie bumps into Orvis, an old friend from 25 years ago who addresses him as 'Fast Eddie', much to the amusement of Vincent. Orvis takes one look at the kid and realises Eddie is 'Stake Horsing' Vincent and out of respect for Eddie he sets up a table for them. Eddie talks Vincent round the room, warning him off playing certain players in case he wins and scares off other players who are more likely to gamble huge amounts. Vincent will play Eddie until one of the men Eddie is staking out comes over and asks for a game. Vincent insists Carmen goes back to the hotel because he's scared for her. She refuses and they row, but Eddie agrees with Vincent and bundles her out of the hall. With Carmen out of the way, Eddie tells Vincent to play it cool, especially as the row attracted attention. But Vincent can't help but show off, and Eddie gives up on him and storms out, telling him this is all a waste of his money. He drives off leaving Vincent behind.

Eddie goes to see Carmen in her hotel room and criticises her for winding Vincent up. He tells her she needs to work like his partner – she makes him feel good so he can teach him. Just then, Eddie notices the Balabushka cue is not in the room. Carmen tells him Vincent came back, took it, then went out. Only then does she realise why Eddie is concerned. As Eddie suspected, Vincent has returned to the pool hall and waits to challenge the very man Eddie warned him not to play. Dancing round the table, Vincent's arrogance gets the crowd clapping. Vincent wins, and as Eddie predicted, this scares off the other player, one who would have gambled much more than the supposed best in the room. Leaving the pool hall on a high, Vincent cannot understand Eddie's exasperation with him. Eddie growls that now, thanks to his impatience, the town is dead to him. Instead of making $150 from one game, they could have got $5000 from playing the heavy gambler. Eddie talks plainly to Vincent. He confesses that 25 years earlier, he was stopped from advancing any further, retired before his time. Vincent explains how tough he finds it just to lay down but tells him he'll try to pay more attention. As a further lesson to the kid, Eddie makes sure he still gets his 60 per cent of the $150.

The next day, Eddie teaches Vincent a hustle. He lets Vincent enter a hall and do his overconfident act. This means he struggles to find anyone willing to take him on, but eventually he does. Meanwhile, Eddie and Carmen, posing as May-to-December lovers, fool around at the bar, giggling and generally distracting Vincent. Eventually, Vincent tells him to keep it down as it's a big money game. Eddie mocks him, and asks the other guy what they're playing for. He says $50. Eddie then addresses the room, pointing to Vincent: 'Anyone wanna bet this guy loses?' The other guy asks him why he's causing trouble, but then, from the back of the room, the bartender asks if he wants to go for a thousand. As predicted, the scam works, but Vincent finds he is upset by seeing Carmen play-acting as Eddie's lover. He wants to quit and the others have to talk him into trusting them and to stick at their game. The trio continue on their journey, making money in every pool hall they pass. In one, they encounter Grady Seasons, a man Eddie regards as the best pool player there is. Eddie and Carmen have to explain to Vincent that he needs to dump the game against Grady so that when they reach Atlantic City his odds will be so low they'll clean up when he wins. Grady spends the game boasting and goading Vincent, and Eddie watches him like a hawk. At first, Vincent manages to play it cool, but after one too many jibes from Grady, he can't hold back and he begins to win. Seeing her boyfriend threaten his chances further up the road, Carmen walks over and whispers to him that if he wins one more game she'll finish with him. He gets the message and reluctantly throws the game.

Eddie borrows the Balabushka and takes it to a local hall. He enjoys a few games until he meets a young man called Amis who appears retarded. After a few light games, however, Amis begins to win. Eddie realises all too late that Amis is a hustler and is furious with himself for being suckered by him. Thrown by this, Eddie realises that there's nothing he can teach him that Vincent doesn't already know and tells the kid he wants to quit. Giving him enough money to get them to Atlantic City on their own, Eddie leaves, taking the Balabushka with him. Back at Orvis's club he confides in his old friend that he's realised that he's going blind. While awaiting the results of some eye tests, Eddie stays on at Orvis's club playing games for fun. He starts off losing, even to an old woman, but slowly he starts winning again until he's managed to make enough money for his own stake in Atlantic City.

The tournament begins, with both Vincent and Eddie winning all of their games. Eddie defeats a previous protégé of his, while Vincent finally gets the chance to turn the tables on Grady Seasons. Eventually, Eddie and Vincent find they are drawn to play each other. It is a tense game with both men holding their own. Vincent impresses the crowd with a difficult and very flash trick shot, but then messes up an easier shot later, leaving Eddie open to win. Vincent takes the defeat badly while Eddie enjoys his return to form. But that evening, Vincent and Carmen come to Eddie's room and tell him that Vincent dumped the game to improve his odds in the practice rooms, just as Eddie had suggested at the start. Vincent hands him an envelope containing a 60 per cent cut of the money they made through bets, as they'd arranged. Eddie is furious. The next day, Vincent and Carmen watch Eddie's match. But before he takes a shot, Eddie announces that he forfeits the game to the amazement of everyone. As he leaves the room, he hands Vincent his envelope back and tells Carmen he feels cheated – he wants to play Vincent on his best game. The two men square up to each other in a practice room. Vincent boasts that the older man can't handle his best and they set up a game, the money in the envelope as their stake. As they begin, Vincent asks him what he'll do when he kicks his ass. Eddie smiles and says he'll get right up and let him kick him again. If he doesn't win this game, he'll win next month in Texas. As he makes to break, he cheers 'I'm back!'

WHO'S WHO?: Paul Newman gained some notoriety after he established 'Paul Newman's Own', a brand of salad dressings that forwards its profits to charity. Married to actress Joanne Woodward, Newman's most celebrated roles include Eddie Felson in *The Hustler* (Robert Rossen, 1961), the eponymous *Cool Hand Luke* (Stuart Rosenberg, 1967), and Butch Cassidy opposite Robert Redford in *Butch Cassidy and the Sundance Kid* (George Roy Hill, 1969). Tom Cruise is currently one of Hollywood's major players, having starred in some of the highest-grossing and critically acclaimed pictures of the last two decades, which include *Top Gun* (Tony Scott, 1986), *Rain Man* (Barry Levinson, 1988), *Mission Impossible* (Brian De Palma, 1996), *Jerry Maguire* (Cameron Crowe, 1996) and *Eyes Wide Shut* (Stanley Kubrick, 1999). Mary Elizabeth Mastrantonio had recorded a scene for *After Hours* which ended up cut from the picture. She starred in *The Abyss* (James Cameron, 1989), the hugely successful Kevin Costner-vehicle *Robin Hood: Prince of Thieves* (Kevin Reynolds, 1991) and *The Perfect Storm* (Wolfgang Petersen, 2000) as well as balancing a successful stage career. John Turturro worked with Spike Lee in *Do The Right Thing* (1989), *Mo Better Blues* (1990) and *Jungle Fever* (1991) (among others), and the Coen Brothers in pretty much everything – including *Miller's Crossing* (1990), *Barton Fink* (1991) and *O Brother, Where Art Thou* (2000). Ron Dean had the semi-regular role of Detective Crumb in the TV series *Early Edition*. Iggy Pop – aka James Newell Osterberg – is the obscenely skinny punk/rockstar famed for hits like 'Real Wild Child (Wild One)', 'Did You Evah' (with Deborah Harry) and 'Lust For Life'. Forest Whitaker makes an early cameo appearance here. He went on to star as the legendary jazz musician Charlie Parker in *Bird* (Clint Eastwood, 1988) and Jody in *The Crying Game* (Neil Jordan, 1992) as well as directing Whitney Houston in *Waiting to Exhale* (1995). Two cast-members of the HBO mob drama *The Sopranos* appear. Bill Cobbs guest-starred in the episode 'Do Not Resuscitate', while Paul Herman played Beansie Gaeta in the episodes 'Full Leather Jacket' and 'Toodle-Fucking-Oo'.

THE USUAL SUSPECTS: Helen Shaver (*Amazing Stories*: 'Mirror Mirror'); John Turturro (*Raging Bull, Grace of My Heart*); Paul Herman (*The Last Temptation of Christ, New York Stories, GoodFellas, Casino*); Richard Price (*Bad, New York Stories*: 'Life Lessons'); Barbara De Fina (*Bad, The Last Temptation of Christ, New York Stories*: 'Life Lessons', *The Grifters, Made in Milan, GoodFellas, Cape Fear, Mad Dog and Glory, The Age of Innocence, Casino, Kundun, My Voyage to Italy, Bringing Out the Dead, Dino*); editor Thelma Schoonmaker (*Who's That Knocking At My Door?, Street Scenes, Raging Bull, The King of Comedy, After Hours, Bad, The Last Temptation of Christ, New York Stories, GoodFellas, Cape Fear, Age of Innocence, Casino, A Personal Journey with Martin Scorsese Through American Movies, Kundun, Bringing Out the Dead, My Voyage to Italy, Gangs of New York*); title designer Dan Perri (*Taxi Driver, New York, New York, The Last Waltz, Raging Bull, The King of Comedy*).

SOURCE: Trying to pay his way through college, Walter Tevis took a job working in a pool hall where he met the real 'Fast Eddie' – pool player Eddie Parker. Being a money player, Eddie would sometimes use assumed names. As well as Eddie Ezzell, Eddie Santee and Terry McKee, he used the name Eddie Felsen, and it was the latter (with a slight change in spelling) that Tevis would use for the name of the central character in his 1959 novel *The Hustler*. Though Parker would claim that only a third of the novel was based on truth, there were a number of incidents that made it to the fictional life of Eddie Felson, such as his friendship with 'New York Fats' (who became 'Minnesota Fats' in his novel). Fast Eddie didn't get his two thumbs broken, as depicted in the movie; his right forefinger was broken during an attack on him.

Starring Paul Newman as Eddie Felson, the film version of *The Hustler* (Robert Rossen, 1961) quickly soared to the top of many people's top ten lists, creating a memorable anti-hero and resulting in a Best Actor nomination for Newman at the Oscars the following year. When Walter Tevis's sequel to *The Hustler* was released in 1984, Newman knew straight away that he wanted to resurrect 'Fast Eddie' (see **PRODUCTION** below) but in the discussion between himself, Martin Scorsese and screenwriter Richard Price, they all agreed that a number of changes would be required. For a start, Scorsese was not convinced that Eddie would have been running a pool hall, feeling that he'd have probably become a second-hand car salesman instead. This evolved into a liquor salesman in the finished script. Flashbacks to Eddie's childhood and a reunion with Minnesota Fats from *The Hustler* (in which Eddie tries to persuade him to join him in a TV documentary playing pool across America) were dropped, as was the idea that Eddie was fighting desperately to emerge from under a mountain of debt. In the script, Eddie is a successful businessman who nevertheless feels unfulfilled because his real potential was denied him all those years ago. The character that would eventually be played by Tom Cruise is actually closer to that of Julian (John Turturro), a cocaine-sniffing opposite to the calm Eddie. Early versions of the script retained the character of 'Minnesota Fats', portrayed by Jackie Gleason in *The Hustler*, but when they sent a copy of the script to Gleason he turned it down, recognising that the character as represented in the script was clearly an afterthought and not integral to the story. Thus, 'Fats' was removed from the script, his role of a link to Eddie's past effectively served by Orvis in the finished film.

PRODUCTION: Looking round for a director for *The Color of Money*, Paul Newman approached Martin Scorsese, having been impressed by

Raging Bull (and, it seems, *The Deer Hunter*, as his introductory letter was, according to Scorsese, addressed to 'Martin Cimino'). In bringing *The Color of Money* to the screen, Paul Newman had already begun to assemble a script. Walter Tevis, author of the novel, had drafted a version before his death, and another writer had been brought in to shape the script to Newman's suggestions. Discussing concerns over the existing script with Newman, Scorsese suggested bringing in a fresh new writer and hired Richard Price, a novelist who'd written *The Wanderers* and *Bloodbrothers*, to have a go at a rewrite. Price saw a number of problems with what his predecessors had done, namely writing a literal sequel that required the audience to be at least partly familiar with *The Hustler*. Price suggested that they take the basic premise, 'Eddie Felson – 25 years on', and drafted a completely new story around that character. Price met with Scorsese and Newman in Malibu where the three brainstormed potential routes they could take. Price began to study pool players and produced a script of around eighty pages, but Newman still wasn't happy, feeling this version deviated too far from their initial discussions. Scorsese suggested to Price that he consider the script a suit shaped to fit Newman. The problem appeared to be that, although Newman wanted to play an anti-hero, he still wanted to retain an essence of likeability. Marty and Richard, meanwhile, liked the meanness of the character and were struggling to bring that to the fore to make the eventual redemption at the end all the more effective. Out of this came a workable script that seemed to appease all sides. After nine months, Scorsese knew he could make something of Price's version and finally committed to directing the picture. Still, a lot of money had already been spent on the script, and on paying off Walter Tevis's estate.

Initially, the picture was set to be produced at Fox, but after disputes over the script and even the casting, they took it to Jeffrey Katzenberg and Michael Eisner, who had left Paramount for Touchstone (see **TESTAMENT OF FAITH** later on). With the picture installed in a new home, production could finally begin. Cast as Eddie's protégé was Tom Cruise, who was at the time a promising young newcomer who'd starred in the film *Risky Business*. During production though, Cruise's *Top Gun* would be released, catapulting him into the big league.

Keen to bring the picture in on time and under budget, but mindful of the amount of time-consuming pool tricks required for the shoot, Scorsese prepared his traditional storyboards and hired cinematographer Michael Ballhaus, who had ensured *After Hours* was completed so swiftly. Scorsese's wife, Barbara De Fina, along with Newman's lawyer, Irving Axelrod, produced. To ensure they remained within budget,

Scorsese and Newman put up a third of their salaries to help fund the picture. Two weeks were put aside for rehearsals, mainly because Newman was not a fan of improvisation, although Scorsese did allow Richard Price to sit in on the rehearsals just in case any interesting improvisations arose. The team managed to hire a number of top pool players of the time, such as Steve Mizerak ('The Miz'); Jimmy Mataya ('Pretty Boy Floyd'); Keith McCready (who would play Grady Seasons); and others such as Michael Sigel and Eva Mataya Laurence (who at the time was Jimmy Mataya's wife) acting as pro shot makers and advisers. Both Newman, an experienced pool player, and Cruise did their own trick shots for the film, except for one seen in the match between Eddie and Vincent where Cruise had to jump two balls to sink another. Scorsese was sure that Cruise could have learned the shot, but that it would have taken an extra two days of practice, holding up production and costing money. The shot was instead performed by Michael Sigel.

The picture was completed one day short of their fifty-day schedule, and a million and a half shy of their $14.5 million budget. With its mix of nostalgia for the original and the sudden rise in Cruise's popularity thanks to *Top Gun*, *The Color of Money* became Scorsese's most profitable film so far. Paul Newman went on to win an Oscar, Tom Cruise began his ascendancy to the position of biggest star in Hollywood and Scorsese signed a two-year deal with Touchstone, offering them first option on his future projects. More importantly, Scorsese was now in a position to return to a project he'd been close to making half a decade earlier – *The Last Temptation of Christ*.

EDITING: Obviously, the frenetic pool scenes are the ones that we all remember here, with the tight, fast editing that almost hurts the eyes. But a more subtle aspect of the look of the picture came after Scorsese suggested making the picture in black and white to tie in with the original film. Touchstone vetoed this, aware of the effect this would have on the picture's box office, so instead, Scorsese, with Michael Ballhaus and Boris Leven, designed the film to look as monochromatic as possible, capturing the winter of Chicago, and then for the final third of the picture they brought up the colour to really bring the scenes in Atlantic City alive.

MUSIC: Scorsese once again called on Robbie Robertson to come up with a soundtrack for the picture. Robertson contributed about twenty minutes of original music, including 'The Blues Suite', which was orchestrated by Gil Evans. The opening 'riff' track, just Robertson moaning over a drum beat, had been recorded on to an ⅛-inch cassette and then played through the stereo. Strangely, as Robertson was contracted to Geffen Records, Katzenberg and Geffen could not come to a happy negotiation on the use of Robertson's voice. Robertson was, however, able to negotiate with MCA for artists like Eric Clapton, Don Henley, Phil Collins and Robert Palmer.

ROOTS: Though it's a sequel to *The Hustler*, any similarity between the two films really begins and ends with the central character, and even he is removed from the optimistic young man from 1961. The inspiration for Fast Eddie, Ed Parker (see **SOURCE** above) produced a video and wrote a workbook on pool in the early 80s called 'What You've Always Wanted To Know About Pocket Billiards, But Were Afraid To Ask' which Paul Newman consulted prior to filming.

QUOTE/UNQUOTE

Narrator: ' "Luck" plays a part in 9-ball. But for some players, luck itself is an art.'

Eddie: 'You couldn't find big time if you had a road map!'

Eddie: 'Straight pool you gotta be a real surgeon to get it. It's all finesse. Now everything is 9-ball because it's fast, good for TV, good for a lot of break shots. . . . Oh well, what the Hell, checkers sells more than chess.'

Eddie: 'Vincent, get in the car, this is embarrassing. You're acting like some girl who got felt up at the drive-in.'

Eddie: 'Money won is twice as sweet as money earned.'

THEMES AND MOTIFS: Vincent, on seeing the Balabushka, exclaims that 'John Wayne carries something like this,' and later on we see him hold his cue like a rifle, point at Eddie and then act as if he himself has been shot down.

CONTROVERSY: Eddie tells Julian off for snorting cocaine, snarling 'I hate that shit'. It was Scorsese's cocaine habit that was partly responsible for his near-death experience prior to the production of *Raging Bull*. This line to some degree acknowledges this. That it's delivered by Newman, an actor who always appears to be in possession of common sense, adds greatly to the scene.

KEEP IT IN THE FAMILY: Marty's father Charles plays one of the High Rollers. Producer Barbara De Fina would eventually become Scorsese's wife. Elizabeth Bracco is the sister of Lorraine Bracco (*GoodFellas*), and at this time, sister-in-law of Harvey Keitel.

THERE HE IS!: In the Atlantic City casino, Scorsese plays the man walking a dog on a leash. The dog is his own dog Zoe. Zoe is credited in the closing credits as 'Dog Walkby'. The director also provides the voice-over explaining the 9-ball.

LEGACY: Just as *Raging Bull* had forever changed the way boxing in the movies would be viewed, so too did pool become revived. Indeed, pool halls across the USA were reporting a massive rise in newcomers, unseen, in fact, since the release of *The Hustler*.

TRIVIA: Considering Scorsese's *The Color of Money* is a sequel to *The Hustler*, it might strike some as a major coincidence that, making his acting debut in the 1961 film as a bartender was one Jake LaMotta.

POSTER: Artwork depicting Tom Cruise, cue in hand, while a huge portrait of Paul Newman overshadows him. Newman appears to have acquired a handy pocket-sized Mary Elizabeth Mastrantonio, which sits comfortably on his chest. Alluding to the original 'Fast Eddie' movie, the tagline tells us: 'The hustler isn't what he used to be, but he has the next best thing: a kid who is.'

AWARDS: It truly was Paul Newman's year, and deservedly so. Both the National Board of Review and the American Academy of Motion Picture Arts and Sciences gave their Best Actor awards to him. Also nominated at the Academy Awards were Mary Elizabeth Mastrantonio (Best Actress in a Supporting Role), Boris Leven and Karen O'Hara (Best Art Direction–Set Decoration), Richard Price (Best Screenplay Based on Material from Another Medium). At the Golden Globes, Paul Newman and Mary Elizabeth Mastrantonio were nominated for Best Actor and Best Actress in a Motion Picture (Drama).

AVAILABILITY: The laserdisc release was a basic three-sided pan-and-scan presentation. Touchstone Home Video have released a similarly bare DVD edition with no extras but a decent widescreen presentation. VHS copies are still available.

WHAT THE CRITICS SAID: Rita Kempley of the *Washington Post*, 17 October 1986 observed that 'No stranger to grit, Scorsese surprisingly opts for glitz, directing this table sports saga as if it were *Rocky II* with nine-balls.' She was impressed by Mastrantonio, to whom she attributes the film's 'needed edge' but was disappointed by the final act, which focuses more on Eddie. By the script, Kempley was, overall, unimpressed: 'On many levels, [Price's] story works. It's a positive portrait of bravado and bonding, of come-uppance and corruption, of ageing and rejuvenation. And it's a showcase for our heroes, a passing of the pool cue, from pretty face past to pretty face present, from cool hand to top gun. But in the end, "Money" is a scratch, a contrived cliffhanger that sets us up for *Hustler III*.'

FINAL ANALYSIS: It's often the case that sport makes for great movies, and considering Scorsese has never been a fan of sports (having spent his childhood indoors due to his asthma) it's all the more surprising that he's managed to create two completely different definitive films on the subject. As ever, the reason it works so well is because it's not actually about sport at all, but about power and its hold over others. Scorsese envisaged Eddie as a dormant hustler, a man whose addiction to the game is so great it scares him. In contrast, the rising star, Vincent, plays the game for the sheer adrenaline-rush he gets from winning, but this could be a video-game to him: he has no respect for pool like Eddie, and he doesn't understand the manipulation or the rush he could get from cheating. In effect, he's too honest to be a successful pool player, something Eddie tries and fails to change. Even at the end, when Vincent dumps the game to con Eddie into thinking he won, we see how Vincent feels he must confess this to his 'Master' and pay him off. In this way, it's a story about corruption, of Eddie corrupting the innocence of Vincent and showing him a new path. Eddie has become the thing he hated the most – a stake-horse, a man who exploits the talents of younger pool players. In effect, he has become the character George C Scott played in the original. Only through ditching that relationship and playing the game for himself does he stand any chance of redemption, which is, after all, the objective of almost every lead character in Scorsese's work.

EXPERT WITNESS: 'He lets you find your own way, but the marvellous thing about him which most directors can't do, if you find yourself in trouble and you come to the director and say "I'm in trouble" the director sure as hell better know how to get you out of there, and that's what he can do.' Actor Paul Newman (*Eddie Felson*).

Barbara Hershey as
Boxcar Bertha

Below: Robert De
Niro and Harvey
Keitel, *Mean Streets*

Alice (Ellen Burstyn) and Flo (Diane Ladd), *Alice Doesn't Live Here Anymore*

De Niro as Travis Bickle, *Taxi Driver*

Jimmy (De Niro) and Francine (Liza Minnelli), *New York, New York*

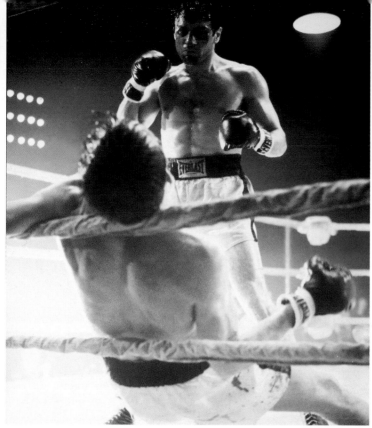

De Niro as Jake LaMotta in the 1940s ...

... and a decade and 60 lbs later

Tom Cruise and Paul Newman, *The Color of Money*

Willem Dafoe, *The Last Temptation of Christ*

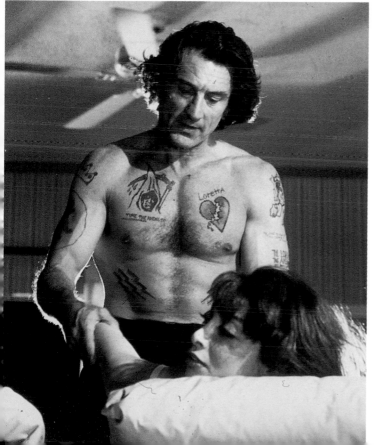

(Left to right) Ray Liotta, Robert De Niro, Paul Sorvino, Joe Pesci – *GoodFellas*

Max Cady (De Niro) with soon-to-be victim Lori (Illeana Douglas), *Cape Fear*

Newland (Daniel Day-Lewis) and May (Winona Ryder) visit Mrs Mingott (Miriam Margolyes), *The Age of Innocence*

Ginger (Sharon Stone), *Casino*

The fourteenth Dalai Lama is revealed, *Kundun*

Frank (Nicolas Cage) reaches breaking point as a stunned Marcus (Ving Rhames) looks on, *Bringing Out The Dead*

Keep it in the family – Charles and Catherine Scorsese, from *Italianamerican*

There he is! – Martin Scorsese, c.1989

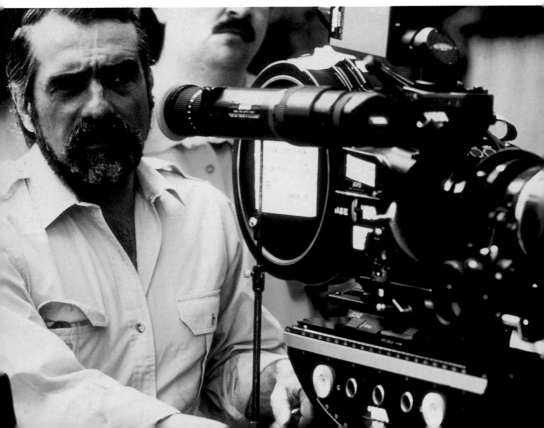

'Sometimes Newman would say, "Guys, I think we're missing an opportunity here". And the minute I heard that I would groan, "Oh, no, here we go again." Unfortunately, he was rarely wrong. But there were points when I thought, "If I hear 'we're missing an opportunity' one more time, you're going to be missing a writer".' Screenwriter Richard Price.

SCORSESE ON *THE COLOR OF MONEY:* 'There will always be people who will look at this picture and say, "Well that's it – that's a sequel." But through the torturous process of the film's production, I think I've done something that's personal. And if I can do something personal and Paul Newman can do something personal and it's all in the same place, then that's great.'

Armani Commercial (1986)

(35 mm – 30 sec – B & W)

Produced for Emporio Armani
Producer: Barbara De Fina
Screenplay: Martin Scorsese
Cinematography: Néstor Almendros

CAST: Christophe Bouquin, Christina Marsilach.

SUMMARY: A woman and a man sit in bed. She teaches him Italian by pointing to different parts of her body.

PRODUCTION: Made for his friend Giorgio Armani, this commercial was originally planned with the couple naked in bed, until Scorsese remembered that the ad was supposed to be an advert for a clothes designer.

Bad (1987)

35 mm – 16 mins – colour/B & W)

Production Company: Optimum Productions
Producers: Quincy Jones, Barbara De Fina
Screenplay: Richard Price

Director of Photography: Michael Chapman
Editor: Thelma Schoonmaker
Choreography: Michael Jackson, Gregg Burge, Jeffrey
Daniel
Stunt Co-ordinator: Edgard Morino

CAST: Michael Jackson (*Darryl*), Adam Nathan (*Tip*), Pedro Sanchez (*Nelson*), Wesley Snipes (*Mini Max*), Greg Holtz Sr (*Cowboy*), Jaime Perry (*Ski*), Paul Calderon (*Dealer*), Alberto Alejandrino (*Hispanic Man*), Horace Daily (*Street Bum*), Marvin Foster (*Crack Customer*), Roberta Flack (*Darryl's Mother*), Dennis Price (*Conductor*).

UNCREDITED CAST: Granville Adams III, Steve Glavin, Roger G (*Dancers*).

TITLES: The Bad logo appears, red on a black background, as if graffiti on an underground wall.

SUMMARY: On the last day of term at Duxton School, Darryl says goodbye to his schoolfriends and then catches the train back home to New York. He gets home to find a note from his mom: who's at work and won't be back until 7. She's left food for him in the fridge. He meets up with some old friends who nickname him 'college' and crack jokes about his life as a student. At first, Darryl takes their mockery with good humour, but as the night goes on, his friends becomes more and more hostile, asking him, 'Are you bad, are you down?' Bowing to pressure, Darryl goes to the subway and prepares to help his friend mug an old man. But at the last moment Darryl changes his mind and tells the man to run. The gang are furious and tell him 'you ain't down with us no more! You ain't bad!' He screams at them '*You* ain't NOTHIN'' and then as the picture goes to colour, Darryl changes his appearance and his crew appears – a massive gang of . . . dancers!

After their performance, they all chant 'Who's bad?' While Darryl sings 'You're doing wrong – y'know it.' Darryl and his new gang shake hands, but his old friends walk away leaving Darryl alone.

WHO'S WHO?: Singer Roberta Flack is probably best known for the songs 'The First Time Ever I Saw Your Face', 'Killing Me Softly with His Song' and, with Peabo Bryson, 'Tonight, I Celebrate My Love'. Wesley Snipes has emerged as one of the biggest action heroes and one of the most well-known African–American actors in Hollywood. His films include *Passenger 57* (Kevin Hooks, 1992), *Demolition Man* (Marco Brambilla, 1993), *The Fan*, opposite Robert De Niro (Tony Scott, 1996) and *Blade* (Stephen Norrington, 1998). Granville Adams III later played Sergeant Jeff Westman in the TV cop show *Homicide: Life on the Streets* and Arif in prison drama *Oz*. Choreographer Gregg Burge appeared in *The Cotton Club* (Francis Coppola, 1984), and *School Daze* (Spike Lee, 1988) and choreographed the closing ceremony of the 1992 Summer Olympics in Barcelona. He also spent three and a half years on Broadway in *The Wiz* as the scarecrow, the role Michael Jackson played in the film version (Sidney Lumet, 1978).

THE USUAL SUSPECTS: Richard Price (*The Color of Money, New York Stories*: 'Life Lessons'); Barbara De Fina (*The Color of Money, The Last Temptation of Christ, New York Stories*: 'Life Lessons', *The Grifters, Made in Milan, GoodFellas, Cape Fear, Mad Dog and Glory, The Age of Innocence, Casino, Kundun, My Voyage to Italy, Bringing Out the Dead, Dino*); cinematographer Michael Chapman (*Taxi Driver, The Last Waltz, American Boy, Raging Bull*); editor Thelma Schoonmaker (*Who's That Knocking At My Door?, Street Scenes, Raging Bull, The King of Comedy, After Hours, The Color of Money, The Last Temptation of Christ, New York Stories, GoodFellas, Cape Fear, Age of Innocence, Casino, A Personal Journey with Martin Scorsese Through American Movies, Kundun, Bringing Out the Dead, My Voyage to Italy, Gangs of New York*).

PRODUCTION: Having recorded with his brothers since the age of six, Jackson went solo in 1979, releasing *Off the Wall* with producer Quincy Jones. His follow-up, *Thriller*, sold 38 million records worldwide and won 58 platinum awards, helped largely by the video to the title-track, a big-budget tribute to horror movies directed by John Landis (*An American Werewolf in London*, 1981). It was Quincy Jones who initially contacted Scorsese on behalf of Michael Jackson to direct the video for the title song for his video *Bad*. The first ten minutes of the video were filmed in black and white, with the final six minutes – predominantly the music video – filmed in colour, but in a white subway with everyone wearing black. Jackson himself came up with the coda to the video, and the entire picture cost $2 million. The video premiered on a CBS television special that aired on 31 August 1987.

EDITING: Listen out for the comic book whooshes as Darryl moves his hands and turns his head (see **Cape Fear**).

ROOTS: The nature of Scorsese's cameo (see **THERE HE IS!**) owes more than a little to Hitchcock, who made appearances in both *Lifeboat* (1949) and *Dial M for Murder* (1954) in similar ways. The black-and-white to colour and back again comes via *The Wizard of Oz*.

CONTROVERSY: Darryl watches a drug dealer in action in his old neighbourhood and barely hides his contempt for him. Later, he assists in the planning of a mugging.

THERE HE IS!: Scorsese's face appears on a fly-poster underneath the words WANTED FOR SACRILEGE which is then torn from the wall.

LEGACY: The album *Bad*, which included the further US No. 1 hits 'Dirty Diana,' 'I Just Can't Stop Loving You,' and 'Man in the Mirror', would eventually go eight-times platinum, helped in no small part by Jackson's decision to tour solo for the first time. Screenwriter Barry Michael Cooper created *New Jack City*'s starring role specifically for Snipes after watching his portrayal of the rival gang leader in *Bad*. The Marvel comic book anti-hero 'Ace', who styled himself after Jackson, wore a costume similar to Jackson's *Bad* suit in issue 5 of Spider-Man, 1986. Weird Al Yankovic's spoof 'I'm Fat', which portrayed the comedian as a grotesquely obese tough guy, was shot on the same subway set used by Scorsese; the video won Yankovic his second Grammy. 'Badder', a segment of the movie *Moonwalker* was Jackson's own parody of the video performed by children. The video for Alien Ant Farm's 2001 rendition of Jackson's 'Smooth Criminal' features references to other Jackson videos, including *Bad*.

ALTERNATIVE VERSIONS: *Bad* is almost always screened in its cut-down form, showing just the dance section. The video release on Michael Jackson's *History Part I* video consisted of the dance section with an additional tag of Jackson wrecking a car.

AVAILABILITY: The full-length edit was finally released in November 2001 on the *Michael Jackson History – Greatest Hits* DVD (ASIN: B00005RSCH).

FINAL ANALYSIS: *Bad* was the first time that most of the public had seen Michael Jackson's new image. Unlike previous restylings, however, Jackson's new look extended to more than just the bondage trousers and leather jacket – he now had almost white skin. Though this was later explained as a side-effect of the pigment condition viteligo, for those that knew Jackson as a 'black' singer it proved to be quite a shock. Overall, working with Scorsese seems to have had a curious effect on Jackson's performance. Is it possible, with his shoulder-shrugging and the way he holds his hand in a pyramid of fingers, that Michael is playing Italian here? You watch the way he delivers that first line of the song – there's a definite air of Sicily about him.

SCORSESE ON *BAD*: 'I've always been fascinated by Michael Jackson's performances and especially his dancing. For years I'd been watching the Minnelli musicals; and I had applied the same camera techniques in the musical sequences of *New York, New York* as in the songs done in the studio for *The Last Waltz*. So I was dying to do it again ...'

Somewhere Down the Crazy River (1988)

(35 mm – 4 mins 30 secs – colour)

Production Company: Limelight
Director: Martin Scorsese
Producers: Amanda Pirie, Tim Clawson
Treatment: Martin Scorsese
Cinematography: Mark Plummer
Production Designer: Marina Levikova

CAST: Robbie Robertson, Sammy BoDean, Maria McKee.

SUMMARY: Robertson plays his song to camera.

WHO'S WHO?: Maria McKee enjoyed a hit some years later with 'Show Me Heaven'.

THE USUAL SUSPECTS: Robbie Robertson (*The Last Waltz*, *The King of Comedy*, *After Hours*, *The Color of Money*).

PRODUCTION: *Somewhere Down That Crazy River* was the launch single for Robbie Robertson's first solo album since leaving The Band in 1976. Friends with Robertson since *The Last Waltz*, Scorsese, as a favour, directed this simple, yet effective video while in hiding after the backlash to the production of *The Last Temptation of Christ*.

The Last Temptation of Christ (1988)
(Working Title: *Passion*)

(35 mm – 163 mins – colour)

Cineplex Odeon Films/Universal Pictures
Producer: Barbara De Fina
Executive Producer: Harry J Ufland
Screenplay by Paul Schrader, based on the novel by Nikos Kazantzakis
Cinematography: Michael Ballhaus
Film Editor: Thelma Schoonmaker
Original Music: Peter Gabriel
Additional Music: Shankar
Casting: Cis Corman
Production Design: John Beard
Art Direction: Andrew Sanders
Set Decoration: Giorgio Desideri
Costume Design: Jean-Pierre Delifer
Title Designers: Joe Caroff, Lon Kirschner

CAST: Willem Dafoe (*Jesus*), Harvey Keitel (*Judas*), Paul Greco (*Zealot*), Steve Shill (*Centurion*), Verna Bloom (*Mary, Mother of Jesus*), Barbara Hershey (*Mary Magdalene*), Roberts Blossom (*Aged Master*), Barry Miller (*Jeroboam*), Gary Basaraba (*Andrew, Apostle*), Irvin Kershner (*Zebedee*), Victor Argo (*Peter, Apostle*), Michael Been (*John, Apostle*), Paul Herman (*Phillip, Apostle*), John Lurie (*James, Apostle*), Leo Burmester (*Nathaniel, Apostle*), Andre Gregory (*John The Baptist*), Peggy Gormley (*Martha, Sister of Lazarus*), Randy Danson (*Mary, Sister of Lazarus*), Robert Spafford (*Man at Wedding*), Doris Von Thury (*Woman with Mary, Mother of Jesus*), Tomas Arana (*Lazarus/Voice in Crowd*), Alan Rosenberg (*Thomas, Apostle*), Del Russel (*Money Changer*), Nehemiah Persoff (*Rabbi*), Donald Hodson (*Saducee*), Harry Dean Stanton (*Saul/Paul*), Peter Berling (*Beggar*), David Bowie (*Pontius Pilate*), Juliette Caton (*Girl Angel*), Mohammed Mabsout, Ahmed Nacir,

Mokhtar Salouf, Mahamed Ait Fdil Ahmed (*Other Apostles*), Russel Case, Mary Seller, Donna Magnani – credited as Donna Marie – (*People At Sermon*), Penny Brown, Gabi Ford, Dale Wyatt, Domenico Fiore, Ted Rusoff, Leo Damian, Robert Laconi, Jonathan Zhivago, Illeana Douglas, David Sharp (*Voices in Crowd*), Khalid Benghrib, Redouane Farhane, Fabienne Panciatilli, Naima Skikes, Souad Rahal, Otmane Chbani Idrissi, Jamal Belkhayat (*Dancers*).

UNCREDITED CAST: Leo Marks, Martin Scorsese (*Voice of Temptation/Satan*).

TITLES: A quote from the introduction to Kazantzakis's book precedes the film, followed by a card which states that: 'This film is not based upon the Gospels but upon this fictional exploration of the eternal spiritual conflict.' A black and red print of thorns appears, with credits lettering in white. The black fades out to leave a blood-red background.

SUMMARY: Jesus, a carpenter from Nazareth, is tormented by voices telling him he is wanted for a great purpose by God. Unwilling to be anything other than a normal man, Jesus tries to prove himself unworthy of such a task by building crucifixion crosses for the Romans, but the voices continue to come, like birds digging their claws into his mind. An old friend, Judas, has begun working with the zealots, plotting against the Romans and working to undermine their rule. He is disgusted by Jesus, calling him a collaborator – as the Romans can find no other person to make their crosses. After another crucifixion, Jesus tells his mother, Mary, that he's certain that God loves him, and is trying to speak with him, but that he wants to be left alone, so he annoys Him by building the crosses. Mary asks if he's sure it's God's voice he hears. If it's the devil, he can be cast out. Jesus notes that if it's God, then He cannot be cast out.

He decides to leave home to clear his mind, but on the way he has another attack, and this time the voices tell him he must go to Mary Magdalene. Jesus goes to Mary Magdalene's room and waits outside as all nations of man take turns to have sex with her. By late evening the room is empty and Jesus finally steps forward. Mary is shocked to see him there and wraps herself up. There, he tells her he's going to the desert and needs her to forgive him before he leaves. Tears well up in her eyes and she tells him to go away. But Jesus stays and waits patiently with her. She says she remembers when they were children, and the tenderness she felt for him. All she ever wanted was him. She asks him to stay. She promises not to touch him, but he tells her he cannot stay.

In the desert he meets an old man, praying for the recently deceased Master of the Monastery. He invites Jesus to rest in his hut, then confesses that he knows who Jesus is. After he has rested, Jesus joins the mourners and is shocked to discover that the man who is dead is the man who had invited Jesus to rest there and learns from Jeroboam, one of the mourners, that the Master was dead at the time of Jesus's arrival. Jeroboam sits and chats with his guest. Jesus later tells him that he is convinced Lucifer is inside him, telling him he is not the son of King David, he is not a man, he is the son of man, the son of God – and God himself. That night, Jesus is visited by a pair of coiled snakes who speak to him in the voice of Mary Magdalene, telling him she forgives him. Then, witnessed by Jeroboam, the serpents recoil. Jeroboam explains that Jesus's sins have been purified and encourages him to leave the monastery.

Judas finds Jesus with the intent of killing him on the orders of the zealots, but after Jesus tells him that God brought them together for some reason, he recognises the change in Jesus. Cautiously Judas tells him that he'll accompany him until he understands what brought about the change, but that if he strays from the path he'll kill him.

Jesus intervenes in the stoning of Mary Magdalene, picking up some stones and challenging the assembly, asking them which of them has never sinned. An old man, Zebedee comes forward and says he has nothing to hide, but as he prepares to throw the stone Jesus warns him to be careful. He warns him that God knows how Zebedee cheats his workers and consorts with a widow. Zebedee drops the stone and Jesus escorts Mary to safety. Crowds of people gather to hear what the Nazarene has to say. Though some of the crowd dismiss his preaching as 'children's stories', others are convinced enough to follow him. Despite this, Jesus confides in Judas that he still has doubts about his new calling. Judas suggests he goes to see John the Baptist. Jesus finds John, an old preacher, surrounded by the newly baptised in ecstatic reverie. After John baptises him, the two men debate their contrasting views on God's intention. John insists that he must use an axe to cut down evil, whereas Jesus believes Love is stronger. To settle the discussion, John tells the young man he should go out into the desert until God sends him the answers to his questions.

Leaving behind his apostles, Jesus walks for days until finally he finds a spot, draws a circle and says he will not leave until God speaks to him in human words, promising he'll take any path God wants. He sits down. And waits. As the days become weeks, Jesus is visited by a serpent, who offers him life with a wife, then a lion who offers him a kingdom, and finally a pillar of fire that offers him power over life and death if only he will sit alongside the unseen demon. The pillar turns into an apple tree. Jesus plucks an apple and bites into it, but it is full of blood. The flame then returns and threatens that they will see each other again. Jesus throws the apple at the flames and they extinguish once more. In the dust, he finds an axe. A vision of John the Baptist appears. He tells him not to be afraid, that he is The One, and that John's work is done now and he can die. After over a month, Jesus returns to the town starving and weakened. He stumbles into the home of two sisters, Mary and Martha, who take him in and feed him. Mary asks him how he can live in the desert, and if he missed having a home. Jesus is touched by the kindness of the women. But then he learns that John the Baptist is dead, killed by Herod on a whim.

In hiding after the execution of the Baptist, the apostles argue among themselves about the best course of action. Suddenly Jesus is with them. He invites them to join him in a war against Satan. Then he reaches inside his chest and pulls out his heart. He tells them to take it. God is inside them all, he says, but the devil is all around and they will fight him wherever he is: in the sick; in the rich; even in the temple. With his disciples, Jesus returns to Nazareth to preach that the people should give away their wealth and follow him, but his words are not well received, with one man saying that he made better crosses than he makes speeches. Nevertheless, some of the people join him: the poor, the crippled and the needy. As he leaves Nazareth, his mother, Mary runs after him but he claims not to know her. She breaks down crying.

Jesus learns of the death of Lazarus, the brother of Mary and Martha. Though Lazarus has been dead for three days, Jesus orders for the stone to his tomb to be rolled away. At the mouth of the tomb, Jesus commands Lazarus in the name of the most Holy God and calls to him. A hand leaps from the tomb. Jesus pulls Lazarus from the tomb, alive.

Eventually, they reach Jerusalem, but Jesus is disgusted to find the temples full of merchants and money changers. In a rage, he tips over every table and casts the money into the air. The rabbis criticise him, saying they will not allow Roman coins that depict false gods into the temple, that they must be exchanged for shekels, but Jesus tells them they shouldn't be taking the money anyway – he has come to put an end to the old laws and bring new ones. Then, to the shock of all, he explains that when he talks of himself he really means God, and that God isn't for just the rabbis, he's for everyone – he is *not* exclusively an Israelite. This angers the crowd and they tear at him. Some beg him to make them rich, some beg to be cured but he screams that he will not help them as they are filled with hatred. In the scuffle, Judas is pulled aside by Saul who asks why he follows the man they told him to kill. Saul's supposed to be in a war against Rome, but all he can see are Jews against Jews.

News reaches the apostles that Lazarus has been murdered by zealots. Judas tells Jesus he is not surprised – Lazarus was the only proof of his greatest miracle. Now there is nothing. Jesus tells Judas he has a terrible secret: that Isaiah came to him the previous night with a prophecy of the one who has 'borne their faults, wounded for their transgressions and did not open his mouth. Despised and rejected by all he was led like a lamb to the slaughter.' At first Judas doesn't understand until Jesus explains that it is himself who is the lamb that must die. Judas is angry, as his friend's death does not make sense. Does this mean he is not the Messiah? Jesus reassures him that he is, that God only lets him know his will a bit at a time. He realises he has been followed all his life by a shadow – the cross. He must die on the cross willingly.

The apostles are confused. Some await the New Jerusalem with excitement, though they don't really understand what it means. Some are scared, knowing how horrific the crucifixion is. Some are angry. Peter goes to Jesus to ask if angels will greet them. Jesus merely puts his arm on Peter's shoulders. They return to Jerusalem with Jesus proclaimed, by his followers at least, King of the Jews. They set about tearing down the markets from the temple. He speaks to the people and tells them that the Baptist warned them that God was coming. Well, he says, it's too late – he's here, and he's going to baptise everybody with fire. As the Jews run through the city, the guards stop them – they are surrounded. Jesus freezes, awaiting a sign from God, and his apostles panic, waiting for him to lead them. They stare as his palms begin to bleed. Jesus faints and, having had their expectations raised, the people turn ugly. They escape as the guards enter the city to quell the riots.

Jesus tells Judas he wishes there was another way but there isn't – he must die on the cross. He says that without that there can be no sacrifice and without Judas there can be no redemption. Judas says he won't let him die, that he is not strong enough. He tells him the temple guards will be looking for him, and it's up to Judas to lead them to him. He will die, but after three days he will rise again to victory. Judas asks if the situations were reversed could Jesus betray his master and Jesus confesses not, which is why God gave him the easier job – to be crucified. That night, the followers meet for the last time. He asks them to share bread and wine – this is his body and blood. Jesus looks to Judas, who takes this as a sign to leave. Though Peter tells Judas they are not finished, but Jesus says to let him go. After the meal, Jesus prays, begging God for another way, anything other than death. Judas returns with the guards and Jesus is arrested.

Jesus is questioned by Pontius Pilate, who observes that he can change how people live, but that Jesus wants to change how people think, which in many ways is more dangerous. He leaves Jesus to the guards, who beat and whip him and then push a crown of thorns on to his head. Wearing just a loin cloth, he is forced to carry his own cross-bar through the streets while the people laugh at him. Stripped naked, he is nailed to a cross and raised up to hang before the people. He becomes aware of two other men crucified beside him. A great wind whips up, and he cries out 'Father, why have you forsaken me?'

. . . but then – silence. He looks down to see a small child staring at him. She says she is an angel who guards him, sent down to Earth to save him. The angel removes the crown of thorns, pulls the nails from him and brings him down, kissing his wounds. She leads him from the cross and tells him sadly that he does not need to die for he is not the Messiah. She takes him to his marriage – Mary Magdalene is his bride. Mary thanks God for bringing him to her and throws her arms around him tightly. She takes him to their home in a rich forest and bathes him, cleaning his wounds. As they make love, Mary already knows they will have a child. But before the child can reach full term, Mary is taken from him. Jesus is distraught but the angel says God took her when she was happy. She explains that there is but one woman in the world, but with many faces. Mary Magdalene died, but Mary, sister of Lazarus, is already bearing his child. This is how the Messiah will come, gradually. He goes to Mary and Martha.

Years go by. Passing through Bethany, Jesus overhears a preacher speaking his name. It is Saul, the former zealot. Saul tells the people about his discovery of the truth, that he had once been a murderer in God's name, but now he preaches the word of Jesus, who, he says, was crucified and rose again. Jesus is angry, calling Saul a liar, but Saul confidently tells him that the resurrected Jesus is what people need to believe in. Jesus warns him he'll tell people the truth. Saul points out that people need God. They'd die for him. All for the sake of Christ.

Jesus grows old. The angel tells him he's done well. They've both done well. Just then, Mary and Martha come running into the house – the Romans are killing everyone. On his deathbed, Jesus is visited by the apostles Peter, Nathaniel and John, followed by Judas. Judas calls Jesus a traitor, reminding him that his place was on the cross, where God put him. They did what they were supposed to do, but Jesus chose the coward's path. He was going to be the new covenant. Now there is no new Israel. Jesus tells him an angel came to him to save him. But then the angel turns into a pillar of flames and Jesus realises he has been tricked. He falls to the floor and crawls to the hill where he should have died and prays to his Father. He begs for forgiveness for not fighting hard enough, and realises that he wants to bring salvation, he wants to pay the price, to be crucified and rise again, to be the Messiah. Suddenly he is back on the cross. He smiles with happiness, with joy and cries out 'It is accomplished!'

WHO'S WHO?: Willem Dafoe appeared in Oliver Stone's Vietnam films *Platoon* (1986) and *Born on the Fourth of July* (1989), Alan Parker's *Mississippi Burning* (1988) and, as the Green Goblin, in Sam Raimi's *Spider-Man* (2002). Character actor Harry Dean Stanton holds the dubious boast that he's been killed in most of his movies, which include *Alien* (Ridley Scott, 1979), *Escape from New York* (John Carpenter, 1981), *Wild at Heart* (David Lynch, 1990) and *The Green Mile* (Frank Darabond, 1999). King of Pop David Bowie isn't as highly regarded for his acting as his singing. Nevertheless he has made some significant contributions to cinema, starring in *The Man Who Fell to Earth* (Nicolas Roeg, 1976), *Merry Christmas Mr Lawrence* (Nagisa Oshima, 1983) and *Labyrinth* (Jim Henson, 1986).

Poet and actor Roberts Blossom played Robert Redford's father in *The Great Gatsby* (Jack Clayton, 1974), and Macaulay Culkin's elderly neighbour in *Home Alone* (Chris Columbus, 1990). Barry Miller played Ralph Garcy, the would-be comedian in *Fame* (Alan Parker, 1980) and science genius Richard Norvick in *Peggy Sue Got Married* (Francis Ford Coppola, 1986). Irvin Kershner was the director of *The Empire Strikes Back* (1980), as well as *The Eyes of Laura Mars* (1978) and the 'unofficial' Bond movie *Never Say Never Again* (1983). Alan Rosenberg may be familiar to viewers of Cybill Shepherd's sitcom *Cybill*, in which he played her ex-husband, Ira. Nehemiah Persoff provided the voice of Papa Mousekewitz in *An American Tail* (Don Bluth, 1986) and its many sequels.

One of the most interesting examples of unusual casting is Leo Marks, who gives voice to Satan in the picture. Marks was a cryptographer who worked for the Special Operations Executive during World War II. Also a playwright, Marks scripted Michael Powell's controversial film *Peeping Tom* (1959), which all but finished off Powell as a film-maker due to its subject matter. Marks also became a close friend of New York

writer Helene Hanff. Hanff had corresponded with the staff of Marks &
Co, a bookshop owned by Marks's father, and subsequently turned her
letters into the book *84 Charing Cross Road*. Marks appeared in a
number of Hanff's later books detailing her trips to London after the
shop's closure. In 1978, Martin Scorsese oversaw the re-release of
Peeping Tom, when it was re-evaluated and praised by critics. As a
somewhat unusual tribute, Scorsese invited Marks to play the voice of
Satan in *The Last Temptation of Christ*.

Paul Herman played Beansie Gaeta in *The Sopranos*, in the episodes
'Full Leather Jacket' and 'Toodle-Fucking-Oo'.

THE USUAL SUSPECTS: Barbara Hershey (*Boxcar Bertha*); Victor
Argo (*Boxcar Bertha, Mean Streets, Taxi Driver, After Hours*); Harvey
Keitel (*Street Scenes, Who's That Knocking At My Door?, Mean Streets,
Alice Doesn't Live Here Anymore, Taxi Driver*); Verna Bloom (*After
Hours*); Paul Herman (*The Color of Money, New York Stories,
GoodFellas, Casino*); Illeana Douglas (*New York Stories*: 'Life Lessons',
GoodFellas, Cape Fear, Grace of My Heart); writer Paul Schrader (*Taxi
Driver, Raging Bull, Bringing Out the Dead*); producer Barbara De Fina
(*The Color of Money, Bad, New York Stories*: 'Life Lessons', *The
Grifters, Made in Milan, GoodFellas, Cape Fear, Mad Dog and Glory,
The Age of Innocence, Casino, Kundun, My Voyage to Italy, Bringing
Out the Dead, Dino*); editor Thelma Schoonmaker (*Who's That
Knocking At My Door?, Street Scenes, Raging Bull, The King of
Comedy, After Hours, The Color of Money, Bad, New York Stories,
GoodFellas, Cape Fear, Age of Innocence, Casino, A Personal Journey
with Martin Scorsese Through American Movies, Kundun, Bringing Out
the Dead, My Voyage to Italy, Gangs of New York*).

SOURCE: Controversy over this retelling of the Christ tale did not begin
with Scorsese. *The Last Temptation of Christ* almost led to
Kazantzakis's excommunication from the Greek Orthodox Church. The
novel was placed on the Roman Catholic Index of Forbidden Books, and
Protestant fundamentalist groups in the United States tried to have it
banned from libraries (thereby helping to make it a best-seller). Yet
Kazantzakis was a serious spiritual seeker. His search took him through
Bergson, Nietzsche, Buddha, Mussolini, Marx, and Lenin, but ultimately
all roads led him back to Christ. The latter part of his career was devoted
to an exploration of Christian concepts, not only in *The Last
Temptation* . . . but also in other novels, including *The Greek Passion*
(1951), in which a Greek village under Turkish occupation becomes

involved in staging a Passion Play, and *St Francis* (1956). *The Last Temptation of Christ* is prefaced with his remarkable statement of spiritual and artistic purpose, an excerpt of which Scorsese uses to introduce the film.

A number of differences between the book and the finished film are apparent, not least of which is the tone. Kazantzakis's book is written more in the style of Magical Realism, where the supernatural and the everyday co-exist, as if a dream. Significantly, Jesus is described less like the traditional Western view that Scorsese went for: 'His nose was hooked, his lips thick . . . [His eyes] were large and black, full of light, full of darkness.' Jesus's mother is described as being a young woman, for she was little more than a child when she married the elderly Joseph. Joseph was struck by lightning and crippled before they could consummate their marriage, leaving Mary an embittered woman looking after an infirm old husband and a son who might well be mad or possessed. After Jesus and Magdalene are married, Kazantzakis has Mary murdered by Saul the zealot, instead of disappearing in a beam of white light as in the film (in Schrader's first draft, though Mary Magdalene is still killed at the hands of a man, it is not specified whose hands these are).

PRODUCTION: After completing *The King of Comedy*, Scorsese began preparing for this project he'd been considering since he made *Boxcar Bertha* in 1972. Barbara Hershey and David Carradine, the stars of *Bertha*, had introduced Scorsese to Nikos Kazantzakis's novel, *The Last Temptation . . .*, but he'd taken years to finish reading it simply because, so he claims, he was enjoying it so much he didn't want it to end. Scorsese was drawn to a portrayal of the human Christ who had to struggle with fleshly desires and limitations. It is the gradual assimilation of Jesus the man into Jesus the Christ, the quenching of all earthly fears and longings in the movement towards union with God, that brings out the meaning of the Cross. Scorsese talked to Paul Schrader about the book during their collaboration on *Taxi Driver*, but it took the director until 1980 before the rights to the book were his. Considering Schrader's Calvinist upbringing, Scorsese felt he might have an interesting take on the novel. The pair discussed the script and decided to make the dialogue less stylised than normal and have the characters speaking in easily understood contemporary language. After four months, Schrader delivered a ninety-page script that had successfully pared down the epic novel. Schrader had written a script that acknowledged the supernatural – Christ literally baring his heart, and encouraging his disciples to eat his flesh and drink his blood – as well as adding elements that he knew would be controversial, such as the embrace between John the Baptist and Jesus which goes into detail, via a voice-over, to tell us that the Baptist's tongue was like 'hot coal in my mouth'. Schrader confessed, however, that much of this was just a Calvinist teasing his Catholic friend and in subsequent drafts the scenes had been removed or toned down.

United Artists passed on the script, but Scorsese managed to get Paramount to agree to take on the picture, with Irwin Winkler and Bob Chartoff as producers. Scorsese worked for nine months on casting and location hunting in different countries, including Morocco, but finally settled on Israel after receiving a hearty and enthusiastic welcome from the Mayor of Jerusalem. Paramount's executives were nervous about the idea of a well-known director filming outside Hollywood, let alone outside the USA. Michael Cimino's three-hour Western, *Heaven's Gate*, had left everyone worried by spiralling budgets. But Scorsese stood his ground and managed to persuade them to give him a $12 million budget and a ninety-day shooting schedule.

Already cast were Barbara Hershey as Mary Magdalene, Harvey Keitel as Judas, British popstar Sting as Pontius Pilate, Lew Ayres as an angel and Aidan Quinn (who would later appear in Susan Seidelman's *Desperately Seeking Susan*) as Christ. Schrader had written the script with De Niro in mind as Christ, aware that he and the director worked well together, though De Niro felt he wouldn't be right for the part. But after nine months' preparation, Scorsese and Winkler calculated that they'd need another $2–4 million and an extra ten weeks to complete the picture. By then Irwin Winkler – whose partnership with Bob Chartoff was coming to an end – had decided that he couldn't produce the picture. Without a producer attached, Paramount had simply lost interest. This, coupled with the campaigns from religious groups against the picture, forced Paramount's hand. Despite having already spent $5 million on sets in Israel, *The Last Temptation of Christ* was dropped from the production schedules. Scorsese scrambled to revise his budget, make it at half the cost and in half the time, but was turned away from every studio.

With Schrader's permission, and on the understanding they would not receive a co-writer's credit, Jay Cocks and Scorsese began to rewrite the script with a mind to a film with a much lower budget than Schrader had been briefed for. Over the years, they produced six drafts of the script. The possibility of a co-production with French funding arose after the French Minister of Culture, Jack Lang, offered his support to any non-French film-makers of standing. Predictably, the offer was damaged by pressure from the Archbishop of Paris, Cardinal Lustiger, who warned President Mitterand not to fund potentially blasphemous works. After the recent scandal over Godard's *Je Vous Salue, Marie*, the French government was understandably nervous of causing more offence. Then offers were made to film the picture in Egypt, or Greece.

At about this time, Scorsese decided to change agents, leaving Harry Ufland, who he'd been with for twenty years, and moving to CAA with the infamous Michael Ovitz. Ovitz began to speak to people at Universal Studios, one of the only studios Scorsese had yet to work with, and gained the interest of Tom Pollock. Together they convinced Cineplex Odeon, the biggest cinema chain in the USA, to put up half the budget to get the picture under way. By April 1987, Scorsese was scouting new locations. By the end of the year, *The Last Temptation of Christ* was finally under way.

There was still the matter of appeasing Paramount, who had yet to recoup their initial investment. But in the meantime, Scorsese and Cocks began working on a further two rewrites of the script. Scorsese's original choice for Christ, Aidan Quinn, was now unavailable, having just completed a troublesome shoot in the Seychelles on *Crusoe* (Caleb Deschanel, 1988) and about to marry. He then considered Eric Roberts, who had recently won an Oscar for *Runaway Train*, and Christopher Walken. But Willem Dafoe won the part, largely because of his appearances in *Platoon* and *To Live and Die in L.A.* Most of Scorsese's original choices were recalled, with the exception of Sting, who was committed to one of the fund-raising tours for Amnesty International. Pontius Pilot would instead be played by fellow popstar David Bowie. Bowie would be on set for just two days: one to rehearse, one to film his short scene.

By September 1983, the sets were built, and filming was finally ready to begin. Dafoe's first scene to be filmed was his journey into the desert. He was worried about the number of scorpions he had seen. With Dafoe in almost every scene of the film, there was tremendous pressure on him throughout the shoot. Scorsese insisted that he should not be seen to be smoking in case someone took his photograph and the image of him as 'Christ' might be ruined. But it was a tough shoot for Dafoe for other reasons. Firstly, he came down with a fever the night before he shot the scene with the cobras at the monastery. Next, to give him a look of madness after his return from the wilderness, one of the make-up artists used eye-drops on him; unfortunately the measures were wrong and Dafoe spent three days unable to see. Locations included Oumnast, a village outside Marrakesh, the Atlas Mountains and around the Roman ruins of Volubilis. Jesus's baptism was filmed high in the hills to avoid upsetting the Moroccan authorities with the nudity, while the temple scenes were filmed in Meknes. During these scenes Dafoe was nervous about the possibility of injuring someone as he ransacked the temple. Despite reassurances from the crew that everything would be OK, Dafoe did indeed end up accidentally injuring Michael Ballhaus – he threw a gold plate which collided with Ballhaus's head.

In creating the illusion of the talking animals during the first temptations, it was initially suggested that an animatronic snake might be a solution. In the end, both the snakes and the lion were simply filmed and then overdubbed in post-production by Hershey and Keitel. For the third temptation, Scorsese wanted something elemental. He initially considered a beam of light, but realised the connotations of that would be misleading, so he selected a pillar of fire. The voice of Satan was created by combining Scorsese's own voice with that of Leo Marks.

In the temple scene where Jesus and his apostles are surrounded by guards, Scorsese had been hampered by bad weather and was in a rush to complete the scene. He had just five stuntmen to create the illusion of an army surrounding the temple, so he used flash pans to sweep up to the scene to disguise the fact that in each scene it was the same five men. At a time when Bertolucci was making *The Last Emperor* and Spielberg was making *Empire of the Sun,* Scorsese couldn't help but feel resentful at the scale of their extras budget compared to his own.

Having created his storyboards and worked out the amount of set-ups that would be required, the challenge for Scorsese was to see just how quickly they could capture each required shot. They began setting up many shots in the early-morning darkness so that as soon as the light came up they began working their way through the shot-list, with a time limit on each one.

The crucifixion scenes would cause more misery for Dafoe, who would be hoisted up in five-minute sets. The crucifix was made with a small seat for Dafoe to sit on, and false fronts to show the nails through his hands and feet. The longest shot, where the camera tilts horizontal, took about an hour to set up, and was difficult because Ballhaus wasn't able to check through the viewfinder to see if the shot had turned out. The final shot of the film flickering through the camera was, surprisingly, not intentional. The camera used to film this scene was faulty and light leaked on to the film, causing a white-out at the exact point in the scene at which Jesus expires, and this was not discovered until the film was processed. Serendipity or divine intervention? It provided them with a unique ending to a difficult production.

EDITING: How unlikely is the idea of an interpretation of the life of Christ made in the style of *GoodFellas*? Yet many of the techniques Scorsese and Schoonmaker employ here are familiar from their other collaborations. In the first scene, the camera zooms through the groves like we have seen it do through boxing rings and pool halls. The strange multiple lap-dissolve over the traveller dismounting from his camel, which would traditionally denote the passage of time, here serves to show us how Jesus sees things differently. Later, we see Jesus and his disciples walk through a crowd of possessed people, and their approach through the throng is filmed almost like a posse coming into a Western town. And as Mary Magdalene works her way through a roomful of punters, we see a pale-skinned man on top of her, then a cut to a black-skinned hand denotes the change of partner. Compare this to the wedding scene in *GoodFellas* where Karen is handed money from the wedding guests, with the hands and faces not matching to speed up the line.

MUSIC: Robbie Robertson first introduced Scorsese to Peter Gabriel in 1983. Scorsese invited him to compose the soundtrack of *The Last Temptation of Christ*; even after the production was scrapped, Gabriel continued to develop ideas, confident the picture could be revived at a later date. Scorsese had already recommended some sounds to him, including Sardinian shepherds and the Moroccan group Nas El Ghiwane. When the film was recommenced, Gabriel created the score from his studio in Bath, UK, before taking the raw materials to New York to fine tune in collaboration with Scorsese and Schoonmaker. The opening came from Armenian doudouk, a piece of music that Gabriel found at the British National Sound Archive called 'The Wind Subsides'. The rhythm had come from Manny Elias who Gabriel had been working with for a number of years. The introduction music was originally created for another project entirely. Gabriel later released two soundtrack albums covering both his own work on the movie and the source music he appropriated.

QUOTE/UNQUOTE
Judas: 'You're worse than them [The Romans]! You're a Jew killing Jews! You're a coward! How will you ever pay for your sins?'
Jesus: 'With my life, Judas. I don't have anything else.'

Judas: 'You're not afraid of dying?'
Jesus: 'Why should I be? Death isn't a door that closes. It opens. It opens and you go through it.'

Jesus: (to John, The Baptist) 'If I was a woodcutter I'd cut, if I was a fire I'd burn but I'm a heart and I love.'

Jesus: 'You think God belongs only to you? He doesn't. God is an immortal spirit who belongs to everybody, to the whole world. You think you're special? God is not an Israelite.'

ROOTS: The decision to cast British voices as the Romans was inspired by *Ben Hur* (William Wyler, 1958). In fact, Scorsese spent many years studying earlier versions of the story of Christ: both Cecil B De Mille's and Nicholas Ray's versions of *The King of Kings* (1927, 1961), *Quo Vadis* (Mervyn LeRoy, 1951), *The Robe* (Henry Koster, 1953), *The Greatest Story Ever Told* (George Stevens, 1965), *The Bible . . . In The Beginning* (John Ford, 1966), *Barrabas* (Richard Fleischer, 1964), and *The Gospel According to St Matthew* (Pier Paolo Pasolini, 1964).

Mary Magdelene's tattoos were inspired by an article in *National Geographic*. Research had shown that tattoos were common among Arabic women, though not those from respectable Jewish houses. Boris Leven had done extensive production design work for the cancelled 1983 production. He'd shown Scorsese a picture of Hieronymous Bosch's painting *The Ghent Christ Carrying The Cross*. The influence of this work can be seen when Christ carries the cross through small, narrow streets and the faces of the crowd seem to adopt the two-dimensional nature of Bosch's painting. Antonello da Messina's *Crucifixion*, which shows Christ on a long, high cross, flanked by the two thieves who are tied to trees. Scorsese and his team also examined texts from the *Jewish Encyclopaedia* and the *Biblical Archaeology Review* as well as, predictably, consulting the Shroud of Turin, one of a number of artefacts believed by some to have direct connections with Christ. The crucifixion scenes draw heavily on Scorsese's own work, specifically the crucifixion scene at the end of *Boxcar Bertha* (1972).

Jay Cocks notes how, being city boys, he and Scorsese looked at the film almost as a Western and, indeed, when Jesus returns from the desert, the shot of him framed in the doorway is a nod to *The Searchers*. In the scene where the Romans surround Christ and his followers in the temple, the guards are directed in a similar way to the guards from *The Wizard of Oz*.

THEMES AND MOTIFS: Mary Magdalene's reaction to Jesus, telling him to leave, recalls The Girl's response to JR's insensitivity in *Who's That Knocking . . .* while the crucifixions are both filmed to match the similar shots in *Boxcar Bertha*. Comparisons also abound in the red-soaked scene where Jesus reveals his heart to his disciples with the scene where the mobsters in *GoodFellas* bury the body of Billy Batts, illuminated by their car's rear lights.

KEEP IT IN THE FAMILY: Verna Bloom is the wife of (uncredited) co-screenwriter Jay Cocks.

LEGACY: A title like this really is prime for spoofing, and so that year we found ourselves with *The Toxic Avenger Part III: The Last Temptation of Toxie* (Michael Hertz, Lloyd Kaufman, 1989). In the HBO mob drama *The Sopranos*, Carmela Soprano cites the picture as one of her all-time favourites.

TRIVIA: Some historians claim Pontius Pilate was born in Scotland, where his father was posted as a Roman Centurion guard. On hearing this, Scottish comedian Billy Connolly tried (and failed) to convince David Bowie to play Pontius Pilate as a Scotsman.

AWARDS: Scorsese was nominated for an Academy Award for best director, but lost out to the less controversial Barry Levinson for *Rain Man* (which starred Tom Cruise and Dustin Hoffman). Barbara Hershey was nominated at the Golden Globes for Best Performance by an Actress in a Supporting Role, and Peter Gabriel was nominated for best score. At the 'Razzies' (The Golden Raspberry Awards), Harvey Keitel was cruelly nominated for worst supporting actor. Maybe they didn't like his hair.

AVAILABILITY: MCA Home Video's laserdisc release was a rather bare pan-and-scan affair. Compare this to the Criterion Collection's version, which contained an audio commentary by Scorsese, Paul Schrader and Jay Cocks, production stills, research materials and costume design galleries, location footage shot by Scorsese, and an exclusive interview with Peter Gabriel talking about his score for the movie. A similar situation to the laserdisc releases: Columbia TriStar Home Video's DVD version (available in Europe) is a decent enough anamorphic widescreen transfer accompanied by a trailer; however, the Criterion Collection (which, though released in the USA is region coding-free, meaning it can be viewed on most DVD players) contains all the materials from the Criterion laserdisc, but with an added 5.1 Dolby Stereo soundtrack. A fullscreen VHS version is also available.

WHAT THE CRITICS SAID: Amidst the outrage over the filming of the controversial book, the critics seemed more perturbed by the accents, with *Time Out* calling the dialogue 'astonishingly banal' and saying that, 'Scorsese fails to illuminate the soul of Christ – essentially what the film is all about. Nevertheless,' the reviewer conceded, 'it remains a sincere, typically ambitious and imaginative work from America's most provocatively intelligent filmmaker.'

EXPERT WITNESSES: 'When you think of Marty, everyone always thinks of him as The Actor's Director, because of his collaboration with great actors and his films always have great performances in, certainly his association with De Niro for example. He is a great actor's director but what surprised me was he's not in the way that you'd think he'd be. He's a dream for an actor because he gives you such a complete world and such a complete set-up. Maybe it's specific to this role but in many, many ways I felt so guided by him, so protected and so excited by what we were doing, but there was very little discussion when I think back to it, everything became very practical. There was a logic to it that doesn't always mean simple; you knew what you had to do and you did it.' Willem Dafoe (*Jesus*).

'I thought we were going to change the world – and we did in some ways. In the way religious people viewed the relationship between Judas and Jesus. There's more to the story of what made him betray Jesus than what I had read. People have been steered down a narrow, bigoted road. It was important to make the film to help people bridge the gap between Christianity and Judaism and perhaps to overcome their prejudices that exist because they've been fed the line that Judas betrayed Jesus.' Harvey Keitel (*Judas*).

FINAL ANALYSIS: A genuine labour of love, and one that marked Scorsese's move towards . . . acceptance in Hollywood as his patience and resilience had won through. *The Last Temptation* is, not surprisingly, a difficult movie for a Catholic to watch, but only because of the burden of guilt that comes with it, like the pictures Scorsese himself struggled with as a teenager, knowing they were 'forbidden fruits'. It's a film that invites us to question the traditional teachings and blind faith and, in the process, actually encourages a deeper understanding of the supreme sacrifice Christ made.

SCORSESE ON *THE LAST TEMPTATION OF CHRIST*: 'It was supposed to be nothing more than what they call an Art movie in

America. It's the kind of movie that should be played in one little theatre in New York, LA, Chicago maybe, Toronto, for about six, seven months. The performers are good, the music is great – Peter Gabriel – the camerawork's terrific, the clothes are terrific, the production design – all that. And I just hope it can be viewed as a movie these days because the controversy that was stirred up by its release kind of overshadows the fact that it's a movie also. A *long* movie – two hours and forty-two minutes, but there was a lot to say. I guess I got hung up on the Catholic iconography of the crucifixion, the Last Supper. I mean, it would have been much quicker if I'd have cut out the Last Supper but I kind of like the fact that it's the Covenant. The cup of wine goes from person to person, then the bread goes from person to person and the music is on the soundtrack but I kind of enjoy that.'

Testament of Faith:
The Battle for The Last Temptation

As soon as *The Last Temptation of Christ* was first announced, the religious organisations of America were campaigning against it, telephoning key individuals at Gulf and Western, who owned Paramount, and asking them why they were making such an offensive picture.

In 1988, as Scorsese was finally making *The Last Temptation of Christ*, with Universal Pictures and Cineplex Odeon, people were baying for the destruction of the film before it had even begun. Protests came from fundamentalists who had read an earlier version of the script by Paul Schrader (for the version planned with Paramount Pictures), a version Scorsese suspected, from actors who had auditioned for the original production back in 1983. In January 1988, Universal hired born-again Christian Tim Penland, head of a marketing company that specialised in fundamental issues, as a consultant on the film. But he resigned some five months later, complaining that Universal had broken their promise to screen a cut of the picture to fundamentalists. Universal explained that Scorsese was behind schedule, but that they expected to see a finished film just one month later.

By the time of the film's completion, the chairman of MCA (Universal's parent company), Lew Wasserman, was under attack for discrediting the Jewish faith by supporting the film. Evangelist Bill Bright offered to compensate Universal for their costs if they would hand over the film for destruction. Scorsese felt compelled to issue a statement: 'My film was made with deep religious feeling. I have been working on this film for fifteen years; it is more than just another film project for me. I believe it is a religious film about suffering and the struggle to find God. It was made with conviction and love, and so I believe it is an affirmation of faith, not a denial. Further, I feel strongly that people everywhere will be able to identify with the human side of Jesus as well as his divine side.'

Universal also issued a statement confirming their support for the picture, expressing the hope that the public would give the film a fair chance.

On 16 July 1988, Reverend RL Hymers led two hundred members of the Fundamentalist Baptist Tabernacle of Los Angeles in a picket of Universal Studios, decrying the company with banners that claimed 'Universal are like Judas Iscariot' and that the film was 'The Greatest Story Ever Distorted'. The American Family Association (who had been behind the campaign that stopped the film from being made by Paramount five years earlier) contacted 170,000 pastors across the USA in their bid to halt the film being released. When the film was eventually screened for a selected audience of religious leaders in New York, Tim Penland held a press conference attacking the film and rejecting any need to see it for himself. However, Reverend William Fore of the National Council of Churches declared on television that the picture was 'just an idea which should be debated openly', and the Episcopal Bishop of New York, Paul Moore, said that he saw nothing blasphemous about it, but other leaders were not so open-minded.

On 27 July, Mother Angelica, head of the Eternal Word TV Network, described the film as 'the most satanic movie ever made' and claimed it would destroy Christianity (prompting Jack Valenti, president of the MPAA, to argue that it was unlikely that one film could destroy an entire faith). In Britain, campaigner Mary Whitehouse threatened to invoke the laws regarding blasphemy (and having done so against a gay magazine in 1977, she was certainly taken seriously), while Cardinal Basil Hume was advised to persuade Catholics not to see the film. However, the British Board of Film Classification decided to pass the film with an 18 certificate, angering Whitehouse, who announced her intention to convince local councils to ban the film. London Transport refused to allow the poster to be shown on any of their billboards.

The picture was scheduled to be released on 23 September. But then the decision was made to bring its release forward to 12 August, with MCA chairman Tom Pollock making a statement that he felt the best thing all round was to make the picture available to the American public and let them make up their own minds. This had the effect of sending the Christian campaigners into panic. Across the country, religious leaders stepped forward to add their voice to the groundswell of opinion against Universal. The US Catholic Conference decided that the film should not be viewed by any of its 40 million followers.

In New York, extra police had to be called to restrain over a thousand protestors outside the Cineplex Odeon Ziegfeld cinema. Despite protests springing up across the country, the campaigns backfired somewhat as wherever the protestors went the film was shown to sell-out houses. However, four major chains declined to screen the picture, and in Salt Lake City, a screen was slashed and the print stolen, presumably to be burned. On 28 September, *The Last Temptation of Christ* opened in France to violent demonstrations. The film was banned in Israel, and in Greece, where Kazantzakis's novel had been listed as a forbidden book for over thirty years. Yet, in West Germany, it was granted an 'especially outstanding' classification, and in Ireland, with its mainly Catholic population, the film was passed on the condition that no one was admitted after the film had started, in case they missed the declaration at the beginning regarding the film's status as a work of fiction. After two months on release, *The Last Temptation of Christ* had grossed around $8 million, boosted in no small part by the protests. The following spring, the picture received a low-key video release.

Armani Commercial II (1988)

(35 mm – 20 sec – colour)

Production Company: Emporio Armani
Producer: Barbara De Fina
Director: Martin Scorsese
Screenplay: Martin Scorsese
Cinematography: Michael Ballhaus

CAST: Jens Peter, Elisabetha Ranella.

SUMMARY: A woman searches a man's apartment to confront him over a photograph she has found of him with another woman. He hides, watching her, before he picks up his coat and leaves undiscovered. As he leaves, he knocks over a bottle of perfume. The woman scours the apartment for him. All that is left is the bottle of perfume, which she brings to her face.

PRODUCTION: Scorsese managed to film this small vignette of domestic disharmony in between the end of shooting and the beginning of editing *New York Stories*.

New York Stories: 'Life Lessons' (1988)

(35 mm – 44 mins (segment) – colour)

Production Company: Touchstone
Producers: Barbara De Fina, Robert Greenhut
Screenplay: Richard Price
Director of Photography: Nestor Almendros
Editor: Thelma Schoonmaker
Production Designer: Kristi Zea

Casting: Ellen Lewis
Costume Designer: John Dunn
Production Manager: Bruce S Pustin
First Assistant Director: Joseph Reidy
Second Assistant Director: Vebe Borge
Production Co-ordinator: Alesandra Cuomo
Script Supervisor: Martha Pinson
Assistant to Mr Scorsese: Julia Judge
Art Director: Wray Steven Graham
Painting by Chuck Connelly courtesy of the
Lennon/Weinberg Gallery, Paulette's work by Susan
Hambleton courtesy of the Trabia-MacAffee Gallery
Performance piece written and performed by Steve Buscemi
Costumes by Giorgio Armani

SOUNDTRACK: 'Whiter Shade of Pale', 'Conquistador' by Procul Harum; 'Politician' by Cream; 'The Right Time' by Ray Charles; 'Like a Rolling Stone' by Bob Dylan/The Band; 'It Could Happen to You' written by Johnny Burke and Jimmy Van Heusen; 'That Old Black Magic' written by Johnny Mercer & Harold Arlen; 'Stella by Starlight' written by Ned Washington and Victor Young; 'Nessun Dorma' from Puccini's *Turandot* performed by Marto del Monaco; 'Sex Kick' by Transvision Vamp; 'What Is This Thing Called Love', 'Bolero De Django' by The Hot Club of France with Django Reinhardt and Stéphane Grappelli.

CAST: Nick Nolte (*Lionel Dobie*), Patrick O'Neal (*Phillip Fowler*), Rosanna Arquette (*Paulette*), Phil Harper (*Businessman*), Kenneth J McGregor, David Cryer (*Suits*), Jesse Borrego (*Reuben Toro*), Gregorij von Leitia (*Kurt Bloom*), Steve Buscemi (*Gregory Stark*), LoNardo (*Woman at Blind Alley*), Peter Gabriel (*Himself*), Mark Boone Jr (*Hank*), Illeana Douglas (*Paulette's Friend*), Paul Mougey (*Guy at Blind Alley*), Deborah Harry (*Girl at Blind Alley*), Paul Herman, Victor Argo (*Cops*), Victor Trull (*Maitre d'*), Richard Price (*Artist at Opening*), Brigitte Bako (*Young Woman*).

UNCREDITED CAST: Michael Powell, Paul Geier.

TITLES: The logo NEW YORK STORIES appears in the night sky with a cut-out tenement block in the foreground. After the prologue, the remaining credits appear on a black background which is splattered by different colours of paint as 'Whiter Shade of Pale' plays.

SUMMARY: Lionel Dobie, celebrated modern artist, is trying to prepare for a forthcoming exhibition of new work. Finding it hard to motivate himself, he instead finds himself playing basketball, drinking and generally avoiding any work at all. The reason? His girlfriend and protégée Paulette has left him. She returns from a trip to Florida and tells him she doesn't want to be with him any more and that she will be moving out as soon as she can. She then tells him she didn't go to Florida with a girlfriend as she told him, but a man, Gregory Stark, a performance artist. Gregory dumped her, but she realises that she still doesn't want to be with Lionel. He decides that if she doesn't want to sleep with him any more then fine, but she doesn't need to move out. If she leaves, she's throwing away a good home, a studio and 'life lessons that are priceless'. He also confesses that her leaving hurts him. She finally gives in – so long as she doesn't have to sleep with him any more.

Lionel tries to work, but is distracted. He goes up to her room and wakes her up to confess that he wants to kiss her foot. She repeats that she won't sleep with him. She asks if he loves her; he says he'd do anything for her. He appraises her work, claiming that it's getting more interesting and ironic. Damned by faint praise she asks him to tell her if she's actually any good because sometimes she thinks she should just quit. He says she shouldn't care what he thinks, it's art and she should feel like she has to do it. If she feels she has to give up she can't be a real artist to begin with. Almost as soon as he's said that he feels bad about it and in private he curses himself.

Lionel talks her into accompanying him to a party. While Lionel plays to the crowd and repeats anecdotes, Paulette is interrogated by others who only speak to her because she lives with Dobie and not because they're interested in her as an artist in her own right. One man does show an interest, a young, handsome Latin man called Toro, and when Lionel sees him talking to Paulette he interrupts them and drags Paulette into a side room to warn her that people are laughing at her out there because the man is a known lothario who only comes to the shows to pick up vulnerable women. She's relieved as she thought they might be laughing at her work, but Dobie says that surely, this is worse, much to her disgust. To spite him, she leaves with Toro anyway. When Dobie gets back from the party he notes that she has taken Toro back to her room. He puts his music on loud and begins to paint, but once he's certain that Paulette's asleep he sits back in a chair and mopes.

The next evening, he leaves a dress out for her to wear to another party, but she tells him she has other plans: she wants to go to where Gregory is performing to rub his nose in it. Lionel suggests she should go with him – if she goes with her friends it'll look like a gang of schoolgirls with a crush. Gregory performs in an old railway siding with searchlights. Lionel talks her into going right up to him, to say 'hello' then just walk away, but just as she does that, some friends of Gregory's barge past and she's excluded. She feels humiliated and blames Lionel for talking her into debasing herself like that. He repeats that he loves her and he'd do anything for her. But he can't let go. As they walk through the rain, she declares that if he does love her as he says, and he'll do anything, then he should kiss a policeman on the mouth and then she will know his love is true. True to his word, he goes to kiss the policeman, but the cop, mistaking him for a drunk or a vagrant, won't let him near, so he just blows him a kiss. When he turns round he sees that Paulette didn't even wait to see what happened. She has vanished.

The next night, Paulette goes out with a friend, but Lionel follows her. Then Gregory comes in and asks how she is, inviting her to his show. Before Paulette can even reply, Lionel intervenes and calls Gregory a 'self-absorbed no-talent son-of-a-bitch'. Paulette storms out, so Lionel grabs Gregory and wrestles him to the floor. When Lionel gets home he finds Paulette preparing to leave him.

The night of Lionel's show finally arrives. In among all the other guests is a beautiful young woman who comes over to touch his hand for good luck. She introduces herself as a painter. He looks her over and is instantly attracted to her. He tells her he needs an assistant, that he offers full board and life lessons that are priceless, and flirtatiously asks if she knows anyone who needs a job. She is stunned.

WHO'S WHO?: Nick Nolte also starred in *48 Hours* (Walter Hill, 1982) opposite Eddie Murphy, *Down and Out in Beverly Hills* (Paul Mazursky, 1986) and *The Prince of Tides* (Barbra Streisand, 1991) for which he picked up an Oscar nomination. Steve Buscemi was just another bit-player until his scene-stealing performance in *Reservoir Dogs* (Quentin Tarantino, 1991). Since then he's starred as similarly slimy characters in films such as *Fargo* (Joel Coen, 1991) and *Armageddon* (Michael Bay, 1998).

THE USUAL SUSPECTS: Nick Nolte (*Cape Fear*); Peter Gabriel (*The Last Temptation of Christ*); Illeana Douglas (*The Last Temptation of Christ, GoodFellas, Cape Fear, Grace of My Heart*); editor Thelma Schoonmaker (*Who's That Knocking At My Door?, Street Scenes, Raging Bull, The King of Comedy, After Hours, The Color of Money, Bad, The Last Temptation of Christ, GoodFellas, Cape Fear, Age of Innocence,*

Casino, A Personal Journey with Martin Scorsese Through American Movies, Kundun, Bringing Out the Dead, My Voyage to Italy, Gangs of New York).

PRODUCTION: Towards the end of 1986, Woody Allen began planning an episodic picture, which he intended to direct along with some other 'name' directors. Initially, he approached Scorsese and Steven Spielberg. Allen explained his idea: that each of them would make a short film of about the same length with the loose theme of being a 'New York' story. After a few months, Steven Spielberg decided not to participate and Francis Ford Coppola came in.

Scorsese approached Richard Price to write his segment, and the pair worked on an idea that had been gestating in Scorsese's mind since the early 1970s (see **Unseen Scorsese**). It was Price who suggested making their lead character a painter, feeling that the initial idea of a writer would be too static. With his original deal with Touchstone still unfulfilled, Scorsese mentioned the project to Jeffrey Katzenberg. Katzenberg had been eager to entice Allen over to Touchstone, and after a few discussions, *New York Stories* (as the picture would be named) became Allen's first picture for the studio.

Scorsese found the production hard going. Having just returned from Europe, he went straight into two weeks of pre-production before the four-week shoot, then went straight into production on a second advert for Armani before commencing the editing on 'Life Lessons'. With Allen and Coppola's segments completed, the film was released on 1 March 1989 and eventually grossed $10.7 million at the US box office – a moderate hit, even by Woody Allen's standards.

EDITING: A curious hark back to the past is visible here, with the circular frames zooming in and out as shots change. Note the reflection in the mirror behind Paulette and Lionel as they row in the closet, with him reflected behind her, and she reflected behind him, so we get to see both sides at the same time. At the show, as we'd expect, flashbulbs from cameras mask cuts, while the sound of the flashes sounds more like guns.

QUOTE/UNQUOTE
Artist: (talking to Lionel) 'When I look at your stuff, I just wanna divorce my wife. I mean, like – thank you!'

KEEP IT IN THE FAMILY: Michael Powell was at this time the husband of editor Thelma Schoonmaker.

ROOTS: The idea of a group of film-makers collaborating on the same picture was almost certainly inspired by *Boccaccio '70* (1962), which was composed of four segments: *La Riffa* (from Vittorio De Sica), *The Temptations of Dr. Antonio* (from Federico Fellini), *Renzo and Luciana* (from Mario Monicelli) and *Il Lavoro* (from Luchino Visconti). Scorsese's episode is a liberal reworking of Dostoevsky's *The Gambler*.

WHAT THE CRITICS SAID: 'Easily the most impressive segment of the Scorsese/Coppola/Allen omnibus . . . simultaneously funny and deadly serious, it packs more into 40 minutes than most Hollywood directors manage in a career.' Andy Gill, *Empire*.

EXPERT WITNESS: 'That the project was called *New York Stories* wasn't my idea or any of our ideas. That was just the working title for the company, Disney. And they liked that title, and they used it. I didn't think that was a good title for it myself, because I felt it was limiting. But it was as good as any.' Fellow director Woody Allen.

FINAL ANALYSIS: Woody Allen's 'Oedipus Wrecks' is a light-hearted comedy, while Scorsese's 'Life Lessons' is an examination of middle-aged angst, something Allen has also studied over the years. They both work well together and generally, reviewers choose one or the other to single out for praise as they're both equally good examples of small-scale stories by their respective directors. The same cannot, sadly, be said for Coppola's 'Life Without Zoe', which is almost universally despised.

SCORSESE ON 'LIFE LESSONS': 'What interested me was the pain of this situation, how much of it is needed for his kind of work, and how much he creates himself.'

GoodFellas (1990)

(35 mm – 146 mins – colour)

MPAA Rating: R

Production Company: Warner Bros
Screenplay: Nicholas Pileggi, Martin Scorsese, based on the book *Wise Guy: Life in a Mafia Family* by Nicholas Pileggi
Producer: Irwin Winkler

Executive Producer: Barbara De Fina
Associate Producer: Bruce S Pustin
Cinematographer: Michael Ballhaus
Film Editor: Thelma Schoonmaker
Co-editor: James Y Kwei
Casting: Ellen Lewis
Production Design: Kristi Zea
Art Direction: Maher Ahmad
Set Decoration: Leslie Bloom
Costume Design: Richard Bruno
Title Designers: Saul Bass, Elaine Bass

SOUNDTRACK: 'Rags to Riches'*, 'The Boulevard of Broken Dreams' by Tony Bennett; 'Can't We Be Sweethearts' by the Cleftones; 'Hearts of Stone' by Otis Williams and the Charms; 'Sincerely'* by the Moonglows; 'Firenze Sogna', 'Parlami d'Amore Mariu' by Giuseppe di Stefano; 'Speedo'* by the Cadillacs; 'Stardust'* by Billy Ward and His Dominoes; 'This World We Live In' ('Il Cielo in una Stanza') by Mina; 'Playboy' by the Marvelettes; 'It's Not for Me to Say' by Johnny Mathis; 'I Will Follow Him' by Betty Curtis; 'Then He Kissed Me', 'He's Sure the Boy I Love' by the Crystals; 'Look in My Eyes'* by the Chantells; 'Roses Are Red' by Robby Vintono; 'Life is but a Dream'* by the Harptones; 'Leader of the Pack', 'Remember (Walkin' in the Sand)'* by the Shangri-las; 'Toot, Toot, Tootsie Goodbye', 'Happy Birthday to You', 'Ain't That a Kick in the Head' by Dean Martin; 'Atlantis' by Donovan; 'Pretend You Don't See Her' by Jerry Vale; 'Baby I Love You'* by Aretha Franklin; 'Beyond the Sea'* by Bobby Darin; 'Gimme Shelter', 'Monkey Man', 'Memo from Turner' by the Rolling Stones; 'Wives and Lovers' by Jack Jones; 'Frosty the Snowman' by the Ronettes; 'Christmas (Baby Please Come Home)' by Darlene Love; 'Bells of St Mary's' by the Drifters; 'Unchained Melody' by Vito and the Salutations; 'Danny Boy', 'Sunshine of Your Love'* by Cream; 'Layla'* by Derek and the Dominos; 'Jump into the Fire' by Harry Nilsson; 'The Magic Bus' by the Who; 'What is Life' by George Harrison; 'Mannish Boy'* by Muddy Waters; 'My Way' by Sid Vicious.

CAST: Robert De Niro (*James 'Jimmy' Conway*), Ray Liotta (*Henry Hill*), Joe Pesci (*Tommy DeVito*), Lorraine Bracco (*Karen Hill*), Paul Sorvino (*Paul 'Paulie' Cicero*), Frank Sivero (*Frankie Carbone*), Tony Darrow (*Sonny Bunz*), Mike Starr (*Frenchy*), Frank Vincent (*Billy Batts*), Chuck Low (*Morris Kessler*), Frank DiLeo (*Tuddy Cicero*), Henny Youngman (*Himself*), Gina Mastrogiacomo (*Janice Rossi*), Catherine

Scorsese (*Mrs DeVito*), Charles Scorsese (*Vinnie*), Suzanne Shepherd
(*Karen's Mother*), Debi Mazar (*Sandy*), Margo Winkler (*Belle Kessler*),
Welker White (*Lois Byrd*), Jerry Vale (*Himself*), Julie Garfield (*Mickey
Conway*), Christopher Serrone (*Young Henry Hill*), Elaine Kagan (*Mrs
Hill*), Beau Starr (*Mr Hill*), Kevin Corrigan (*Michael Hill*), Michael
Imperioli (*Spider*), Robbie Vinton (*Bobby Vinton*), John Williams
(*Johnny Roastbeef*), Daniel P Conte (*Dr Dan*), Nancy Ellen Cassaro (*Joe
Buddha's Wife*), Tony Conforti (*Tony*), Frank Pellegrino (*Johnny Dio*),
Ronald Maccone (*Ronnie*), Tony Sirico (*Tony Stacks*), Joe D'Onofrio
(*Young Tommy DeVito*), Steve Forleo (*City Detective 1*), Richard
Dioguardi (*City Detective 2*), Frank Adonis (*Anthony Stabile*), John
Manca (*Nickey Eyes*), Joseph Bono (*Mikey Franzese*), Katherine
Wallach (*Diane*), Mark Evan Jacobs (*Bruce*), Angela Pietropinto
(*Cicero's Wife*), Marianne Leone (*Tuddy's Wife*), Marie Michaels (*Mrs
Carbone*), LoNardo (*Frenchy's Wife*), Melissa Prophet (*Angie*), Illeana
Douglas (*Rosie*), Susan Varon (*Susan*), Elizabeth Whitcraft (*Tommy's
Girlfriend at the Copa*), Clem Caserta (*Joe Buddha*), Samuel L Jackson
(*Stacks Edwards*), Fran McGee (*Johnny Roastbeef's Wife*), Paul Herman
(*Dealer*), Edward McDonald (*Himself*), Edward Hayes (*Defense
Attorney*), Daniela Barbosa (*Young Henry's Sister 1*), Gina Mattia
(*Young Henry's Sister 2*), Joel Calendrillo (*Young Henry's Older
Brother*), Anthony Valentin (*Young Michael*), Edward D Murphy
(*Liquor Cop 1*), Michael Citriniti (*Liquor Cop 2*), Peter Hock
(*Mailman*), Erasmus C Alfanio (*Barbecue Wiseguy*), John Di Benedetto
(*Bleeding Man*), Manny Alfaro (*Gambling Doorman*), Thomas Lowry
(*Hijacked Driver*), Margaret Smith (*School Guard*), Richard Mullally
(*Cop 1*), Frank Albanese (*Mob Lawyer*), Paul McIsaac (*Judge – 1956*),
Bob Golub (*Truck Driver at Diner*), Louis Eppolito (*Fat Andy*), Tony
Lip (*Frankie the Wop*), Mikey Black (*Freddy No Nose*), Peter Cicale
(*Pete the Killer*), Anthony Powers (*Jimmy Two Times*), Vincent Pastore
(*Man with Coatrack*), Anthony Alessandro, Victor Colicchio, (*Henry's
60s Crew*), Mike Contessa, Philip Suriano (*Cicero's 60s Crew*) Paul
Mougey (*Terrorised Waiter*), Norman Barbera (*Bouncer*), Anthony
Polemeni (*Copa Captain*), James Quattrochi (*Henry Greeter 1*),
Lawrence Sacco (*Henry Greeter 2*), Dino Laudicina (*Henry Greeter 3*),
Thomas E Camuti (*Mr Tony Hood 1*), Andrew Scudiero (*Mr Tony Hood
2*), Irving Welzer (*Copa Announcer*), Jesse Kirtzman (*Beach Club
Waiter*), Russell Halley (*Bruce's Brother 1*), Spencer Bradley (*Bruce's
Brother 2*), Bob Altman (*Karen's Dad*), Joanna Bennett (*Marie 1*), Cayle
Lewis (*Marie 2*), Gaetano Lisi (*Paul 3*), Luke Walter (*Truck Driver*), Ed
Deacy (*Detective Deacy*), Larry Silvestri (*Detective Silvestri*), Johnny

'Cha Cha' Ciarcia (*Batts's Crew 1*), Frank Aquilino (*Batts's Crew 2*), Vito Picone (*Vito*), Janis Corsair (*Vito's Girlfriend*), Lisa Dapolito (*Lisa*), Michael Calandrino (*Godfather at Table*), Vito Antuofermo (*Prizefighter*), Vito Balsamo, Peter Fain, Vincent Gallo (*credited as Vinnie Gallo*), Gaetano LoGiudice, Garry Pastore (*credited as Garry Blackwood*) (*Harry's 70s Crew*), Nicole Burdette (*Carbone's Girlfriend*), Stella Keitel (*Henry's Older Child, Judy*), Dominique DeVito (*Henry's Baby, Ruth*), Michaelangelo Graziano (*Bar Patron*), Paula Gallo (*Janice's Girlfriend 1*), Nadine Kay (*Janice's Girlfriend 2*), Tony Ellis (*Bridal Shop Owner*), Peter Onorati (*Florida Bookie*), Jamie De Roy (*Bookie's Sister*), Joel Blake (*Judge – 1971*), H Clay Dear (*Security Guard with Lobsters*), Thomas Hewson (*Drug Buyer*), Gene Canfield (*Prison Guard in Booth*), Margaux Guerard (*Judy Hill at 10 years*), Violet Gaynor (*Ruth Hill at 8 years*), Tobin Bell (*Parole Officer*), Berlinda Tolbert (*Stacks's Girlfriend*), Adam Wandt (*Kid*), Joseph P Gioco (*Garbage Man*), Isiah Whitlock Jr (*Doctor*), Alyson Jones (*Judy Hill at 13 years*), Ruby Gaynor (*Ruth Hill at 11 years*), Bo Dietl (*credited as Richard 'Bo' Dietl*) (*Arresting Narc*).

UNCREDITED CAST: Matthew T Gitkin (*Warehouse Worker*).

TITLES: Considering the opening titles came from legendary designer, Saul Bass (working with his wife Elaine), they're amazingly simple. In the pre-teaser titles, the credit cards (white text on black) zoom past the camera, accompanied by the sound of cars passing by. Then a simple caption: THIS FILM IS BASED ON A TRUE STORY. A second caption card tells us it's NEW YORK 1970 before cutting to the car containing Henry, Jimmy and Tommy. As Henry drives, bleary-eyed through the night, the other two sleep until a noise coming from the trunk disturbs them. Outside the car, lit red by the car's rear lights, Henry struggles with his car-keys as Tommy slips out a huge kitchen knife from his jacket. The trunk opens to reveal a man wrapped in a white shroud, his face a bloody mess. Surprised that he's still alive, Tommy lunges at him and stabs him repeatedly; Jimmy then shoots the man at point blank range four times. As Henry closes the trunk, the frame freezes, the screen cuts to black and the title GOODFELLAS appears in bold red. The remaining credits appear as before in white text.

SUMMARY: For as long as he can remember, Henry Hill has wanted to be a gangster. In his early teens he had watched the wiseguys in his neighbourhood and was impressed by the way they could seemingly do what they wanted when they wanted, like parking their cars in front of fire hydrants and never getting a parking ticket. Henry gets a part-time job running errands for Paulie Cicero, a powerful man in the neighbourhood, who comes from the same part of Sicily as Henry's mother. At first, his parents are pleased that Henry is showing some initiative in getting work, but as the job begins to take up more and more of his time, Henry stops going to school and starts earning more money than his father. Every day, Henry is learning new ways to score money, and is introduced to two major players in Paulie's crew, Jimmy 'The Gent' Conway and Tommy DeVito.

Eventually, Henry is arrested for selling cigarettes known to be stolen, but his reluctance to give evidence or reveal anything that might incriminate others goes down well with Paulie's crew and as Henry gets older, so his power and influence grow.

By 1963, Henry is working for Jimmy, who is effectively managing the entire illegal operations surrounding Idlewild Airport. Though things are going well for everyone, Tommy DeVito is becoming a frightening personality, with many people unsure of when he is likely to explode. When Sonny, a local businessman, comes to see Paulie for help after Tommy's violent behaviour in his bar, Paulie's solution is to buy into Sonny's business, putting Henry in charge of things. They use the business as a front, ordering stock and then selling it from the back door with no intention of honouring the bill. Once the bills become too great, they simply torch the place.

Henry is asked by Tommy to go on a double date with him – Henry's date is a Jewish girl called Karen. Henry has no interest in the girl, but eventually they begin dating, though Karen is forced to lie to her parents about Henry's Catholic background and claims he is half Jewish. She herself still believes he is a construction union delegate. Meanwhile, Henry sets up a heist for Jimmy which results in them stealing $420,000 from Air France. This heist sets Henry up as a major player, especially after he pays Paulie his tribute.

Henry and Karen eventually get married – twice! – once with a traditional Jewish ceremony for her family, and again with his extended mafia family. It isn't long before Karen realises her husband isn't in construction, especially after spending time with the wives of the other crew-members. When police officers come to search their house, she begins to treat it as routine.

However, everything begins to change for the crew on 11 June 1970, at Henry's bar, the Suite Lounge in Queens, New York. A welcome home party for Billy Batts, a 'Made Man' recently released from jail, turns sour after Batts mocks Tommy in front of his friends. Later that night, Tommy and Jimmy beat Batts to death and, with Henry's help, bury him in a shallow grave. As Batts was a 'Made Man' and therefore untouchable, Tommy has broken one of the biggest rules in the Wiseguys' code of honour and the trio are forced to deny all knowledge of the event.

The relationship between Karen and Henry deteriorates, especially when Henry takes a mistress, Janice Rossi. After Karen pulls a gun on Henry while he is sleeping, he leaves her and moves in with Janice. But Paulie and Jimmy intervene and he returns home. To ease the situation, Paulie sends Henry with Jimmy to force one of Paulie's debtors to pay what he owes, but the man's sister works as a secretary at the FBI and Henry is arrested and sent to prison. To Henry's surprise, prison life is not the punishment he'd feared, but it is a hard period for Karen, who feels cut off and abandoned by the 'family'. Henry begins to peddle drugs to earn a living. When he is released, and against Paulie's direct orders, Henry secretly continues to deal in narcotics through contacts in Pittsburgh. Slowly Henry begins to involve Jimmy and Tommy, his children's baby-sitter Lois and his new girlfriend, Sandy, in his business.

Via Morris Kessler, a contact of Henry's, Jimmy orchestrates an immaculate robbery – the notorious Lufthansa heist in which he manages to steal an estimated $4 million. Despite warnings from Jimmy to his crew not to buy anything that might attract the attention of the cops, many of the crew buy new cars and fur coats for their wives. Then, when the getaway vehicle, covered in fingerprints, is found due to the carelessness of the driver, Stacks, Jimmy hires Tommy to kill him. Then, as Morrie begins to make a nuisance of himself, pestering Jimmy for his share of the money, Jimmy has Morrie killed.

Soon, bodies are being discovered all over the city as more and more of Jimmy's crew become liabilities. The only thing that cheers Jimmy's spirits is the news that Tommy is finally going to be 'Made', which would mean increased power for his friends. But on the morning of the ceremony, Jimmy receives a call. The murder of Billy Batts has finally caught up with him and Tommy has been executed.

On Sunday 11 May 1980, Henry's life in the Mafia comes to an end after he is arrested for dealing in drugs. In a panic, Karen flushes Henry's entire drugs supply down the toilet, a $60,000 investment. Disgusted that Henry lied to him, Paulie finally cuts him out of the 'family' and makes it known that he is no longer welcome. Henry is convinced that at any point he might be killed by any of his former friends. Eventually, seeing no other way out, he turns state's witness and informs on his friends, including Paulie and Jimmy. Entering the witness protection programme, Karen and Henry begin a new life with new identities, but in 1989, after 25 years of marriage, they finally separate.

WHO'S WHO?: From his first major role in *Something Wild* (Jonathan Demme, 1986) to the psychotically obsessive cop in *Unlawful Entry* (Jonathan Kaplan, 1992) and his brief appearance in *Hannibal* (Ridley Scott, 2001), Ray Liotta has tended to play relatively unsympathetic characters living on the edge – *Field of Dreams* (Phil Alden Robinson, 1989) and *Corrina, Corrina* (Jessie Nelson, 1994) being exceptions. Paul Sorvino is the father of Oscar-winning actress Minra Sorvino, as well as an opera singer and the founder of the Sorvino Asthma Foundation.

Former model Lorraine Bracco has enjoyed a career high thanks to her role of Dr Melfi in HBO mobster drama *The Sopranos*. Fellow *Sopranos* cast-member Michael Imperioli also co-wrote, produced and acted in Spike Lee's *Summer of Sam* (1999), while other *Sopranos* regulars here include: Tony Sirico who plays Paulie 'Walnuts' Gaultieri; Tony Darrow who played Larry Boy Barese in the first series of *The Sopranos*, as well as other gangsters in *Bullets over Broadway*, *Sweet and Lowdown*, *Small Time Crooks*, (Woody Allen, 1994, 1999, 2000), *Analyze This* (Harold Ramis, 1999) and *Mickey Blue Eyes* (Kelly Makin, 1999); Suzanne Shepherd plays Mary DeAngelis; Nicole Burdette was Tony's elder sister, Barbara; Paul Herman played Beansie Gaeta in series 2; and Vincent Pastore was hapless traitor Salvatore 'Pussy' Bonpensiero in the first two series. Debi Mazar can also be seen as Two-Face's moll 'Spicc' in *Batman Forever* (Joel Schumacher, 1995) and numerous promo videos by Madonna, including 'Papa Don't Preach' and 'Music'.

Frank Sivero had small roles in *The Godfather* and *The Godfather Part II* (Francis Ford Coppola, 1972, 1974). Mike Starr often plays slow-witted heavies in films such as *Mad Dog and Glory* (John McNaughton, 1993) *Summer of Sam* (Spike Lee, 1999); Beau Starr is Mike Starr's brother, and appeared as Sherrif Meaker in *Halloween 4: The Return of Michael Myers* (Dwight H Little, 1988) and *Halloween 5* (Dominique Othenin-Girard, 1989). Frank DiLeo was at one time Michael Jackson's manager. Comedian Henny Youngman (who appears as himself) is attributed with the monkier 'King of the One-Liners', producing such classic lines as 'Take my wife . . . please!' A good friend of Frank Sinatra, Jerry Vale was part of that Italian–American crooner set that took over Vegas in the 70s and 80s. It's said that Martin Scorsese's mother, Catherine, was a huge fan of his (check out his website, www.jerryvale.com). Samuel L Jackson appeared in a number of Spike Lee's pictures, including *Do the Right Thing* (1989) and *Jungle Fever*, before appearing in Quentin Tarantino's *Pulp Fiction* (1994) as cool bible-quoting hitman Jules, the role that propelled him to the position of America's number one black actor. Vinnie Gallo would become better known as outspoken actor Vincent Gallo, star of *Palookaville* (Alan Taylor, 1995) and director/writer/star of *Buffalo '66* (1998).

Nicholas Pileggi worked as a reporter for the Associated Press from 1956 until 1968 when he moved to *New York* magazine, where he's worked ever since. He took four years to research his second book, *Wiseguy*, which formed the basis of his co-written script with Scorsese. He later co-wrote *City Hall* (Sidney Lumet, 1996) with Paul Schrader. Pileggi is the husband of fellow writer Nora Ephron (*When Harry Met Sally*, *Sleepless in Seattle*).

Saul Bass was one of the industry's most celebrated title designers, having worked with Alfred Hitchcock in creating the spellbinding visuals for films such as *Vertigo* and *North by Northwest*. Elaine was his wife and collaborator in the last few years of his life.

THE USUAL SUSPECTS: Robert De Niro (*Mean Streets, Taxi Driver, New York, New York, Raging Bull, The King of Comedy, Cape Fear, Casino*); writer Nicholas Pileggi (*Casino*); Peter Fain (*Mean Streets, New York, New York, Raging Bull, The King of Comedy*); Jerry Vale (*Casino*); producer Irwin Winkler (*New York, New York, Raging Bull*); Margo Winkler (*New York, New York, The King of Comedy, After Hours*); Frank Vincent, Joe Pesci, Frank Adonis, Joseph Bono, Daniel P Conte (*Raging Bull, Casino*); Richard Dioguardi, Katherine Wallach, Chuck Low (*The King of Comedy*); Frank Aquilino (*After Hours*); Paul Herman (*The Color of Money, The Last Temptation of Christ, New York Stories, Casino*); John Manca, Ronald Maccone, Melissa Prophet, Clem Caserta, Philip Suriano (*Casino*); producer Barbara De Fina (*The Color of Money, Bad, The Last Temptation of Christ, New York Stories*: 'Life Lessons', *The Grifters, Made in Milan, Cape Fear, Mad Dog and Glory, The Age of Innocence, Casino, Kundun, My Voyage to Italy, Bringing Out the Dead, Dino*); editor Thelma Schoonmaker (*Who's That Knocking At My Door?, Street Scenes, Raging Bull, The King of Comedy, After Hours, The Color of Money, Bad, The Last Temptation of Christ, New York Stories, Cape Fear, Age of Innocence, Casino, A Personal Journey with Martin Scorsese Through American Movies, Kundun, Bringing Out the Dead, My Voyage to Italy, Gangs of New*

York); title designers Saul and Elaine Bass (*Cape Fear, The Age of Innocence, Casino*).

SOURCE: Writer Nicholas Pileggi was approached by Simon & Schuster to write the story of Henry Hill, an ex-mafia foot-soldier turned state-witness. Initially, Pileggi wasn't at all interested, feeling there were already enough gangster stories out there. Additionally, he got the impression that Hill really had no intention of writing a book but was merely trying to scam some money from the publisher. But, as he learned more about Henry Hill, he began to recognise something unique about his story. He wasn't a 'Godfather', he was only half Italian and didn't seem to have been that high up in the world of organised crime – but his connections put him in a unique position. Though he interviewed both Henry and his wife Karen, as well as the arresting officers on the case that propelled Henry towards the Witness Protection Programme, Pileggi saw the story not as an investigative book, but as a sociological book, looking at how these people lived.

Henry was raised at 392 Pine Street, between Brownsville and East New York. The cab-stand was opposite, at 401 Pine Street, while Paulie's pizza joint, Presto Pizza (where Henry witnessed his first hit, and got told off for wasting aprons), was nearby on Pitkin Avenue, between Crescent and Pine on the north side of the street. Though named Paulie Cicero in the movie, the man who took the young Henry under his wind was actually Paul Vario. Running a large crew for the Lucchese family, Vario had the help of his four brothers: Lenny, a union official, was the oldest, then Paul; next was Tommy, who had joined Lenny in helping to control the unions; Vito (known as Tuddy), lost a leg in the Korean War and took the decision to hire Henry as a 'gofer'; and their youngest brother Salvatore, or 'Babe'. Through the Varios, Henry became friends with Jimmy 'the gent' Burke and Tommy DeSimone, two other associates from Vario's huge crew whose operations were based in Brooklyn. For the film, Jimmy was renamed Conway after his mother's name, with Tommy given the surname DeVito.

At sixteen, Henry was arrested for the first time, caught with Paulie's son Lenny trying to use a hot credit card in a gas station to buy a couple of tyres for Tuddy's wife's car (not for selling un-taxed cigarettes with young Tommy as in the film). On the day of Henry's first court appearance, Paulie was away in prison for contempt, and couldn't be there. It was Tuddy who Henry remembers saying, 'You broke your cherry.'

The following year, Henry joined the US Army Paratroopers and was stationed at Fort Bragg, North Carolina. He stayed in the Army until

1963 but always stayed in touch with Tuddy and Paulie, and after leaving the army, Henry was given a job as a maitre d' at The Azores, a restaurant owned by Thomas Lucchese. Later, Henry took over The Suite Lounge after discussions with Paulie. He began to enjoy running the restaurant as a legitimate business and ordered the rest of his crew to stay away from the place, to keep the place clean. But one by one his friends began to drop by and soon it turned into a regular hangout. Hill was also the mastermind behind the 1978 Boston College basketball point shaving scheme where he and his associates rigged nine games, an episode omitted from the film.

As we learn at the end of the film, Paul Cicero died of respiratory illness in 1988 in Fort Worth Federal Prison, aged 73. The character Jimmy Conway was, at the time of the film's release, serving twenty years-to-life for murder in a New York State prison, not eligible for parole until 2004 when he would have been 78 years old. The real Jimmy died in prison of cancer in 1996 aged 65.

PRODUCTION: During production of *The Color of Money*, Scorsese obtained galley proofs of Nicholas Pileggi's *Wise Guy* and enquired with his friend and producer Irwin Winkler about buying the rights. Approaching Pileggi with a mind to adapting the book into a screenplay, Scorsese showed the writer Truffaut's *Jules et Jim* to give him an idea of the narration technique he felt they could use to structure the film. Then Scorsese and Pileggi separately worked out which bits of the book they'd like for the movie, with Scorsese convincing Pileggi that, because they didn't have to follow a proper narrative structure they could have fun with it, taking it episode by episode to show the rise and fall, rather than the highs and lows and highs again. From 1986 to 1987, the two worked on eleven drafts of the script while Scorsese secretly worried if it was wise to commit himself to making yet another gangster movie. He began looking for other projects should he decide to pass on *Wise Guy* (see **Unseen Scorsese**). *The Last Temptation of Christ* finally entered production in 1987, and after that he began work on Woody Allen's *New York Stories*. Out of courtesy, Scorsese's old friend Michael Powell offered to appraise the script for *Wise Guy*. His eyesight was so poor that his wife, editor Thelma Schoonmaker, read it to him. Powell quickly realised what had drawn Scorsese to the subject was a fresh approach to the whole gangster lifestyle, and convinced Scorsese that it was a worthwhile project.

Warner Brothers had been attached to the script from the outset, but had patiently waited as Scorsese completed his other projects. Now they decided that they'd do the picture only if Scorsese could attract a major star to appear. Robert De Niro had read the script a couple of years earlier and when Scorsese suggested they work together again for the first time in seven years, De Niro agreed to take the comparatively small role of Jimmy Conway. With De Niro confirmed, Warners offered an increased budget of approximately $26 million. With the script approved, Scorsese spent two weeks annotating it with storyboards.

Some years earlier, Scorsese had met with actor Ray Liotta and after seeing him in Jonathan Demme's *Something Wild*, decided he'd be good for the role of Henry. Aside from Paul Sorvino, most of the cast turned out to be old friends and previous collaborators of the director, with Joe Pesci cast as the fiery Tommy and Lorraine Bracco as Karen Hill. As was usual, Scorsese encouraged improvisation among his actors, leading to Joe Pesci scripting and largely directing the memorable 'How am I funny' scene. Paul Sorvino remembers how, in a scene where his character had to rebuke Henry, he found himself slapping Ray Liotta across the face to the surprise of both actors. Meanwhile, despite the part only requiring him to be on set for three weeks, De Niro engaged in detailed research into his character, speaking to Henry Hill via pre-arranged phone calls. The detail even extended to the way his character poured ketchup by rolling the bottle between his palms instead of patting it.

Location filming took place over the summer and autumn of 1989, with Queens, New York providing the backdrop for Henry's old neighbourhood. Scorsese hired cinematographer Michael Ballhaus, whose experience in swift set-ups and limited budget once more proved invaluable. Production designer Kristi Zea was amused when Scorsese told her early on of his belief than the picture 'never should have been made by anyone but an Italian'. The essential idea would be that there'd be no parody of the Italian lifestyle, except towards the end of the picture when Karen and Henry's house should show their garish lack of taste. Scorsese hand-picked the costumes for his actors, even down to the ties and suit worn by young Henry for the scene where his mother accuses him of looking like a gangster.

The celebrated steadicam shot through the back of The Copacabana came about by accident when the management at The Copa refused permission for them to film through the front. A false corridor was built to prologue the sweeping seduction of Karen into this lifestyle – a corridor that had to be put in place and then swept out of line of the shot during the take. With so many complicated shots and the biggest ensemble cast Scorsese had had to face so far, the production understandably went a couple of weeks over schedule. However, Scorsese also had a long-standing acting commitment to director Akira Kurosawa, having agreed to play Van Gogh in his film *Dreams* so, while he was in Japan doing that, he left his assistant director Joe Reidy to finish off the last few shots. Scorsese then settled down with Thelma Schoonmaker to edit the picture in spring 1990 in line with a release in the autumn of that same year. For the first time, he was forced by the studio to preview the film in California, a practice that was becoming all too common. The previews were well received, though the audience claimed they felt agitated by the last day sequence, which was exactly the response Scorsese was after. After taking on board some of the suggestions made during the previews, Scorsese and Schoonmaker re-edited the picture slightly to tighten up the last two reels.

With this out of the way, Scorsese went on to appear alongside De Niro as a McCarthy-era film director in *Guilty by Suspicion*, the directorial debut of his producer, Irwin Winkler. One side effect of this was the disappearance of Scorsese's trademark beard as few directors sported facial hair in the 1950s.

GoodFellas was finally released in the USA in September 1990 to generally enthusiastic reviews and strong box-office takings, eventually grossing nearly $49 million in the USA.

EDITING: *Raging Bull* might have bagged Schoonmaker an Oscar, but it's *GoodFellas* that arguably represents her greatest achievement (even though the Academy Award that year went to Neil Travis's *Dances with Wolves*). Here, Schoonmaker and Scorsese utilise every trick in the book to convey emotion and astounding breakneck speed of narrative, with cameras swirling round the actors and crash-zooming in at moments of great significance.

The freeze-frames, inspired by Truffaut's *The 400 Blows* (1959) and by TV documentaries Scorsese saw as a child, allow the narration time to catch up with the visuals, often to denote a significant development in Henry's life: the very beginning, where Henry's voice-over tells us he always wanted to be a gangster just as he closes the boot on the corpse of Billy Batts; when his father beats him, and so on. Invariably, these freeze-frames occur at just the moment we want them to speed up, such as the many acts of physical or moral violence committed around Henry.

Some scenes don't pause, but are slowed down to prolong the moment again. Two such shots come to mind: Karen leaving her house as she watches Henry pistol-whip her neighbour; and Jimmy standing at the end of the bar planning to whack Morrie Kessler (to the tune of Cream's 'Sunshine of Your Love').

Karen and Henry's wedding is a lesson in editing on its own. Leading in from a shot where Karen hides Henry's gun, we see the Jewish ceremony with the breaking of the glass (see **BIBLE CLASS**). Schoonmaker here uses a number of jump cuts to propel us through this segment, from the glass being placed in cloth and then broken on the floor up to the camera flash as we cut to the huge function room where the second wedding celebration is held. Now we pan across the room, seeing the men huddled together discussing business, Tommy's mother berating him for 'bouncing around from girl to girl' and then the wives. Now we circle round Karen as she describes how she was introduced to Henry's two families and comments on how they're all called Peter or Paul and all their wives are called Marie. In the giving of gifts, Karen is kissed by Paulie, but the next shot is of another man handing her money, then a woman kisses her, then two different male hands give her money – which all gets placed inside a pillow-case by Henry as if it's stolen loot. Then Henry points Karen to look across the room to see the long line of people still waiting to give them their tributes. The final shot of the scene, with Henry and Karen dancing happily, then cuts to Karen's mother at home, nagging her about her husband's lifestyle – a deliberate attempt to show that as soon as they are married things began to go downhill.

Three shots come directly from Hitchcock: the first is where young Henry, from his bedroom, spies on the gangsters across the street, inspired by the scene in *Psycho* where Norman watches Marion through a peephole in the wall; another *Psycho* reference is the top-down shot of Henry in the shower where he learns of the Lufthansa robbery; and finally, possibly the most subtle trick in the entire picture occurs in the scene where Jimmy and Henry meet at the café for the last time. As the camera approaches their table from side on, note the gentle zoom in/pull back trick (where the foreground image stays in the same position in the frame, but the background seems to move closer) that Hitchcock first developed for *Vertigo*. As if this wasn't enough, we also have the astounding one-take tracking shot right through the back of the Copa and out to the front of the stage. Which goes to prove Scorsese was really just showing off . . .

MUSIC: Scorsese's two-hour, twenty-minute rock music promo offers over forty contemporary pieces of music, which makes the soundtrack album as released, with less than half of the featured tracks, something of a disappointment. Still, from the opening note of Tony Bennett's 'Rags to

Riches' we know we're in for a treat as Scorsese takes us for a spin through some of his favourite songs from the last forty years, with some interesting results. The menace of De Niro planning to kill Morrie Kessler is dramatically enhanced by the sound of Cream's 'Sunshine of Your Love' suddenly erupting over the scene. For the scenes where the bodies begin to appear all over the city, Scorsese uses a song he actually played on the set while filming, the piano section from Eric Clapton's 'Layla', while the paranoid mania of Henry's last day as a wise-guy features a superb mixing of Nilsson's 'Jump into the Fire' with the Who's 'Magic Bus' (the 'Live at Leeds' version), the Rolling Stones' 'Monkey Man' (which features the line 'I'm a flea-bit peanut monkey and all my friends are junkies') and George Harrison's 'What is Life?' Inspired is the use of Sid Vicious's version of 'My Way', complete with the lyric, 'Regrets, I've had a few/But then again, too few to mention.' Incidentally, Vito Picone (playing himself) was the lead singer of Vito and the Elegants, who had a number one hit in the US charts with 'Little Star' in 1958.

QUOTE/UNQUOTE

Henry: (narrating) 'As far back as I can remember, I've always wanted to be a gangster.'

Jimmy: (to young Henry) 'Never rat on your friends . . . and always keep your mouth shut.'

Tommy: (to a nervous Henry) 'Let me understand this, cos I dunno, maybe it's me, I'm a little fucked up maybe, but I'm funny how? I mean, funny like I'm a clown, I amuse you? I make you laugh, I'm here to fuckin' amuse you?' Whadda you mean "funny", funny how? How am I funny?'

Karen: (narrating) 'I know there are women like my best friends who would've gotten out of there the minute their boyfriend gave them a gun to hide. But I didn't. I gotta admit the truth – it turned me on.'

Karen: (narrating) 'After a while it got to be all normal. None of it seemed like crime, it was more like Henry was enterprising in that he and the guys were making a few bucks hustling while the other guys were sitting on their asses waiting for handouts. Our husbands weren't brain-surgeons – they were blue-collar guys!'

Henry: (narrating) 'If you're part of a crew, nobody ever tells you that they're going to kill you. Doesn't happen that way. There aren't any arguments or curses like in the movies. See, your murderers come with smiles. They come as your friends.'

Henry: (narrating) 'That's the hardest part. Today everything is different. There's no action. I have to wait around like everyone else. Can't even get decent food. Right after I got here I ordered some spaghetti with marinara sauce and I got egg noodles and ketchup. I'm an average nobody. I get to live the rest of my life like a schnook.'

ROOTS: The last shot of the film, with Tommy shooting straight into the camera combines the shock of *The Great Train Robbery* (Edwin S Porter, 1903) and punk caper movie *The Great Rock 'n' Roll Swindle* (Julien Temple, 1980). In the shooting of the barman, Spider, Tommy refers to *The Oklahoma Kid* (Lloyd Bacon, 1939) and *Ben Casey*, the TV medic played by Vince Edwards from 1961 to 1966, while Jimmy mentions *Shane* (George Stevens, 1953). The use of voice-over and many of the editing techniques come from Truffaut's *Jules et Jim* (1961). We see a brief clip from Al Jolson's *The Jazz Singer* (Alan Crosland, 1927). Jimmy Conway's nickname comes from James Cagney's character in *Jimmy the Gent* (Michael Curtiz, 1934).

THEMES AND MOTIFS: Typically, for Scorsese, the last shot sees the hero alone (although this is more implied by the 'Where are they now' cards informing us that Henry and Karen split up than by the shot of Henry in his towelling bathrobe outside on the lawn). The long introduction to Henry's crew round the bar recalls De Niro's entrance in *Mean Streets*, and of course, the bar-rooms are invariably lit red. We also get judicious uses of red in the scenes where Henry, Tommy and Jimmy dig the grave for Billy Batts, giving the effect that their digging is unearthing Hell. The bridge between the recap of the stabbing of Batts in the trunk and the next scene is created with a bleed to red. Forever linking the way of the gangster to that of the old West, as shown by Hollywood, we have Tommy claiming to be the Oklahoma Kid (see **ROOTS**) and shooting his gun into the air during a robbery like a cowboy. During the birthday of Jimmy's son we catch a glimpse of the cake, decorated with little plastic Western figures. This birthday sequence leads into a montage of holiday and birthday photographs – there is a similar sequence in *Raging Bull*.

CONTROVERSY: Not a film to show your mother. *GoodFellas* at one time held the record for the most instances of swearing onscreen ever (losing that title in 1999 to *South Park: Bigger, Longer and Uncut*). The F-word alone is used over 240 times, mostly by Joe Pesci. As we've seen before, racism is a common flaw with these people. The truck driver Jimmy pays off to let them steal his cargo rushes into a nearby diner to report that 'two niggers' stole his truck. Tommy is affronted when he learns that a girl he's dating is apparently 'prejudiced against Italians', although this doesn't prevent Tommy becoming angered by his girlfriend claiming to understand the attraction of black entertainer Sammy Davis Jr.

If the profanity doesn't startle you, the violence almost definitely will. The stabbing and shooting of Billy Batts in the prologue is genuinely upsetting, although for sheer brutality the shooting of Stacks (Samuel L Jackson) comes close.

The sexual content in the film is very tastefully handled, there is a suggestion that Karen delays her husband leaving for work by performing oral sex on him.

BIBLE CLASS: For Karen's family, it's important that their daughter marries a Jewish boy, hence her concern when Henry wears a cross on a chain to his first visit to their house, revealing him to be a Catholic. In real life, Henry converted to Judaism for Karen's sake, though his lifestyle didn't really leave time for either religion. On the wall of Tommy's mother's dining room, a picture of the Last Supper can be seen. This is later mirrored in the scene where we see the crew Jimmy has assembled for the Lufthansa job. Significantly, everyone in that shot will end up dead by the end of the film, apart from Jimmy and Henry, whose eventual removal from that lifestyle leaves them emotionally dead at least. Significantly, Tommy's last words to his mother are: 'Don't paint any more religious pictures', which can be taken as a slight dig at the director in the light of events surrounding *The Last Temptation of Christ*.

The symbolism of the smashing of the glass by the Chatan at the conclusion of the ceremony has a variety of explanations. One is that the shattering breaks the silence of the ceremony and cues the assembled guests to cheer; guests usually respond with 'Mazel Tov!' ('Congratulations!'). The breaking also reminds us of the fragility of personal relationships: the glass is shattered with the implication that the marriage should always remain intact; as well as symbolising the breaking of the bride's hymen after the marriage is consummated.

KEEP IT IN THE FAMILY: Scorsese's parents make their most significant contribution to their son's work since *Italianamerican*.

Catherine Scorsese plays Tommy's mother in three scenes. The scene where she makes a meal for Tommy and his friends was largely improvised. Charles Scorsese plays Vinnie, one of the older members of Paulie's crew. It's Charlie whose voice we hear telling De Niro about Tommy's execution. Lorraine Bracco was, at the time of production, the wife of Harvey Keitel. Their daughter Stella plays Henry and Karen Hill's daughter, Judy.

LEGACY: *The Simpsons* episode 'Bart The Murderer' pinches from both *GoodFellas* and De Niro's *A Bronx Tale*, with Bart becoming the bartender at a local Mafia-owned bar and falling under the protection of 'Fat Tony' (voiced by Joe Mantegna). In *Swingers* (Doug Liman, 1996) Jon Favreau and Vince Vaughn discuss the 'Through-the-back-of-the-Copa' scene. *Harry Enfield's Television Programme* did a sketch where Enfield and Paul Whitehouse remade *GoodFellas* (or as their continuity announcer described it, 'completely ruined for television') with the swearing overdubbed with words like 'fun'. A certain pizza company would also be without a name, were it not for the film. And of course, the HBO drama series *The Sopranos*, is frequently described by critics as '*GoodFellas* – the TV series'.

ALTERNATIVE VERSIONS: A television version of the film was prepared by Martin Scorsese, retaining a good portion of the film's graphic violence. It also retained much of the profanity, minus the F-and S-words which were dubbed over. Martin Scorsese did a televised introduction upon the film's network premiere.

DELETED SCENES: Thelma Schoonmaker refers to one brief scene that was cut from the finished movie, in which the young Henry is taught how to drink espresso coffee.

TRIVIA: Pity actor Frank Vincent, meanwhile, who suffered the indignity of having a car door slammed into him by Joe Pesci in *Raging Bull*, and here takes the most violent assault ever seen on a human being in a movie. Fear not though, for Vincent manages to get his own back in *Casino*. Former US Attorney and former head of the eastern district's Organized Crime Strike Force, Edward McDonald, plays himself in the movie, re-enacting what he did in real life: convincing Henry and Karen to enter the Witness Protection Programme. Despite the efforts of Scorsese and his team to make the film as accurate as possible, some small errors do creep in. In the scene that's identified as being set in 1963, Henry is leaning on a 1965 Chevy Impala and a Boeing 747 is seen landing six years before the first 747 took off. When Tommy whacks Stacks, he shoots him a total of four times in the first shot, but then, in the slow-motion reprise, he fires five times. The uncropped full-screen video release reveals a continuity error not visible in the theatrical version, namely the cross on Henry's neck-chain when he hears of the Lufthansa robbery that suddenly changes to a Star of David and back.

POSTER: A classic image, De Niro centre, Liotta to the left, Pesci to the right, with just their collars and De Niro's cuffs visible, their black suits invisible against the background. At the bottom of the US quads, there was also the image of a man lying shot in the street. The tagline announced: 'Three Decades of Life in the Mafia'.

TRAILERS: The main trailer, lasting three minutes, is almost a cut-down mini-version of the film itself, beginning with the line 'As long as I can remember . . .', running through the establishing narration of Henry's neighbourhood and through the main plot-points in the film. There's a nice edit where we see the crushing of a glass at the Jewish wedding overdubbed by a gunshot. Over this, the voice-over tells us: 'In a world that's powered by violence, on the streets where the violent have power, a new generation carries on an old tradition.' A shorter version of this trailer runs at just 1 minute 25 seconds.

AWARDS: In 1991, there was one film that won critical acclaim for itself, its director, lead actor and its screenplay. Sadly, that film was not the violent, foul-mouthed *GoodFellas* but the more family-friendly *Dances with Wolves*, Kevin Costner's brave revival of the Western genre. Still, at the Golden Globe Awards, *GoodFellas* was nominated for Best Motion Picture (Drama), Best Director, Best Screenplay and best supporting actor/actress (for Joe Pesci and Lorraine Bracco respectively). It was a similar story at the American Academy Awards, with *Dances with Wolves* collecting the best film and best director statuettes, though *GoodFellas* received nominations for Best Picture, Best Director, Best Screenplay, Best Supporting Actress (Bracco) and Best Editing (Thelma Schoonmaker). The night wasn't a complete washout though, as the first award of the night, Best Supporting Actor, went to Joe Pesci, who with great humility gave possibly one of the shortest acceptance speeches in history – 'It's my pleasure'. However, having been released too late to be eligible, *Dances with Wolves* did not sweep the board at the 1991 British Academy Awards. *GoodFellas* found itself the proud winner of five BAFTAs for Best Adapted Screenplay, Best Costume Design (Richard Bruno), Best Direction, Best Editing and Best Film, with further nominations for De Niro (Best Actor) and Michael Ballhaus (Best Cinematography). (Incidentally, the following year, *Dances with Wolves* lost out to Alan Parker's *The Commitments*.)

Scorsese won Best Director at the National Society of Film Critics Awards (along with Best Film for *GoodFellas*); the Boston Society of Film Critics named the picture Best Film, Scorsese the Best Director and Joe Pesci Best Supporting Actor; at the Chicago Film Critics Association Awards the Best Director went to Scorsese, with trophies also awarded for Best Picture, Best Screenplay and Best Supporting Actor (Lorraine Bracco and Joe Pesci); at the New York Film Critics Circle Awards, it won Best Film, Robert De Niro won a Best Actor Award (in a combined win for his performance in Penny Marshall's *Awakenings*, 1990) and Scorsese bagged Best Director; the Los Angeles Film Critics Association named *GoodFellas* Best Picture, Scorsese Best Director, Ballhaus for Best Cinematography, Pesci Best Supporting Actor and Bracco Best Supporting Actress; the National Board of Review gave Pesci their award for Best Supporting Actor; the American Cinema Editors gave their Eddie to Thelma Schoonmaker, while Michael Ballhaus was nominated for a trophy from the British Society of Cinematographers; the Danish critics gave the picture their Bodil Award for Best American Film, and Scorsese was awarded a Silver Lion for Best Direction at the Venice Film Festival. The Writers Guild of America nominated the script for the Best Screenplay Based on Material from Another Medium, the film also received nominations at the César Awards in France (for Best Foreign Film) and the Edgar Allan Poe Awards. And, in 2000, *GoodFellas* was registered with the American National Film Preservation Board.

AVAILABILITY: Originally released on DVD in the USA in 1997, with the European version released the following year, the disc was a widescreen presentation, though unfortunately due to the picture's length it was also a dreaded 'flipper' – the film was split on to two sides of the disc. *GoodFellas* has also been released on VHS a number of times, in both fullscreen and widescreen editions.

WHAT THE CRITICS SAID: Reviews tended to follow a similar pattern, with praise for the director always undermined by criticism of the violence or the lifestyle portrayed. Barry McIlheney of *Empire* gave a fairly even-handed review: 'Violent in the extreme – this is a movie where heads literally get kicked on – and simply relentless in its grip over more than two hours, *GoodFellas* falls short only in its limited emotional range, never quite achieving the full sweep of Coppola or Leone over the same terrain. In its own narrow, near-claustrophobic perspective, however, driven along by a classic soundtrack and with no shortage of master directorial brush strokes, it is hard to imagine a bigger picture than this.' Geoff Andrew of *Time Out* summed up popular opinion, calling it a 'return to form', although he was concerned by the screenplay's apparent lack of a clear moral stance, observing how Pileggi and Scorsese seem 'less concerned with telling a lucid, linear story than with providing sociological evidence of an ethically (ethnically?) marginalised society united by the desire to make a fast buck.'

In *The New York Times* Pauline Kael, declared the picture 'a triumphant piece of filmmaking – journalism and sociology presented with the biro of drama.' Though Kael did concede the film lacked a strong central lead in the manner of Howard Hawks' *Scarface*, she admitted that 'what you respond to is Scorsese's bravura: the filmmaking process becomes the subject of the movie. Watching it is like getting strung out on pure sensation.' Over on the *Washington Post*, Desson Howe wrote: 'By the time a key witness comes forward and puts a stop to all the crime in *GoodFellas*, the relief is practically serene. It means no more horrifying murders, no more husbands cheating on their wives, no more double-crossings, no more red-eyed cocaine binges, and no more having to stir that tomato sauce. But it also signals the conclusion to one of Martin Scorsese's most brutal but stunning movies, an incredible, relentless experience about the single-minded pursuit of crime.'

EXPERT WITNESSES: 'My husband would come home and I'd say, "So, Charlie, what did you do today?" And he'd say, "Well today they killed so-and-so." And the next day he'd come home and say "Well, they dumped the bodies today." I said, "Marty, what's going on? What's this movie about? Only killing?" He said, "Ma, it's the book. It's the way it is." I played the mother of Tommy and he's always killing too!' Catherine Scorsese (*Mrs DeVito, Tommy's Mom*).

'I saw *GoodFellas* three times. Before I saw it the first time, my anxiety and fear were very high. But as it turned out, I was able to relive 25 years of my life on the screen. The second time, I was actually frightened by all the blood. The third time, I concentrated on the players. Robert De Niro had really done his homework. Paul Sorvino was just terrific as Paulie. Ray Liotta was the Henry I had fallen madly in love with all those years ago – good-looking, well dressed, immaculately clean. He'd light up a room when he came in. It was all there. Tommy was as frightening as a killing machine with no "off" button. I thought the movie was fast and furious. And correct.' The real Karen Hill.

FINAL ANALYSIS: While Coppola was struggling to revive his career after a decade of bankruptcy and Spielberg was working on an ill-advised sequel to *Peter Pan*, Scorsese produced what many consider to be the jewel in his crown. Seductive, terrifying, fascinating and almost never dull, *GoodFellas* represents a lifetime's achievement from one of cinema's most dedicated students. Taking the best from only the best film-makers, Scorsese also improved upon his own work in a compilation of sequences that hark right back to *It's Not Just You, Murray!* and *Who's That Knocking At My Door?* as well as *Mean Streets* and *Raging Bull*. As we watch Henry and later Karen become seduced and consumed by the lifestyle, 'living good', it's hard not to feel some empathy for them when it all inevitably comes to an end. Henry's gradual decline into coke-fuelled paranoia offers us one last dizzying whirl around his rapidly disintegrating life before he comes crashing back down to Earth. In his world, making the evening meal is just as important as dropping off a consignment of guns and planning a drugs run. And why not? For we see throughout the film that the rewards of living a life of crime are the luxuries of garlic sliced with a razor or veal shanks for the tomato sauce (no doubt made to Mama Scorsese's famous recipe). The last reel of the picture, from Henry's arrest until the shots of him standing in his bathrobe collecting his newspaper, come as an intentionally disappointing anticlimax. For all our feelings of morality, we almost envy the freedom, the wealth and the excitement. We almost want to start addressing our friends as 'Fat Andy', 'Freddie No-Nose', 'Pete the Killer' and 'Jimmy Two-Times', but only so long as we don't have to face the consequences at the end of it.

SCORSESE ON *GOODFELLAS*: 'What fascinated me most were the details of everyday life. What they (the local goodfellas) eat, how they dress, the nightclubs they go to, what their houses look like, and how, around that, life organises itself, day by day, minute by minute. Their wives, their kids.'

Made in Milan (1990)

(35 mm – 20 min – colour)

Production Company: Emporio Armani
Producer: Barbara De Fina
Director: Martin Scorsese
Screenplay: Martin Scorsese
Cinematography: Nestor Almendros
Editor: Thelma Schoonmaker
Music: Howard Shore

CAST: Giorgio Armani, Howard Shore

SUMMARY: As he prepares for a show, designer Giorgio Armani discusses his life, his family and his Italian background.

USUAL SUSPECTS: Editor Thelma Schoonmaker (*Who's That Knocking At My Door?*, *Street Scenes*, *Raging Bull*, *The King of Comedy*, *After Hours*, *The Color of Money*, *Bad*, *The Last Temptation of Christ*, *New York Stories*, *GoodFellas*, *Cape Fear*, *Age of Innocence*, *Casino*, *A Personal Journey with Martin Scorsese Through American Movies*, *Kundun*, *Bringing Out the Dead*, *My Voyage to Italy*, *Gangs of New York*).

PRODUCTION: Having already made two commercials for fashion house Armani, Scorsese shot this documentary over five days in May 1990 in between attending the Cannes Film festival and returning home to complete the editing on *GoodFellas*.

LEGACY: The notoriously shy Armani has only allowed one other recorded interview since *Made in Milan: A Man For All Seasons*, made by Julian Ozanne.

WHAT THE CRITICS SAID: Film critic Woody Hockswender quipped: 'Employing Scorsese to direct such flimsy material is as absurd and wasteful as hiring George Cukor to film your wedding.'

SCORSESE ON *MADE IN MILAN*: This film is about style. About a man with style from a terribly impoverished background. I had no idea. He is such an elegant man. I didn't know until he started talking about it and introduced us to his parents. They were always well dressed but the mother made the clothes for him. She taught him. And he's self-made. He created the empire out of his energy and his vision.'

Cape Fear (1991)

(70 mm – 128 mins – colour)

Produced by Amblin Entertainment, in association with
Cappa Films and TriBeCa Productions for Universal Pictures
Producers: Barbara De Fina, Robert De Niro (not credited)
Executive Producers: Kathleen Kennedy, Frank Marshall
Director: Martin Scorsese
Written by Wesley Strick based on the novel *The Executioners* by John D MacDonald
Cinematography: Freddie Francis
Editor: Thelma Schoonmaker
Production Designer: Henry Bumstead
Music: Bernard Herrmann
Music Adaptation: Elmer Bernstein
Cinematographer: Freddie Francis
Casting: Ellen Lewis
Art Direction: Jack G Taylor Jr
Set Decoration: Alan Hicks
Costume Design: Rita Ryack
Miniature Special Effects Supervisor: Derek Meddings
Title Designers: Saul Bass, Elaine Bass

SOUNDTRACK: 'Tiptina' by Professor Longhair; 'Patience' by Guns N' Roses; 'Do Right Woman – Do Right Man' by Aretha Franklin; 'The Bog' by Bigod 20; 'Been Caught Stealing' by Jane's Addiction; 'The Creature from the Black Leather Lagoon' by the Cramps.

CAST: Robert De Niro (*Max Cady*), Nick Nolte (*Sam J Bowden*), Jessica Lange (*Leigh Bowden*), Juliette Lewis (*Danielle Bowden*), Joe Don Baker (*Claude Kersek, Private Investigator*), Robert Mitchum (*Lieutenant Elgart*), Gregory Peck (*Lee Heller, Cady's Attorney*), Martin Balsam (*Judge*), Illeana Douglas (*Lori Davis*), Fred Dalton Thompson (*Tom Broadbent*), Zully Montero (*Graciela, The Bowdens' Maid*), Craig Henne, Forest Burton, Edgar Allan Poe IV, Rod Ball, W Paul Bodie (*Prisoners*), Joel Kolker (*Corrections Officer*), Antoni Corone (*Corrections Officer*), Tamara Jones (*Ice Cream Cashier*), Roger Pretto,

Parris Buckner (*Racquetball Colleagues*), Margot Moreland (*Secretary*), Will Knickerbocker (*Detective*), Robert L Gerlach, Bruce E Holdstein (*Arresting Officers*), Richard Wasserman, Paul Nagle Jr, Paul Froehler, Mary Ellen O'Brien, Jody Wilson (*Parade Watchers*), Kate Colburn (*Waitress*), Domenica Scorsese (*Danielle's Girlfriend*), Garr Stevens (*Big Man 1*), Billy D Lucas (*Big Man 2*), Ken Collins (*Big Man 3*), Linda Perri, Elizabeth Moyer (*Ticket Agents*), Catherine Scorsese, Charles Scorsese (*Fruit Stand Customers*), Jackie Davis (*Jimmy the Dockmaster*).

TITLES: The Universal Logo turns blue and ripples as if reflected in water. The logo fades, replaced by golden water, against which the credits appear in a white font that appears to have been slashed. We see distorted images of an eagle swooping down, a startled eye, a mouth grimacing, then a face lit from above, a distorted body and finally a single drop of blood which colours the water red just as the credit, DIRECTED BY MARTIN SCORSESE appears. Through the blood we see a negative image of a pair of eyes, which turn blue, then positive black and white then colour as the opening narration begins and we see the face of Danielle Bowden smirking coquettishly back at us. The images in the title sequence, by the way, came from unused footage from the titles for *Seconds* (John Frankenheimer, 1966), which Saul and Elaine Bass projected on to a pool of oil.

SUMMARY: Leigh Bowden, a successful designer, her husband Sam, a lawyer, and Danielle, their daughter, have a seemingly perfect life. But the Bowdens' life is not a happy one, with Sam having enjoyed a number of affairs in the past and possibly on the verge of another with his secretary Lori, Leigh increasingly frustrated by her husband's infidelity and Danielle, misbehaving at school and experimenting with marijuana. All these cracks in their relationships are waiting to be prised slowly open when Max Cady comes to their town.

Cady was once a client of Sam's accused of a vicious sexual assault on a young woman. Sam buried evidence that might have helped lessen Cady's sentence, leaving Cady facing fourteen years in prison. On his release, Max comes looking for Sam obsessed with the idea of making Sam pay for his own loss. At first he merely annoys the family, laughing gregariously and smoking in a cinema. But after he casually reintroduces himself to Sam one afternoon, he mumbles that Sam is going to 'learn about loss'. That night, Sam tells Leigh about Cady, claiming that he can't remember the details of Cady's case, but that he thinks the man might be holding a bit of a grudge against him.

At work, Sam explains to his senior partner, Tom Broadbent, that he believes Cady is harassing him and that he's filed a restraining order against him, which will be heard in the courts in ten days. Then he confides the details of the case: that Cady was convicted of a serious sexual assault on a young girl and that Sam buried the information that the victim in Cady's case was promiscuous. Sam is certain that there's no way the illiterate Cady could have known about that. Later, though, Cady drives up beside Sam and tells him that he learned to read during his stretch, starting with children's books but soon gravitating towards law until he was able successfully to represent himself in his parole hearings. It wasn't long before he learned about Sam's deception. Panicking, Sam offers to give Cady $10,000, but Cady ridicules his offer, pointing out that even $50,000 wouldn't cover minimum wage, never mind the loss of his wife and the child who believes him to be dead.

Back at his office, Sam works towards finding a reason for the authorities to restrict Cady, but then he receives a call from Leigh that sends him racing back home. That afternoon, her dog Ben died in front of her, howling in agony. The vet told her the dog was poisoned. A friend in the police force arranges for Cady to be brought in on a vagrancy charge while they inspect his bank details. It turns out that, while he was in prison, Cady's mother died, leaving him $30,000. With no evidence to place Cady on the Bowden's property, the police are forced to let him go. When Sam next sees Cady in the street staring lustfully at Leigh, Sam punches him, unable to control his temper any longer. Unfortunately, he does so in front of a number of witnesses who see Cady as the victim in the dispute.

That night, Cady meets Sam's secretary in a bar. Lori has a bit of a crush on Sam and is drowning her sorrows at being continually stood up by him. Max takes advantage of the situation, seducing the lonely woman, taking her back to her apartment and then savagely beating her and biting a chunk out of her cheek. Though neighbours call the police on her behalf and positively identify Max's car at the scene, Lori is too terrified to testify, knowing how women in her position are treated in cases like this. Worried for Lori, Sam calls her from home, but when Leigh overhears him talking, she accuses him of having an affair with Lori. Sam tries to reassure her that the girl is merely infatuated with him and that there is nothing going on between them, but the incident has clearly opened up old wounds and Sam is forced to sleep on the couch that night.

Sam decides to hire Claude Kersek, a private investigator, to keep tabs on Cady. Kersek learns that, while in prison, Cady murdered a fellow inmate, which was why his sentence was doubled to fourteen years. Though Sam tells his family that he is reassured by Kersek's expertise, it's obvious that he is still very concerned and on edge. While Kersek is on surveillance, however, Max reveals that he knows he's been followed and Kersek is forced to step forward and threaten Cady. Cady, however, doesn't seem at all worried, confident that nobody can legally stop him from being in the town and going wherever he pleases. To prove the point, he brazenly drives up to the Bowden house and hands Leigh a dog-collar, pretending he found it further up the road. Leigh explains to him, unknowing, that their dog died recently, but when Max deliberately lets slip that he knows their dog was big and friendly and that Leigh is an artist she realises who he is. Leigh bravely stands up to the man, telling him she finds him repulsive, but when she hears Danielle leave the house she panics and orders her daughter back inside. Unfortunately, Cady has already caught a glimpse of the girl. He drives off purposefully.

That night, Danielle receives a call at home from Max Cady posing as her new drama teacher. He tells her their summer class has been moved to the theatre and then proceeds to show how much he understands her and her problems, including how her parents won't let her grow up and become a woman. The next morning, Danielle heads off alone to the theatre, in the basement of her school. There she finds her 'teacher' waiting for her on the stage, smoking a joint. He offers her some, saying it will relax her, and then, stubbing it out on his tongue, gives it to her. He talks sympathetically with her until she realises that he's not her teacher, but the man who has been hanging around her home. She asks him if he's the man who killed their dog and Max seems genuinely upset to hear that her dog has died. He tells her he has no anger in him, that he prays for her father as she should. Then, slowly, he touches her face, slides his thumb into her mouth and then kisses her passionately before walking off into the back of the theatre's stage. Suddenly aware of how vulnerable she is, Danielle runs out of the theatre.

Kersek breaks the news to Sam that Cady has spotted him. He suggests that he knows some people who might be able to work outside the law. Sam insists he's not willing to go that far, but, after he learns of Danielle's close encounter with Cady, he can see no alternative and asks him to hire the thugs to put Cady in hospital. Sam goes to see Cady in a restaurant to warn him to leave town. Cady, however, repeats that he is happy staying there and that he's come to save Sam. Sam leaves, disgusted. Later that night, Sam watches, hidden, as the hired thugs jump Cady and begin to beat him with bars. At first, Max is curled on the floor, defenceless, but then he manages to fight all three men to the ground.

The next morning, Sam tries to obtain the services of a top lawyer, Lee Heller. Heller is courteous and friendly, having fought in Korea with Sam's boss. But when Sam mentions he needs an injunction against Cady, Heller is forced to cut the conversation short – Cady hired him the previous day. At the hearing, Sam's case crumbles when it's revealed that Max had taped his earlier threat. Sitting in the courtroom, bruised and battered, Max looks every inch the victim and the judge awards the restraining order, not to Sam, but to Max Cady.

Sam goes to Kersek and asks him to get him a gun. Kersek points out that, having never fired a gun before, he might as well hand the gun over to Cady straight away. Sam tells him that he's to face a hearing to see if he'll be allowed to practise law in the state again. Kersek realises that, if Sam is forced to attend the hearing, that will leave Leigh and Danielle alone for two days. Cady, he points out, is an opportunist. And, if Cady enters his house illegally, then he can be shot within the bounds of the law. The night before the hearing, Sam drives out to the airport with his wife and daughter, certain that Max will be following him. Sure enough, once Danielle and Leigh drive away, Max tries to find out from the check-in attendant if Sam left on the flight.

Sam sneaks back out of the airport and makes his way home. Back at the house, while Sam lies out of sight from the windows, Kersek sets up a system of tripwires to alert him if Cady breaks in. Despite Kersek sitting up all night, gun in hand, there's no sign of an intruder, but the next morning, as Danielle takes out the trash she finds a copy of Henry Miller's *Sexus* left there by Cady. Their talk has had a profound effect on Danielle, and, believing the man has made a connection with her, she smuggles it into the house. The Bowdens' maid, Graciela, is asked to stay overnight as she would if Sam was actually away. In the night, Kersek is alerted by his tripwires, but is relieved to find they have been activated by an unlocked door. Sitting down for a drink in the family kitchen, Kersek is grabbed from behind by Cady dressed as Graciela. Upstairs, Sam and Leigh hear a gunshot and cautiously venture into the kitchen to find Kersek lying dead on the floor, garrotted with a piano wire and shot in the head with his own gun. Then Danielle discovers the body of Graciela.

The Bowdens flee their home and make their way to their houseboat, moored in Cape Fear, unaware that Cady is clinging to the underside of their car. Sam steers the boat upriver and drops anchor just as a storm begins to brew. As Sam checks the moorings on the boat, Max grabs him and strangles him until he passes out. Severing the moorings and leaving the boat to float free, Max boards, terrorising the women: he locks Danielle in the hold while he forcibly molests Leigh. As Leigh tries to get hold of Max's gun, he handcuffs her to a railing and then drags Sam, his hands tied behind his back, into the cabin. With both parents bound, Max pulls Danielle out of the hold and prepares to rape her. Leigh pleads with him to take her instead and Max listens patiently before telling the petrified mother that her begging will just make him enjoy taking her daughter all the more. As he insolently lights his cigar, Danielle grabs a bottle of lighter fluid and squirts it at Max. His upper body is engulfed in flames and he throws himself headfirst into the river.

The family breathe a sigh of relief, but not for long, As Sam struggles to maintain control of the boat, Max, his face badly burned, manages to climb back on board and he once more holds the family at gunpoint. In a manic fervour, Cady stages his own mock trial of Sam, with legal terms and biblical quotes intermingled. As Cady tries to pass sentence, the boat enters uncharted waters. Thinking swiftly, Sam cuffs Cady's leg to a rail just as the boat is torn apart on the rocks. Both men are thrown ashore, with Cady linked to a large section of decking. Sam and Cady continue to fight until, as Sam picks up a rock, vowing to kill his tormentor, the section of decking is swept underwater, dragging Cady down with it. Sam watches, exhausted, as Cady slowly drowns.

WHO'S WHO?: Jessica Lange shot to fame as the Fay Wray replacement for the remake of *King Kong* (John Guillermin, 1976), clocked up another remake opposite Jack Nicholson with *The Postman Always Rings Twice* (Bob Rafelson, 1981) and picked up her first Oscar for Best Supporting Actress for *Tootsie*. More recently, she starred opposite Liam Neeson in *Rob Roy* (Michael Caton-Jones, 1995). Cornering the market in disturbed teenage girls, Juliette Lewis followed *Cape Fear* with *Kalifornia* (Dominic Sena, 1993), *Natural Born Killers* (Oliver Stone, 1994) and *From Dusk Till Dawn* (Robert Rodrigues, 1996). Joe Don Baker is perhaps more familiar, to British audiences at least, from his role in the groundbreaking TV thriller *Edge of Darkness* and for his guest appearances in the James Bond films *The Living Daylights* (John Glen, 1987), *GoldenEye* (Martin Campbell, 1995) and *Tomorrow Never Dies* (Roger Spottiswoode, 1997).

Tough guy Robert Mitchum and eternally earnest Gregory Peck swap sides from their roles in the original *Cape Fear*, 1962. Mitchum played a Cady-esque preacher in *The Night of the Hunter* (Charles Laughton, 1955), and showed his many critics just how underrated an actor he truly was with a stunning performance in David Lean's *Ryan's Daughter* (1970). Peck is probably most famous for his early starring role in Hitchcock's *Spellbound* (1945), *Duel in the Sun* (King Vidor, 1946) – which was a major influence on the young Scorsese – Atticus Finch in *To Kill A Mockingbird* (Robert Mulligan, 1962) and Robert Thorne in *The Omen* (Richard Donner, 1976). Martin Balsam also appeared in the original *Cape Fear*, and played Detective Arborghast, Norman Bates's second on-screen victim in Hitchcock's *Psycho* (1960). Derek Meddings shaped visions of the future for generations of children, having been responsible for model work on hundreds of episodes of Gerry Anderson's many puppet series, including *Thunderbirds*, *Stingray* and *Captain Scarlet*. His final project was overseeing model effects on *GoldenEye*.

THE USUAL SUSPECTS: Robert De Niro (*Mean Streets*, *Taxi Driver*, *New York, New York*, *Raging Bull*, *The King of Comedy GoodFellas*, *Casino*); Illeana Douglas (*The Last Temptation of Christ*, *New York Stories*, *GoodFellas*, *Grace of My Heart*); editor Thelma Schoonmaker (*Who's That Knocking At My Door?*, *Street Scenes*, *Raging Bull*, *The King of Comedy*, *After Hours*, *The Color of Money*, *Bad*, *The Last Temptation of Christ*, *New York Stories*, *GoodFellas*, *Age of Innocence*, *Casino*, *A Personal Journey with Martin Scorsese Through American Movies*, *Kundun*, *Bringing Out the Dead*, *My Voyage to Italy*, *Gangs of New York*).

SOURCE: John Dann MacDonald was born in Sharon, Pennsylvania on 24 July 1916. Like Scorsese, MacDonald was bed-ridden at the age of 12 due to illness, a near-fatal double whammy of mastoiditis and scarlet fever. He first began to write during the war, while stationed in Ceylon. Instead of sending his wife letters he knew would be censored, he began to send his wife short stories. To his surprise, she managed to sell one of the stories for publication. After the war, he turned to writing full-time. In 1958 he wrote *The Executioners*, a novel which, strangely, takes place nowhere near the Cape Fear river.

MacDonald's novel differs from both film versions. Sam is married to Carol, and has three children, six-year-old Bucky, eleven-year-old Jamie and their daughter, Nancy, who is fourteen. The book opens with Sam telling his wife that he's learned of the release of Max Cady, a man he testified against in the army having witnessed him rape a girl no older than their own daughter. Sam is an idealist who believes in the law, telling his wife: 'If the law can't protect us, then I'm dedicated to a myth, and I'd better wake up.' Although his menace runs through the book, with many scenes either anticipating his arrival or following on from his departure, Cady himself appears in just one scene. Addressing Sam as 'Lieutenant', Cady tells him about going to find his own wife, who divorced Cady while he was in prison and has since remarried. Cady boasts that he kidnapped her and forced her to write him an incriminating love letter to prevent her from ever testifying against him. Cady is described as being five foot nine, balding with 'small brown eyes set in deep simian sockets' and artificial-looking teeth. When Sam has Cady beaten, the assailants are defeated as in the films, but the end result is Cady is arrested and held for thirty days for disorderly conduct, which buys Sam enough time to allow his children to go to summer camp. After Cady is released, he disappears. At the summer camp, Jamie is shot from long-range, though only wounded. Driving their other son to a hideout, Carol nearly crashes their car when the wheel of their caravan falls clean away; the wheel-nuts had been loosened so that they were only partially threaded. The climax to the book comes after Cady breaks into the Bowdens' house and kills the police officer guarding the family (a young deputy named Kersek). Sam shoots blindly into the night and the next morning the police find Cady's body up in the woods behind their house. The Bowdens' boat, the Sweet Sioux III, never leaves its moorings, and the family go nowhere near Cape Fear, with the bulk of the novel set in up-state New York.

Three years after its publication, *The Executioners* made the jump to the big screen thanks to actor Gregory Peck, who had acquired the rights to the novel and approached British director J Lee Thompson to direct the film version. Thompson had struck up a friendship with Peck when the two worked together on *The Guns of Navarone*. Originally, Thompson had approached Telly Savalas to play Cady, but, after testing Robert Mitchum, Savalas took the part of the private detective, Sievers, with Martin Balsam as Police Chief Mark Dutton, characters whose roles would be amalgamated into one for the remake. Polly Bergen was cast as Bowden's wife, now called Peggy, with Lori Martin as their sole child, Nancy. Cady's preferred term of address for Sam is changed from 'Lieutenant' to 'Counselor', and instead of simple revenge, Cady's motivation is to even the miscarriage of justice he feels was served against him by Bowden. Indeed, it's implied that, as Bowden is a supporter of the Civil Rights movement, his apparent desire to restrict Cady's civil rights is all the more ironic. Cady takes a young woman for a drive, but after she goads him he beats her viciously. Ashamed and scared, she refuses to testify against Cady and instead leaves town. A new sequence, not in the novel, sees Cady slowly stalk a terrified Nancy around her school until she dashes out into the road and is nearly knocked down by a car. The attack of the hired thugs goes wrong, as in the novel, but one of the thugs reveals who hired him and Sam Bowden finds himself facing a disbarment hearing. Sam hatches the plan with Chief Dutton to lure Cady into committing a crime. Dutton's deputy, Kersek, is murdered by Cady, who goes after Sam's wife. The climax to the film is similar to that of the remake, except after the protracted fight in the swamp, Sam pulls a gun on Cady and tells him that he's going back to jail.

PRODUCTION: Having remade *A Guy Named Joe* (Victor Fleming, 1943) in 1989 as *Always*, and made a flawed sequel to *Peter Pan* in the form of *Hook* two years later, Steven Spielberg began to consider reworking another film he held the rights to, J Lee Thompson's *Cape Fear*. After Stephen Frears and Donald Westlake left the project, Spielberg approached Wesley Strick, a young writer who'd already scored success with *Arachnophobia* (Frank Marshall, 1990), produced by Spielberg's company, Amblin. Strick was sent a tape of the original movie, but was not impressed, seeing it as a failed Hitchcock-style movie. Strick met with Spielberg and outlined the many flaws in the story that convinced him he had to pass on the project. At the end of the meeting, according to Strick, Spielberg told him he was glad the writer was coming aboard, clearly seeing his resistance as yet another indication that he was right for the job. Indeed, soon after, Spielberg decided to produce the picture instead of directing.

Looking to his old friend Martin Scorsese to take the helm, Spielberg staged a read-through of the script in New York for Scorsese with Robert De Niro (as Cady) working alongside Kevin Kline (as Sam Bowden) and Kline's wife Phoebe Cates (as Bowden's daughter). Scorsese still wasn't sold on the idea. For him, the family were too squeaky-clean, the morality too black and white. Hearing Scorsese's criticisms, Spielberg encouraged him to make whatever changes he felt necessary to make it interesting for him. Additionally, as he'd done with *Raging Bull*, Robert De Niro began the hard-sell on the Max Cady character, persuading Scorsese that they could really do something with him. The pair hadn't worked closely in nine years (*GoodFellas* being little more than an extended cameo for De Niro), and slowly, Scorsese came around and committed to the project, later claiming that he saw it more as an apology to Universal for all the 'suffering and madness' he'd caused them with *The Last Temptation of Christ*.

Scorsese and De Niro invited Wesley Strick to New York to meet him properly for the first time and discuss a number of changes that they drafted. Strick wasn't surprised to see that many of them were to undo elements he had specifically written with Spielberg in mind to direct. One significant difference between the original movie and the remake was, however, already in Strick's first script, the change of Sam's job from prosecutor to defence attorney.

Turning his mind to casting, Scorsese originally considered movie idol Robert Redford for the role of Sam, as he seemed to embody many of the virtues the character originally had. He certainly didn't consider Nick Nolte, who, when they'd previously worked together on *New York Stories*, was overweight and bearded. But at a screening of *GoodFellas* at the Museum of Modern Art, Scorsese bumped into Nolte, who had lost a lot of weight and was clean-shaven and wearing a suit and tie and glasses. The change of image surprised Scorsese enough to feel he'd be perfect for the part, especially as, underneath the respectable exterior, Scorsese knew Nolte also had the capability to suggest a darker side to the character. Jessica Lange and Nolte teased each other between takes, with Nolte dropping his trousers on one occasion and Lange refusing to come back until 'everything is put away'. Jessica Lange and Scorsese had already met, Lange having auditioned for the role of Vickie LaMotta in *Raging Bull*. Lange would be cast as Sam's wife, Karen – later changed to Leigh. For the role of Danielle, De Niro conducted the initial interviews alone in Beverly Hills. Though Juliette Lewis was the first person De Niro auditioned, both Scorsese and he continued to audition other girls in subsequent casting calls. After a fourth audition, Scorsese reassured Lewis by telling her that they simply didn't believe they could have been so lucky to have found their Danielle with their very first audition which was why they kept auditioning just to make sure. As a tribute to the original movie, Scorsese managed to persuade three of the original cast-members to take supporting roles in the remake. The original Sam Bowden, Gregory Peck, would spend a day on the set playing Max Cady's slippery lawyer, Lee Heller. Robert Mitchum, who'd played Max Cady, was Sam's friend in the police department, Lieutenant Elgart, while Martin Balsam was given the part of the judge who awards the restraining order to Max Cady.

Robert De Niro had begun work on the character some months earlier, beginning a strict work-out regime with his trainer Dan Harvey, working out for three hours a day before coming in for rehearsals. Scorsese left shooting the scenes with De Niro shirtless until near the end, to allow the actor to reach maximum physique. While working on the accent he'd decided to use for the film, De Niro interviewed rapists and killers in prison, read court depositions of rapist killers and spoke with doctors and other specialists who could help with his research. One case revealed an incident where a man had bitten the cheek of his victim, inspiring De Niro to suggest a similar act in his character's attack on Lori. And reading the suggestion in the script that Cady should cling to the underside of the Bowdens' car, De Niro insisted that he'd only perform the scene if it could be proven that such a stunt could actually be done. A stuntman was despatched to test it out and, satisfied, De Niro approved the scene. One other skill De Niro picked up during preproduction was the ability to speak 'Glossolalia' – a form of ecstatic language that is found in extreme fundamental Christian organisations, often called 'speaking in tongues'. De Niro had heard audio tapes of the phenomenon and incorporated this into the final moments of Cady's life as he begins to drown.

Wesley Strick's script had indicated that Cady sported a couple of tattoos. This inspired De Niro to come up with the idea of having Cady's body covered in ink. Artist Ilona Herman took guidance from De Niro and Scorsese on the designs, taking quotes from the Bible and working with Temptu Inc, a make-up company that specialised in temporary tattoos. Temptu's founder, Roy Zuckerman, had worked with De Niro before, providing faded Navy tattoos for his character in *GoodFellas*. The biggest problem they faced was making the tattoo waterproof and visible through the burns towards the end of the film. De Niro also caused them problems by bulking up for the role, so the tattoos expanded by about eight per cent, requiring Temptu to retouch some of the designs. De Niro's own tattoo, a black panther he had done during *Mean Streets*, was incorporated into their work.

For the first time, Scorsese allowed his writer on to the set, and Strick quickly proved his worth by making corrections to the dialogue during filming. One such instance occurred early on, when Strick first saw De Niro's extensive tattoo work. Having been unaware of this development, Strick hastily rewrote a line for Mitchum about not knowing whether to look at Cady or read him. He also wrote the scene where Cady hands Leigh the dog-collar at the request of Jessica Lange, who pointed out that her character should have an opportunity to meet Cady prior to the big climactic boat sequences (see **DELETED SCENES**).

Location filming would take place in Fort Lauderdale, Florida. Production designer Henry Bumstead (a former collaborator with Hitchcock) found the Bowdens' house just one month before shooting, adding shutters to the exterior and a wooden banister to the showpiece staircase. One major problem with the location of the house was that it lay directly under the flight path from the nearby airport, so crew-members had to be stationed at the airport to communicate back to the unit to co-ordinate shooting.

Cape Fear marked the first time Scorsese had used Cinemascope. He'd shied away from it previously, aware of how 70 mm films tend not to transfer well to the television screen. But, as this was his first attempt at a 'genre' picture, with matte paintings, special effects and a hefty budget ($34 million, his biggest to date), the temptation was too great.

The scene set in Danielle's school was originally closer to the original, with Cady terrorising the girl to the point where she hangs out of a window and is caught by the school janitor. However, De Niro and Scorsese decided it would be more effective if, instead of terrorising her, Cady tries to seduce her, and Strick worked out the scene in improvisations with De Niro and Lewis. In the final shoot, Scorsese planned to allow De Niro a little freedom, and so set up the scene with two cameras. Lewis, who later confessed she'd developed a crush on De Niro, was already nervous at the idea of being kissed by him, so when he delivered the line about putting his arm around her she began to giggle. But she had no idea that De Niro (having discussed an idea with his director) planned to push his thumb into her mouth. It was that first take that ended up in the final cut.

For the climactic boat sequence, a 90×100-foot tank of water was constructed in a sound stage in Florida. With over two hundred drawings prepared by Scorsese for these scenes alone, it took nearly seven weeks to complete the shoot. These scenes had to be completed in time for veteran model-maker Derek Meddings to match the miniatures he would prepare for the boat's journey along the river and its gradual disintegration.

Another first for Scorsese was the use of optical special effects. The 4th of July fireworks that are seen behind De Niro as he sits on the Bowdens' wall were created with computer graphics, merging a number of different layers to create a larger-than-life display of colours. The darkening skies throughout the film were created with matte paintings, most notably for Max Cady's departure from prison and for the backdrop to the Bowdens' house. For the shot of Max being doused in flames by Danielle, De Niro acted out the scene in the studio, then a stuntman was hired to mimic his performance against a blue screen so that the flames could then be digitally grafted on to the shots of De Niro.

Cape Fear opened in November 1991 to generally positive reviews, although the levels of violence, particularly against women, came under attack. But for the first time in his life, Scorsese had an undisputed commercial success on his hands, with the picture raking in over $79 million in the USA alone. His most expensive project to date had also become his most lucrative, and his reward would be the freedom to make the kind of films he wanted to. His next project, however, would not be quite what most people would have expected . . .

EDITING: Scorsese's take on *Cape Fear* is more self-consciously stylistic than the original, with his customary dizzying camerawork and editing playing on the idea that this is high melodrama, not the documentary realism of his previous work. His use of negatives and colour stands out, with the opening shot of Danielle bleeding in red/negative, then turning blue/negative before turning blue/positive and finally colour. The close to the film reverses this process, moving from colour through to red before fading to black for the closing titles. The negative technique also appears during the sex scene between Nolte and Lange, adding to the idea that the Bowdens' relationship is not a satisfying one, for Leigh at least. In that scene we also have two colour fades, to yellow as Leigh looks up from underneath Sam, and then to pink-red as she puts on lipstick. Earlier, as Sam and Leigh talk about how they might spend the summer, we see Sam in the foreground and Leigh also in focus in the background. The reverse shot shows Leigh reflected in the mirror next to Sam, akin to the scene with Nolte and Arquette in *New York Stories*. There is the use of negative images again when Sam wakes up and thinks he sees Max standing at the foot of his bed.

Twice in the film, Sam closes all the shutters, locks every window and bolts the doors, in a series of jump-cuts that echo a similar scene in Scorsese's *Amazing Stories* episode, 'Mirror, Mirror'. As Max Cady turns the tables on the three thugs, look out for the 'Hitchcock' manoeuvre again, where the background seems to fall away as he stands still. Scorsese manages to fully utilise the widescreen format of the picture to convey the idea that these characters feel they are on their own. Characters are often framed to the extreme left or right of a shot, or, in the case of the scene where the family leave for the airport, we see a great amount of space between the characters – they don't leave the house together, but in a broken chain. As Sam watches the attack on his wife through the blinds of the boat, the frame shows us just one eye staring out in horror. This came from cinematographer Freddie Francis who suggested that focusing on just the one eye made Nolte look fishlike. And note the shot of Jessica Lange pulling herself out of the mud near the end; the shot was reversed to make it look less natural.

MUSIC: It was while on a break during preproduction that Scorsese first came up with the idea of using Bernard Herrmann's original score. Herrmann's last work with Scorsese had been for *Taxi Driver* back in the winter of 1975. Having created the music for the Scorsese-produced *The Grifters*, Elmer Bernstein offered to rework Herrmann's score. With the length and structure of the film differing from the original, it wasn't just a case of playing the score over the scenes. Bernstein reworked a number of sections, constructed a new opening piece based around Herrmann's F C B F motif and utilised segments from Herrmann's unused score for Alfred Hitchcock's *Torn Curtain*.

QUOTE/UNQUOTE

Danielle: (narrating) 'My Reminiscence. I always thought that for such a lovely river the name was mystifying – *Cape Fear* – and that the only thing to fear in those enchanted summer nights was that the magic would end and real life would come crashing in.'

Lieutenant Elgart: (looking at Cady's tattooed body) 'I don't know whether to look at him or read him . . .'

Max: 'All that prison time made me coarse. Guess I'm covered in too many tattoos, huh? But you see there's not a whole Helluva lot to do in prison except desecrate your flesh.'

Max: 'Grandaddy used to handle snakes in church, Granny drank strychnine. I guess you could say I had a leg up, genetically speaking.'

Danielle: (narrating) 'We never spoke about what happened – at least not to each other. Fear, I suppose; that to remember his name and what he did would mean letting him into our dreams and I hardly dream about him any more. Still, things won't ever be the way they were before he came, but that's alright because if you hang on to the past, you die a little every day, and for myself, I know I'd rather live . . . The End.'

ROOTS: On Cady's wall we see pictures of the dictators Mussolini and Stalin, Civil War General Robert E Lee, St Sebastian (speared through both sides like a cross), super-heroes Black Bolt and Captain Marvel, and an illustration of Alexander the Great. His mini-library includes *The Holy Bible, 100 days; Eat right and Stay Fit, American Judgements*, Nietzsche's *The Will to Power* and *Thus Spake Zarathrustra*, Dante's *The Inferno, Southern Reporter, The Cell Within, Criminal Law and its Processes, Contracts* and a book on Federal Rules Decisions. We see clips from *Problem Child* (Dennis Dugan, 1990), in which John Ritter parodies Jack Nicholson from *The Shining* (Stanley Kubrick, 1980) and a clip of Jane Wyman from *All That Heaven Allows* (Douglas Sirk, 1955). When Cady first meets Danielle, he sings a line from pop princess Tiffany's teen anthem 'I Think We're Alone Now'. As we'd expect, with the genre and Herrmann's music, there are a number of Hitchcock references. The invulnerability of Cady is inspired in part by a sequence from *Torn Curtain*, which was designed to show how long it actually takes to kill a man. Spielberg originally suggested Max should disguise himself as the Bowdens' maid in a tribute to *Psycho*. Another reference from that film is a shot of Sam lying wet on the boat deck as he watches Max attack Leigh, which recalls the shot of Janet Leigh's body lying lifeless on the bathroom floor (and surely the decision to rename Sam's wife from Karen to Leigh is a further tribute to the *Psycho* star). The fireworks outside the Bowdens' house is reminiscent of a shot from *To Catch a Thief*. Cady watching the family during the parade comes from *Strangers on a Train*, where the nutjob Bruno watches tennis player Guy Haines and his girlfriend. And the framing of the characters in the extreme left or right of the shot is possibly inspired by Hitchcock's *North by Northwest*, in which Cary Grant spends the entire film on the left of the frame. Cady's silhouette in the way of the cinema screen is reminiscent of so many Loony Tunes and Warner Bros cartoons, while there are a number of subtle suggestions that he sees himself as a comic book super-hero. Aside from the illustration on his cell wall, on the night he meets Lori he is seen wearing a shirt with a webbing design like that of Spider-Man's costume, and later he hangs from the ceiling via the chin bars like Spider-Man. Clinging to the underside of the Bowdens' car, while also very Spider-Manlike, was, according to Strick, inspired by the face-huggers from *Aliens* (James Cameron, 1986). Danielle reads Thomas Wolfe's *Look Homeward, Angel* (see also **Taxi Driver**). She tells Cady that she hasn't read Henry Miller's trilogy of *Plexus*, *Sexus* and *Nexus* but has read parts of *Tropic of Cancer* (see **After Hours**). She also has a poster on her wall of Robert Smith, the tousle-haired singer from British band the Cure, and another of Megadeath.

THEMES AND MOTIFS: Guilt, and the ideas that your sins will find you out, are the forces at work here, with Cady cast both as the demon aggressor and the Angel of the Apocalypse. Though many of Scorsese's characters are less than politically correct when it comes to women, Max Cady is Scorsese's first out and out villain. If his excessive tattoos aren't a giveaway, or his saucy cigar lighter (a cheap bikini-clad torso with no head or arms), then the mere fact that he smokes in a public cinema and finds *Problem Child* funny should do it. Scorsese's traditional signifier, the colour red, can be seen in Max's clothes (he owns at least three shirts that feature the colour red) and his bright red convertible (in no way a Freudian compensation on Cady's part). Some of the sound effects that accompany Cady, particularly in the latter scenes such as the swish when he turns his head fast, recall the similar effects used for Michael Jackson's *Bad* video. We also have the test of fire: Max can stump a cigarette out on his tongue and hold a burning flare, which would probably make *Who's That Knocking . . .*'s JR, *Mean Streets*'s Charlie and *Taxi Driver*'s Travis jealous. One other motif, but it's not Scorsese's: fans of Spielberg often keep a lookout for a shooting star across the night sky. In *Cape Fear*, we see that just after Kersek has tied up Danielle's teddy bear with fishing wire.

CONTROVERSY: Understandably, the levels of violence and intimidation towards women in the picture proved too much for some viewers. But there is also the legal aspect of the film, which some law-minded critics have pointed out doesn't stand up to scrutiny. At the time of J Lee Thompson's film, the law allowed information about a woman's sexual activity to be admissible in a rape trial to show consent or to impeach her credibility as a witness. But in the 1970s, during the heyday of the women's liberation movement, pressure mounted to restrict the admissibility of evidence concerning an alleged rape victim's past sex life. Michigan passed the first such statute in 1974, and, by 1976, this rape shield legislation had been enacted in more than half the states in one form or another. One of those states was Georgia, where it's stated Max Cady had been tried for rape in 1977. That Sam Bowden had felt the need to bury the report on his victim's promiscuity would therefore be unnecessary. In all this, few people were concerned by the idea of Max handing a joint to the fifteen-year-old Danielle on school property, no doubt because of the thumb-sucking scene that followed.

BIBLE CLASS: Max is a walking bible, literally The Word made Flesh: on his back we see the Scales of Truth and Justice; on his left forearm: 'Vengeance is Mine' NT. Romans; on his left bicep: I have put my trust in the LORD GOD in him will I trust. Ps 91,2/'THE LORD IS THE AVENGER'. NT: I Hassq lonig ii 817/'My time is not yet full come'; on his right arm: 'My Time IS AT HAND'. NT: Matthew, XX. Max advises Sam to read the Bible, the book between 'Esther' and 'Psalms', which of course, is the book of Job, where God tests Job's faith by taking everything from him. He tells Danielle not to judge her parents, quoting

Christ's words from the cross when he tells her to 'Forgive them, for they know not what they do.'

KEEP IT IN THE FAMILY: Domenica Scorsese is the daughter of Martin Scorsese and producer Julia Cameron. Her grandparents, Catherine and Charles Scorsese, appear as customers at a fruit stand in the background of the scene where Sam phones Lieutenant Elgart.

LEGACY: The film was parodied in 1993 by the wonderfully subversive animated sitcom, *The Simpsons* in an episode called 'Cape Feare: Not Affiliated with the Film "Cape Fear".' The episode features young Bart terrorised by Sideshow Bob (voiced by Frasier's Kelsey Grammer), who Bart helped convict for the robbery of the Kwik-E-Mart three seasons earlier, and who has just been released from Springfield Penitentiary. References to the film include Sideshow Bob's newly acquired taste for Hawaiian shirts; a scene in a cinema with Sideshow Bob chomping on a cigar and laughing loudly (while watching *Ernest Goes Somewhere Cheap*); Bob's tattoos, including ink on his knuckles which, considering the character only has three fingers, spell 'LUV' and 'HĀT'; string tied through the house as tripwires; Bob hiding under the Simpsons' car (shortly before Homer decides to drive through a cactus patch for absolutely no reason; a pastiche of Bernard Herrmann's *Cape Fear* score; a wacky, fast-talking DJ called Marty; a vigilante who looks strangely like Robert Mitchum; and in a possible reference to the director of the original film, the Simpsons are temporarily put into the witness protection programme and change their name to The Thompsons. The episode also contains references to *The Last Temptation of Christ* (a talking snake) and *GoodFellas* (the witness protection programme).

Not to be outdone, *The Ben Stiller Show*, which ran for twelve episodes on the Fox network in 1992–1993, featured a trailer-style sketch in its first episode called 'Cape Munster', in which Stiller, as Eddie, the werewolf son from the horror sitcom *The Munsters*, terrorises Sam Bowden (Bob Odenkirk) and his daughter Danielle (the sublime Janeane Garofalo). Eddie was seen to leave prison (telling his guard he didn't need his books as he'd 'already read 'em') and walk straight into the camera with a bump. The strip-search of Eddie reveals tattoos with the legends 'FESTER IS MINE' and 'GRANDPA SUCKS', a broken heart with the name 'Lily' above it, and a drawing of Herman Munster. The investigator quips, 'I don't know whether to look at him or go trick-or-treating.' The trailer ends with a parody of the thumb-sucking scene, where Danielle (Garofalo) is hindered by her retainer.

DELETED SCENES: A number of scenes were deleted or changed from how they appeared in the script:

- The scene where 'Karen' Bowden struggles to design a logo would have been followed by one where she wakes in the morning to find that a very simple, effective design has been drawn on her pad. She assumes it's Danielle's work, but it isn't. Though this was intended to further imply that Cady can come and go as he pleases in the house, the idea was dismissed due to the implausibility of Cady being a graphic artist (even though this could have been suggested by the tattoos possibly being self-designed).
- On seeing the muscled torso of Cady during the strip search, Lieutenant Elgart was scripted to exclaim: 'Jeez. Couldn't hurt that with an axe.' This was changed to the a comment about not knowing whether to look at him or read him.
- The scene where Sam sees the brutally beaten Lori for the first time would have ended with her telling him how Cady had told her he intended to kill Sam four times (which comes from a line in the book): his dog, his wife, his daughter and finally himself.
- In anticipation of summer school, Danielle reveals that she's thinking of becoming an actress, which is why meeting the new drama teacher is so important to her.

From the scenes that were filmed, a fair few have been included on the Universal DVD collectors' edition:

- Sam calls Leigh at home and she asks him why they never got an alarm system installed, mocking that it's just because 'This town is so very nice and everything is just so very, very nice.' The scene does appear, in part, in the trailer.
- After the murder of their dog, Sam calls a colleague with a description of Cady while Leigh puts the dog-bowl in the trash. She then changes her mind and recovers the bowl.
- Danielle chats with the maid about how things always seem to go wrong when things are right, and how she used to love going to their houseboat in Cape Fear.
- Danielle wakes her mother in the middle of the night saying she can't sleep. Leigh combs her daughter's hair. Leigh recalls a summer when Danielle cut off her hair, and Danielle asks Leigh why she cut her hair short. Leigh replies that she just thought it might change something.
- Sam and Leigh argue and then Sam pulls her up for saying Cady 'probably' killed her dog, asking her if she has doubts that it was him. She says honestly that she doesn't know.

- Max brags to Sam about how he kidnapped his ex-wife, took her to a hotel, photographed her and then forced her to write him a letter thanking him for the weekend, thereby ensuring her silence with the threat of sending copies of the photos and letter to her new husband should she ever think of speaking against him to the police. He points out that he did all that just because she spurned him, implying that something worse is coming to Sam for his betrayal. He also spouts bible stories of Lazarus and the rich man (who was told by Christ that he would be less likely to enter the kingdom of Heaven than a camel was to pass through the eye of a needle).
- Sam phones the police after Cady murders the cop, but Leigh stops him when she sees that Cady has put one of his shirts on Kersek the cop to make it look like Sam killed him in the belief it was Cady. Leigh insists that they cannot stay in the house any longer.

POSTER: A superbly eerie poster had a close-up of De Niro's eyes as if his face was half submerged in water, and floating just on the surface was a photograph of the Bowdens huddled together but ripped to separate Danielle from her parents. The taglines for the different posters read: 'There is nothing in the dark that isn't there in the light. Except fear' and 'Sam Bowden has always provided for his family's future. But the past is coming back to haunt them.'

TRAILER: With the caption: THE BOWDEN FAMILY HAVE MOVED TO NEW ESSEX, the trailer proceeds to tell the entire story of the film. Gregory Peck's one day's work manages to get him a credit though, and both he and Robert Mitchum appear in the trailer, clearly linking the remake to the past.

AWARDS: The film was Oscar-nominated and Golden Globe-nominated for Best Actor (De Niro) and Best Supporting Actress (Juliette Lewis); and BAFTA-nominated for best cinematography (Freddie Francis) and best editing (Thelma Schoonmaker). Scorsese collected a nomination at the 1991 Berlin Film Festival for a Golden Berlin Bear Award, while the picture received a few nominations at the MTV Music Awards, including Best Villain and Best Male Performance (both De Niro) and Best Kiss (De Niro and Lewis).

AVAILABILITY: MCA Home Video released both pan-and-scan and widescreen versions of the picture on laserdisc in 1996. Universal Home Video's DVD, released in 2000, is an impressive special edition to rival Columbia TriStar's *Taxi Driver* release. The film itself, an anamorphic widescreen transfer, is on one disc, while a second disc contains a 'making of' documentary, a selection of deleted scenes, behind the scenes footage from the 4th of July parade and houseboat sequences, photograph and production matte painting montages, the opening sequence without credits, a trailer and production notes. The picture has also been available on VHS in both widescreen and fullscreen editions and enjoys occasional screenings on cable and satellite movie channels.

WHAT THE CRITICS SAID: *Variety* reviewer Todd McCarthy perhaps fairly accused Scorsese of 'taking on an obviously commercial project involving material outside his interests', while David Ansen of *Newsweek* described it as a 'swell B movie dressed in haute cinematic couture'. In the UK, Matt Mueller of *Empire* criticised the 'nerve-wracking but rather ludicrous finale on the Bowden's unmoored houseboat, lapsing into standard Hollywood shock-schlock, as in the old he's-dead-or-maybe-he-isn't ploy'. Mueller was happy to agree that the director's reputation as 'a brilliant maverick is still intact, however, and with *Cape Fear*, Scorsese solidifies his position as America's greatest living film-maker. Stylish, harrowing and brilliantly compelling.'

EXPERT WITNESSES: 'I had seen the original. I liked it. I liked the idea of revenge and all that, and this sort of single-mindedness to get this person like a heat-seeking missile locking in on somebody and just wanting to get even. I thought that's a pretty clear simple thing.' Actor Robert De Niro (*Max Cady*).

'There's total trust between [De Niro] and Marty. If Marty says it's fine, then Bob just walks away. I think they both realise how important they are to each other. In some ways it's very strange being on the set with the two of them because they're so close. Obviously, they've discussed their ideas beforehand, so there's very little discussion or rehearsing on set. There's usually just a few words between Marty and Bob, and then off we go.' Cinematographer Freddie Francis.

'I think Marty's use of violence is very valid. He never uses it gratuitously, he always makes a very strong point, and I think if anyone who thinks that violence doesn't exist in this world or thinks it should be avoided at all costs is ... it's a dangerous state of mind. One has to be aware of the terrible things that are out there to prepare oneself for them and to try and counter them. So I think if you're going to show violence and it's done with conviction the way Marty does it then it is correct.' Editor Thelma Schoonmaker.

'*Cape Fear* ... was a great experience, because I was given the chance to take material and, by shaping it around me, create a memorable character. It's the break that, as actors, we all look for.' Actress Illeana Douglas (*Lori Davis*).

FINAL ANALYSIS: Often lumped in with *Basic Instinct* and *Fatal Attraction* as examples of the way the exploitation genre has been absorbed by the mainstream, *Cape Fear* is a surprising picture for Scorsese. Having tried to achieve acceptance from Hollywood in the 70s and having been in the wilderness for much of the 80s, for Scorsese to be allowed to make a commercial movie with a big budget *and* for it to make money must have seemed like a double-edged sword. On the one hand, it allowed him the flexibility and power to finally make the kind of pictures he wanted to. But on the other, he would never be able to return to the smaller, low-budget pictures of the past. Showing the makers of tired, tawdry schlock-horror flicks how to do it is the real appeal of *Cape Fear* though – balancing the severe realism of Cady's attack on Lori in the early sequences with the almost cartoon aspect to the final boat scene, but never once descending into pastiche.

SCORSESE ON *CAPE FEAR*: '*Cape Fear* really felt like going to work in a way, I wasn't really exploring anything new there. Except a Hollywood theatricality, with the thriller and boat aspect. It was really a hard picture for me to make because it was another genre.'

The Age of Innocence (1993)

(Super 35 mm – 139 min – colour)

Produced by Columbia Pictures
Producer: Barbara De Fina
Co-Producer: Bruce S Pustin
Associate Producer: Joseph P Reidy
Cinematographer: Michael Ballhaus
Film Editor: Thelma Schoonmaker
Casting: Ellen Lewis
Production Design: Dante Ferretti
Art Direction: Speed Hopkins, Jean-Michel Hugon
Set Decoration: Robert J Franco, Amy Marshall, Philippe Turlure
Costume Design: Gabriella Pescucci
Title Designers: Saul and Elaine Bass

SOUNDTRACK: 'Faust' by Charles Gounod; 'Piano Sonata No. 8 in C Minor, Op 13' ('Pathetique') written by Ludwig Van Beethoven; 'Radetzky March' written by Johann Strauss Sr.; 'Emperor Waltz Op 437', 'Artist's Life', 'Tales from the Vienna Woods' written by Johann Strauss; 'Quintet In B Flat Op 87, 3rd Movement' written by Felix Mendelssohn-Bartholdy; 'Marble Halls' by Enya.

CAST: Daniel Day-Lewis (*Newland Archer*), Michelle Pfeiffer (*Ellen Olenska*), Winona Ryder (*May Welland*), Linda Faye Farkas (*Female Opera Singer*), Michael Rees Davis, Terry Cook, Jon Garrison (*Male Opera Singers*), Richard E Grant (*Larry Lefferts*), Alec McCowen (*Sillerton Jackson*), Geraldine Chaplin (*Mrs Welland*), Mary Beth Hurt (*Regina Beaufort*), Stuart Wilson (*Julius Beaufort*), Howard Erskine (*Beaufort Guest*), John McLoughlin, Christopher Nilsson (*Party Guests*), Miriam Margolyes (*Mrs Mingott*), Siân Phillips (*Mrs Archer*), Carolyn Farina (*Janey Archer*), Michael Gough (*Henry Van Der Luyden*), Alexis Smith (*Louisa Van Der Luyden*), Kevin Sanders (*The Duke*), WB Brydon (*Mr Urban Dagonet*), Tracey Ellis (*Gertrude Lefferts*), Cristina Pronzati (*Countess Olenska's Maid*), Clement Fowler (*Florist*), Norman Lloyd (*Mr Letterblair*), Cindy Katz (*Stage Actress*), Thomas Gibson (*Stage Actor*), Zoe (*Herself*), Jonathan Pryce (*Monsieur Riviere*), June Squibb (*Mingott Maid*), Domenica Scorsese (*Katie Blenker*), Mac Orange (*Archer Maid*), Brian Davies (*Philip*), Thomas Barbour (*Archer Guest*), Henry Fehren (*Bishop*), Patricia Dunnock (*Mary Archer*), Robert Sean Leonard (*Ted Archer*), Joanne Woodward (*Narrator*)

UNCREDITED CAST: Claire Bloom, Charles Scorsese, Martin Scorsese

TITLES: One of Saul and Elaine Bass's greatest opening sequences. The Columbia logo appears, and then turns to sepia. With white text on a black background, the credits begin: COLUMBIA PICTURES PRESENTS ... A CAPPA/DE FINA PRODUCTION ... A MARTIN SCORSESE PICTURE ... Next, against the backdrop of scrolling text, the names of the principal cast members appear. As the logo appears, white inside a scrolling boarder, and the rest of the credits roll, we see a succession of time-lapsed flowers bloom behind a feint gauze of lace.

SUMMARY: New York City, the 1870s. Newland Archer is introduced to the Countess Ellen Olenska, a cousin of his fiancée, May Welland. Countess Olenska is known to Newland as they used to play together as children, but he has not seen her since she left New York to marry a Polish Count. Now she has returned, having left her husband, and New York Society prepares for the impending scandal. Wanting to be seen to support his fiancée's family, and secretly despising the formal rituals of the New York High Life, Newland persuades May to announce their engagement at the Beauforts' annual ball. In the event, Olenska decides not to come as she feels her dress isn't smart enough for the ball. Soon after, May and Newland visit May's grandmother, Mrs Mingott, to tell her of their engagement – Granny Mingott is considered by many to be the matriarch and 'dowager Empress' of New York society. As they are about to leave, Ellen Olenska arrives, accompanied by Julius Beaufort, a renowned businessman who is well known for his many affairs behind his wife's back. It looks like he intends Countess Olenska to be his next conquest.

Newland's mother decides to invite a few guests to dinner, including Sillerton Jackson, a cousin of the Archers and a reliable source for gossip. Jackson takes great pleasure in sharing his extensive knowledge of the Countess Olenska's past with the other guests. Apparently, Olenska was kept a virtual prisoner by her philandering husband until his secretary helped her escape. Jackson explains that it is said that Olenska and the secretary lived together for a year before she returned to New York.

Mrs Mingott surprises all by announcing a formal dinner in honour of Countess Olenska. But the invitations are returned, society unwilling to be seen to condone the Countess. Believing the snub to be the work of grand snob Larry Lefferts, Newland appeals to the Van Der Luydens for support; the Van Der Luydens are considered the most powerful and influential family in society. Perceiving that Lefferts has snubbed the Welland family in his actions, the Van Der Luydens decide to invite the Countess to a dinner they are having for their cousin, the Duke of St Austrey, knowing that no one else would refuse such an invitation, whether Olenska was present or not. There, Newland and the Countess strike up a conversation and Newland is taken by the Countess's lack of worry about formality. They arrange to meet the next day and Ellen confesses to him that despite everyone's kindness she feels very lonely, as if she only has everyone's support as long as they don't hear anything upsetting.

Mr Letterblair, Newland's employer, reveals that the Welland family have told him that Countess Olenska plans to divorce and are concerned about the scandal that would surely follow. Letterblair says the family have requested that, with his impending marriage to May, they feel he would be the best person to be the Countess's legal adviser in this matter so that he might persuade her to consider the consequences of divorce. Newland visits Ellen and dutifully explains to her the effects that a divorce could have on her should her husband decide to air certain private matters in public. She reluctantly agrees to take his counsel, but soon after she takes flight and goes to stay with the Van Der Luydens. Newland slowly realises he is growing attached to Ellen. To distract himself, he travels to see May in Florida and asks her if they might bring their marriage forward, despite her mother's wishes that their engagement be a long one. His desire to hurry things worries May and she asks him if there is someone else between them. Newland reassures her that there is no one else, though he also realises that May is somewhat lacking in imagination and no match for Ellen.

Newland visits Mrs Mingott and asks if she might use her influence on her family to enable him and May to be married sooner. Mrs Mingott observes that her family can be difficult and that none of them seem to take after her except Ellen. She asks him why he didn't marry Ellen when he had the chance and then tells him that she has heard that Count Olenski wants her back. Newland rashly tells her he'd rather she died than allow that to happen. Mrs Mingott reminds him that Ellen is still the Count's wife, regardless. Ellen arrives, and Newland makes to leave, but not before arranging to see Ellen again. In private, Newland confesses his love for Ellen, but the news upsets her – it was Newland who made marriage impossible for them when he talked her into not divorcing her husband. He tells her there is nothing done that cannot be undone and kisses her. She then confesses that she knows just how much he has already done for her, announcing his engagement to May at the Beauforts' ball so there would be two families supporting her, and going to the Van Der Luydens on her behalf. She knows that to ask him to leave May would be cruel; it would be asking him to throw away the very aspect of him she loves most.

Thanks to the influence of Mrs Mingott, May and Newland are married only a month later. On their honeymoon in Paris, Newland meets a Monsieur Riviere and enjoys a fine conversation with him about literature; after dinner he suggests to May they might invite Riviere for dinner. However, May's reluctance to risk being embarrassed in the company of such an erudite man makes Newland change his mind. He realises all too late that his wife's ignorance in matters of art, music and life in general will cause him problems in the future. He worries that her niceness and charm are merely a curtain that hides her emptiness.

A year and a half goes by. Newland learns that Ellen has been staying with a family in Portsmouth. Taking advantage of his wife and family's invitation to yet another party, he goes to see Ellen who is clearly overjoyed. She tells him that her husband sent his secretary to offer her a great deal of money for her to return to him. The secretary is still waiting for her at her hotel, so Newland convinces her to abandon the secretary to spend the day with him instead. They both acknowledge their forbidden love for each other, and agree that seeing each other at parties, at the theatre, from whatever distance is preferable to not seeing each other at all. She tells him she will not be returning to her husband.

Back in New York, Newland once again meets Monsieur Riviere, and learns that Riviere is in fact the secretary to the Count Olenski. Riviere is all too aware of the sacrifice Olenska would be making were she to return to her husband and, much to Newland's surprise, he begs Newland to use his influence on the Countess's family to ensure she never goes back to him.

Thanks to the ever up-to-date gossip of Sillerton Jackson, Newland learns that Julius Beaufort's business has collapsed, affecting many of their closest friends – including the Countess, who had invested almost all of her money in Beaufort and now finds herself near penniless. Newland prepares to leave for Washington to see Ellen, but then May receives a telegram telling her that her grandmother has had a stroke. It seems the previous night, Julius Beaufort's wife, Regina, came to see Mrs Mingott to beg her to back Julius and stand behind their common lineage. Regina threatened that if she didn't support him, then all of them would be dishonoured. Mrs Mingott told her that she couldn't begin to claim lineage to her old family when she'd been perfectly content to be known by her married name after all this time. So incensed was Granny Mingott that she had a stroke there and then. Now, with the whole family notified, Granny Mingott worries about looking after so many relatives as they await what they imagine will be her imminent funeral. She tells May and Newland that Ellen will be arriving the next day and Newland quickly volunteers to collect her from the station. Though Ellen and Newland manage to find some time together, it is clearly still painful for them both. Newland decides to tell his wife everything, but before he can begin, May tells him that Ellen is to return to Europe.

May and Newland hold their first formal dinner since their marriage – in honour of Countess Olenska's departure. As he watches the crème of New York society treat Ellen with the utmost respect, he realises for the first time that their good manners are a clear sign that in truth they believe her to be Newland's lover, and that his wife believes that too. Once their guests have departed, May sits with her husband in his study. Newland once again tries to tell his wife of his emotional troubles and begins by saying that he plans on going travelling for a while. But then May tells him he cannot, not unless he takes her with him, and she doubts her doctors would allow that, since she is expecting his child. He asks her if she has told anyone, and she confesses that she told Ellen, shortly before she left. It is obvious to Newland that his wife has been more manipulative than he ever gave her credit for.

In time, their first child, Theodore, is joined by Bill and Mary. Their children grow up. Mary marries one of Larry Leffert's sons; May nurses Bill through a near life-threatening bout of pneumonia, then she herself dies. Newland genuinely mourns her passing. In his 57th year, Newland finds himself in Europe at the request of his eldest son, now fully-grown. While touring Paris, Ted makes arrangements to meet the Countess Olenska, who he has heard of through other members of the family, but later, Ted reveals that he knows that Olenska and his father were once close as his mother told him the day she died. He also hints that he feels it's not too late for his widowed father to make up for lost time. Though Newland is surprised by his son's indiscretion, he is moved by the thought that his wife had known his pain and pitied him.

Accompanying his son to see Olenska, Newland changes his mind at the last minute and returns to his hotel, leaving his son to see her alone.

WHO'S WHO?: Daniel Day-Lewis shot to fame in 1985 with two films released simultaneously in the States – *My Beautiful Laundrette* (Stephen Frears) and *A Room with a View* (James Ivory). He won an Oscar for playing artist Christy Brown in *My Left Foot* (Jim Sheridan, 1989) and achieved blockbuster success with *The Last of the Mohicans* (Michael Mann, 1992). Michelle Pfeiffer is probably best known for her appearances in *The Witches of Eastwick* (George Miller, 1987), *Dangerous Liaisons* (Stephen Frears, 1989) and, as Catwoman, in *Batman Returns* (Tim Burton, 1992). More usually associated with more off-beat roles, Winona Ryder starred in *Beetlejuice* (Tim Burton, 1988), *Heathers* (Michael Lehmann, 1989), *Bram Stoker's Dracula* (Francis Ford Coppola, 1992) and *Little Women* (Gillian Armstrong, 1994). Ryder's co-star in Dracula, Richard E Grant was born in Swaziland, though he is thought of as the epitome of Englishness. He's most readily identified with the cult picture *Withnail and I* (Bruce Robinson, 1987).

Alec McCowen memorably portrayed Chief Inspector Oxford in Alfred Hitchcock's last British picture, *Frenzy* (1972) and stood in as Q in the unofficial Bond movie *Never Say Never Again* (Irvin Kershner, 1983). Geraldine Chaplin is the daughter of legendary comic Charlie Chaplin. In Richard Attenborough's biopic about her father (1992), she played her own grandmother. Stuart Wilson's most high-profile role is probably that of Don Rafael in *The Mask of Zorro* (Martin Campbell, 1998). Character actress Miriam Margolyes is a familiar face on British television from shows such as the sketch-based *A Kick up the Eighties* (1981) and *Blackadder*. Though she's appeared in numerous pictures, her most familiar role, to children at least, is the voice of Fly, the maternal dog in *Babe* (Chris Noonan, 1995). Siân Phillips came to fame thanks to the role of Livia in the BBC TV series *I Claudius* (1976) and as Alec Guinness's wife in the series *Tinker, Tailor, Soldier, Spy* (1980) and *Smiley's People* (1982). For American audiences, she's possibly better known thanks to her iconic appearance as the Reverend Mother Gaius Helen Mohiam in the sci-fi epic *Dune* (David Lynch, 1984). Recently, she's had a recurring role in the TV series *La Femme Nikita*, as Alice.

Michael Gough has enjoyed a revival of his career thanks to Tim Burton, who cast him as Alfred in *Batman* (1990) – a role he played in all three sequels – and as the notary, Hardenbrook, in *Sleepy Hollow* (1999). His early career saw him play Arthur Holmwood in the Hammer version of *Dracula* (Terence Fisher, 1958 – known as *Horror of Dracula* in the States), as well as roles in the ITV series *The Avengers* (as Dr Clement Armstrong, inventor of The Cybernauts, 1965) and the BBC sci-fi series *Doctor Who* (The Celestial Toymaker, 1966). Norman Lloyd may be familiar as Doctor Daniel Auschlander from *St. Elsewhere*. Earlier in his career, he was the producer and occasional director of the TV anthology series *Alfred Hitchcock Presents*, having also appeared in two of the great director's pictures, *Saboteur* and *Spellbound*. Thomas Gibson would later star in the sitcom *Dharma & Greg*. Versatile Welsh actor Jonathan Pryce played Juan Perón opposite Madonna in *Evita* (Alan Parker, 1996) and the megalomaniac Elliot Carver in the Bond film *Tomorrow Never Dies* (1997). Robert Sean Leonard is one of a number of 'graduates' from the inspirational rites of passage picture *Dead Poets Society* (Peter Weir, 1989). Joanne Woodward starred in *The Three Faces of Eve* (Nunnally Johnson, 1957), for which she won an Oscar. She also appeared in *Rachel, Rachel* (1968) and *The Glass Menagerie* (1988) both directed by her husband, actor Paul Newman.

THE USUAL SUSPECTS: Daniel Day-Lewis (*Gangs of New York*); Mary Beth Hurt (*Bringing Out the Dead*); credited writer Jay Cocks (*Made in Milan, Gangs of New York*); editor Thelma Schoonmaker (*Who's That Knocking At My Door?, Street Scenes, Raging Bull, The King of Comedy, After Hours, The Color of Money, Bad, The Last Temptation of Christ, New York Stories, GoodFellas, Cape Fear,*

Casino, A Personal Journey with Martin Scorsese Through American Movies, Kundun, Bringing Out the Dead, My Voyage to Italy, Gangs of New York).

SOURCE: Born in 1862, Edith Wharton belonged to an aristocratic New York family of English and Dutch descendants at the heart of fashionable Society. Though she was schooled in the etiquette and rituals of the society from an early age, her knowledge of art and literature was largely self-taught, with encouragement from her governess. In 1885, Edith married Edward 'Teddy' Wharton, a Boston banker from a similar social background but with no artistic or intellectual interests. Though Teddy didn't stand in the way of her writing career, their marriage was not a happy one with Edith suffering a nervous breakdown. After discovering her husband had used her money to set up a mistress, she deserted him and moved to Paris where she lived for the rest of her life (only returning once to the USA, in 1920, to accept the Pulitzer prize for her novel, *The Age of Innocence*).

Like much of Wharton's work, *The Age of Innocence* is a book of contrast between the old traditions, old money, and the new. This contrast is shown through the growth and development of the book's central character, Newland Archer, who begins the novel as much a part of the established order as anyone else. At the theatre, his interest in Countess Olenska is not attraction but concern that his innocent new fiancée might have her reputation tarnished by association with the decidedly undesirable Countess. Olenska is described as being dark haired, in binary opposition to the fair-haired May (a contrast that is swapped for the film, mainly down to casting). Significantly, with flowers playing such an important part in the story, May is associated with lilies of the valley, a bloom connected with virginity and purity. Yet Newland begins to suspect that this innocence is merely an act, with May appearing too concerned with whether she is fashionable and doing the done thing; he slowly finds himself drawn to the Countess Olenska because of her seeming lack of awareness of society's expectations. The film's immaculate attention to detail is already there in the text, with Wharton describing every buttonhole, every fork or hair accessory. A few small changes occur towards the end, with Newland's eldest son Dallas renamed Theodore and his daughter Mary married to one of Larry Leffert's sons instead of Chivers, a character omitted from the film.

PRODUCTION: Jay Cocks gave Martin Scorsese a copy of the novel in 1980 just before he began work on *The King of Comedy*, but he didn't read the book until 1987, during his tour of the *Guardian* lectures in the UK. With the backing of 20th Century Fox, Scorsese and Jay Cocks began work on an adaptation of the novel shortly before the director began filming *GoodFellas*, taking three weeks to complete the first draft. Scorsese and Cocks felt it important to stick closely to the text, and decided upon retaining the novel's third-person narrator for the screenplay to convey the essence of the film being a work of literature. With *GoodFellas* and then *Cape Fear* on the cards, *The Age of Innocence* slipped back in Scorsese's schedule until the spring of 1992, by which time Fox had decided to drop the project and Columbia Pictures, under the guidance of new arrival Mark Canton, picked it up. In the two and a half years since Scorsese had first decided to make the picture, his visual research consultant, art history graduate Robin Standefer had been compiling 25 'bible' references on the look and manners of the period, using sources such as the Frick Collection, the New York Historical Society, the Library of Congress and various Wharton and Art history scholars such as RWB Lewis and Linda Nochlin. For the many paintings that adorned the houses of Granny Mingott and Countess Olenska, they used works from the Macchiaioli, a long-forgotten school of Italian preimpressionists.

The production used a number of existing locations: the academy of music in Philadelphia stood in for the opera house; the National Arts Club in Gramercy Park became the Beaufort Mansion; and Troy, New York – with its three-storey brownstones – provided many of the film's exteriors. Production designer Dante Ferretti built just three period sets: Archer's library, the ballroom at the home of Julius Beaufort and the main hall of the Metropolitan Museum of Art, circa 1880. Though both Scorsese and producer Barbara De Fina were deliberately vague in interviews about the overall cost, the rumoured budget was between $30–40 million, most of which went on the period detail needed. A chandelier was built from scratch at a cost of $25,000, and over 80 extras populated the ballrooms. Lily Lodge, whose grandmother had known Wharton, was hired as etiquette coach and was on call at all times.

Scorsese's father Charlie had been ill for some time, and the director's frequent visits to the hospital necessitated a delay to the editing of the picture and a slip in the release date of five months (although the original date was never felt, by Scorsese at least, to be realistic). Charlie died in August 1993, just a week before the film's premiere at the Venice Film Festival, and a last minute change to the film's end credits dedicated the picture to 'Luciano Charles Scorsese'.

EDITING: Possibly Scorsese's and Schoonmaker's most ostentatiously flashy work, *The Age of Innocence* is almost fetishistic in the way the camera picks up details like cufflinks, watch-chains and cutlery and darts from face to face, plate to plate. The first big 'trick' of the picture comes when Larry Lefferts lifts his opera glasses and sees Olenska for the first time. The traditional way of filming this would be to mask off the frame and leave a figure-of-eight window to simulate the lenses. Scorsese wanted something different. In collaboration with cinematographer Michael Ballhaus, by doing stop-motion photography where they took one frame at a time, he printed it three times and then lap-dissolved between each set of frames to give a juddering effect. We do, however, see some more traditional examples of masking, such as the scene in the theatre where a circular frame is used to focus on Newland and Ellen and exclude the other characters from the frame. Towards the end, as Newland reads Ellen's letter to May, his eyes are picked out by the light, just as we saw Francine's in *New York, New York*. As with *Cape Fear*, some shots end with the screen filled with a primary colour, such as the shot of Ellen looking up just as the screen flares red. At the museum, the reflections of Newland and Ellen appear on the glass of an exhibit while we hear the dialogue from the next shot. As the pair sit together, the effect is reminiscent of the scene on the ferry in *Who's That Knocking* . . . with JR chatting to the girl.

MUSIC: Aside from Bernstein's score, the music here is mainly contemporaneous with the setting. One piece, 'Marble Halls' from Michael William Balfe's opera *The Bohemian Girl*, was first performed in November 1843, but the arrangement is by twentieth Century Irish singer-songwriter Enya, and can be found on her 1991 album *Shepherd Moons*.

QUOTE/UNQUOTE

Narrator: 'This was a world balanced so precariously that its harmony could be shattered by a whisper.'

Countess Olenska: 'May I tell you what most interests me about New York? Not all the blind obeying of tradition, someone else's tradition. It seems stupid to have discovered America only to make it a copy of another country. Do you suppose Christopher Columbus would have taken all that trouble just to go to the opera with Larry Lefferts?'

Countess Olenska: 'Is New York such a labyrinth? I thought it was all straight up and down like Fifth Avenue. All the cross streets numbered and big honest labels on everything.'

Newland: 'Everything is labelled, but every*body* is not.'
Countess Olenska: 'Then I must count on you for warnings too.'

Countess Olenska: 'Newland. You couldn't be happy if it meant being cruel. If we act any other way I'll be making you act against what I love in you most. And I can't go back to that way of thinking. Don't you see? I can't love you unless I give you up.'

ROOTS: In the published screenplay, Jay Cocks supplies notes on some of the films he and Scorsese took their inspiration from in the construction of the film, which include: the ironic narration and the slow zooms from *Barry Lyndon* (Stanley Kubrick, 1975); director William Wyler's use of contrasts between space and claustrophobia in *Carrie* (1952); and from *The Heiress* (1949), Wyler's adaptation of Henry James's *Washington Square* they were impressed by the way 'Wyler shoots drawing rooms, ballrooms and dining rooms as if they were antechambers of the soul, with deep shadow and stalks of light'; the shot of the light across Newland's eyes from *Detour* (Edgar G Ulmer, 1945); Visconti's trilogy of *The Innocent* (1977), *The Leopard* (1963) and *Senso* (1954).

As he sifts through a consignment of books, Newland reads 'The House of Life: The Sonnet' from Dante Gabriel Rossetti, *Ballads and Sonnets*, while the opera that appears throughout the film is Gounod's *Faust*. Incidentally, in the novel, Wharton mocks the fact that the German text of a French opera sung by Swedish performers should be translated into Italian to make it easier to understand for an English audience. The painting in Mrs Mingott's room of two Indian warriors about to kill a young woman depicts the murder of Jenny McCrae, an actual historical event that happened in upstate New York during the Revolutionary War. The event took place in 1777, shortly before the battle of Saratoga, and was a key event in rallying Patriot militia.

THEMES AND MOTIFS: The picture opens with the show-within-a-show that we've seen right from *What's a Nice Girl Like You . . .*, *Alice Doesn't Live Here Anymore*, *New York, New York* and *New York Stories*. As with *The Last Temptation of Christ* and *GoodFellas*, *The Age of Innocence* is as much about ritual as it is about the story: from the carefully considered arrivals and departures of people at events (Regina Beaufort's routine of leaving the opera after a specific act as a sign that her ball will begin a half-hour later, the comment that Ellen Olenska's late arrival at the Van Der Luyden's dinner party – and her rather revealing red dress – is something to be frowned upon) to the extremely detailed ritual of the presentation and multiple courses of food.

CONTROVERSY: There's a wonderful aside where the narrator informs us that the ostentatious Beauforts have 'The Return of Spring', the 'much-discussed nude by Bougereau', which Beaufort 'had the audacity to hang in plain sight'. Sillerton Jackson asks Newland if he believes women should share the same freedoms as men. Ellen Olenska notes how Newland is happy with the idea of women being equal so long as it doesn't actually happen.

THERE HE IS!: Scorsese plays the photographer taking May's wedding picture.

KEEP IT IN THE FAMILY: Catherine Scorsese appears without her customary glasses as a passenger on the ferry, while Scorsese's daughter Domenica plays Katie Blenker. The film was dedicated to Charles Scorsese, who died during production, and was the first of Scorsese's Cappa Productions, named after Catherine Scorsese's maiden name.

POSTER: With a picture of Newland and Ellen embracing, the tagline ran: 'In a world of tradition. In an age of innocence. They dared to break the rules.' *Empire* magazine later pointed out that the publicity still used for the poster had a rather embarrassing anachronism – peeking out of the period handbag of Countess Olenska was a packet of very modern mints.

TRAILER: Playing up the historical epic angle, the trailer shows off the costumes, the spectacle and the ritual of the story. A wonderfully cheesy voice-over tells us that: 'In a time of tradition . . . in a place of privilege . . . Newland Archer lived his life by the rules of his society . . . until he met a woman who lived by her own rules. From the Pulitzer-Prize-winning novel, Columbia Pictures is proud to present Daniel Day-Lewis, Michelle Pfeiffer, Winona Ryder . . . The Age Of Innocence, A Martin Scorsese Picture.'

AWARDS: At the Academy Awards, the picture won Best Costume Design (Gabriella Pescucci), and was nominated for Best Actress in a Supporting Role (Winona Ryder), Best Art Direction-Set Decoration (Dante Ferretti and Robert J Franco), Best Music, Original Score (Elmer Bernstein), and Best Writing, Screenplay Based on Material from

Another Medium (Jay Cocks and Martin Scorsese). At the Bodil Awards it won Best American Film for Martin Scorsese. The British Academy Awards, perhaps predictably, gave the Best Supporting Actress award to Miriam Margolyes, while nominations went to Winona Ryder (also in the Best Supporting Actress category), Michael Ballhaus (Cinematography) and Dante Ferretti (Production Design). At Camerimage, Michael Ballhaus was nominated for a 'Golden Frog'. At the Golden Globes, Winona Ryder won the award for Best Performance by an Actress in a Supporting Role in a Motion Picture, with nominations for Best Director, Best Motion Picture – Drama and Best Performance by an Actress in a Motion Picture – Drama for Michelle Pfeiffer. The Italian National Syndicate of Film Journalists gave their Silver Ribbons for Best Costume Design to Gabriella Pescucci and Best Production Design to Dante Ferretti. The National Board of Review awarded Scorsese with their Best Director award, with Winona Ryder winning Best Supporting Actress. Ryder also won the Southeastern Film Critics Association for Best Supporting Actress.

Oh, and the cast of *The Age of Innocence* awarded Scorsese both the Most Grumpy award and the Best Able to Clear a Path award.

AVAILABILITY: Columbia TriStar released a 3-sided widescreen laserdisc in 1994. VHS copies have been released in both full- and widescreen format, and in the autumn of 2001, Columbia TriStar released a DVD with a selection of trailers (*The Age of Innocence*, *Sense and Sensibility* and *Remains of the Day*) and filmographies of the principal cast.

WHAT THE CRITICS SAID: 'Scorsese is known for his restless camera,' wrote Roger Ebert in his four-star review, 'he rarely allows a static shot. But here you will have the impression of grace and stateliness in his visual style, and only on a second viewing will you realize the subtlety with which his camera does, indeed, incessantly move, insinuating itself into conversations like a curious uninvited guest.'

EXPERT WITNESS: 'My performance was very minimalist. He kept saying "Less". I thought I was a Stepford Wife . . . I learned more than I've ever learned. He has incredible energy. It's not just that he talks fast; he's incredibly soothing. He made me feel not only that I was proud of my work and made sense; he made me feel great. I actually looked forward to showing up at 6 a.m. I think he affected my life in a deep way that doesn't even have to do with movies.' 'Actress Winona Ryder (*May*).

FINAL ANALYSIS: For those of us used to Scorsese's macho bloodthirsty dramas, the idea of him 'doing a Merchant Ivory' might seem a little strange. Yet the world of Newland, May and Countess Olenska is in some ways just as vicious and dangerous as those of Henry Hill and Jake LaMotta. One wrong word, one misplaced allegiance and your life could, effectively, be over. A caustic, ironic script serves the source material well and I cannot be the only person to be surprised that this, of all films did not bag Scorsese the Academy Award that has eluded him for so long.

SCORSESE ON *THE AGE OF INNOCENCE*: (on the budget for the picture) 'Where that extra three or four million went was for the structure and the anthropology of the scenes. In other words, the look of the dishes has to be a certain way, and that's what I thought would give it the extra love and care. And maybe the audience can feel that, get a sense of sumptuousness.'

A Century of Cinema: 'A Personal Journey with Martin Scorsese Through American Movies' (1995)

(Various – 224 min – colour/B & W)

Part I: 'The Director's Dilemma'; 'The Director as Storyteller'; 'The Western'; 'The Gangster Film'; 'The Musical' (73 min)
Part II: 'The Director as Illusionist'; 'The Director as Smuggler' (80 min)
Part III: 'The Director as Smuggler – part II'; 'The Director as Iconoclast' (74 min)
A BFI Production for Channel 4 in Association with Miramax Films
Line Producer: Dale Ann Stieber
Associate Producer: Raffaele Donato
Producer: Florence Dauman
Executive Producers: Colin MacCabe, Bob Last
Director: Martin Scorsese

Written and Directed by: Martin Scorsese, Michael Henry
Wilson
Director of Photography: Jean Yves Escoffier
Supervising Editor: Thelma Schoonmaker
Editors: David Lindblom, Kenneth I Levis
Music: Elmer Bernstein
Titles: Saul Bass

PRESENTER: Martin Scorsese

SUMMARY: Martin Scorsese offers an intentionally subjective view of American movies up to the end of the 1950s.

THE USUAL SUSPECTS: Editor Thelma Schoonmaker (*Who's That Knocking At My Door?*, *Street Scenes*, *Raging Bull*, *The King of Comedy*, *After Hours*, *The Color of Money*, *Bad*, *The Last Temptation of Christ*, *New York Stories*, *GoodFellas*, *Cape Fear*, *The Age of Innocence*, *Casino*, *Kundun*, *Bringing Out the Dead*, *My Voyage to Italy*, *Gangs of New York*); Saul Bass (*GoodFellas*, *Cape Fear*, *Age of Innocence*, *Casino*).

PRODUCTION: Commissioned by the British Film Institute to front and co-write an edition of their series *A Century of Cinema*, Scorsese chose to present a unique, personal journey through the history of American Cinema. The main production was completed in the summer of 1994, with just the voice-over needing to be recorded, which he did during the filming of *Casino*. *A Personal Journey* . . . premiered at the Cannes Film Festival in May 1995.

WHAT THE CRITICS SAID: In a glowing five-star review, Philip Thomas wrote: 'Scorsese's prose radiates pent-up energy and deep knowledge, and this incredibly readable book will not only add to anyone's understanding of movie history but also to the huge lake of respect most people hold for the man.'

Casino (1995)

(70 mm – 172 min – colour)

A Universal Pictures Production
Producer: Barbara De Fina
Associate Producer: Joseph P Reidy

Written by Nicholas Pileggi and Martin Scorsese, based on
the book by Nicholas Pileggi.
Cinematographer: Robert Richardson
Film Editor: Thelma Schoonmaker
Casting: Ellen Lewis
Production Design: Dante Ferretti
Art Direction: Jack G Taylor Jr
Set Decoration: Rick Simpson
Costume Design: John A Dunn, Rita Ryack
Title Designers: Saul Bass, Elaine Bass
Technical Advisers: Frank Cullota, Murray Ehrenberg, Marty
Jacobs, John Manca

SOUNDTRACK: 'Sweet Virginia', 'Gimme Shelter', 'Heart of Stone' by
The Rolling Stones; 'House of the Rising Sun' by The Animals;
'Contempt – Théme de Camille'* by Georges Delerue; 'Angelina/Zooma,
Zooma Medley'*, 'Basin Street Blues/When It's Sleepy Time Down
South Medley'* by Louis Prima; 'Hoochie Coochie Man'* by Muddy
Waters; 'I'll Take You There'* by The Staple Singers; 'Nights in White
Satin'* by The Moody Blues; 'How High the Moon'* by Les Paul and
Mary Ford; 'Hurt'* by Timi Yuro; 'Ain't Got No Home'* by Clarence
'Frogman' Henry; 'Without You'* by Nilsson; 'Love is the Drug'* by
Roxy Music; 'I'm Sorry'* by Brenda Lee; 'Go Your Own Way'* by
Fleetwood Mac; 'The Thrill is Gone'* by BB King; 'Love is Strange'* by
Mickey and Sylvia; 'The "In" Crowd'* by Ramsey Lewis; 'Stardust'* by
Hoagy Carmichael; 'Walk on the Wild Side'* by Jimmy Smith;
'Fa-Fa-Fa-Fa-Fa (Sad Song)'* by Otis Redding; 'I Ain't Superstitious'* by
Jeff Beck; 'The Glory of Love'* by The Velvetones; 'Whip It', '(I Can't
Get No) Satisfaction'* by Devo; 'What a Difference a Day Makes'* by
Dinah Washington; 'Working in a Coalmine'* by Lee Dorsey; 'House of
the Rising Sun'* by Eric Burdon; 'Those Were the Days'* by Cream;
'Who Can I Turn To (When Nobody Needs Me)'* by Tony Bennett;
'Slippin' and Slidin''* by Little Richard; 'You're Nobody Till Somebody
Loves You'* by Dean Martin; 'Compared to What'* by Les McCann
and Eddie Harris; 'Wir Setzen Uns Mit Thraenen Nieder' from
'Matthaus Passion'* by Johann Sebastian Bach, performed by The
Chicago Symphony Orchestra, conducted by Sir Georg Solti.

CAST: Robert De Niro (*Sam 'Ace' Rothstein*), Sharon Stone (*Ginger
McKenna-Rothstein*), Joe Pesci (*Nicholas 'Nicky' Santoro Sr*), James
Woods (*Lester Diamond*), Don Rickles (*Billy Sherbert*), Alan King
(*Andy Stone*), Kevin Pollak (*Phillip Green*), LQ Jones (*Commissioner*

Pat Webb), Dick Smothers (*Senator*), Frank Vincent (*Frank Marino*), John Bloom (*Don Ward*), Pasquale Cajano (*Boss Remo Gaggi*), Melissa Prophet (*Jennifer Santoro*), Bill Allison (*John Nance*), Vinny Vella (*Artie Piscano*), Oscar Goodman (*Sam Rothstein's Attorney*), Catherine Scorsese (*Mrs Piscano*), Philip Suriano (*Dominick Santoro*), Erika von Tagen (*Older Amy*), Frankie Avalon (*Himself*), Steve Allen (*Himself*), Jayne Meadows (*Herself*), Jerry Vale (*Himself*), Joseph Rigano (*Vincent Borelli*), Gene Ruffini (*Vinny Forlano*), Dominick Grieco (*Americo Capelli*), Richard Amalfitano (*Casino Executive*), Casper Molee, David Leavitt (*Counters*), Richard F Strafella (*Casino Executive*), Peter Conti (*Arthur Capp*), Catherine T Scorsese (*Piscano's Daughter*), Steve Vignari (*Beeper*), Rick Crachy (*Chastised Dealer*), Larry E Nadler (*Lucky Larry*), Paul Herman (*Gambler in Phone Booth*), Salvatore Petrillo (*Old Man Capo*), Joey DePinto (*Stabbed Gambler*), Heide Keller (*Blonde at Bar*), Millicent Sheridan (*Senator's Hooker*), Nobu Matsuhisa (*Ichikawa*), Toru Nagai (*Ichikawa's Associate*), Charlene Hunter (*Ticket Agent*), Dom Angelo (*Craps Dealer*), Joe Molinaro (*Shift Manager*), Ali Pirouzkar (*High Roller*), Frankie J Allison (*Craps Dealer*), Jeff Scott Anderson (*Parking Valet*), Jennifer M Abbott (*Cashier*), Frank Washko Jr (*Parking Valet*), Christian A Azzinaro (*Nicholas 'Little Nicky' Santoro Jr–7 Years*), Robert C Tetzlaff (*Custom's Agent*), Anthony Russell (*Bookie*), Carol Wilson (*Classroom Nun*), Joe Lacoco (*Detective Bob Johnson*), John Manca (*Wiseguy Eddy*), Ronald Maccone (*Wiseguy Jerry*), Buck Stephens (*Credit Clerk*), Joseph P Reidy (*Winner*), Joe La Due (*Signaller*), Fred Smith, Sonny D'Angelo, Greg Anderson (*Security Guards*), Stuart Nisbet (*LA Banker*), Tommy DeVito (*Crooked Poker Dealer*), Frank Adonis (*Rocky*), Joseph Bono (*Moosh*), Craig Vincent (*Cowboy*), Daniel P Conte (*Doctor Dan*), Paul Dottore (*Slim*), Richard T Smith (*Security Guard/Cowboy*), David Rose (*David*), Jonathan Kraft (*Jonathan*), Michael McKensie Pratt (*Showgirls' Stage Manager*), Patti James, Ruth Gillis, Carol Cardwell (*Country Club Women*), Dean Casper (*Elderly Man*), Nan Brennan, Karyn Amalfitano, KC Carr (*Wives*), David Varriale (*Flirting Executive*), Darla House (*Baby Amy*), Carol Krolick (*Slapping Woman*), Frank Regich (*Slapped Man*), Herb Schwartz (*Maitre d'*), Bret McCormick – credited as Max Raven (*Bernie Blue*), Clem Caserta (*Sal Fusco*), Jed Mills (*Jack Hardy*), Janet Denti (*Receptionist*), Cameron Milzer (*Secretary*), Leain Vashon (*Bellman*), Jim Morgan Williams, Jed L Hansen (*Pit Bosses*), Brian Le Baron (*Valet Parker*), Mortiki Yerushalmi (*Jewellery Store Owner*), Mufid M Khoury, Khosrow Abrishami (*Jeweller Fences*), Richard Riehle (*Charlie Clark*), Mike Maines, Bobby Hitt (*Cops in Restaurant*), Shellee Renee (*Showgirl*

in Parking Lot), Alfred Nittoli (*Chastised Gambler*), Carl Ciarfalio
(*Tony Dogs*), Jack Orend (*Baker*), Linda Perri (*Ace's Secretary*), Ffolliott
Le Coque (*Anna Scott*), J Charles Thompson (*Judge*), Michael Paskevich,
Mike Weatherford, Eric Randall (*Reporter at Airport*), Gwen Castaldi
(*Business Week Reporter*), Brian Reddy, Roy Conrad (*Board
Investigators*), Mike Bradley, David Courvoisier (*TV Newsmen*), George
Comando (*Piscano's Brother-in-Law*), Andy Jarrell (*Commissioner
Bales*), Robert Sidell, Tyde Kierney (*Control Board Members*), Paige
Novodor (*Female Newscaster*), Claudia Haro (*Trudy/Announcer*), Sasha
Semenoff (*Orchestra Leader*), Gil Dova (*Juggler*), George W Allf, Joe
Anastasi, F Marcus Casper, David Arcerio, Richard Wagner (*FBI
Agents*), Madeline Parquette (*Woman Black Jack Dealer*), Nick Mazzola
(*Blackjack Dealer*), Gino Bertin (*Maitre d'*), Mitch Kolpan, Csaba
Maczala (*Detectives*), Peter Sugden (*Lip Reader*), Rudy Guerrero
(*Maitre d' at Disco*), Randy Sutton, Jeff Corbin (*Cops at Ace's House*),
Sly Smith (*FBI Agent 1*), Jeffrey Azzinaro (*Nicholas 'Little Nicky'
Santoro Jr–10 Years*), Carrie Cipollini (*Piscano's Wife*), Loren Stevens,
Gary C Rainey (*Agents, Piscano Raid*), Haven Earl (*Haley Judge*), Sam
Wilson (*Ambulance Driver*), Michael Toney (*Fat Sally*)

UNCREDITED CAST: Walt G Ludwig (*Bartend Joe*), Steve Schirripa
(*Man in Bar*)

TITLES: We're told the film is ADAPTED FROM A TRUE STORY, then we see,
from 1983, Ace walk to his car. As he turns on the ignition, the car
explodes. We see him falling against a backdrop of flames, which then
turn into close-ups of neon and signs of multi-coloured bulbs. Ace's
silhouette begins its descent, the screen fills with flames and the caption
appears A MARTIN SCORSESE PICTURE.

SUMMARY: Mr Big, Remo Gaggi, hands over control of the Tangiers,
the biggest casino in Las Vegas, to expert gambler Sam 'Ace' Rothstein.
Sam is worried that his previous convictions will restrict him from
obtaining a gambling licence but he is reassured that with the ten-year
licence processing backlog and a convenient law that allows a man to
work at a casino while his application is being processed, he can simply
take on a variety of different job titles while effectively running the
casino untroubled. At first, things couldn't be better; the takings have
doubled since he took over, which means his employer, Gaggi, is better
off. For Sam, it's a chance to turn legit and, although he still pays his
tribute to Gaggi, the casino floor is run for him by a crew of ex-cheats

who can spot all the scams and ensure that no one steals from the casino who isn't meant to. But the arrival of two people threatens to complicate Sam's life – Nicky Santoro, an old friend from 'back home' with an uncontrollable temper, and Ginger McKenna, a wild but beautiful hustler and ex-call girl with her old pimp, Lester Diamond in tow.

Having spent some time enjoying Ginger's company, Sam asks her to marry him, but she tells him she doesn't love him. Worried he's getting old, Sam tells her that doesn't matter to him. He offers to set her up for the rest of her life – in effect, he offers to 'buy' her. They have a child and get married, even though Ginger's pimp, Lester, continues to hassle her. He even trusts her with the only key to a safe deposit box containing $2 million, an insurance policy against the possibility of him ever being kidnapped. Meanwhile, Nicky begins to run gambling scams in Sam's casino, paying off dealers and bringing in friends who are so keen on signalling to each other that it's obvious what's going on. Sam warns Nicky that his game has been spotted, but Nicky, whose only intent is to steal, is a 'Made' man, which makes him effectively untouchable. Eventually, Nicky manages to get himself registered in the State's 'Black Book', banned from every casino in Vegas. But Nicky doesn't want to leave the city and begins to organise heists all over the joint. With a couple of legitimate businesses as a front, such as his jewellers and his restaurant, he manages to turn himself into a bit of a star, with politicians and showgirls lining up to be seen at his restaurant. And when Nicky helps Gaggi identify some rival gangsters who made the mistake of sticking up one of Gaggi's bars, Nicky is established as 'the new boss of Las Vegas'.

Ginger takes $25,000 out of the safe deposit box to give to her ex-pimp Lester. Sam interrupts her meeting with him and tells Lester to leave town. To make his point, he has some of his goons beat Lester up. Ginger is furious and confides in Nicky that Sam has put aside a million dollars in jewellery for her. Nicky tells her she should just take things easy and points out that he's never seen Sam so happy. Sam begins to worry about Ginger's drinking, and when he finds that she's been stealing his painkillers he realises she's depressed and offers to get her some professional help.

Sam finds himself in trouble with the authorities when he fires Don Ward, an incompetent employee who just happens to be related to half the town. When Ward's brother-in-law, County Commissioner Pat Webb comes to plead Ward's case, Sam explains that three of his slot machines made a huge pay-out and Ward did nothing about it. Either he was in on a scam or he was too stupid to notice. Either way, Sam feels he cannot have a liability like that in his casino. Webb is disappointed in Sam's inflexibility and tells him he should regard himself as a guest in Las Vegas and not to feel he can call it home. Then it's discovered that somewhere in the process, one of the Tangiers employees is stealing from the money that's stolen for the gangsters back home. To make matters worse, the president of the Tangiers, a man by the name of Phil Green who was hired as a respectable figurehead for the corporation, has had a silent business partner all along, and when she tries to collect some money from him and he refuses her, she takes the matter to court. Green is forced by the court to open up the Tangiers' books to show where his financing comes from. This obviously worries the mob who don't wish their involvement to be revealed. Nicky is hired to kill Green's business partner which has the effect of widening the police's investigation and putting Sam under the spotlight. When an interview with Sam is printed in the newspapers declaring him 'The Boss' of the Tangiers, Commissioner Webb decides to investigate Sam's gaming licence, putting Sam's future in Las Vegas in jeopardy.

Sam warns Nicky about letting things get out of control – he's stopped asking permission from back home and has been questioned for over two dozen murders. Every move Nicky makes brings the attention back to Sam; every newspaper report on Nicky associates him with Sam, threatening his impending licence hearing. But matters grow really serious when Piscano, the under-boss in Kansas responsible for arranging the mob collections from the Tangiers, is taped by an FBI wire moaning to his mother about the situation in Vegas. By the time Sam's hearing comes around, the board reject his application for a licence without even hearing the case.

Sam speaks to his bosses about Nicky, feeling that his friend's high-profile activities have brought too much attention on him and caused him to lose his licence. Nicky is furious, believing Sam owes him for his success and warns him to never speak about him behind his back again. Ginger, now a serious alcoholic and drug user, asks Sam for a divorce. Sam tells her that, in her condition, he's not willing to let her take custody of their daughter, Amy. Ginger runs away to California with Amy and plots with Lester to steal the rest of the $2 million from the safe box. She calls Nicky and asks for his help; she's worried that Sam will kill her. Nicky goes to Sam and tells him the situation and advises him to speak to her. After a fraught phone call in which Ginger confesses to spending $25,000 of Sam's money, he persuades her to return home with their daughter. But almost as soon as she returns Sam knows it's the end. He overhears her plotting to have him killed and ends up booting her out. Once more though he accepts her back. One afternoon, Sam comes home to find Ginger has tied their daughter to her bed and left her on her own. Sam has finally had it and throws Ginger out. To spite him, she clears out the bank vault to escape Sam forever, but then the FBI pull her in for questioning. Ginger doesn't tell them anything, but the FBI don't need her anyway; thanks to the evidence from Piscano, they're able to arrest a number of key figures in the mob. When Piscano himself is arrested, he dies of a sudden, massive heart attack, and, though Nicky himself escapes, most of his crew are arrested and his home and business premises are searched thoroughly. The mob bosses manage to get off the charges due to being elderly – and instantly begin putting their house in order with a series of executions. After Ginger takes off, she ends up dying of a massive drugs overdose. Meanwhile, a bomb is placed under Sam's car. Through luck, Sam escapes his car unharmed. But the attack was unauthorised and, Made or not Made, the powers that be deem Nicky to be too much of a liability. He too is executed, along with his brother: the pair are beaten to a pulp and buried, still alive, in a shallow grave.

The old life is over. The Tangiers corporation turns Vegas into a theme park while Sam finds himself back where he started, the master gambler, making money for the bosses 'back home'.

WHO'S WHO?: From beauty contest winner and model, Sharon Stone had auditioned, unsuccessfully, for the role of Vicky LaMotta in *Raging Bull*. Ten years later, she appeared as Arnold Schwarzenegger's wife in Paul Verhoeven's *Total Recall* (1990) before Verhoeven cast her as the duplicitous Catherine Tramell in the controversial *Basic Instinct* (1992). Although the infamous leg-crossing scene made her a megastar, it also eclipsed her acting talent and set her back as an actress to be taken seriously, a trend *Casino* helped to put right. Intelligent, intense actor James Woods starred in *Videodrome* (David Cronenberg, 1983), was Oscar-nominated for his role in *Salvador* (Oliver Stone, 1986) and appeared opposite De Niro in *Once upon a Time in America* (Sergio Leone, 1984).

Don Rickles, comedian, host of numerous TV shows in the States and scene-stealer in *Kelly's Heroes* (Brian G Hutton, 1970), is probably more familiar to younger viewers as the voice of Mr Potato Head in *Toy Story* and *Toy Story 2* (John Lassiter et al, 1996, 1999). Fellow comedian Alan King plays himself in the *Taxi Driver*-inspired *You Talkin' To Me?* (Charles Winkler, 1987) and played a casino owner in *Rush Hour 2* (Brett Ratner, 2001). Kevin Pollak is another comedian who's made the leap to acting, though he's tended to play less and less on the comedy as his career's progressed. He played Aidan Quinn's brother in *Avalon* (Barry Levinson, 1990) and Tom Cruise's colleague in *A Few Good Men* (Levinson again, 1992), and, in the same year as *Casino*, he appeared as one of *The Usual Suspects* (Bryan Singer). LQ Jones can be seen in one of Scorsese's favourite Westerns, *The Naked and the Dead* (Raoul Walsh, 1958), and a number of Sam Peckinpah's pictures, including *The Wild Bunch* (1968) and *Pat Garrett and Billy the Kid* (1973). John Bloom is probably better known by his alter ego, satirist and film reviewer Joe Bob Briggs from TNT's *Monstervision*. As a real-life attorney, Oscar Goodman is alleged to have defended a number of suspected mobsters. In 1999 he was elected Mayor of Las Vegas.

A slew of people appear as younger versions of themselves in *Casino*: 60s teen heartthrob Frankie Avalon had a second career peak thanks to his appearance as the Teen Angel in the hit musical *Grease* (Randal Kleiser, 1978); legendary entertainer Steve Allen was the man responsible for launching *The Tonight Show*, America's top talk show, and was a regular panellist on *What's My Line?*; the crooked poker dealer is played by Tommy DeVito, ex-member of the original Four Seasons.

THE USUAL SUSPECTS: Robert De Niro (*Mean Streets, Taxi Driver, New York, New York, Raging Bull, The King of Comedy, GoodFellas, Cape Fear*); Joe Pesci, Frank Vincent, Frank Adonis, Joseph Bono, Daniel P Conte (*Raging Bull, GoodFellas*); Dean Casper (*Alice Doesn't Live Here Anymore*); Melissa Prophet, Philip Suriano, Jerry Vale (*GoodFellas*); Paul Herman (*The Color of Money, The Last Temptation of Christ, New York Stories, GoodFellas*); Linda Perri (*Cape Fear*); writer Nicholas Pileggi (*GoodFellas*); Barbara De Fina (*The Color of Money, Bad, The Last Temptation of Christ, New York Stories, The Grifters, Made in Milan, GoodFellas, Cape Fear, Mad Dog and Glory, The Age of Innocence, Kundun, My Voyage to Italy, Bringing Out the Dead, Dino*); editor Thelma Schoonmaker (*Who's That Knocking At My Door?, Street Scenes, Raging Bull, The King of Comedy, After Hours, The Color of Money, Bad, The Last Temptation of Christ, New York Stories, GoodFellas, Cape Fear, The Age of Innocence, A Personal Journey with Martin Scorsese Through American Movies, Kundun, Bringing Out the Dead, My Voyage to Italy, Gangs of New York*).

SOURCE: *Casino* is, as the closing titles inform us, a fictional story with fictional characters, but adapted from a true story, that of Frank 'Lefty'

Rosenthal, who took control of mob activity in Las Vegas in the early 70s. His right-hand man was Tony 'The Ant' Spilotro, a childhood friend from Chicago, renamed Nicky Santoro for the film. Frank fell in love with Geri McGee (renamed Ginger McKenna) a chip hustler, prostitute and topless dancer. Frank proposed to her, promising to set her up for life, but her pimp began muscling in, and then she began having an affair with Tony. Piscano, whose complaints to his mother are recorded by the FBI, is based on Carl DeLuna, who kept all their records, while Mr Nance, who brings the money from the casino to Kansas was based on Carl Thomas. Frank Rosenthal was blown up in 1982, as we see happen to Sam, but survived to tell Nicholas Pileggi the tale.

PRODUCTION: Almost as soon as he had finished scripting *GoodFellas* with Scorsese, Nicholas Pileggi was looking to write about the gangsters of Las Vegas. Taking the story of Frank 'Lefty' Rosenthal as his basis, Pileggi spoke to Scorsese about his idea and the director quickly latched on to it as a possible future movie. Pileggi showed Scorsese a news clipping about Rosenthal and his wife fighting on their lawn and the police being called. FBI agents already staking out the house had managed to photograph the scene (in the first draft of the script, this formed the opening of the film). Scorsese wanted to do something different to *GoodFellas*, to look at the 'family' aspect of organised crime but also to look at the bigger picture, including everyone in the chain. Whereas with *GoodFellas* the book was already published by the time he began work on the script, Pileggi was writing his book and collaborating with Scorsese on the screenplay simultaneously. This of course meant that the script had to be inspected by the legal department before anything could be approved and Scorsese found himself in drawn-out battles with lawyers who clearly didn't understand the subject matter. The lawyers sent Scorsese over forty recommendations for changes and deletions, including Nicky's voice-over where he claims that a man had an ice pick put into his testicles and still didn't talk; the lawyers felt that this must be inaccurate – surely he would talk at this point? Another comment claimed that Pileggi's research was lacking as they believed a victim being subjected to ten seconds with a cattle prod would be too long, while another insisted they could not name Chicago as the mob city, suggesting it should be changed to Detroit or Cleveland. Scorsese threatened to change the title card to 'Back Home' if they persisted (indeed, many of the references to Chicago were replaced with this euphemism).

Scorsese began preproduction in June 1994, though Universal were holding off to see a script before officially greenlighting the project.

Scorsese had to call them to explain they'd have a long wait as the script was being formulated in his head – this would not be the normal film they'd expect. Scorsese felt pressured by the studio into ramping up production for a September start date, too early for the scale of the film he envisaged.

To ensure accuracy throughout, Scorsese hired former gangster Joe Russo to act as technical adviser. Russo described the offices of the character that inspired Nicky, and on location, he pointed out that one of the rooms selected for the shoot had a large floor-to-ceiling window, which would have been too easy for someone to shoot Nicky through, so the production team were told to build a wall with high, narrow windows. Coincidentally, Mark Caspar, the former FBI agent who arrested the real Nicky, was also on hand as an adviser, and it turned out that Mark and Joe knew each other – Mark had once been assigned to tail Joe.

Some of the actresses Scorsese wanted to see for the role of Sam's wife Ginger felt unhappy about actually having to read for him. He knew they could act, but he needed to hear the words of the character coming out of their mouths to be sure. Sharon Stone was desperate for the part of Ginger and, although Scorsese interviewed lots of other actresses, he saw Stone first. His agent and Stone's agent were working together to bring Stone to the project and, after six weeks, they set up a meeting between Stone and Scorsese, but Scorsese missed the meeting because the train he was on from Las Vegas broke down. Scorsese was forcing to contact Stone and convince her he was still interested in her. She read for him with De Niro. De Niro was impressed with her and she was cast. Her first scene to be filmed was Ace's proposal.

Robert De Niro was attached even before they began work on the script, and the actor began meeting with Frank Rosenthal to research for the role. Rita Ryack and John Dunn, in charge of wardrobe for the production, also met with Frank Rosenthal and borrowed his clothes to get an approximation of them for Rothstein's clothes. Sharon Stone worked with Ryack herself to get her own look, while Scorsese chose the suits, shirts and ties for De Niro and Pesci personally; there were fifty-two suits for De Niro that track the changes in his personality and forty changes for Stone.

On 14 September 1994, filming began. To commemorate the occasion, Joe Pesci gave Scorsese a gift – a bullet inscribed with Scorsese's name, while his agents presented him with a camera engraved with the start date. Filming was scheduled to take place out of continuity because they were shooting according to location. The scenes outside the fictional

Tangiers casino were shot in front of the then-closed Landmark casino. Filming in the fifth biggest casino in Las Vegas offered both benefits and hindrances, but the depth of the room and the hundreds of real extras were things they could never have achieved on a soundstage. However, even in the early hours of the morning, the constant sound of the slot machines made the shoot a tense one, and they had to work around the noises of people cheering when they won. Even outside the casinos, the shoot would not prove to be an easy one. As they shot one late-night scene, two drunks in a car drove on to the set unaware that a film was being shot; the set police stopped them before they crashed into one of the prop police cars parked up for the scene. A small incident with a sprinkler delayed filming of the scene where Nicky's wife removes the smuggled diamonds from her hair – the sprinkler reacted to the heat of the lights. The scene was already planned to take up some time due to the different camera speeds being used.

Having preferred to stick with traditional methods for so long, editor Thelma Schoonmaker finally relented against using modern equipment for this picture. She was surprised by the speed at which the Avid editing suite allowed her to prepare a cut, and how its saving facilities allowed her to experiment more with form. Even with this technological breakthrough, the editing took almost eleven months, with much of the structure of the film being developed at this stage. Initially, the fight between Ginger and Sam on their lawn – the incident that had grabbed Scorsese's interest in the first place – was to have appeared at the beginning, and the long tracking shot following Nace through the counting room of the Tangiers appeared much later. This counting-room scene was brought forward at Scorsese's request to show right from the start the level of corruption involved. The scene where Nicky's brother was beaten to death was important in that it had to ensure the audience could still sympathise with someone as despicable as Nicky, which is why the camera focuses most on his reaction to the scene.

Casino was released on 22 November 1995, grossing just under $42.5 million on its domestic run.

EDITING: Arguably, one of the reasons *Casino* is often cruelly known as 'GoodFellas 2' is down to the editing. As in *GoodFellas*, the camera is moving almost constantly: flash photography cuts, freeze-frames and, at the beginning, a huge tracking shot as the camera follows a man with a suitcase into the counting room, round all the counters, into the safe and out again through the casino, out of the front doors and into a waiting cab.

MUSIC: Considering which music to use for the film, Scorsese spoke with Robbie Robertson who suggested Scorsese use more Vegas-sounding music. This led him to using Louis Prima – he'd already used 'Just a Gigolo/I Ain't Got Nobody' in *Raging Bull* (and De Niro sang it in the Scorsese-produced *Mad Dog and Glory*). He realised that, like *GoodFellas*, he didn't want to use a composed score, because that would detract from the documentary feel to the picture – composed scores tend to act as signifiers that the movie is a movie. Remembering how movie scores often became chart hits, he selected Elmer Bernstein's 'Walk on the Wild Side', which had also been a hit for Jimmy Smith, and music from two films by Godard, *Le Mépris* and *Vivre Sa Vie*. He'd originally planned to use the Bach only at the end, but title designer Saul Bass suggested using it at the opening of the picture too. There's some nice irony in the choice of songs here, such as where Sam narrates the scene with the senator staying at the hotel and we hear 'The In Crowd'. After Sam marries Ginger and we see her crying, the scene cuts to Sam showing her their new luxury home, a fur coat and a million and a half in jewels to the tune of 'What a Difference a Day Makes'.

QUOTE/UNQUOTE

Nicky: (narrating) 'A lot of holes in the desert, and a lot of problems are buried in those holes. 'Cept gotta do it right. I mean, you gotta have the hole already dug before you show up with a package in the trunk. Otherwise, you're talking about a half-hour to forty-five minutes of digging. And who knows who's gonna be coming along in that time? Before you know it, you gotta dig a few more holes. You could be there all fuckin' night.'

Sam: (narrating) 'No matter how big a guy was, Nicky would take him on. You beat Nicky with fists, he comes back with a bat; you beat him with a knife, he comes back with a gun; and if you beat him with a gun, you better kill 'im, 'cause he'll be coming back and back, until one of you is dead.'

Sam: (narrating) 'For guys like me, Las Vegas washes away your sins. It's like a morality car wash. It does for us what Lourdes does for humpbacks and cripples.'

Nicky: (calmly, to banker Charlie Clark) 'If you don't have my money for me, I'll crack your fucking head wide open in front of everybody in the bank. And just about the time I'm coming out of jail, hopefully, you'll be coming out of your coma. And guess what? I'll split your fucking head open again. 'Cause I'm fucking stupid! I don't give a fuck about jail! That's my business. That's what I do.'

THEMES AND MOTIFS: Scorsese's three gangster films share the use of a subjective first-person narrator (as do *The Last Temptation of Christ*, *Bringing Out the Dead* and his early student films). The narration is split roughly three ways here, with Sam and Nicky narrating the majority of the picture and Frank Marino narrating one scene that could not be told from the point of view of any of the main characters. Significantly, we don't get Ginger's view of things, which adds to the feeling that Sam controls her. Nicky's narration presents Scorsese with the opportunity for a nice trick – although we've seen Sam blown up at the beginning of the picture, we might already assume that he survives as he's here to tell the tale, but right in the middle of the reprise of the car explosion, Nicky's narration is dramatically cut short as he is executed by Marino. This then has the knock-on effect that we don't know whether or not Sam will survive.

CONTROVERSY: Nicky has a choice turn in racist terms, referring to Sam as 'The Golden Jew' and his Arabian contacts as 'Sand Niggers'. Unsurprisingly, with De Niro and Pesci onboard, the word 'Fuck' is said 362 times, an average of 2.05 times per minute. Scorsese stated before the film's release that he created the 'head in the vice' scene as a sacrifice, certain the MPAA would insist it be cut. He hoped this would draw fire away from other violent scenes that would seem less so by comparison. When the MPAA made no objection to the vice scene, he left it in, albeit slightly edited.

KEEP IT IN THE FAMILY: Catherine Scorsese plays Piscano's mother, telling him off for his bad language. Mrs Scorsese's onscreen granddaughter is played by her real-life granddaughter and namesake from Scorsese's first marriage, Cathy.

DELETED SCENES:
- (rehearsed, but ultimately dropped) Ace asks Ginger if she's seen Nicky since he spoke to her about him and she says she hasn't. He asks her to swear on the life of their daughter and she repeats she hasn't spoken to him. He again asks her to swear on Amy's life and when she does he produces a tape recording of a conversation with her arranging to meet Nicky, then he lunges at her and she runs inside and grabs their kid.

The trailer reveals an additional scene filmed but cut from the final cut:
- Sam tells Nicky 'I tried to do everything for you, even though I knew, deep down inside, you would bury me', to which Nicky responds 'I buried you? You buried yourself!'

ALTERNATIVE VERSIONS: There are two network television versions: the original three-hour theatrical cut minus objectionable footage, and a re-edited 140 minute version put together under sole supervision of Martin Scorsese. The version shown in Swedish cinemas in 1996 removed 43 metres of footage, mainly from the vice torture and baseball beatings.

POSTER: There were two main posters. One depicted De Niro in semi-shadow holding a red die between his thumb and forefingers, with insets of Pesci and Stone; another poster had a montage of De Niro, Stone and Pesci (holding the red die). Taglines read: 'No one stays at the top forever', and 'Luck has nothing to do with the games they play.'

TRAILER: The gravelly-voiced man does the voice-over again: 'They had it all . . . they ran the show and it was paradise, while it lasted. Robert De Niro, Sharon Stone, Joe Pesci . . . A Martin Scorsese Picture – Casino.'

AWARDS: Sharon Stone was nominated for an Academy Award for Best Actress in a Leading Role. At the American Cinema Editors Awards, Thelma Schoonmaker was nominated for an 'Eddie' for Best Edited Feature Film. At the Golden Globes, Sharon Stone won for Best Performance by an Actress in a Motion Picture – Drama, with Scorsese picking up a nomination for Best Director. The Italian National Syndicate of Film Journalists gave a Silver Ribbon for Best Dubbing, Male to Luigi Proietti for dubbing the voice of Robert De Niro, and to Dante Ferretti for Best Production Design. At the MTV Movie Awards, meanwhile, Sharon Stone was nominated for Best Female Performance, while Joe Pesci picked up a nod for Best Villain.

LEGACY: For more inventive (and violent) uses of a pen, you could do worse than check out the sublime *Grosse Pointe Blank* (George Armitage, 1997).

AVAILABILITY: There were a number of different versions of *Casino* on Laserdisc. The original MCA/Universal release was a three-sided widescreen presentation with Dolby Digital sound. A subsequent four-sided release boasted enhanced DTS digital sound. But the Pioneer version was the most impressive, being a slightly longer cut than the theatrical release and containing additional trailers for *Waterworld* (Kevin Reynolds, 1995) and *Apollo 13* (Ron Howard, 1995).

WHAT THE CRITICS SAID: Neil Jeffries of *Empire* wrote: 'You can say what you like about this being *GoodFellas Part 2* or *GoodFellas In Vegas*, but it's impossible not to be impressed. *Casino* screams quality at every turn . . . Weaving narration by Pesci and De Niro with one of the best period soundtracks ever assembled, this is as good to listen to as to watch – but the visuals are something else again; long, swooping, tracking shots; overhead views of gaming tables; fast-moving and slickly cut montages; burst of Pesci-perpetrated sickening violence; and more costume changes than in six series of Dallas . . . okay, so it might have worked just as well if an hour shorter, but complaining that this numbs your arse is like whingeing that the roof of the Sistine Chapel gives you a crick in the neck.' This seems a fairer assessment than that of David Ansen of *Newsweek*, who claimed that: 'It's not the actors' fault that no one is able to break through the film's gorgeous but chilly surface. You watch *Casino* with respect and appreciation, revelling in its documentary sense of detail. Filled with brilliant journalism, *Casino* leaves you hungry for drama.'

EXPERT WITNESS: 'I'm very fortunate. I speak to other actors who say "I wish I had somebody I could work with all the time, could always rely on and go back to . . ." It's considered that your work is special, and I like that. I know that if [Marty] says it, it's going to be what he says. I also support him as a director. I'll do whatever he wants.' Actor Robert De Niro (*Sam 'Ace' Rothstein*)

FINAL ANALYSIS: As the critics noted at the time, it's hard to be enthusiastic about *Casino* for all its wonders. Firstly, it's very light on plot – the first half-hour of screen time seems to be taken up with background detail while the rest of the film seems to be a string of anecdotes that fail to be as entertaining as either *Mean Streets* or *GoodFellas*. Ultimately, there's a strong feeling that, despite the new characters and setting, we've seen it all before. As ever though, one can't fault the performances Scorsese gets from his cast. Sharon Stone manages to play a selfish 'greedy bitch' and incompetent mother yet still maintain our sympathies; De Niro gives his most restrained, dignified performance since *The Last Tycoon* (Elia Kazan, 1976); and Pesci . . . well Pesci provides us with the entertainment, as he does in *GoodFellas* and the *Lethal Weapon* movies, playing an utterly repellent character who is truly mesmerising, even when he's stabbing someone in the neck with a pen.

SCORSESE ON *CASINO*: 'This story has to be on a big canvas. There's no sense in my getting Bob De Niro and Joe Pesci and making a 90-minute picture, about only one aspect of one story out of Vegas for the past 40 years. It has to be set in the context of time and place, it has to be about America. Otherwise, why make another mob story? I couldn't care less.'

Kundun (1997)

(70 mm – 114 mins – colour)

MPAA Rating: PG-13

A Cappa/De Fina Production for Refuge Productions/Touchstone Pictures
Producer: Barbara De Fina
Executive Producer: Laura Fattori
Associate Producer: Scott Harris
Co-Producer: Melissa Mathison
Screenplay: Melissa Mathison
Director of Photography: Roger Deakins
Music: Philip Glass
Production/Costume Design: Dante Ferretti
Editor: Thelma Schoonmaker
Casting: Ellen Lewis
Art Direction: Franco Ceraolo. Massimo Razzi
Set Decoration: Francesca LoSchiavo

CAST: Tenzin Thuthob Tsarong (*Dalai Lama*, adult), Gyurme Tethong (*Dalai Lama*, age 12), Tulku Jamyang Kunga Tenzin (*Dalai Lama*, age 5), Tenzin Yeshi Paichang (*Dalai Lama*, age 2), Tencho Gyalpo (*Mother*), Tenzin Topjar (*Lopsang*, aged 5–10), Tsewang Migyur Khangsar (*Father*), Tenzin Lodoe (*Takster*), Tsering Lhamo (*Tsering Dolma*), Geshi Yeshi Gyatso (*Lama of Sera*), Lobsang Gyatso (*The Messenger*), Sonam Phuntsok (*Reting Rimpoche*), Gyatso Lukhang (*Lord Chamberlain*), Lobsang Samten (*Master of the Kitchen*), Tsewang Jigme Tsarong (*Taktra Rimpoche*), Tenzin Trinley (*Ling Rimpoche*), Ngawang Dorjee (*Kashag/Nobleman 1*), Phontso Thonden

(*Kashag/Nobleman 2*), Chewang Tsering Ngokhang (*Layman 1*), Jamyang Tenzin (*Norbu Thundrup*), Tashi Dhondup (*Lobsang*, adult), Jampa Lungtok (*Nechung Oracle*), Karma Wangchuck (*Deformed Face Bodyguard*), Kim Chan (*Second Chinese General*), Henry Yuk (*General Tan*), Ngawang Kaldan (*Prime Minister Lobsang Tashi*), Jurme Wangda (*Prime Minister Lukhangwa*), Robert Lin (*Chairman Mao*), Selden Kunga (*Tibetan Doctor*), John Wong (*Chinese Comrade*), Gawa Youngdung (*Old Woman*), Tenzin Rampa (*Tenzin Chonegyl*, age 12), Vyas Ananthakrishnan (*Indian Soldier*).

UNCREDITED CAST: R Gern Trowbridge (*Monk*), Yoon C Joyce (*Chinese Officer*)

TITLES: The Touchstone logo appears in red, with the flash across the logo appearing to the sound of Tibetan cymbals. The film logo appears reflected against the surface of black water, then disperses with a ripple. Rolling captions reveal that the sons of Genghis Khan gave the Dalai Lama his name, which means 'Oceans of Wisdom'. In a war-torn Asia, Tibetans have practised non-violence for over a thousand years, with the Dalai Lama as their ruler – he's believed to be the human manifestation of the Buddha of Compassion. In 1933, after the death of the thirteenth Dalai Lama, a holy man began the quest for the fourteenth, a search that would take him four years to complete.

SUMMARY: A holy man, disguised as a servant, stops at the house of a family with a two-year-old boy, Lhamo Dhondrub. The man is immediately taken by the child, who somehow sees through his disguise and calls him 'Lama'. Revealing himself to the family, the Lama sets out a table of objects and asks the child to pick out those objects he feels belong to him. Instinctively, the child picks out the possessions once owned by the thirteenth Dalai Lama. To the shock of his family, the holy man addresses the child by his spiritual name – 'Kundun' – and proclaims him the latest in a long line of Dalai Lamas. Two years later, Lhamo is taken away in a procession to meet Reting Rimpoche, a man who saw him in a vision and followed the signs to him. Reting explains to him that he has been reborn, as we will be again as long as all life continues. He is here to love and care for all living things. Soon after, he is presented to the people of Tibet as the fourteenth Dalai Lama and taken to Lhasa to begin a life of training and study. But, after Reting Rimpoche is banished from the Monastery for breaking his vows, the responsibility for taking care of the boy falls to the Lord Chamberlain.

When he is old enough, the Dalai Lama is warned by the Lord Chamberlain, he will face great responsibilities. The previous Dalai Lama had to look after his people's physical and spiritual wellbeing during an invasion by the Chinese. Though they managed to drive the Chinese back, he is told that the Chinese are once again laying claim to Tibet and, after learning that India and Britain are unable or unwilling to help them, he decides to write to President Truman of America. Mao Tse Tung, leader of the Communists of China, presents Tibet with three demands: that Tibet must accept that it is part of China; that their defences must be conducted by China; all political and trade with foreign countries must be conducted through China. The Dalai Lama rejects all three points. In retaliation, the Chinese invade Tibet, claiming they come at the request of the 'Tibetan minority' to liberate them from 'the tyranny of the Dalai Lama'. Though he himself feels he is too young, his advisers realise that he must be enthroned as the leader of Tibet immediately and then leave Lhasa for his own safety.

The Government moves to Dungkhar Monastery, but this merely has the effect of convincing the Chinese that they have won. The Dalai Lama agrees to meet with General Chang Ching-Wu, who presents his Holiness with a seventeen-point agreement the Chinese Government wish him to sign. The Dalai Lama greets the General with silence, but secretly he is surprised that, having been expecting a demon, perhaps with horns, he is just a man after all. Though they receive a letter from America, his Holiness realises that it is unsigned. America is far away, and the Chinese are close. Reluctantly, he decides to return to Lhasa. He finds the Chinese administration installed and demanding more and more from the Tibetan people. They insist on absorbing the Tibetan army into their own ranks and replacing the Tibetan flag with that of Communist China.

After the United Nations refuse to hear their appeal and Britain, India, Nepal and America refuse to meet with their representatives, the Dalai Lama concedes to travel to Peking to negotiate with Chairman Mao. He sees many parallels between socialism and Buddhism, but is surprised by Mao's assertion that religion is a poison that has kept the Tibetan people weak. On his return to Tibet, however, he finds his people terrified and oppressed. The Chinese have bombed and desecrated the monasteries, and forced children to shoot their own parents. When the Chinese instruct him that they intend to send the Tibetan army to fight against a revolt in the East, the Dalai Lama tells him he will not approve such a decision. With tanks in the streets and aeroplanes sitting outside Lhasa, the Lord Chamberlain again advises his Holiness that he must flee Tibet.

Finally, after hearing his own people plead with him, he relents. Dressed as a soldier, he is escorted to sanctuary in India.

The Dalai Lama has not yet returned to Tibet. He hopes one day to make the journey.

WHO'S WHO?: Melissa Mathison was the writer of Steven Spielberg's *E.T. – the Extra Terrestrial*, and, until recently, the wife of actor Harrison Ford.

THE USUAL SUSPECTS: Producer Barbara De Fina (*The Color of Money, Bad, The Last Temptation of Christ, New York Stories, The Grifters, Made in Milan, GoodFellas, Cape Fear, Mad Dog and Glory, The Age of Innocence, Casino, My Voyage to Italy, Bringing Out the Dead, Dino*); editor Thelma Schoonmaker (*Who's That Knocking At My Door?, Street Scenes, Raging Bull, The King of Comedy, After Hours, The Color of Money, Bad, The Last Temptation of Christ, New York Stories, GoodFellas, Cape Fear, The Age of Innocence, Casino, A Personal Journey with Martin Scorsese Through American Movies, Bringing Out the Dead, My Voyage to Italy, Gangs of New York*); production/costume designer Dante Ferretti (*The Age of Innocence, Casino, Bringing Out the Dead, Gangs of New York*).

PRODUCTION: During *The Age of Innocence*, Scorsese was handed Melissa Mathison's script, *Kundun*, by his agent at CAA, Jay Maloney. Scorsese had known Mathison back in the 1970s and at one time it looked like he and Mathison would work together on Mark Helprin's book *Winter's Tale* (see **Unseen Scorsese**). He had been interested in the Dalai Lama ever since his Holiness was awarded the Nobel Peace Prize in 1989, and what appealed to him about the script was its sense of simplicity with everything told from the child's point of view. Mathison and her husband Harrison Ford introduced Scorsese to the Dalai Lama and his Holiness advised Mathison on a number of technical aspects of her script. Scorsese and Mathison then worked on fourteen different drafts of the script, ultimately settling on one that was close in style to their second draft. Open auditions were held in the spring of 1996 to find Tibetan and Chinese actors who would bring a sense of honesty to the film. Indeed many of the supporting cast were not trained actors at all, but, coming from Tibet, they had lived the lives of these characters for real. During the two weeks of rehearsals, Scorsese allowed the Tibetans themselves to coach the children.

With the possibility of filming in Tibet out of the question, the production was instead taken to Morocco. There, production designer

Dante Ferretti had the sets built as accurately as possible, with the exception of the monastery throne room, which was designed deliberately to seem like the memory of a child rather than a realistic depiction of the room. Although the production was lucky enough to have a large number of extras, one shot was, by necessity, created digitally: the scene where the Dalai Lama dreams of standing in a square surrounded by slaughtered monks was achieved by filming a number of extras lying at the feet of the Dalai Lama, then the extras were duplicated digitally to create a devastating image of mass slaughter. Scorsese and Schoonmaker worked from January to October 1997 cutting the picture. They found the last three months the hardest as they worried that the length of the film might lose people's interest. As they worked on a rough cut, composer Philip Glass began work on the score for the picture. Scorsese had wanted to work with Glass ever since he heard the work he'd done for Paul Schrader on *Mishima: A Life in Four Chapters* (1985). *Kundun* was released in the USA on Christmas Day 1997 with staggered releases across Europe throughout the following year.

QUOTE/UNQUOTE
Norbu: 'Today you lose, Kundun. Tomorrow you may win. [clicking his fingers] Things change, Kundun.'

Chairman Mao: 'You need to learn this: religion is poison. *Poison*. Like a poison, it weakens the race. Like a drug, it retards the mind of people and society. "The opiate of the people." '

Dalai Lama: 'Just like a dream experience, whatever things I enjoy will become a memory. Whatever is past will not be seen again . . . I will liberate those not liberated. I will release those not released. I will relieve those unrelieved. And set living beings in Nirvana.'

ROOTS: Just as the Westerns of old Hollywood stole from the films of the East, so Scorsese shoots this film of the East like a Western, with sun-bleached vistas and dusty journeys. But he also reviews a number of key Eastern films such as Akira Kurosawa's *Yojimbo* (1961), Satyajit Ray's *Panther Panchali* (1955) and *Jalsaghar* ('The Music Room', 1958), and Zhuangzhuang Tian's *Dao Ma Zei* ('The Horse Thief', 1986). The Dalai Lama is seen to watch *La Poule aux Oeufs d'or* ('The Hen That Laid The Golden Egg' 1905) and *Henry V* (Laurence Olivier, 1944). The shot of the Dalai Lama standing in the middle of hundreds of dead monks is inspired by a similar scene in *Gone with the Wind* (Victor Fleming, 1939).

THEMES AND MOTIFS: The film, as we'd expect in a film about religion, is one of cycles and ritual. We hear the story of Lhamo's birth, which he insists his family tell him again and again. When he first meets Reting Rimpoche, he learns of the story of the first Dalai Lama, who, like Reting, was attended by crows at his birth, while the phrase 'I see a safe journey . . . I see a safe return' is passed from brother to brother in the film. There's an important motif of vision, both a spiritual vision (such as the ones experienced by both the Dalai Lama and Reting Rimpoche) and sight, in the gaze of the Dalai Lama, who watches movies and looks through a telescope; significantly, he is a short-sighted man with the greatest 'vision' in his country.

CONTROVERSY: Understandably, the announcement that Disney would be filming the story of the Dalai Lama did not sit well with the Chinese government. Chinese Foreign Ministry spokesman Cui Tiankai declared that, 'To sing the praises of the Dalai Lama – this kind of action does not conform with reality,' with veiled threats that Disney's interests in China would suffer as a consequence. Disney called on former Secretary of State Henry Kissinger to advise them on the best way forward but ultimately backed Scorsese completely.

LEGACY: Scorsese's name was added to a list of people banned from setting foot in Tibet by the Chinese government.

KEEP IT IN THE FAMILY: The film is dedicated to Catherine Scorsese, who died during production.

AWARDS: *Kundun* received nominations from the American Academy of Motion Picture Arts and Sciences for Best Art Direction and Set Decoration (Dante Ferretti and Francesca LoSchiavo), Best Cinematography (Roger Deakins), Best Costume Design (Ferretti again) and Best Original Dramatic Score (Philip Glass). Roger Deakins won Best Cinematography awards from the Boston, New York and National Society of Film Critics and was also nominated for an award by the American Society of Cinematographers. Philip Glass's score was nominated at the Golden Globes, though he won in the same category at the Los Angeles Film Critics Association Awards. *Kundun* was also nominated for best Foreign Film by the Australian Film Institute (which was won, and deservedly so, by Curtis Hansen for *L.A. Confidential*).

AVAILABILITY: *Kundun* is, at the time of writing, still not available in any format in the UK, but in the USA Buena Vista Home Video have released both VHS and DVD editions.

WHAT THE CRITICS SAID: 'Filming in lush, warm tones,' Helen Van Kruyssen noted in her review for the late, lamented *Neon* magazine, 'Scorsese demonstrates an admirable respect for the subject matter. The result is an unsentimental, informative and striking film. If a cynical heart prevented you from seeing this on the big screen, think again: *Kundun* is a compelling accomplishment, confirming yet again Scorsese's unmatched filmmaking talents.' Ian Freer, awarding the film four stars in *Empire*, wrote that, 'Even if *Kundun* lacks the commitment and penetration set by his own high standards, much of Scorsese's stock-in-trade is still present; impeccable performances (Tsarong as the 18-year-old Lama effortlessly embodying sedate wisdom), the evocation of private milieus, and a fascination with rite and ritual. Indeed, Scorsese's documentary style accumulation of exotic detail occasionally serves to distance rather than illuminate the sacred world . . . the net result is difficult and demanding viewing yet strangely thrilling.'

FINAL ANALYSIS: Though it's easy to compare *Kundun* with its spiritual brother in Scorsese's canon, the equally overtly religious *The Last Temptation of Christ*, in many ways it is actually closer to the spirit of *The Age of Innocence*, both in the way the lifestyles of the characters are revealed more by an attention to detail than any incident in particular, and in the way that, like Newland and the Countess's story, the drama is routed in the *inaction* of the Dalai Lama. A man of peace, and one of such inspirational goodness, is hard to build a dramatic film around – indeed the first real incident of conflict comes with the Chinese invasion of Tibet, when the film is already halfway gone. Many of the real-life events that affect the Tibetan people happen offscreen, meaning we only hear of the oppressive control of the Chinese, but don't see any evidence of it ourselves, aside from the installation of obtrusive speakers pumping Chinese music right into the heart of Lhasa. Rather than turning this into an over-detailed and dull but worthy tale, this level of inaction has the effect that we find ourselves so drawn into the life and ritual of the monastery that even something as innocuous as the Chinese music feels like a much stronger invasion of Tibet than the colourful and rather attractive images of the Red Army marching across the border. When we finally see the after-effects of the Chinese occupation – or rather the imaginings of the Dalai Lama, who sees himself surrounded by thousands of slaughtered monks – it feels almost excessive. We understood that the Chinese were bad when we saw the rather fey, grotesque figure of Chairman Mao leaning over the young Dalai Lama and lecturing him on the corruptive influence of religion. What we're left with, however, is a film that might be light on drama, but is still utterly compelling even if from the point of view that a person surely couldn't remain so dedicated and resolute to peace after being driven from their own home by a force like the Communists.

SCORSESE ON *KUNDUN*: 'I don't want the picture to have a message, let me put it that way, if it does, maybe it'll be good that it has a message, but it may not be a good work of art. That's something else. Whether it should be a good work of art or not, I don't even know, whether it's a work of art. I just know that I was kind of burning to make it. But I think one thing is – the Dalai Lama is an example. When the little boy tells him toward the end, his youngest brother says, "I'll go to war," and he looks at the boy after all this is happening and all that's going to happen, and he looks at the little boy, and he says "Dalai Lama doesn't believe in war." And I think that's what we have to think about.'

Bringing Out the Dead (1999)

(70 mm – 121 mins – colour)

MPAA Rating: R

A Scott Rudin – Cappa/De Fina production for Touchstone
Pictures and Paramount Pictures
Producers: Barbara De Fina, Scott Rudin
Associate Producers: Jeff Levine, Mark Roybal
Executive Producers: Bruce S Pustin, Adam Schroeder
Director: Martin Scorsese
Screenplay: Paul Schrader, based on the novel by Joe
Connelly
Director of Photography: Robert Richardson
Editor: Thelma Schoonmaker
Music: Elmer Bernstein; orchestrated and conducted by
Emilie Bernstein
Casting: Ellen Lewis
Production Design: Dante Ferretti
Art Direction: Robert Guerra
Set Decoration: William F Reynolds
Costume Design: Rita Ryack

SOUNDTRACK: 'Nowhere to Run'* by Martha & The Vandellas; 'Too Many Fish in the Sea'* by The Marvellettes; 'Bell Boy'* by The Who; 'What's the Frequency Kenneth'* by REM; 'I'm So Bored with the USA'*, 'Janie Jones'* by The Clash; 'T.B. Sheets'* by Van Morrison; 'These Are Days' by 10,000 Maniacs; 'You Can't Put Your Arms Around a Memory'* by Johnny Thunders; 'Ring Tang Ding Dong (I Am a Japanese Sandman')* by The Cellos; 'Rivers of Babylon'* by The Melodians; 'Red Red Wine'* by UB40; 'Combination of the Two'* by Big Brother & The Holding Company.

CAST: Nicolas Cage (*Frank Pierce*), Patricia Arquette (*Mary Burke*), John Goodman (*Larry*), Ving Rhames (*Marcus*), Tom Sizemore (*Tom Walls*), Marc Anthony (*Noel*), Mary Beth Hurt (*Nurse Constance*), Cliff Curtis (*Cy Coates*), Nestor Serrano (*Dr Hazmat*), Aida Turturro (*Nurse Crupp*), Sonja Sohn (*Kanita*), Cynthia Roman (*Rose*), Afemo Omilami (*Griss*), Cullen Oliver Johnson (*Mr Burke*), Arthur J Nascarella (*Captain Barney*), Martin Scorsese (*Dispatcher*), Julyana Soelistyo (*Sister Fetus*), Graciela Lecube, Marylouise Burke, Mary Diveny (*Neighbour Women*), Phyllis Somerville (*Mrs Burke*), Tom Riis Farrell (*John Burke*), Aleks Shaklin, Leonid Citer (*Arguing Russians*), Jesus A Del Rosario Jr (*Man with Bloody Foot*), Larry Fessenden (*Cokehead*), Bernie Friedman (*Big Feet*), Theo Kogan, Fuschia Walker (*Prostitutes*), John Heffernan (*Mr Oh*), Matthew Maher, Bronson Dudley, Marilyn McDonald, (*Mr Oh's Friends*), Ed Jupp Jr, J Stanford Hoffman (*Homeless Men in Waiting Room*), Rita Norona Schrager (*Concerned Hispanic Aunt*), Don Berry (*Naked Man*), Mtume Gant (*Street Punk*), Michael Noto (*Grunt*), Omar Sharif Scroggins (*Bystander*) muMs (*Voice in Crowd*), Michael Kenneth Williams (*Drug Dealer*), Andrew Davoli (*Stanley*), Charlene Hunter (*Miss Williams*), Jesse Malin (*Club Doorman*), Harper Simon (*IB Bangin'*), Joseph Monroe Webb (*Drummer*), Jon Abrahams (*Club Bystander*), Charis Michaelson (*IB's Girlfriend*), Lia Yang (*Dr Milagros*), Antone Pagan (*Arrested Man*), Melissa Marsala (*Bridge & Tunnel Girl*), Betty Miller (*Weeping Woman*), Rosemary Gomez (*Pregnant Maria*), Luis Rodriguez (*Carlos*), Sylva Keleglan (*Crackhead*), Frank Ciornei (*Dr Mishra*), Catrina Ganey (*Nurse Odette*), Jennifer Lane Newman (*Nurse Adviser*), John Bal, Raymond Cassar (*Policemen in Hospital*), Tom Cappadona, Jack O'Connell, Randy Foster (*Drunks*), Richard Spore (*Homeless Suicidal*), James Hanlon, Chris Edwards (*Firemen*), Mark Giordano (*Police Sergeant*), Michael Mulheren, David Zayas (*Cops in Elevator*), Terry Serpico (*Cop 1*), Brian Smyj (*Cop 2*), Floyd Resnick (*Cop 3*), Megan Leigh (*Surgeon*), David Vasquez

(*Screaming Man*), Judy Reyes, Joseph P Reidy (*ICU Nurses*), Queen Latifah (*Dispatcher Love*) Bart DeFinna (*Restaurant Cashier*), Carolyn Campbell (*Policewoman*).

TITLES: A caption card reads: 'This film takes place in New York City in the early 90s.' The credits appear white on a black background in a bitty, typewritten font. The credits are interspersed with shots of Frank and the ambulance.

SUMMARY: Frank Pierce is an exhausted and embittered ambulance driver. Months of dead patients and time spent with the lowlifes of the city have taken their toll and he feels ready to quit his job. He becomes obsessed by the memory of one particular patient, a homeless asthmatic girl called Rose who died as he fought to save her life. Now he finds himself haunted by feelings of guilt and by visions of Rose wherever he looks. During one shift he and his partner, Larry, are called to the house of Mr Burke who has suffered a heart attack. Though it looks as if Burke is dead, Frank manages to resuscitate him and they take him to Our Lady of Perpetual Mercy hospital (known to the ambulance drivers as 'Misery'). Mr Burke was unconscious for a long time and there are fears he may never recover. As the doctors monitor his progress they are forced to shock him a number of times just to keep his heart going. Through his shift Frank becomes acquainted with Burke's daughter, Mary. Mary hasn't spoken to her father in three years, ever since she became involved with drugs, though she claims she's now clean.

After a second night saving and losing lives, Frank sees Mary heading towards an apartment block. He follows her and finds her asleep in the bedroom of a drug dealer called Cy. Exhausted and worried for both his own sanity and for Mary, Frank breaks down crying and Cy gives him a pill to help him relax. Within minutes he is asleep, dreaming about pulling ghosts out of the streets and remembering the day Rose died. He wakes screaming. With a surge of energy, he picks up the sleeping Mary, throws her over his shoulder and carries her out of the building. Mary wakes up groggy and bad-tempered. Frank escorts her home and follows her up to her apartment but finds himself falling asleep on her couch. Mary leaves him there while she goes back to see her father and Frank doesn't wake until the next evening. Before his next shift, Frank goes to see Mr Burke and thinks he can hear his cries, begging to die. Later that night, Frank is dispatched to the apartment block where he met Cy the previous night. There he finds Cy hanging from the side of the building impaled on a railing, having tried to escape from a gang of rival drug dealers via his apartment window. With the help of the fire brigade, Frank manages to pull Cy to safety.

Returning to the hospital, Frank visits Patrick Burke one more time. His eyes plead with Frank to let him go, so Frank assists him by removing his ventilator and placing the heart monitor pads on himself to allow Mr Burke enough time to pass without the risk of being forced alive again by the doctors. He goes to tell Mary that her father has died. Mary tells him she cannot believe he had the strength to carry on living as long as he did and then invites Frank in. They lie together on her bed, Frank's head cradled on her lap.

WHO'S WHO?: The career of oddball actor Nicolas Cage received an early boost thanks to his uncle, Francis Ford Coppola, who cast him in *Rumble Fish* (1983), *The Cotton Club* (1984) and *Peggy Sue Got Married* (1986). His turn as the one-armed lover of Cher in *Moonstruck* (Norman Jewison, 1987), plus starring roles in *Raising Arizona* (Joel Coen, 1987), *Vampire's Kiss* (Robert Bierman, 1989) and *Wild at Heart* (David Lynch, 1990) further solidified him as an unpredictable actor, and his Oscar-winning performance in *Leaving Las Vegas* (Mike Figgis, 1995) propelled him to the A-list. Recent hits include *Face/Off* (1997), *City of Angels* (Brad Silberling 1998) and *Captain Corelli's Mandolin* (John Madden, 2001). Cage's ex-wife Patricia Arquette is the sister of fellow actors David, Richmond, Alexis and Rosanna. Her starring role in *A Nightmare on Elm Street 3: Dream Warriors* (Chuck Russell, 1987) barely prepared us for the star she'd become after appearing opposite Christian Slater in the Quentin Tarantino-scripted *True Romance* (Tony Scott, 1993).

Despite an extensive film career, including roles in the majority of the Coen Brothers pictures, John Goodman will always be remembered as Dan Conner, the put-upon husband in the long-running US sitcom *Roseanne*. A graduate of *ER*, Ving Rhames made an instant impression as Marsellus Wallace in *Pulp Fiction* (Quentin Tarantino, 1994) and also appeared in *Mission: Impossible* (Brian De Palma, 1996), *Mission: Impossible II* (John Woo, 2000), *Con Air* (opposite Nicolas Cage) and *Out of Sight* (Steven Soderbergh, 1996). Tom Sizemore appeared in the third series of US drama series *China Beach* before pegging a role in Oliver Stone's second Vietnam picture *Born on the Fourth of July* (1989). He played the slimy Jack Scagnetti in Stone's *Natural Born Killers* (1995) and also appeared in *Heat* (Michael Mann, 1995), *The Relic* (Peter Hyams, 1997), *Saving Private Ryan* (Steven Spielberg, 1998) and *Pearl Harbor* (Michael Bay, 2001). Afemo Omilami played the drill sergeant in *Forrest Gump* (Robert Zemeckis, 1994). Marylouise Burke played Connie in *Series 7: The Contenders* (Daniel Minahan, 2001).

Harper Simon is the son of singer/songwriter Paul Simon. Jon Abrahams starred in *Scary Movie* (Keenen Ivory Wayans, 2000) and played Robert De Niro's son in *Meet the Parents* (Jay Roach, 2000). Aida Turturro plays Tony Soprano's sister Janice in *The Sopranos*, while Antone Pagan also appeared in the series as Detective Ramos in the episode 'Bust Out'.

THE USUAL SUSPECTS: Charlene Hunter (*Casino*); writer Paul Schrader (*Taxi Driver, Raging Bull, The Last Temptation of Christ*); producer Barbara De Fina (*The Color of Money, Bad, The Last Temptation of Christ, New York Stories, The Grifters, Made in Milan, GoodFellas, Cape Fear, Mad Dog and Glory, The Age of Innocence, Casino, Kundun, My Voyage to Italy, Dino*); editor Thelma Schoonmaker (*Who's That Knocking At My Door?, Street Scenes, Raging Bull, The King of Comedy, After Hours, The Color of Money, Bad, The Last Temptation of Christ, New York Stories, GoodFellas, Cape Fear, The Age of Innocence, Casino, A Personal Journey with Martin Scorsese Through American Movies, Kundun, My Voyage to Italy, Gangs of New York*); production/costume designer Dante Ferretti (*The Age of Innocence, Casino, Kundun, Gangs of New York*).

SOURCE: Although the bulk of the novel is faithfully adapted for the screen, one major omission from the film is Frank's battle to repair his broken marriage – it ends after he realises his ex-wife has fallen in love with another woman.

PRODUCTION: Producer Scott Rudin read Joe Connelly's semi-autobiographical novel when it was still at the galley stage. He quickly acquired the rights and instinctively knew he wanted Scorsese to direct the film version. In turn, Scorsese knew that Paul Schrader was the perfect writer to capture the spirit of the novel. Schrader read the book and promptly agreed to take on the script, which he completed with his customary speed in just three weeks. Scorsese had been interested in working with Nicolas Cage ever since the actor's uncle, Francis Ford Coppola, introduced them some years earlier. By this time, Cage was riding high after an Oscar win for his starring role as a drunkard in Mike Figgis's *Leaving Las Vegas* and a succession of high-profile action movies. After Scorsese's old friend Brian De Palma informed him of the good working relationship he'd enjoyed with Cage on *Snake Eyes* (1998), Scorsese contacted the actor to star in *Bringing Out the Dead*.

Cage spent time working with emergency crews in both New York and Los Angeles and was surprised to find the LA experience more harrowing than the New York one, with the paramedics fitting him with a bulletproof vest to attend the scene of a drive-by shooting. Joe Connelly was also on hand as an adviser to the actors and crew, helping Cage in particular achieve the psychological depths of his character.

Filming began on 18 September 1998 with the majority of the shoots taking place at night on the streets of 'Hell's Kitchen'. Although almost contemporary, *Bringing Out the Dead* was specifically set at the beginning of the 1990s, before Mayor Guiliani's reforms had cleaned up the streets, and when the city's drug problem was reaching record levels. Dante Ferretti and his team scouted for locations on the City's West Side and proceeded to dirty up the streets for the look they needed. As if the technical aspect of filming in The City That Never Sleeps wasn't enough, the crew often found themselves waiting around for complicated shots to be set up. With the actors enduring copious amounts of blood and grime being splattered all over them throughout the shoot, costumer Rita Ryack had to have massive numbers of duplicate costumes on hand, with as many as ten costume changes prepared for Nicolas Cage alone. The hardest task she faced, however, was preparing the looks of the extras on the street, maintaining a balance between believability and the almost surreal aspect of the characters to convey the growing sense of Frank's despair and alienation. With location filming drawing to a close after two months, the team were ready for the interiors, which would be shot at Bellevue Hospital – which Dante Ferretti transformed into the emergency rooms of Mercy Hospital – and the Bedford Avenue Armory in Brooklyn – which housed the apartments of Mary, the Burkes and Cy. Technicians at Industrial Light and Magic were then hired to meld the interiors with previously shot location footage for the scenes below Cy's apartment with the dealer suspended over the edge of the building. The production finally wrapped on 8 January 1999 after over 70 days at a cost of $32 million. It was released the following October.

EDITING: As the film opens, we see an ambulance and then Frank's eyes in almost a mirror of the opening titles to *Taxi Driver*, but at a much faster pace. In a number of sequences, notably in those where Frank accompanies the manic Tom Walls, the action is sped up to almost comic levels, really adding to the mania raging in Frank's mind. In the dream sequence where Frank remembers Rose's death, the actors acted out their movements backwards and then the sequence itself was reversed, a process also seen in *Cape Fear*.

QUOTE/UNQUOTE
Griss, the Security Guard: 'Don't make me take off my sunglasses!'

Radio Operator: 'You'll be driving to the man that needs no introduction. Chronic caller of the year, three straight and shooting for number four. The Duke of Drunk. The King of Stink. Our most frequent flyer – "Mr Oh".'

Frank: 'You swore you'd fire me if I came in late again. You swore, you swore!'
Captain Barney: (apologetic) 'I'll fire you tomorrow.'

Frank: 'I gotta get a drink. Sobriety's killing me.'

Frank: (to a suicidal patient) 'With all the poor people of this city who wanted only to live and were viciously murdered, you have the nerve to sit here, wanting to die, and not go through with it?! You make me *sick*!'

Mary Burke: 'This city, it'll kill you if you aren't strong enough.'
Frank: 'Ah, the city doesn't discriminate. Gets everybody.'

THEMES AND MOTIFS: Aside from the visual nods to *Taxi Driver* (the use of rear-view mirrors, the focusing on Frank's eyes, shots of prostitutes and the practical similarities from shooting in the same locations), we have the scene where Frank enters the apartment of Cy, the drug-dealer. Echoing Sport from *Taxi Driver*, Cy talks a lot of crap and exhibits a shocking lack of taste in his interior décor – a pink/red apartment filled with kitsch. When we return to Cy's apartment towards the end of the film, the pink-red has been replaced with blood red from the body of Cy's companion. One of the street teens watching Noel the dreadlocked vagrant uses his fingers to mime shooting a gun.

THERE HE IS!: Stealing the show, Scorsese plays the voice of the radio dispatcher.

AWARDS: Robert Richardson won Best Cinematography at the Florida Film Critics Circle Awards, the Italian National Syndicate of Film Journalists gave their Silver Ribbon for production design to Dante Ferretti and Ving Rhames received a nomination for Best Supporting Actor at the Golden Satellite Awards.

AVAILABILITY: Available in both VHS and DVD format, with the latter also containing a short behind-the-scenes featurette.

POSTER/TRAILER: Featuring a black-and-white image of Cage's eyes as seen through a cross against a red background, the poster featured the tagline: 'Any call can be murder, any stop can be suicide, any night can be the last. And you thought your job was hell?' This tagline also appeared in the trailer.

WHAT THE CRITICS SAID: 'With tremendous visual imagination, Scorsese creates a phantasmagoric view of the city's underbelly, and of the wretched souls there that can't always be saved. And while the milieu and the director's signature themes of guilt and redemption may seem familiar, the film takes some surprising turns, ending on a hopeful note that's as satisfying as it is moving.' Chris Cronis *Premiere*, awarding the picture four stars.

EXPERT WITNESS: 'The *Taxi Driver* comparison is there; it's unavoidable. [But] there are marked differences. Frank is a different character from Travis Bickle. This is not someone who's cooking in a broth of anger and violence. He's searching for peacefulness. He wants to sleep; to have his reward. But he feels that God has taken his hand off him, and he's become an instrument of death.' Writer Paul Schrader.

FINAL ANALYSIS: It's no wonder Scorsese found himself drawn to Joe Connelly's novel. *Bringing Out the Dead* is full of pop music references, which suggests Connelly wrote the novel with a film version in mind; many of the references seem to act as possible suggestions for a soundtrack. It almost feels as if we've come full-circle here, with Joe Connelly writing about a spiritually hollow man on the edge of a breakdown, only instead of turning this into a pseudo-documentary as they might have done in the past, Scorsese and Schrader head more towards a bible-black comedy populated by a series of grotesques: Griss, the security guard whose darkest threat is to warn people not to make him take off his shades; Noel, the dreadlocked lunatic who we learn is a victim of the crueller side of seductive drug-dealer Cy; Tom Walls, Frank's explosive co-driver (played by a barely recognisable Tom Sizemore) and a comedy nun preaching against 'Mexican divorces' for good measure (you can't go wrong with a comedy nun). Though the overall effect leaves one feeling emotionally distant from the characters, it's an interesting departure for Scorsese who wrong-foots expectations and, as with *Taxi Driver*, reserves the best lines for himself.

SCORSESE ON *BRINGING OUT THE DEAD*: 'There's a correlation to *Taxi Driver*, there's no doubt . . . only it's twenty-five years later and we're a little mellower now. Instead of killing people, our protagonist is trying to save people. We were all about thirty, thirty-one years old – Schrader, De Niro and myself – when we made *Taxi Driver*. But now we're fifty-six. It's a different world, and we're different, too.'

My Voyage to Italy (2001)

(35 mm – 246 mins – colour/B & W)

MPAA Rating: PG-13

A Mediatrade Presentation
in association with Cappa
Productions/Pasa Doble productions
Producers: Barbara De Fina, Giuliana Del Punta, Bruno
Restuccia
Executive Producers: Giorgio Armani, Ricardo Tozzi, Marco
Chimenz
Co-Executive Producers: Raffaele Donato
Assistant Producer: Caterina D'Amico
Screenwriters: Suso Checchi D'Amico, Raffaele Donato,
Kent Jones, Martin Scorsese
Director of Photography: Phil Abraham
Editor: Thelma Schoonmakor
Assistant Editor: Jeffrey M Werner
Presented by Martin Scorsese

SUMMARY: In the spirit of Scorsese's contribution to *A Century of Cinema* 1995, here he appraises some of the great Italian directors whose work has influenced his own career.

THE USUAL SUSPECTS: Producer Barbara De Fina (*The Color of Money, Bad, The Last Temptation of Christ, New York Stories, The Grifters, Made in Milan, GoodFellas, Cape Fear, Mad Dog and Glory, The Age of Innocence, Casino, Kundun, Bringing Out the Dead, Dino*); editor Thelma Schoonmaker (*Who's That Knocking At My Door?, Street Scenes, Raging Bull, The King of Comedy, After Hours, The Color of Money, Bad, The Last Temptation of Christ, New York Stories, GoodFellas, Cape Fear, The Age of Innocence, Casino, A Personal Journey with Martin Scorsese Through American Movies, Kundun, Bringing Out the Dead, Gangs of New York*).

PRODUCTION: Planned very much as a work-in-progress, the documentary was first screened at the Venice Film Festival in 1999 in a ninety-minute form, while a fuller-length version, at a staggering four hours and six minutes, received its world premiere at the Cannes Film Festival two years later. The project is ongoing, however, with Scorsese planning a further instalment dealing with more recent developments in Italian cinema.

ALTERNATIVE VERSIONS: A ninety-minute version, then called *Il Dolce Cinema*, was shown at the Venice Film Festival in 1999. The version shown at Cannes in 2001, renamed *Il Mio Viaggio In Italia*, ran at 243 minutes.

AVAILABILITY: A DVD release is, at the time of writing, scheduled for June 2002.

SCORSESE ON *MY VOYAGE TO ITALY*: 'Those films showed the hard reality of life with images that were so moving that our older relations wept and even we children were overcome ... It was through film that I really began to discover my family, who they were and from where they came. Many questions that came to me then found their answers only through the films.'

Gangs of New York (2002)

(70 mm – Duration TBC – colour)

A Cappa Production for Miramax Films

Producers: Alberto Grimaldi, Martin Scorsese
Associate Producer: Gerry Robert Byrne
Executive Producers: Maurizio Grimaldi, Michael Hausman,
Harvey Weinstein
Line Producer: Laura Fattori
Written by Steven Zaillian, Kenneth Lonergan, Jay Cocks
and Martin Scorsese, based on the book by Herbert Asbury
Music: Elmer Bernstein
Cinematography: Michael Ballhaus
Editing: Thelma Schoonmaker
Casting: P Larry Kaplan, Ellen Lewis
Production Design: Dante Ferretti
Art Direction: Robert Guerra

Set Decoration: Francesca LoSchiavo
Costume Design: Sandy Powell

CAST: Leonardo DiCaprio (*Amsterdam Vallon*), Daniel Day-Lewis (*Bill 'The Butcher' Poole*), Cameron Diaz (*Jenny*), Jim Broadbent (*Boss Tweed*), John C Reilly (*Happy Jack Mulraney*), Henry Thomas (*Johnny Sirocco*), Brendan Gleeson (*Monk Eastman*), Roger Ashton-Griffiths (*PT Barnum*), Gerry Robert Byrne (*Draft Official*), Liam Carney (*Fuzzy*), Barbara Bouchet (*Jenny's Mother*), Gary McCormack (*Stick*), Liam Neeson (*Priest Vallon*), Cara Seymour (*Hellcat Maggie*), Peter-Hugo Daly (*Priest*), Gary Lewis, Devon Murray, Pete Postlethwaite, Stephen Graham, Yoon C Joyce.

SUMMARY: New York, 1863. As a child, Amsterdam Vallon witnessed his father's murder at the hands of gang leader Bill 'The Butcher' Poole. After leaving reform school, Vallon returns to the area known as 'The Five Points' to bring together his father's old gang, The Dead Rabbits, and avenge his death.

WHO'S WHO?: Thanks to his lead roles in the updated version of *Romeo and Juliet* (*William Shakespeare's Romeo + Juliet*, Baz Luhrmann, 1996) and *Titanic* (James Cameron, 1997), Leonardo DiCaprio is one of the biggest young heart-throbs in America. His love interest in *Gangs . . .*, Cameron Diaz, first wowed audiences in *The Mask* (Chuck Russell, 1994) and followed it up with *My Best Friend's Wedding* (PJ Hogan, 1997), *A Life Less Ordinary* (Danny Boyle, 1997) and *There's Something about Mary* (The Farrelly Brothers, 1998). Jim Broadbent tends to go for comic roles in films such as *Life is Sweet* (Mike Leigh, 1990) and *Bullets Over Broadway* (Woody Allen, 1994). John C Reilly has one of those faces that often sees him cast as an officer of the law in films such as *Shadows and Fog* (Woody Allen, 1992), *Dolores Claiborne* (Taylor Hackford, 1995) and *Magnolia* (Paul Thomas Anderson, 1999). Henry Thomas will forever be remembered as 'that cute kid from *ET*' (Steven Spielberg, 1982). Ironically, it was as a Scottish rebel in *Braveheart* (Mel Gibson, 1995) that Irish actor Brendan Gleeson first came to international prominence, though since then he's carved an impressive career for himself in films like *The General* (John Boorman, 1998) and *Mission: Impossible II* (John Woo, 2000). Barbara Bouchet might be familiar to modern audiences, thanks to the recent revival of interest in James Bond, as Miss Moneypenny from the Bond spoof *Casino Royale* (Val Guest et al, 1967) though, when casting her,

Scorsese was probably thinking more of her collaborations with Otto Preminger and Bob Fosse. Liverpool actor Stephen Graham starred in Guy Ritchie's *Snatch* (2000) and the TV series *Band of Brothers*. Irish giant Liam Neeson has been immortalised in action figure form thanks to his part in *Star Wars: Episode I – The Phantom Menace* (1998), though thankfully no one thought of releasing similar merchandising for *Schindler's List* (Steven Spielberg, 1993) or *Michael Collins* (Neil Jordan, 1996). Cara Seymour played Björk's neighbour in *Dancer in the Dark* (Lars von Trier, 2000). Gary Lewis played the dad in *Billy Elliot* (Stephen Daldry, 2000) and Shanks in *My Name is Joe* (Ken Loach, 1998).

THE USUAL SUSPECTS: Daniel Day-Lewis (*Age of Innocence*); producer Barbara De Fina (*The Color of Money, Bad, The Last Temptation of Christ, New York Stories, The Grifters, Made in Milan, GoodFellas, Cape Fear, Mad Dog and Glory, The Age of Innocence, Casino, Kundun, My Voyage to Italy, Bringing Out the Dead, Dino*); editor Thelma Schoonmaker (*Who's That Knocking At My Door?, Street Scenes, Raging Bull, The King of Comedy, After Hours, The Color of Money, Bad, The Last Temptation of Christ, New York Stories, GoodFellas, Cape Fear, The Age of Innocence, Casino, A Personal Journey with Martin Scorsese Through American Movies, Kundun, Bringing Out the Dead, My Voyage to Italy*); production/costume designer Dante Ferretti (*The Age of Innocence, Casino, Kundun, Bringing Out the Dead*).

PRODUCTION: On New Year's Day, 1970, Martin Scorsese found a copy of Herbert Asbury's 1928 non-fiction book on a friend's shelf. The book, which told of the battles between Irish immigrants and existing inhabitants of New York, stirred memories in the young director's mind of stories he was told as a child – of the time before the Italians settled in the Little Italy of the Lower East Side – and he knew he wanted to make a film of it. But he also knew it would have to be a story on an epic scale and, by the time his reputation was big enough to tackle such a project, Michael Cimino's disastrous *Heaven's Gate* had convinced the film studios that epics were too risky to invest money in. But, by the time of *Bringing Out the Dead*, Scorsese was finally able to bring his long-awaited production together. The script had been co-written with Jay Cocks, though additional rewrites came from Steven Zaillian and Kenneth Lonergan.

Having discounted London as a location due to the cost of the production, Scorsese managed to set up shop in the celebrated Cinecittà studios in Rome, where great films such as *Cleopatra* and *Ben Hur* had been made.

The star of the film would be Leonardo DiCaprio, who went in to nine months of intensive street-fighting school with celebrity trainer Dominique Vandenberg. The press took great delight in reporting the gossip that Scorsese forced the young star to apologise to the cast and crew after turning up late to the set one morning after a heavy night of partying in Rome with his supermodel girlfriend, Gisele. The irony of a former wildman of Hollywood lecturing DiCaprio on excessive partying was lost on no one.

For the role of the main adversary in the film, Bill 'The Butcher' Poole, Scorsese approached his long-time collaborator Robert De Niro. But when De Niro backed out for 'personal reasons', and Scorsese's second choice, Willem Dafoe, was also unavailable, the director selected Daniel Day-Lewis, who had starred in *The Age of Innocence*. Strangely, Day-Lewis had been in semi-retirement working as a shoemaker in Florence until Scorsese summoned him. Though the press reported that the female lead, the knife-wielding pickpocket Jenny, would be played by actresses such as Anna Friel, Claire Forlani, Heather Graham, Monica Potter and Mena Suvari, the role went instead to Cameron Diaz.

Among Martin Scorsese's faithful collaborators working on the picture would be Thelma Schoonmaker (who, breaking tradition, began editing the picture after just two days of shooting, as Scorsese was so eager to see how it was all looking), director of photography Michael Ballhaus, assistant director Joseph Reidy, casting director Ellen Lewis (who would have to find over 1,200 extras) and production designer Dante Ferretti. Ferretti was given six months to recreate nineteenth-century New York, including Paradise Square, the Old Brewery, Broadway, the brothel, Sparrow's Pagoda, the harbour (including an almost full-sized ship) and an entire Catholic cathedral, named St Thomas's after Scorsese's friend, actor Tom Cruise, who came out to Italy to visit him. Beginning principal photography on 30 August 2000, the scale of the picture meant that filming would drag on to 14 April the following year. Production then moved to San Francisco, where special effects wizards Industrial Light & Magic began to paint in the backdrops of New York while Scorsese and Schoonmaker battled on with the task of a lengthy editing process. *Gangs of New York* was originally scheduled to be in cinemas by December 2001, just in time to qualify for the 2002 Academy Awards nominations. But in the midst of editing to an ambitious deadline, the bombing of the World Trade Center in September 2001 caused Hollywood to reassess its entire output. With schedules rejigged to avoid causing offence or upset, *Gangs of New York* was moved back to the summer of 2002, allowing Scorsese and Schoonmaker more time to complete editing.

QUOTE/UNQUOTE

Bill 'The Butcher' Poole: (watching the Irish immigrants arrive in New York) 'I don't see no Americans. I see trespassers.'

Amsterdam Vallon: (discussing the violence and hatred in the city) 'I give you my word, this'll all be finished tomorrow.'
Jenny: 'No . . . it won't . . .'

TRAILER: With the film's delayed release, the trailer was all that Scorsese/DiCaprio/Diaz fans had to keep them entertained for nearly a year. Displaying just a hint of the spectacular work of the production team in rebuilding a New York from over 140 years ago, a voice-over describes Amsterdam Vallon as: 'A man who will fight for freedom. A man who will kill for power.' The trailer ends with a tagline all the more poignant after the destruction of the World Trade Center: 'America was born in the streets.'

SCORSESE ON *GANGS OF NEW YORK*: 'I've been dying to make this picture for years because it's more about the history of the city, and the history of the city being the history of America really, I think, particularly in the nineteenth century. And I don't know, I mean it's difficult because there is so much action in the picture, how does one deal with violence these days in cinema? Especially after making *Casino*, where at the end of the film, Joe Pesci and his brother are beaten to death with baseball bats by their best friends? And when you do that, I don't know, there's no place to go in a sense. It is the dead end of organised crime, it is the dead end of that kind of life style, that's where you wind up. And here, I've got to be careful, I have to think of other ways to infer violence, rather than be blunt about it.'

Unseen Scorsese

As with any prolific director, Scorsese has considered many different projects over the years that have either fallen by the wayside or have yet to see the light of day. These are just some of the projects that have sat on Scorsese's desk over the years:

Jerusalem, Jerusalem (c. 1966)

The first part of Scorsese's 'Little Italy' trilogy, *Jerusalem, Jerusalem* would have introduced JR, who would later be at the centre of *Who's That Knocking At My Door?* JR is one of a gang of eighteen-year-old Catholic boys on retreat. The boys confess their sins and listen to sermons about sex and marriage. As the boys are lectured on the Stations of the Cross, JR mentally pictures the violence inflicted upon Christ, seeing the blood pour from nailed wrists (see **Boxcar Bertha** and **The Last Temptation of Christ**). Later, back home, JR is lying in bed when his room is bathed in light. The end caption would have read 'For the greater glory of God'. Though the script would never be made, many of the themes and anecdotes resurfaced in *Who's That Knocking At My Door?* and *Mean Streets*.

Unable to find anyone willing to let him film such a religious passion back in the late 60s, Scorsese briefly considered making it for television in the 1980s but as yet *Jerusalem, Jerusalem* remains unproduced.

This Film Could Save Your Marriage (c. 1966–8)

Desperate to make movies, Scorsese and co-writer Mardik Martin worked on a script that would be partly about the hassles they got from their wives for messing about with movies all the time.

The Honeymoon Killers (1969)

Scorsese was originally hired to direct this low-budget biopic about Martha Beck and Ray Fernandez, who were executed in Sing Sing Prison in 1951. But after a number of creative differences, largely down to Scorsese's insistence on filming everything in master shots, he was replaced as director (after just one week) by Donald Volkman, who was in turn replaced by scriptwriter Leonard Kastle. The finished film starred Shirley Stoler and Tony Lo Bianco and is currently available on DVD in the UK.

Untitled 'Soldier' project (c. 1969)

After being sacked from *The Honeymoon Killers*, Scorsese tried to develop a historical documentary on the history of soldiering, though nothing more came of this.

I Escaped From Devil's Island (1973)

After completing *Boxcar Bertha*, producer Roger Corman was suitably impressed by the young director to offer him another blaxploitation picture. Due to be shot in Costa Rica, it passed to William Witney after Scorsese decided to make his pet project *Season of the Witch* (later retitled *Mean Streets*) instead. To keep Scorsese on the team, Corman even offered to fund *Season of the Witch* himself – as long as Scorsese rewrote it as a blaxpoitation flick. Scorsese politely declined the offer.

The Arena (1973)

Another Corman project, this time boasting the novel genre mix of sword-and-sandal-meets-blaxploitation as two slave girls – one black, one white – are thrown into the gladiatorial ring for the titillation of the masses. Based on a script by *Boxcar Bertha* scribes John William Corrington and Joyce Hooper Corrington, it was instead lensed by Steve Carver and Joe D'Amato. It starred queen of the blaxpoitation genre, Pam Grier.

Badge 373 (1973)

Scorsese directed a few segments of this very minor follow-up to William Friedkin's *The French Connection* with Robert Duvall trying to fight a New York crime syndicate single-handedly. The picture was ultimately completed by Howard W Koch.

Unnamed 'Life Lessons' Project (1973)

A story inspired by Dostoevsky's *The Gambler*, in which the young mistress of an older artist asks him to prove his love for her by insulting a respectable older noblewoman. Though fellow Dostoevsky-phile Paul Schrader worked on a basic outline for a possible script, the project never advanced further. The general concept behind the film did eventually evolve into Scorsese's segment of *New York Stories*, released some fifteen years later.

Haunted Summer (1976)

A film about Mary (Godwin) Shelley, her husband, poet Percy Bysshe Shelley and that infamous summer's evening where a competition to create the ultimate horror story resulted in Mary producing what became her celebrated novel *Frankenstein*. Though Scorsese eventually passed on the project, a film version was released in 1988, directed by Ivan Passer and starring Alice Krige as Mary Shelley and Eric Stoltz as Percy.

Prize Fighter (c. 1976)

While Marty desperately tried to put off the persistent De Niro, who was dogging him about making a film version of boxer Jake LaMotta's autobiography, he briefly considered producing it as a stage play before giving in and putting together the film *Raging Bull*.

Untitled 'Indian' Project (1976)

Believed to have been under discussion while *Alice Doesn't Live Here Anymore* was in post-production, this would have been a film about the Battle of Wounded Knee, starring Marlon Brando, who had publicly announced his interest in the rights of Native Americans when he sent an actress posing as a squaw to decline his Oscar for *The Godfather*.

Unnamed 'Mother Cabrini' biopic (c. 1978)

Scorsese has spoken of his intention to make a biographical picture telling the story of Frances Cabrini, an ordinary, fragile woman who, in 1880, founded the Institute of the Missionary Sisters of the Sacred Heart of Jesus. At the request of Pope Leo XIII, Mother Cabrini went to New York to help Italian immigrants instead of going to China as she had expected, and she went on to found over sixty other missions throughout the United States and the world. Mother Cabrini died on 22 December 1917, at Columbus Hospital in Chicago. She was beatified in 1938 and canonised Saint Frances Xavier Cabrini on 7 July 1946. To date, this project has not progressed any further.

The Act (1978)

A stage play starring Liza Minnelli, which Scorsese was directing until he realised how out of his depth he was. He bowed out of the production two weeks before it was due to open. He was replaced by dancer and Broadway star Gower Champion.

Night Life (1978)

Written with Jay Cocks, this was the story of two rival brothers. However, the collapse of Scorsese's second marriage, his severe ill health and his subsequent involvement in *Raging Bull* took him in another direction.

The Lives of the Saints (c. 1980)

Convinced he'd thrown everything at *Raging Bull* and had nothing more to say, Scorsese was considering going to Rome to make documentaries on the lives of the Saints. Much of his research would later be ploughed into both attempts to bring *The Last Temptation of Christ* to the screen.

Night and the City (1985)

Richard Price wrote a screenplay for a remake of Jules Dassin's 1950 film. At the time Scorsese wasn't keen on doing remakes, but Irwin Winkler (*New York, New York, Raging Bull, GoodFellas*) eventually directed it in 1992, starring Robert De Niro and Jessica Lange, the year after Scorsese's own remake of *Cape Fear*.

Dick Tracy (1986)

Warren Beatty cast around for a director for his film version of the comic-book detective Dick Tracy. Though Scorsese, eager for a commercial hit, appeared interested, he ultimately bailed to take up Paul Newman's invitation to direct *The Color of Money*. Beatty would eventually direct and star in the picture himself in 1990.

Winter's Tale (1986)

A $15 million fantasy based on a book by Mark Helprin, to have been scripted by either Tom Benedek (author of *Cocoon*) or Melissa Mathison (*ET, Kundun*). Again, this was pushed aside to make way for *The Color of Money*.

Sea of Love (1989)

As part of their deal with Scorsese, Universal offered him this script by Richard Price. Eventually the film, starring Al Pacino and Ellen Barkin, would be made by Harold Becker.

White Palace (1990)

Another proposal from Universal, this was a script by Ted Tally (before his *Silence of the Lambs* Oscar glory) of a young executive and his passionate affair with a middle-aged waitress. *GoodFellas* suddenly became a go-project for Scorsese and *White Palace* was eventually made by Luis Mandoki, starring James Spader and Susan Sarandon.

Mine – The Gershwin biopic (1985/1993)

Scorsese has had two attempts at developing the story of songwriter George Gershwin as a musical for the screen. The first version was scripted by Paul Schrader. Schrader's script had, by 1993, been replaced by one by John Guare. The Gershwin project seems to have stalled in recent years as Scorsese's commitments have grown.

Robbie Robertson and Friends (1988)

A Cinemax special, with Robbie Robertson in concert, joined by U2 and Peter Gabriel. When Robertson's guests proved unavailable, the project was canned. A later suggestion that the project might become a full-length feature 'rockumentary' also failed to materialise.

Schindler's Ark (*c.* 1988)

After completing *The Last Temptation of Christ*, Scorsese was approached by producer Tom Pollock to consider a project that Steven Spielberg had been working on, an adaptation of Thomas Keneally's true story of the Nazi capitalist who saved the lives of hundreds of Jews from the death camps in Poland. Scorsese worked with Steve Zaillian on the script, but still felt Spielberg should make the picture himself. The script was the element that convinced Spielberg to have confidence in himself and he took the project back. The film was eventually released in 1993 as *Schindler's List*, starring Liam Neeson.

Unnamed Gore Vidal script (1990s)

Gore Vidal had been head of the jury at the Venice Film Festival where *GoodFellas* was in competition and had persuaded the panel to award the Golden Lion to *Rosencrantz and Guildenstern Are Dead* because he hated *GoodFellas* so much. Despite this, during the 1990s, Vidal and Scorsese collaborated on a script together, though nothing has come of this as yet.

Clockers (1995)

Scripted by Richard Price based on his own novel and bought for
Scorsese to direct, Scorsese eventually stepped aside and produced the
picture, with Spike Lee as director. starring Harvey Keitel.

... and in the waiting zone:

Dino

Warner Bros have patiently sat and waited for Scorsese to complete *Gangs
of New York* before ramping up on the proposed biopic of Dean Martin,
so this looks like being the main contender for next out of the stalls.
Rumoured casting projections for *Dino* include Tom Hanks as Dean
Martin, Jim Carrey as Jerry Lewis and Hugh Grant as Peter Lawford.

Alexander

In October 2001, Graham King's Initial Entertainment Group (IEG)
announced that, fresh from *Gangs of New York*, Leonardo DiCaprio
and Martin Scorsese would team up again on the story of Alexander The
Great, based on a script by Peter Buchman (*Jurassic Park III*) and
Christopher McQuarrie (*The Usual Suspects*), who would also produce
the picture alongside DiCaprio's company, Appian Way, and Scorsese's
Cappa Productions. However, with both Oliver Stone and Ridley Scott
having also announced Alexander projects, we'll have to wait and see
who gets their version on to the screen first.

The Blues

Produced by Offline Entertainment with Clear Blue Sky Productions and
Cappa Productions, this is a six-part documentary mini-series about the
blues, charting the geographical and chronological evolution of
African–American music's influence on popular music worldwide. In
addition to one edition from Scorsese, a self-confessed blues fan, other
episodes will apparently be directed by Michael Apted, Charles Burnett,
Spike Lee, Marc Levin and Wim Wenders.

The Neighborhood

Another collaboration with Nicholas Pileggi about three generations of
an Italian family, which they began thinking about during the

production of *GoodFellas*. It's the story of Scorsese's family starting with his parents in Elizabeth Street with flashbacks to his grandparents in Sicily and how they came to America, their courtship during the Second World War and the arrival of the 60s. The script was written in three weeks and Scorsese has suggested that at two hundred pages it's very lengthy and might make a good mini-series.

Walter Winchell

A biopic of the New York-born journalist and broadcaster.

Gucci project

Possibly along the same lines as Scorsese's *Made in Milan*, which looked at Armani, this is a picture about the fashion house of Gucci.

High and Low

After Akira Kurosawa bequeathed the rights for his film *Tengoku to Jigoku* (1963) to Scorsese's Cappa Productions, an announcement was made in 2001 that Scorsese would produce a remake, directed by Brazilian film-maker Walter Salles. Disney's Touchstone Pictures has been linked to the project, though, at the time of writing, it has not received the green light.

Silence

From the novel by Shusaku Endo, about a Portugese priest in seventeenth-century Japan.

Oceans of Storm

An astronaut love story to star and be produced by Warren Beatty.

Additional Credits

As Actor

Cannonball (1976)
Director: Paul Bartel
as Mafioso

Il Pap'occhio 30 (1981)
Director: Renzo Arbore
as TV director

Pavlova: A Woman for All Time (1983)
Director: Emil Lotianou
as Gatti-Cassaza

'Round Midnight (1986)
Director: Bertrand Tavernier
as Goodley

Akira Kurosawa's Dreams (1990)
Director: Akira Kurosawa
as Vincent Van Gogh

The Grifters (1990)
Director: Stephen Frears
Opening voice-over (not credited)

Guilty by Suspicion (1991)
Director: Irwin Winkler
as Joe Lesser

Quiz Show (1994)
Director: Robert Redford
as Sponsor

Search and Destroy (1995)
Director: David Salle
as Accountant

The Muse (1999)
Director: Albert Brooks
as Himself

As Producer

The Grifters (1990)
Director: Stephen Frears

Mad Dog and Glory (1993)
Director: John McNaughton

Con Gli Occhi Chiusi (1994) (executive producer)
Director: Francesca Archibugi

Search and Destroy (1995)
Director: David Salle

Clockers (1995)
Director: Spike Lee

In the Spotlight: 'Eric Clapton – Nothing But the Blues' (1995) (executive producer)

Grace of My Heart (1996) (executive producer)
Director: Allison Anders

Kicked in the Head (1997) (executive producer)
Director: Matthew Harrison

The Hi-Lo Country (1998)
Director: Stephen Frears

You Can Count on Me (2000) (executive producer)
Director: Kenneth Lonergan

The Blues (2002) TV Series (executive producer)
Directors: Charles Burnett, Leslie Harris, Spike Lee, Marc Levin, Wim Wenders

As Editor

Woodstock (1970)
Director: Michael Wadleigh

Medicine Ball Caravan (1971)
Director: François Reichenbach

Elvis on Tour (1972)
Director: Pierre Adidge, Robert Abel

Unholy Rollers (1972)
Director: Vernon Zimmerman

Miscellaneous Credits

Inesita (1963) (photographer)
Director: Robert J Siegal

Obsessions (1969) (scriptwriter)
Director: Pim de la Parra

Woodstock (1970) (assistant director)
Director: Michael Wadleigh

Minnie and Moskowitz (1971) (sound editor)
Director: John Cassavetes

Presented by . . .

Films that enjoyed either a first release or a rerelease in the United States thanks to support from Scorsese.

A Matter of Life and Death (1946)
Directors: Michael Powell, Emmerich Pressburger

Pursued (1947)
Director: Raoul Walsh

A Double Life (1947)
Director: George Cukor

Force of Evil (1948)
Director: Abraham Polonsky

The Golden Coach (1952)
Director: Jean Renoir

Les Orgueilleux/The Proud Ones (1953)
Director: Yves Allegret

Johnny Guitar (1954)
Director: Nicholas Ray

La Strada (1954)
Director: Federico Fellini

Peeping Tom (1960)
Director: Michael Powell

Rocco and his Brothers (1960)
Director: Luchino Visconti

El Cid (1961)
Director: Anthony Mann

Mama Roma (1962)
Director: Pier Paolo Pasolini

I Am Cuba (1963)
Director: Mikhail Kalatozov

Belle De Jour (1967)
Director: Luis Buñuel

Intervista (1987)
Director: Federico Fellini

Scorsese the Activist

In 1980, Martin Scorsese spearheaded a campaign against Eastman Kodak and the 'Eastmancolor' film stock the company introduced in the 1950s. Scorsese had realised that the lifespan of a negative could be as little as thirteen years, and declared that 'Everything we are doing now means nothing!' He rallied film-makers to insist in their contracts for access to the very latest in film stock, and encouraged them to boycott Eastman Kodak until the company could provide film stock that was less likely to fade. Scorsese began touring film festivals with a lecture on colour fading and eventually, at no extra cost, Eastman Kodak offered new film stock less likely to deteriorate over time.

Index of Quotations

MS refers to Martin Scorsese

It's Not Just You, Murray!
11 'Of all my films . . . began to die out.' MS quoted in Mary Pat Kelly, *Martin Scorsese: A Journey*, New York, Thunder's Mouth, 1991, p11.

The Big Shave
12 'Consciously it was . . . a very bad period.' MS quoted in Kelly, *Martin Scorsese: The First Decade*, p19.

Who's That Knocking At My Door?
18 'never done a nude scene' Marshall Fine, *Harvey Keitel: The Art of Darkness*, p xi.
19 'That whole first . . . exciting but unnerving.' Zina Bethune, ibid, p48.
19 'I dislike it . . . Who's gonna see it? Nobody.' MS quoted in Anthony Decurtis, 'What The Streets Mean', *Martin Scorsese Interviews*, edited by Peter Brunette, p162.

Street Scenes
22 'I see the movie . . . social meaning.' Harvey Keitel quoted in Marshall Fine, *Harvey Keitel: The Art of Darkness*, p57.
22 'I used footage . . . it was godsent.' MS cited in Lawrence S Friedman *The Cinema of Martin Scorsese*, p43.

Boxcar Bertha
27 'costumes and guns'. MS quoted in David Thompson and Ian Christie, *Scorsese on Scorsese*, p31.
28 'the first reel . . . it turned out.' MS quoted in *Scorsese on Scorsese*, p34.
30 'I liked the way . . . seen piercing flesh.' MS quoted in *Scorsese on Scorsese*, p36.
31 'You spent . . . piece of shit.' Quoted in *Scorsese on Scorsese*, p38.
31 '*Boxcar Bertha* eschews . . . in the Depression.' Andy Gill, *Empire*, November 1990.
32 'Mostly I attempted . . . to the picture.' MS quoted in *Cinema of Martin Scorsese*, p51.

Mean Streets
39 'A lot of places . . . black and Italian.' MS quoted by Gavin Smith, *Film Comment*, 1990.
44 'A true original . . . sense of evil.' Pauline Kael, *New York Times*, quoted in *5001 Nights At The Movies*, p473.
44 'Perhaps I got . . . rebelled against it.' *Harvey Keitel: The Art of Darkness*, p60.
44 'Sometimes as an actor . . . work with Marty.' Robert De Niro quoted in 'Bobby's Back', Nick Tosches, *Esquire*, March 1996, p50.

45   '*Mean Streets* is always . . . It's too personal.' MS in *Martin Scorsese interviews*, p181.

Alice Doesn't Live Here Anymore
54   'Full of funny . . . all fouled up.' Pauline Kael, *New York Times*, quoted in *5001 Nights At The Movies*. p15.

55   'We never intended . . . with no choice.' MS in *Scorsese on Scorsese*, p51.

Italianamerican
58   'He felt he'd . . . signed autographs.' MS in *Martin Scorsese Interviews*, p38.

Taxi Driver
67   'They'd made hundreds . . . worked with Marty before.' Michael Chapman in the 'Making of Taxi Driver', Taxi Driver Collector's Edition DVD.

72   'Part of the horror implicit . . . he could be legion.' Pauline Kael, *New Yorker.*, quoted in *5001 Nights At The Movies*.

72   'First and last . . . diagram of social unease.' Jack Kroll, *Newsweek*, cited in *Robert De Niro Movie Top Ten*, pp51–52.

72   'It is a measure . . . a vintage year.' David Castell, *Films Illustrated*, issue 61.

73   'You can work . . . are no values.' Paul Schrader in the 'Making of Taxi Driver', Taxi Driver Collector's Edition DVD.

73   'Paul Schrader, Marty and myself . . . they can relate to that.' Robert De Niro, interviewed by James Lipton, *Inside the Actor's Studio*.

74   'I remember . . . in a new way.' Jodie Foster quoted by Rachel Abramowitz, 'Fearless', *Premiere* January 1995, Vol. 8, No. 5, ed. Susan Lyne, p64–5.

75   'I felt all . . . acceptance of an audience.' MS in the 'Making of Taxi Driver', Taxi Driver Collector's Edition DVD.

New York, New York
87   '*New York, New York* has superb . . . of the mature Judy Garland.' David Castell, *Film Illustrated*, October 1977.

87   'In all those . . . actor around today.' Liza Minnelli quoted by Keith McKay, *Robert De Niro, The Hero Behind The Masks*, New English Library, London, UK. 1988, p73.

88   'I was extremely . . . I love it.' MS in *Scorsese on Scorsese*, p72.

The Last Waltz
91   'There was a rock . . . travelling booger matte.' Jonathan Taplin quoted in *Premiere*, November 1991, p68. Reprinted in *Scorsese Interviews*, p193.

91   'I had the feeling . . . the audience anymore?' MS quoted in Terry Curtis Fox, 'Martin Scorsese's Elegy for a Big-Time Band', *The Village Voice*, 29 May 1978, cited in *Martin Scorsese Interviews*, p81.

Raging Bull
109   'a swollen puppet . . . and kills it.' Pauline Kael, reprinted in *Taking It All In*, pp107 and 111.

110 'I thought it . . . out of shape.' Robert De Niro in *Inside The Actor's Studio*.
110 'I've never seen . . . making the film.' Jake LaMotta in Andy Gill, 'The Godfather', *Premiere* UK, Emap Metro, October 1993, p73.
110 'Knowing Jake personally . . . make this picture.' MS quoted by Gavin Smith, *Film Comment*, January/February 1998, reprinted in *Martin Scorsese Interviews*, p252.

The King of Comedy
121 'Putting a grossly . . . ordinary bad movies.' Pauline Kael, reprinted in *Taking It All In*, p456.
122 '. . . perhaps the funniest film ever . . .' Mat Snow, *Premiere* UK, Emap Metro, October 1993, ed. Barry McIlheney, p77.
122 'Before we started . . . I understood it.' Jerry Lewis quoted by Andy Gill, 'The Godfather', *Premiere* UK, Emap Metro, October 1993, ed. Barry McIlheney, p74–5.
123 'I must say . . . it's a problem.' MS quoted by Peter Biskind, 'Slouching Toward Hollywood', *Premiere*, November 1991, ed. Susan Lyne, published by K-III mags, NY, USA. reprinted in *Scorsese Interviews*, p195.

After Hours
133 'This is the work . . . year's best.' Roger Ebert, *Chicago Sun-Times*, 10 November 1985.
134 'The anxiety of . . . he was laughing.' Griffin Dunne quoted by Mary Pat Kelly, *Martin Scorsese: A Journey*, p186.
134 'The final cost was . . . for so little.' MS in *Scorsese on Scorsese*, p101.

Amazing Stories: 'Mirror, Mirror'
139 'I just wanted to . . . too much time.' MS quoted in 'Amazing Anthologies' By Elvis Mitchell, *Film Comment*, September/October 1985, Vol.: 21, pp. 63–65.

The Color of Money
152 'No stranger to grit . . . for *Hustler III*.' Rita Kempley, *Washington Post*, 17 October 1986.
152 'He lets you . . . he can do.' Paul Newman interviewed in *The Directors*, The American Film Institute, USA, 2000.
153 'Sometimes Newman would . . . missing a writer.' Richard Price in Myra Forsberg 'The Color of Money: Three Men and a Sequel', *New York Times*, 19 October 1986.
153 'There will always . . . then that's great.' MS, ibid.

Bad
157 'I've always been . . . to do it again . . .' MS in *Scorsese on Scorsese*, p113.

The Last Temptation of Christ
173 'When you think . . . and you did it.' Willem Dafoe, Criterion DVD commentary, *The Last Temptation of Christ*.
173 'I thought we . . . Judas betrayed Jesus.' *Harvey Keitel: The Art of Darkness*, p161.

173 'It was supposed . . . kind of enjoy that.' MS in *First Works*.
174 'My film was . . . his divine side.' MS in *Scorsese on Scorsese*, pxxii.

New York Stories: 'Life Lessons'

181 'Easily the most . . . in a career.' Andy Gill, *Empire*, November 1990.
181 'That the project . . . good as any.' *Woody Allen on Woody Allen*, Faber & Faber, p201.
182 'What interested me . . . he creates himself.' *Scorsese on Scorsese*, p148.

GoodFellas

191 'never should have . . . but an Italian.' MS quoted in *Moving Pictures*, 1990.
200 'Violent in the extreme . . . bigger picture than this.' Barry McIlheney, *Empire*, November 1990, pp18–19.
200 'less concerned with . . . make a fast buck.' Geoff Andrew, *Time Out Film Guide*, p314.
200 'a triumphant piece . . . on pure sensation.' Pauline Kael, cited in *5001 Nights At the Movies*, p297.
200 'By the time . . . pursuit of crime.' Desson Howe, *Washington Post*, 21 September 1990.
200 'My husband would . . . always killing too!' Catherine Scorsese quoted in Richard Goodwin, 'The Making Of Goodfellas', *Hotdog*, September 2000.
200 'I saw *GoodFellas* . . . And correct.' Karen Hill quoted in Richard Goodwin, 'The Making Of Goodfellas', *Hotdog*, September 2000.
201 'What fascinated me . . . wives, their kids.' MS in *Empire*, November 1990, p80.

Made in Milan

202 'Employing Scorsese to . . . film your wedding.' Woody Hockswender cited on www.scorsesefilms.com.
202 'This film is . . . and his vision.' MS in *Empire*, November 1990, p84.

Cape Fear

222 'taking on an . . . outside his interests'. Todd McCarthy, *Variety*, cited in Douglas Brode, *The Films of Robert De Niro*, p230.
222 'swell B movie . . . couture.' David Anser, *Newsweek*, cited in *The Films of Robert De Niro*, p231.
222 'nerve-wracking but . . . brilliantly compelling.' Matt Mueller, *Empire*, March 1992, p17.
222 'I had seen the original . . . simple thing.' Robert De Niro, 'Making of Cape Fear', *Cape Fear* DVD commentary.
222 'There's total trust . . . off we go.' Freddie Francis quoted by Andy Gill, 'The Godfather', *Premiere* UK, Emap Metro, October 1993, ed. Barry McIlheney, p75.
222 'I think Marty's . . . it is correct.' Thelma Schoonmaker in 'Making of Cape Fear', *Cape Fear* DVD Commentary.
223 '*Cape Fear* . . . we all look for.' Illeana Douglas in *Premiere*, Special Issue, 'New York and the Movies', K-III Magazine Corp, N.Y. USA, 1994, ed. Cyndi Stivers.

223 '*Cape Fear* really felt . . . was another genre.' MS in *Empire* 107 'Doctor Martin' by Ian Freer, p79.

The Age of Innocence
235 'Scorsese is known . . . curious uninvited guest.' Roger Ebert, *Chicago Sun-Times*, 17 September 1993.
235 'My performance was very minimalist . . . do with movies.' Winona Ryder quoted in 'Clean Streets', by Daphne Merkin, *Premiere*, October 1993, p48.
236 'Where that extra . . . a sense of sumptuousness.' MS, ibid, p122.

A Century of Cinema
237 'Scorsese's prose radiates . . . for the man.' Philip Thomas, *Empire* 102, December 1997.

Casino
251 'You can say . . . in the neck.' Neil Jeffries, *Empire*, ed. Mark Salisbury, October 1996, p122.
251 'It's not the . . . hungry for drama.' David Ansen, *Newsweek*, quoted in *The Films of Robert De Niro*, p269.
251 'I'm very fortunate . . . whatever he wants.' Robert De Niro in *The Films of Robert De Niro*, p271.
252 'This story has . . . couldn't care less.' MS in 'The Filmmaker series: Scorsese', *Premiere*, December 1995, Premiere publishing company NY, LLC., ed. Susan Lyne, p111.

Kundun
257 'To sing the . . . conform with reality,' Cui Tiankai in Reuters news report, Friday, 29 November 1996.
258 'Filming in lush . . . unmatched filmmaking talents.' Helen Van Kruyssen, *Neon*, December 1998, Emap Metro London UK. p109.
258 'Even if *Kundun* lacks . . . yet strangely thrilling. Ian Freer, *Empire* 107, May 1998.
259 'I don't want . . . to think about.' MS on *Frontline*: 'Dreams of Tibet', produced and directed by Ben Loeterman, 28 October 1997.

Bringing Out the Dead
266 'With tremendous visual . . . it is moving.' Chris Cronis, *Premiere*, June 2000, p100, Hatchette Filipacci Magazines inc., L.A., USA.
266 'The *Taxi Driver* comparison . . . instrument of death.' Paul Schroder in an interview on the official *Bringing Out the Dead* website.
266 'There's a correlation . . . we're different, too.' MS, ibid.

My Voyage to Italy
268 'Those films showed . . . through the films.' AG Basoli, 'Rekindling our Love of Italian Cinema: MoMA's Second Act Series', *Moviemaker* Magazine, republished on MovieMaker.com.

Gangs of New York
272 'I've been dying . . . blunt about it.' MS interviewed on *The Charlie Rose Show*, 15 October 1999.

Bibliography

Books

Biskind, Peter. *Easy Riders, Raging Bulls*. London, Bloomsbury Publishing Plc., 1999.

Bjorkman, Stig. *Woody Allen on Woody Allen*, London, Faber and Faber Ltd, 1995.

Boorman, John and Donohue, Walter (ed.). *Projections 7*. London, Faber and Faber Ltd, 1997.

Brunette, Peter (ed.). *Martin Scorsese Interviews*, Mississippi, University Press of Mississippi, 1999.

Christie, Ian and Thompson, David, ed. *Scorsese on Scorsese* (2nd ed), London, Faber and Faber Ltd, 1996.

Dyson, Michael Eric. 'Reflecting Black: African-American Cultural Criticism' *American Culture*, Vol 9. Minnesota, University of Minnesota Press, 1993.

Fine, Marshal. *Harvey Keitel: The Art of Darkness*. NY, Fromm International, 1997.

Friedman, Lawrence S. *The Cinema of Martin Scorsese.*

Hunter, Jack (ed.). *Robert De Niro – Movie Top Tens*. London, Creation Books International, 1999.

Kael, Pauline. *5001 Nights at the Movies*. London, Marion Boyars Publishers, 1993.

Kelly, Mary Pat. *Martin Scorsese: The First Decade*. NY, Redgrave, Pleasantville, 1980.

Kelly, Mary Pat. *Martin Scorsese: A Journey*. New York, Thunder's Mouth, 1991.

Kolker, Robert Phillip. *A Cinema of Loneliness: Penn, Kubrick, Coppola, Scorsese, Altman*. 1980.

McKay, Keith. *Robert De Niro: The Hero Behind The Masks*, London, New English Library, 1988.

Taylor, Bella. 'Martin Scorsese', *Close Up: The Contemporary Director*, ed. Jon Tuska, Vicki Piekarski, David Wilson, Metuchen, Scarecrow Press, 1981.

Weiss, Marion. *Martin Scorsese: A Guide To References and Resources*. Boston, 1987.

Periodicals

Empire 33, Ed. Barry McIlleney. London, EMAP Metro Ltd, March 1992.

Empire 35, Ed. Barry McIlheney. London, EMAP Metro Ltd, May 1992.

Empire 107, May 1998.

Esquire magazine, Vol. 4, No. 1. ed. Rosie Boycott, National Magazine Company Ltd, London, February 1994.

Esquire magazine, ed. Rosie Boycott, National Magazine Company Ltd, London, March 1996.

Films Illustrated, Vol 6. No 61, London, Independent Magazines Ltd, September 1976.

Films Illustrated, Vol 7, No 74, London, Independent Magazines Ltd, October 1977.

Hotdog. London, I Feel Good Ltd, September 2000.
Premiere, ed. Susan Lyne, NY, K-III mags, November 1991.
Premiere, ed. Susan Lyne, NY, K-III mags, January 1995.
Premiere UK, Emap Metro, UK, October 1993.

Video/DVD/Television
The Directors. Media Entertainment Inc./The AFI, dir. Robert J Emery, New York, 2000.
First Works: Scorsese. TAE/Adjosh Productions, USA, 1989.
Moving Pictures: 'The Goodfellas Behind *GoodFellas*'. BBC 2, UK, October 1990.
Inside the Actor's Studio: Robert De Niro. The Film and Arts Bravo Network, Betelgeuse Productions, In The Moment Productions, Ltd., New York, 1998.

Internet
Obviously, any film-fan's first stop-off point on the World Wide Web should be the Internet Movie Database (www.imdb.com). Here are a few less-well-travelled paths.

The Last Temptation of Christ Denied by Bob and Gretchen Passatino was originally meant to be published at the time of Scorsese's controversial film. For whatever reason, the book was subsequently dropped. Answers In Action, a non-profit-making, evangelical Christian organisation, have published the book on their website (www.answers.org/issues/last_temptation.html). It makes fascinating reading for anyone who wishes to learn first hand the arguments against both the book and the film of *The Last Temptation of Christ*.

If you'd like to contact the real Henry Hill, subject of *GoodFellas*, you can do so via his website: www.goodfellahenry.com – if one of the many wiseguys who leave hate messages in his guestbook hasn't got to him first.

Fans of Gib Guilbeau, who provided the music for *Boxcar Bertha*, will be pleased to know he has his own website at www.gibguilbeau.com. The official site for Philip Glass, composer of the score for *Kundun*, is at www.philipglass.com, while the websites for *Bringing Out the Dead* and *Gangs of New York* can be found at www.bringingoutthedead.com and www.gangsofnewyork.com respectively.

There's a complete archive of Roger Ebert's reviews at www.suntimes.com/ebert/ebertser.html.

Picture Credits

The following pictures are courtesy of the Ronald Grant archive: Page 1 (bottom); Page 2 (top); Page 3 (both); Page 5 (bottom); Page 6 (both); Page 8 (bottom).

The following pictures are courtesy of the Kobal collection: Page 1 (top); Page 2 (bottom left and right): Page 4 (both); Page 5 (top); Page 7 (both); Page 8 (top).

Index